DEVELOPMENT IN THE AMERICAS

BEYOND FACTS

Understanding Quality of Life

Eduardo Lora
Coordinator

IDB

Inter-American Development Bank

Co-published by
    David Rockefeller Center for Latin American Studies
    Harvard University
    1730 Cambridge Street
    Cambridge, MA 02138

Distributed by
    Harvard University Press
    Cambridge, Massachusetts
    Phone: U.S.A. and Canada, 1-800-405-1619; all others, 1-401-531-2800
    E-mail: orders@triliteral.org

    London, England
    Phone: +44(0) 1243-779777; Fax: +44(0) 1243-843303
    E-mail: cs-books@wiley.co.uk

Cataloging-in-Publication data provided by the
Inter-American Development Bank
Felipe Herrera Library

Beyond facts : understanding quality of life.

p. cm.
[Development in the Americas ; 2008]
"This special volume [is] the first edition of the IDB's new Development in the Americas series, which replaces its annual Report on Economic and Social Progress as the Bank's flagship publication"—Preface.
"The principal authors ... are ... Eduardo Lora ... [et al.]—Acknowledgments.
Includes bibliographical references and index.
ISBN: 978-1-59782-079-0

1. Quality of life—Latin America.   2. Cost and standard of living—Latin America.   3. Public goods—Latin America. I. Lora, Eduardo. II. Inter-American Development Bank. III. Series.

HN110.5.A8 B45 2008
306.098 B45--dc22   LCCN: 2008939413

The IDB's Office of External Relations was responsible for the design and production of this report.

Publisher	Rafael Cruz
Production Editor	Michael Harrup
Assistant Editor	Sarah Schineller
Graphic Design	Dolores Subiza
Editorial Assistant	Cathy Conkling-Shaker
Translators	Larry Hanlon
	Sarah Schineller
	Richard Torrington
Indexer	Breffni Whelan
Additional Typography	Word Express, Inc.

Contents

Preface

The Inter-American Development Bank observes its fiftieth anniversary at a critical time for Latin America and the Caribbean. The financial crisis in the developed countries has put years of the region's economic and social progress at risk.

The latest test to which this region is being subjected should not, however, cause its inhabitants to lose sight of the achievements of the last half century. Judging from traditional indicators, the region has made some impressive gains. Per capita income (at 2000 prices) has more than doubled, from approximately US$2,000 in 1960 to more than US$4,500 today. The average Latin American can expect to live almost 73 years, compared to just 56 in 1960. The literacy rate has increased from 63 percent in 1960 to 86 percent in 2000. Today, children in the region attend school an average of seven years, compared to only three-and-a-half years in 1960.

In terms of employment growth, Latin American countries have outperformed most other developing nations, creating an average of 12 jobs per year for every thousand people of working age between 1990 and 2004. In addition, although Latin Americans have poured into cities with unprecedented speed, the region has managed to democratize urban home ownership and provide basic services to the vast majority of urban dwellers. Two out of three families own their homes, even among the poor. Nearly 95 percent of the urban population has access to electricity, and over 85 percent has access to running water and telephone service (the latter thanks to the recent expansion of mobile telephones).

Of course, not all the news is positive. International test scores show that Latin American students lag behind their counterparts not only in OECD member states, but in other developing nations as well. Poor education is taking a real toll on the region's competitiveness, reflected in the low productivity growth that has been acting as a brake on higher wages and economic growth throughout Latin America and the Caribbean. Furthermore, while cities have burgeoned around the region, their infrastructure has not always kept pace with the demand and needs of the population, while attendant crime and pollution often go unchecked.

The data from afar paint a heartening picture of a population whose standard of living has improved dramatically, but in too many ways the real quality of people's lives is not measurably better. So how do Latin Americans themselves feel about their lives against the backdrop of the past half century? What do they think of their lives, societies, cities, health, education, and jobs? Are their perceptions in tune with the facts as measured by traditional economic and social indicators? Does it matter for policy?

On the occasion of its fiftieth anniversary, the IDB took on the challenge of consulting its most important constituency—the people of the region—about the quality of their lives. Using data from the Gallup World Poll and other public opinion surveys, the Bank uncovered some fascinating results. Overall, Latin Americans are satisfied with their lives, but interestingly, people in some of the poorest countries are the most optimistic while citizens of some of the most-developed countries are the most pessimistic. Not surprisingly, people with higher incomes are more satisfied with their lives than those with lower incomes, but economic growth actually breeds discontent rather than greater happiness, at least in the short run.

Despite the proliferation of low-skill jobs and informal employment, most Latin Americans are pleased with their work. Perhaps even more startling is the generalized preference to work in the informal economy over the formal, salaried sector because of the flexibility, autonomy, and opportunity for personal growth that informality seems to offer. In terms of social services, the majority of Latin Americans are satisfied with their education systems because they value discipline, safety, and the physical infrastructure of their schools more than the scores their children achieve on academic tests. And even in countries with poor health profiles, people are largely satisfied with their own health and the health care services they receive.

These results have great significance for the Bank's program of activities and for public policy in countries throughout the region. Clearly, there are political costs to growth policies that are likely to increase, rather than decrease, public dissatisfaction. If at-risk countries and social groups are tolerant of their health problems, prevention policies and efforts to improve health services will likely bypass them. And how can the region hope to have human resources capable of competing in the world economy if the majority of its people are blind to the failings of their education systems?

With this volume, the Bank hopes to spark a healthy discussion of these issues, since it has learned that policies must enjoy public support to be effective. Public opinion matters; it matters for politics and it matters for policy. Taking the pulse of our constituent region enriches public discourse and enhances the political viability of public policy.

In the final analysis, the IDB is at the service of the citizens of Latin America and the Caribbean. It is fitting that it should mark its first half century of operation by asking them how they have fared after five momentous decades of economic and social changes. It is also fitting that this special volume on such a special occasion should be the first edition of the IDB's new Development in the Americas series, which replaces its annual Report on Economic and Social Progress as the Bank's flagship publication.

I am pleased to present this volume to the policymakers of the region, to our partners in academia and in the nongovernmental advocacy world, and, most of all, to the people of Latin America and the Caribbean, our inspiration.

Luis Alberto Moreno
President
Inter-American Development Bank

Acknowledgments

Development in the Americas (DIA) is the flagship publication of the Inter-American Development Bank. This issue was produced under the direction of Eduardo Lora, Chief Economist and General Manager, a.i., of the Research Department. Rita Funaro, Publications Coordinator of the department, was the editorial advisor; Carlos Andrés Gómez-Peña, Technical and Research Assistant, provided production coordination. The Bank's Office of External Relations was in charge of editorial review and of the publication process, under the supervision of Pablo Halpern. Carol Graham, a researcher at the Brookings Institution, was the external technical advisor.

The principal authors of each individual chapter are presented below:

Chapters 1 and 2 Eduardo Lora
Chapter 3   Eduardo Lora in collaboration with Juan Camilo Chaparro
Chapter 4   Eduardo Lora in collaboration with Juan Camilo Chaparro and
                  María Victoria Rodríguez-Pombo
Chapter 5   William Savedoff in collaboration with Mariana Alfonso and Suzanne
                  Duryea
Chapter 6   Suzanne Duryea, Juan Carlos Navarro, and Aimee Verdisco
Chapter 7   Carmen Pagés in collaboration with Lucía Madrigal
Chapter 8   Eduardo Lora, Andrew Powell, and Pablo Sanguinetti
Chapter 9   Carlos Scartascini in collaboration with Rita Funaro

Juan Camilo Chaparro, Ted Enamorado, Lucas Higuera, Ana Carolina Izaguirre, Lucía Madrigal, Karla Rodríguez, María Victoria Rodríguez-Pombo, Miguel Rueda, and Mariana Salazni were the research assistants. John Dunn Smith was proofreader.

This study benefited from the results of three projects of the Bank's Research Centers Network:

1. Multidimensional Quality of Life, coordinated by Eduardo Lora; Jere R. Behrman, Carol Graham, and Ravi Kanbur were the academic advisors to this project, in which the following research teams participated:
   • Argentina: Centro de Estudios Distributivos, Laborales y Sociales (CEDLAS), Universidad Nacional de La Plata (UNLP). Leonardo Gasparini, Walter Sosa Escudero, Mariana Marchionni, and Sergio Olivieri.
   • Brazil: Centro de Políticas Sociais, Fundação Getúlio Vargas. Marcelo Côrtes Néri, Aloísio Pessoa de Araújo, Gabriel Buchmann, Samanta dos Reis Sacramento Monte, and Ana Beatriz Urbano Andari.
   • Brazil: Instituto Futuro Brasil and Universidade de São Paulo. Naércio Aquino Menezes-Filho, Raphael Bottura Corbi, and Andréa Zaitune Curi.

- Chile: Departamento de Sociología, Pontificia Universidad Católica de Chile. Carolina Flores and María Soledad Herrera.
- Colombia: Fundación para la Educación Superior y el Desarollo (FEDESAROLLO). Mauricio Cárdenas, Carolina Mejía, and Vincenzo Di Maro.
- Mexico: Spectron Desarrollo SA. Susan W. Parker, Luis N. Rubalcava, and Graciela M. Teruel.
- Mexico: Facultad Latinoamericana de Ciencias Sociales (FLACSO-Mexico) and Universidad Popular Autónoma del Estado de Puebla. Mariano Rojas.

2. Urban Quality of Life, coordinated by Andrew Powell; Pablo Sanguinetti and Bernard van Praag were the academic advisors to this project, in which the following research teams participated:

- Argentina: Centro de Estudios Distributivos, Laborales y Sociales (CEDLAS), Universidad Nacional de La Plata (UNLP). Guillermo Cruces, Andrés Ham, and Martín Tetaz.
- Bolivia: Fundación Aru. Werner L. Hernani-Limarino, Wilson Jiménez, Boris Arias, and Cecilia Larrea.
- Colombia: Universidad EAFIT and Centro Nacional de Consultoría. Carlos Medina, Jairo Núñez, and Leonardo Morales.
- Costa Rica: Environment for Development Initiative at CATIE. Juan A. Robalino, Roger Madrigal, and Luis Hall.
- Peru: Grupo de Análisis para el Desarrollo (GRADE). Lorena Alcázar and Raúl Andrade.
- Uruguay: Universidad de la República and Universidad ORT. Georgina Piani, Néstor Gandelman, and Zuleika Ferre.

3. Educational Quality, coordinated by Suzanne Duryea, Juan Carlos Navarro, and Aimee Verdisco; Eric Hanushek was the academic advisor to this project, in which the following research teams participated:

- Argentina: Fundación de Investigaciones Económicas Latinoamericanas (FIEL). Sebastián Auguste, María Echart, and Francisco Franchetti.
- Bolivia: Fundación Aru. Werner L. Hernani-Limarino, Wilson Jiménez, Miguel Vera, Franz Arce, and Ludwing Torres.
- Brazil: Instituto Futuro Brasil, Escola de Economia de São Paulo, and Escola de Pósgraduação em Economia de la Fundação Getúlio Vargas. Naércio Aquino Menezes-Filho, Creso Franco, Fábio Waltenberg, Aloísio Pessoa de Araújo, Gabriel Buchmann, Marcelo Côrtes Néri, Paulo Picchetti, Vladimir Ponczek, and André Portela Souza.
- Chile: Centro de Medición MIDE UC. Jorge Manzi, Katherine Strasser, Ernesto San Martín, Dante Contreras.
- México: Spectron Desarrollo SA. Susan W. Parker, Jere R. Behrman, and Luis N. Rubalcava.
- Paraguay: Instituto Desarrollo. Rodolfo Elias, Katie Baird, César Cabello, and Jorge Corvalán.
- Peru: ABT Asociados Inc. Javier Luque, Flor Guardia, and José Carlos Saavedra.

The following researchers prepared additional baseline material cited in the References: Marcela Cristini, Rafael Di Tella, Cynthia Moskovits, Ramiro Moya, Joan Nelson, and Ludger Woessmann.

Many other persons contributed their technical input and valuable suggestions to this report, including Sir George Alleyne, Natalie Alvarado, Joseph Antos, Davide Bancolini, Alberto Barreix, Hugo Eduardo Beteta, José Brambila, Oscar Cetrángolo, Alberto Chong, Andrés Dean, Morgan Doyle, Jesús Duarte, Koldo Echebarría, Marco Ferroni, Robert Fogel, Marie Gaarder, Amiran Gafni, Silvia Galleguillos, Oded Galor, Edward Greene, Enrico Giovannini, Antonio Giuffrida, Eduardo González-Pier, Amparo Gordillo, Sally Grantham-McGregor, Meri Helleranta, Carlos Alberto Herrán, Pablo Ibarrarán, Roberto Iunes, William Jack, Michael Jacobs, Fidel Jaramillo, Kei Kawabata, Stanley Lalta, Jorge Lamas, Eduardo Levcovitz, Santiago Levy, Maureen Lewis, Beatriz López, Florencia López Boo, Gregory Marchildon, Reynaldo Martorell, Mercedes Mateo, David Mayer, Jacqueline Mazza, André C. Medici, José Antonio Mejía, Onofre Muñoz, Hugo Ñopo, Israel Osorio Rodarte, Sergio Piola, Claudia Piras, Augusto Portocarrero, Eduardo Rojas, David Rosas Shady, Héctor Salazar, Juana Salazar, Rodrigo R. Soares, José Seligmann, Mitchell Seligson, Ernesto Stein, Leslie Stone, Rubén Suárez, Karl Theodore, Daniel Titelman, Mariano Tommasi, Guillermo Troya, Claudia Uribe, Patricia Vane, Jaime Vargas, Joachim von Braun, and Adam Wagstaff.

On the Bank's behalf, the authors also wish to acknowledge the invaluable support they received from various entities that contributed precious statistical information to this project. The Gallup Organization was our principal support, by virtue of a generous agreement signed with IDB to share its World Poll. The Latin American Public Opinion Project (LAPOP) of Vanderbilt University and the Statistical Institutes of Belize, Ecuador, El Salvador, Guatemala, and Honduras collaborated in conducting specialized surveys.

SETTING THE STAGE

1

Quality of Life Viewed through Another Lens

*We are all very ignorant, but not all ignorant
of the same things*—Albert Einstein

Since Plato and Aristotle, philosophers have debated the topic of quality of life. Everybody seeks a better quality of life, although few people are able to define with precision the objective of their quest. If the key to a good quality of life were simply to have a good income, governments could concentrate their efforts on economic growth and ignore what people need for personal development and what society needs to achieve the public good. Reality, however, is quite different. In any democratic society, governments and the political systems that include them are judged not only by the quality of macroeconomic results, but also by their capacity to interpret and respond to the demands of the electorate on the most varied of fronts, ranging from national security to access to justice, and from the delivery of public utility services to the operation of hospitals and schools. A few basic economic and social statistics and a good dose of intuition to interpret public opinion and the actions of politicians are generally the main sources of information available to government leaders in making judgments and decisions.

Without disregarding these sources, it is also possible to go directly to individuals to find out what they think about the most important aspects of their lives, such as their health, their education, their jobs, and their housing, and how they perceive the main aspects of public policies and of the economic and social environment in which they live. Toward this end, more and more use is being made of surveys sponsored by private organizations or by governments themselves. The Gallup World Poll is the most ambitious effort available today for gathering information on perceptions of quality of life.

Through comparisons of data among various countries, and between the region of Latin America and the Caribbean[1] and the rest of the world, it is now possible to dis-

---

[1] Throughout this study, for brevity and ease of reading, the terms "Latin America" and "Latin Americans" are used inclusively to embrace the countries and people of the Caribbean as well. The databases used include various Caribbean countries.

tinguish the economic and social factors that most influence the perceptions individuals have of their own lives and of the situations in their countries. It is also possible to determine up to what point perceptions reflect reality according to official statistics on income, growth, unemployment, or poverty, or equally or more important, realities such as crime and the quality of education, which are typically ignored in official statistics.

This battery of data and analyses offers a new perspective for governments that want to identify the true needs of their citizens, for politicians who want to detect problems and controversial issues as the basis for their campaigns and decisions, and for companies and economic agents that need to better understand the behaviors of their markets and customers.

A Brief Overview

Are Latin Americans Different?

Although newspaper headlines frequently proclaim that one Latin American country or another is the happiest in the world or the most optimistic about its future, Latin Americans do not belong to another galaxy. In fact, South Asians and Western Europeans are consistently more positive in their opinions than Latin Americans. Nevertheless, there is great diversity within the region: Costa Ricans and Guatemalans stand out as the most optimistic in all aspects of their lives, whereas Chileans are seen as the most pessimistic. Perceptions fit psychological and cultural patterns: individuals are more positive in their opinions of themselves than in their opinions of other people or society as a whole, and the poor are kinder than the rich in their opinions of public policies, which constitutes an "aspirations paradox." This diversity of opinions reflects more the variety of individual viewpoints than the diversity of countries, although the latter does influence the former. Age, gender, employment status, and religious inclinations are a few of the individual factors that affect the opinions people have of themselves and of the situations in their countries.

To illustrate the parallel between subjective opinions and objective indicators, this study introduces a Subjective Human Development Index, comparable to the well-known United Nations Human Development Index. Based on this index, in Latin America, Peruvians demonstrate the widest gap between their perceptions and the reality of their own lives and the situations in their countries. Argentines and Chileans are fairly critical, while Costa Ricans and Bolivians have a very benign opinion of the social situations in their countries.

The Conflictive Relationship between Income and Satisfaction

The direct relationship between income and satisfaction is the basis of all economic theory. But this relationship does not fully reflect what happens in practice. In general, people in countries with higher income levels feel more satisfied in all aspects of their lives. Nevertheless, in countries that experience more rapid growth, people are more likely to feel less satisfied, which implies an "unhappy growth paradox." Also, in general, within each country people with higher incomes feel better off than those with lower incomes. However, when a person is surrounded by others with higher earnings, his or her satisfaction with his or her own work, housing, and all the things he or she can buy and do is reduced. These findings have important implications for policymaking, which are discussed in several chapters of this volume.

Social Policies

Perceptions regarding health, education, and employment are analyzed with revealing results throughout this study. People's toleration of their own health problems is an obstacle for prevention policies and for improving health services among certain social groups and in some of the countries with the worst health indicators. Similarly, acceptance by the majority of Latin Americans of their education systems does not square with the pitiful results achieved by the countries of the region on international academic achievement tests. This acceptance contributes to the fact that the academic quality of schools is not considered important in the decisions Latin American parents make regarding the education of their children. More important factors are discipline, safety, and the physical appearance of schools.

Job Quality

Low-productivity jobs, informal employment, and work instability are palpable realities in all Latin American countries, yet these apparently negative realities stand in stark contrast to the opinions of the workers themselves. Most people in the region are happy with their jobs, and there are more salaried workers who would prefer to work for themselves than informal workers who dream of becoming employees. Although labor policies require that workers have social security, guarantees of stability, paid vacations, and many other benefits, these benefits are not what is valued by those who are happy with their jobs. What is important to them is flexibility, autonomy, respect, and opportunities for personal growth. This suggests the need to redesign labor legislation in the region to take into account the interests and needs of workers so that no conflict arises between their interests and preferences and their opportunities to be employed by high-productivity companies and sectors.

Cities

People's satisfaction with their own housing and cities depends on several variables that are regularly measured in censuses and other standard sources of official information, such as the delivery of services and the quality of housing materials. But it also depends on aspects that are less studied, and in many cases ignored by policies, such as property titling, neighborhood safety, public transportation, sidewalk and road conditions, and proximity to green areas. Some of these features are reflected in home prices, but others are not and therefore tend to be ignored by the market. Problems differ from city to city and neighborhood to neighborhood, highlighting the diversity in tastes and lifestyles among inhabitants. In this study, we propose methods for the valuation of urban public goods that may prove useful for understanding the operation of housing and land markets and for designing public service and taxation policies at the local level.

The Political Economy of Public Opinion

Along with offering policy recommendations for each issue analyzed, this study also draws attention to the effects that perceptions can have on political processes and on public decision making. The beliefs and the perception and interpretation biases of both the electorate and politicians and government leaders exert considerable influence on the supply and demand of public policies. Information possessed by various actors in the political process can affect (in ways that are not always consistent) the perceptions of issues among the different players, which in turn affect the policy discussion, formulation, and implementation process. On those bases, strategies are proposed herein to reduce the information gap and the influence of perception biases so that the public debate may involve better options for producing policies that contribute to improving the quality of life.

In light of the findings of this study, a government strategy focused on efficiency and economic growth has little chance of political success, given that growth in income may not result in increases in satisfaction with different aspects of life, especially if such income growth unequally benefits different groups of individuals, or if it substantially changes expectations for material progress. Hence, it is not surprising that Washington Consensus policies have been the subject of popular rejection, especially in countries where the promoters of such policies have tended to exaggerate their potential benefits.

To avoid the loss in satisfaction with life that typically accompanies periods of accelerated economic growth, it would be effective to reduce the income of those families or individuals who are visible reference points for the social groups most vulnerable to changes in expectations (especially the upwardly mobile urban middle classes). Some expropriations, price controls, or special taxes on successful sectors may serve short-term political purposes, but over the long haul they are unsustainable because they are harmful to growth.

It is more feasible to garner political support through strategies that combine growth policies with initiatives for economic and social inclusion and with measures that address immediate demands for health, education, employment, or housing services. But in any case, inclusion and social service delivery strategies that maximize political support are not necessarily those that produce the greatest improvements in the living conditions of the poor. Because of the "aspirations paradox," generating dissatisfaction with social policies may be a requirement for creating political demand for better services in education, health, or social protection.

These incongruities between what may prove to be politically effective and what is effective in economic and social terms constitute a dilemma confronting politicians and government leaders today, especially in fragmented and high-inequality democracies, such as those of Latin America.

Because policy decisions in a democratic system are the result of conflicts and negotiations between groups with different interests and visions, rarely can these contradictions be resolved solely by appealing to technical arguments. Public debate may be more fruitful if opinion leaders and economic advisers to governments and political organizations begin to mine the riches hidden within the opinions of the people, so as to detect the limitations of traditional economic and social statistics and to better understand the motivations and needs of individuals, with all the opportunities and risks that this implies.

A Question of Approach

This study focuses on the opinions that Latin Americans have of their own lives and of the situations in their countries. This approach stands in stark contrast to the traditional approach of economists, who have avoided the use of subjective data both for theoretical reasons and because of the practical difficulties of measuring and interpreting opinions.

Traditional economic theory is based on the assumption that individuals are "rational" in the sense that they make decisions in order to pursue their own welfare in a coherent manner. According to this approach, the behavior of individuals is sufficient for deducing what advances their welfare ("revealed preferences" in economic jargon). Thus, if people work more, this implies that the welfare they derive from this increased work is greater than that which they would have obtained from the leisure they sacrificed in working more. If individuals spend the income received through this additional effort on luxury cars or upscale clothing instead of on a larger or better-located home, it is because they see the former as having greater utility than the latter. It is deduced, in accordance with traditional theory, that the higher the levels of income or consumption of any individual are, the greater his or her welfare will be, because of the increased options for choosing what will produce greater satisfaction or utility that the increased levels of income or consumption will provide him or her.[2] And if all individuals increase their levels of income or consumption, it is deduced that this group of individuals will necessarily have greater utility, that is, a better quality of life (i.e., the situation is "Pareto superior," in the abstruse parlance of economists).[3]

Although this is an eminently theoretical approach, it exerts an enormous influence on the manner in which economists are accustomed to broaching the quality of life issue. First, it assumes that, because individuals are rational, their decisions must generally coincide with the objective of improving their utility or their quality of life. Second, it assumes that it is people's decisions, more than their opinions, that reveal what brings them well-being and what does not. Third, and as result of the above, it posits that it is not necessary, and it may even be misleading, to try to measure directly the well-being that individuals experience or to attempt to compare the well-being of some individuals with that of others.

These conclusions, however, are debatable. Using a different approach, a growing school of psychologists and, more recently, economists and political scientists has attempted to establish some patterns of behavior of individuals vis-à-vis their consump-

---

[2] Unless the act of working more is not the result of a free decision, but instead an imposition.

[3] In cases in which some individuals have suffered losses in income or consumption, it cannot be deduced with certainty whether society as a whole is better or worse off, because according to traditional economic theory, it is not possible to observe directly or to compare among them the well-being of these individuals. In keeping with this theory, it is necessary to introduce some value judgment to compare the incomes of various people. This value judgment may be reflected in the weighting (negative) that would be given to inequality within a function of social well-being (such a function is the simplified representation of the values that society as a whole or a hypothetical "benevolent social planner" would assign to average income and to its distribution among the population).

tion decisions or their attitudes toward risk. This school has also tried to measure, using various methods, the sensations and perceptions of well-being and is exploring their relationship with individual factors and with the economic, social, and cultural conditions of individuals. This new approach, although still lacking the elegance and conceptual coherence of the theoretical apparatus of traditional neoclassical microeconomic theory, is opening new horizons for understanding such paradoxes as "unhappy growth" or satisfaction amid poverty as the result of a lack of aspirations.

Economists' suspiciousness in regard to opinion surveys is not based solely on theoretical reasons but also on the biases in people's opinions of their satisfaction vis-à-vis the different aspects of their own lives or the situations of their countries, as well as on the errors in measuring such opinions. The morale of the respondents at the time the survey is taken or the phrasing or order of the questions may affect survey results.[4] But inasmuch as better statistical and econometric methods have been developed, these difficulties have been reduced. Additionally, a growing number of surveys have yielded highly consistent results for phenomena once considered impossible to measure, such as happiness. The opinions people have of their well-being tend to reflect accurately the positive and negative sensations that they experience inwardly or that they express physically. These opinions also conform to those of close family members or friends in regard to the individual's well-being and are associated with physical measures, such as high blood pressure or cardiac pulse rate.[5]

This study makes ample use of opinion surveys, not only to find out how individuals perceive their own well-being, but also to explore how they value the different aspects of their lives, how satisfied they are with their health, with their education and that of their children, with their work, and with various public goods—from urban infrastructure to safety. Of course, people's opinions are not all that matter, and they can, in fact, lead to erroneous conclusions. For example, the opinions of individuals regarding their own health may not be accurate, or the manner in which they evaluate the education of their children may be conditioned by the limitations of their own education. Similarly, opinions regarding their work conditions may be affected by conformism, habit, or ignorance of labor rights. Many people may feel quite good about their cities, unaware of serious pollution or safety problems, while others may exaggerate the scale of these problems.

For these reasons, the many quality of life indicators based on perceptions may create confusion. Their usefulness for public policies depends on an understanding of how perceptions are formed and what factors influence them, as well as on recognizing the incongruities between perceptions and the economic and social indicators that society has chosen as its objectives.

Defining Quality of Life

Although quality of life, as applied to persons, has increasingly preoccupied medical, psychological, and social research since the 1970s, there still does not exist sufficient

---

[4] Bertrand and Mullainathan (2001) discuss the most common statistical problems of surveys, and Veenhoven (2007) analyzes the possible biases and measurement errors involved in the questions on life satisfaction.

[5] See the reviews of the validity of well-being measures in Diener (2005) and in Kahneman and Krueger (2006).

consensus on how to define the term, as each discipline has emphasized different aspects of the phenomenon. Multiple definitions of personal quality of life may be found, such as that which deals with the set of necessary conditions for happiness, with subjective life satisfaction, with the potential for adaptation, or with the basic commitment to improve one's life. Multiple meanings of the term as applied to countries may also be found.

However, the various accepted meanings of the term recognize that it is a broad concept that embraces more than the "living conditions" approach, which focuses on the material resources available to individuals. Quality of life also includes the circumstances in which people lead their lives. Accordingly, it is accepted that it is a multidimensional concept, not only because it requires that the diverse aspects of people's lives be taken into consideration, but also because it comprises aspects that are external to individuals and the interrelations among them. There is, however, no agreement on what these dimensions should be or how they should be selected or weighted to obtain a synthetic measure of the quality of life. Although the inclusion of subjective indicators to measure some of these dimensions or quality of life as a whole was the subject of much debate up until a few years ago, it is now accepted that subjective indicators are also relevant, and that the combined use of objective and subjective indicators provides a more comprehensive view.

Various taxonomies have been proposed for ordering the different elements involved in the quality of life. A common objective of these classifications is to organize the variables so as to later construct a comprehensive measure of quality of life (see Box 1.1). However, there is no need to construct a synthetic measure to study quality of life. On the contrary, given that there is no agreement on the definition of quality of life, or on the dimensions that make up the concept, or on how they should be combined with one another, the construction of synthetic indices contributes very little to understanding the complexity of the factors and viewpoints that influence quality of life.

Rather than as a basis for constructing synthetic indices of quality of life, the usefulness of a taxonomy of elements connected with quality of life lies in ordering the different meanings and dimensions of the concept of quality of life and of the variables involved. To quote Veenhoven (2000: 2), "Since we cannot force the use of words, we can better try to clarify their meanings."

The taxonomy used in this study is summarized in Table 1.1. The central structure of the table is provided by the distinction between individual and "national" variables (the table's columns) and by the distinction between "objective" variables and opinion variables (its rows).

Whereas individual variables refer to personal characteristics, to living conditions, or to the opinions of a particular person, "national" variables are aggregates for the country (and occasionally for the city or state, hence the use of quotation marks). In some instances the "national" variables consist of the sums or averages of individual variables, but this is not always the case. Policies or national institutions, for example, are not measured by statistical aggregation of individual observations. Individual variables that prove relevant to the concept of quality of life are not only those that are internal and specific to the individual, such as age, income or one's opinions of oneself, but also those referring to the individual in relation to others, such as marital status, relative income position, and one's opinion of others or of society as a whole.

Box 1.1 Quality of Life Components

Recognizing that quality of life is a multidimensional concept, academics from various disciplines have proposed alternative ways to classify its components, which are the conceptual basis for the hundreds of existing alternative measures of quality of life. A typical example of such measures, from a medical point of view, is Health Survey SF-36 (Ware, 1998), which assesses the quality of life of the respondent through its mental and physical components. The physical component is measured on the basis of 22 questions that inquire about physical limitations in regard to performing everyday tasks and work, the presence of pain, and perception of health status. The mental component combines the responses to 14 questions regarding vitality, emotional or physical limitations to social functioning, emotional limitations to work performance, whether the respondent characterizes him- or herself as nervous, and his or her degree of enjoyment of life.

A scale for measuring quality of life well known in the world of psychology is that proposed by Cummins (1997), which considers quality of life to be an aggregate of objective and subjective components. Each component includes seven domains: material well-being, health, productivity, intimacy, safety, place in the community, and emotional well-being.

One of the first attempts to measure the quality of life of a population in general was the Study of Comparative Welfare for Scandinavia, under the direction of Erik Allardt (Allardt and Uusitalo, 1972). This study considered the following criteria: income, housing, political support, social relations, irreplaceability, doing interesting things, health, education, and satisfaction with life. These indicators made it possible to distinguish between "having," "loving," and "being," considered the three basic dimensions of welfare based on the humanistic psychology prevailing at that time.

Another outstanding effort to measure the progress of societies is that developed by Richard Estes of the University of Pennsylvania through his Weighted Index of Social Progress (WISP), which covers 163 countries. WISP consists of 40 indicators that constitute 10 subindices of the following quality of life components: education, health status, situation of women in the society, military expenditure, economy, demography, environment, social chaos, cultural diversity, and welfare effort.

Source: Based on Veenhoven (2000).

Table 1.1 A Taxonomy of Variables of Interest Concerning Quality of Life

	Individual Variables		"National" variables
	Personal variables	Variables concerning the individual in relation to other people	
"Objective" Variables — Foundations of the lives of individuals or of society	**Abilities** • Age • Gender • Personality • Physical and mental health • Education • Knowledge and experience	**Family conditions** • Marital status • Children • Family structure **Other interpersonal conditions** • Friendships • Community participation	**Policies** • Economic (tax, economic regulation) • Work (hiring and firing laws) • Social (social security and protection) **Institutions** • Rule of law • Political institutions • Quality of public administration
"Objective" Variables — Objective results	**Material conditions of life** • Income • Consumption • Housing conditions (ownership, quality of materials, access to services) • Access to health, education, social security and job quality	**Relative conditions of life** • Income quintile • Income of reference group • Spatial segregation • Discrimination	**"National" results** • Economic (GDP, inflation) • Human development (life expectancy, infant mortality, schooling) • Work (informal, unemployment) • Social (poverty, inequality) • Quality of environment (natural, urban)
Opinion Variables — Assessment of results	**Individual assessment of results** In regard to individuals themselves • Happiness • Satisfaction with own life • Satisfaction with domains of personal life (standard of living, health, education, job, housing)	In regard to the situation of the country or society • General situation of country • Economic situation of country • Opinion on domains of society (health system, education system, employment policies, supply of housing, etc.)	**"National" averages of individual assessment of results** In regard to individuals themselves • Happiness • Satisfaction with own life • Satisfaction with domains of personal life (standard of living, health, education, job, housing) In regard to the situation of the country or society • General situation of country • Economic situation of country • Opinion on domains of society (health system, education system, employment policies, supply of housing, etc.)

In principle, the distinction between objective and subjective variables involves the former being verifiable or externally observable, while the latter are not. Socio-demographic characteristics of individuals, inflation or gross domestic product are objective variables. Opinion variables are by definition subjective. However, the distinction is less clear than it seems at first glance. For example, most indicators of the quality of public institutions contain elements of subjective judgment by experts. Elements of subjectivity are also present in attempts to measure externally the abilities or knowledge of individuals. Nonetheless, for want of a better term, herein "objective" covers all those variables that constitute the foundations of life for individuals or society, as well as the observable results of their individual and collective actions and behaviors.

The taxonomy proposed in Table 1.1 is useful because it makes it possible to situate some of the concepts most commonly used in quality of life studies and relate them to the variables used in this study. For example, the *abilities* with which individuals confront life, such as their personalities, health, education levels, and experiences (the upper left-hand portion of the table) relate to the concept of quality of life understood as the "ability to live" (Veenhoven, 2000). Amartya Sen (1985) in particular has highlighted the importance of this aspect of people's quality of life by emphasizing the development of abilities as a necessary condition for personal fulfillment and social development.

The *material conditions of life*, which include income, consumption, housing, access to health and education services, and employment conditions, are the objective results at the individual level. These results have been the focus of studies that have attracted the attention of economists, sociologists, and anthropologists since the 1970s.

Observing the quality of the economic, social, and institutional environment in which individuals live is another approach to defining quality of life. In this case, the approach involves objective conditions external to individuals that shape their existence and include both the policy and institutional variables that are the foundations for the functioning of society and the *"national" results*, whether economic, social, or environmental, for the country as a whole. This set of variables (the upper right-hand portion of the table) reflects how "livable," to use a term of Veenhoven (2000), a society is.

In contrast to objective variables, or "facts," are opinions (shown in the lower portion of the table). Within the opinion variables, the most important section in quality of life studies is related to *individual assessments of results in regard to themselves* (the lower left-hand section of the table), that is, the subjective evaluation that individuals make in regard to their life in general or to various dimensions of their lives or "domains" (material standard of living, health, education, employment, housing, etc.). In the past, this type of variable was virtually the exclusive preserve of psychologists and philosophers, but increasingly it is attracting the attention of economists as well. When the assessment refers to life as a whole, more precise terms are used, such as "life satisfaction" or the concepts of "happiness" or "overall happiness," all of which are employed interchangeably (depending solely on the questions in the survey). More precisely defined, "overall happiness is the degree to which an individual judges the overall quality of his/her own life as a whole favorably. In other words: How much one likes the life one leads" (Veenhoven, 2007: 8).

In recent years remarkable progress has been made in measuring happiness (or satisfaction with life), as discussed in Chapter 4. Measuring happiness is the only way in which an encompassing evaluation of the quality of life can be attempted. It is not feasible in any of the other approaches to assessing quality of life (through abilities, material conditions of life, or quality of the economic, social, and institutional environment of the country) to have a measure that encompasses the whole set of variables, simply because it is not possible to define a priori which components are valid and which are not, or how to assign a relative weight to each component. Neither does it make sense to combine indicators belonging to different approaches, although this has been the practice in the production of the hundreds of available quality of life indicators.

Although one's level of happiness or satisfaction with life is an encompassing assessment of the quality of life of individuals, this does not imply that public policies should be designed to produce maximum happiness or satisfaction. Since the reasons will be revealed in the chapters that follow, and summarized in the last chapter, suffice it to note here that happiness is an externally manipulable valuation, subject to inconsistencies and contradictions, and affected by biases that tend to favor the opinions that individuals have of themselves.

Happiness or satisfaction with life reflects quite imprecisely—and sometimes inconsistently—the opinions that individuals have of the situations of their countries or their societies (*individual assessment of results in regard to the situation of the country or society* in the lower portion of Table 1.1). Also, these opinions fail to clearly reflect the variables with which the quality of the economic, social, and institutional environment of a country is measured. The same holds true for the opinions of individuals in regard to the different dimensions or domains of their lives or within their societies.

Perhaps for these reasons, governments and analysts have so far paid very little attention to individuals' perceptions regarding their own quality of life or regarding the situations of their countries or societies. Although ultimately this study relates to public policies and their effectiveness, there are nonetheless valid reasons to investigate (in general and in each domain) how perceptions of the quality of life are formed and how they influence the decisions of individuals. First, this is an approach to quality of life that is valid in itself. Second, perceptions can influence the policies that are adopted in a democratic system, through the impact of voters on public decisions and on the control of government officials and public institutions. Third, perceptions can influence the effectiveness of policies so as to produce results, not only for the reasons already stated, but also because they can affect the expectations of individuals, their trust in institutions, and their attitudes of cooperation with state entities. Lastly, perceptions can provide information for the public debate on whether or not the policy objectives of the government correspond to the objectives of the people in their pursuit of well-being or to people's perceptions of happiness.

2

The Personality of Quality of Life Perceptions

Unrealistic optimism is a pervasive feature of human life; it characterizes most people in most social categories. —Richard H. Thaler and Cass R. Sunstein

Latin American and Caribbean public opinion on quality of life is a constant source of surprise. For example, it might be expected that Costa Rica would be the country in the region where the most people declared themselves satisfied with their lives, whereas Haiti would be the country where the lowest proportion of the population would hold the same opinion. This is because, although the average level of earnings among Costa Ricans is not the highest in the region, the vast majority have access to health care, education, and basic public services—a stark contrast to the situation in Haiti. If the same reasoning is applied to other cases, however, it is indeed surprising that Guatemalans declare themselves to be nearly as satisfied with their lives as Costa Ricans, or that Chile is one of the countries where more people express dissatisfaction with their lives.

Latin American and Caribbean perceptions of the quality of education and employment also turn out to be rather disturbing. Although all countries in the region have ranked very low in internationally recognized tests of academic achievement in which they have participated, two out of every three people in the region say they are satisfied with the schools to which their children have access. And although employment informality and the lack of employment stability are endemic phenomena in Latin America and the Caribbean (hereafter "Latin America"), it is one of the world's regions where the highest share of the working population declare themselves to be satisfied with their work.

In light of these contradictions, it may seem reasonable for governments and analysts in the region to continue to concentrate almost exclusively on "objective" quality of life statistics such as the well-known Human Development Index (HDI), which combines income per capita, life expectancy, literacy levels, and schooling coverage, the indicators of unmet basic needs used in many countries, or the wider combination of indicators associated with the Millennium Development Goals (MDGs), which include extreme poverty; gender equality; maternal health; prevalence of AIDS, malaria, and other illnesses; and various indicators of environmental sustainability.

Even though objective indicators are irreplaceable, a knowledge of perceptions is crucial to the understanding of those aspects of quality of life that are impossible to measure via external observation but are central to the decision-making process and implementation of public policy in democratic societies. If the majority of the population are satisfied with their economic situation and standard of living, how will they then be willing to accept the sacrifices and uncertainties that might be entailed, for example, by a free trade agreement that promises to generate higher levels of income and consumption in the future? If parents consider the education system to be working well, how will they then apply pressure in order to raise teaching standards? If the majority of people are satisfied with their work, including those who are self-employed or working without social security or labor protection of any kind, what chance does government then have in its efforts to reduce employment informality?

Given that perceptions of the quality of life cannot be inferred via external observation, opinion polls provide an invaluable source of information. They are, however, a problematic source whose limitations and possibilities must be understood in order to separate the wheat from the chaff.

What Do Latin Americans Think about Their Quality of Life?

In recent years, surveys of quality of life perceptions have become more widespread. Since 2003, the European Foundation for the Improvement of Living and Working Conditions has carried out various polls in 28 European countries (the 27 current EU member states, plus Turkey), with the aim of understanding not only the differences in lifestyles and standards of living in those countries, but also the differing aspirations and needs expressed by the diverse populations that make up the new, expanded European Union.[1] In Latin America, the Latinobarometer (managed by the Corporación Latinobarómetro, based in Chile) has, since the mid-1990s, researched various aspects of the quality of life in 17 Ibero-American countries in the region.

The most ambitious system of surveys on the quality of life is one recently established on a worldwide level by the Gallup Organization. Since 2006, this entity has carried out an annual worldwide poll in more than 130 countries (the Gallup World Poll). It constitutes the most uniform and widely based source of quality of life perceptions currently available (see Box 2.1). The system is therefore the prime source of information on quality of life perceptions used in this book, because it facilitates international comparisons. However, as the samples are representative only at a national level and the coverage of certain topics is limited, in the sectorial chapters of this book other multinational opinion polls are also used, such as the Latinobarometer and Vanderbilt University's Latin American Public Opinion Project (LAPOP), as well as surveys carried out by national institutes of statistics in certain countries.

In order to analyze quality of life perceptions, a distinction must first be made between individuals' perceptions of themselves and their personal living conditions on

---

[1] The results are analyzed in European Foundation for the Improvement of Living and Working Conditions (2004).

Box 2.1 The Gallup Worldwide Quality of Life Survey

In 2006, the Gallup Organization established a survey system that uses uniform methodologies to gather information about various aspects of the quality of life in more than 130 countries around the world. Twenty-two Latin American countries were included in the 2006 round, 20 in the 2007 round, and 22 in the 2008 round (still unavailable for consultation as this volume went to press).

In the majority of countries surveyed, a sample of 1,000 people is used, but in more populous countries such as China, the United States, and Brazil, larger samples are called for. The samples are representative of the entire population aged 15 or older. The polls are carried out by telephone in those countries in which more than 80 percent of the population has access to a landline telephone and by face-to-face interview in all the others. (All of the Latin American countries fall into the latter category.) The interviewees are selected at random among household members, in order to avoid the representativeness bias that often arises when only the first available household member is interviewed.

Interviews given in the home last approximately one hour and those carried out by telephone last 30 minutes. The same basic questionnaire is used in all countries, although in some regions additional questions are included.

At the request of the IDB, additional questions were included in the 2007 survey for the countries of Latin America concerning perceptions of and conditions of access to health and education services, perceptions of the quality of employment, affiliation with a pension system, and perceptions about diverse aspects of urban life, including safety conditions.

_____

Source: Gallup (2007).

one hand and, on the other, those same individuals' perceptions of the city or country in which they live. Using this distinction, the principal Gallup questions on various aspects or "dimensions" of the quality of life analyzed in this study are shown in Table 2.1. These dimensions have been chosen according to their relevance for policymaking in Latin America, not because they are considered, a priori, to be more important than others for the quality of life from an individual's point of view. As will be shown in Chapter 4, friendship, religion, or family relationships can be more important for many people than the dimensions included in the table, although it is doubtful whether these are areas in which the state could, or should, intervene.

The Highs and Lows in Quality of Life Perceptions

Newspapers often point out that one country or another in Latin America is the "happiest" or most optimistic in the world. This has given rise to the belief that Latin Americans tend to express more positive opinions than people in other regions. If the region as a whole is considered, however, there is no firm basis for this belief.

Table 2.1 Questions on Satisfaction in Gallup World Poll

Area	Self-perceptions and perceptions of immediate surroundings	Perceptions of society and other external circumstances
General	"Please imagine a staircase with the steps numbered from zero to ten, where zero is the lowest step and ten the highest. Suppose that the highest step represents the best possible life for you and the lowest step represents the worst possible life for you. On what step of the staircase do you presently see yourself?"	"Imagine a staircase with the steps numbered from zero to ten, where zero is the lowest step and ten the highest. Suppose that the highest step represents the best possible situation for your country and the lowest step represents the worst possible situation for your country. Please tell me the number of the step where you believe your country is at this time."
Standard of living	"Are you satisfied or dissatisfied with your standard of living, that is, with all the things you can buy and do?"	"Would you say that current economic conditions in your country are good, or not?"
Health	"Are you satisfied or dissatisfied with your health?"	"Do you have confidence in the medical and health system of your country?"
Education	No questions in this area	"In the city or area where you live, are you satisfied or dissatisfied with the education system and the schools?"
Work	"Are you satisfied or dissatisfied with your work or job?"	"Are you satisfied or dissatisfied with efforts to increase the number and quality of jobs in your country?"
Housing	"Are you satisfied or dissatisfied with your housing or the place you currently live?"	"In the city or area where you live, are you satisfied or dissatisfied with the availability of good homes at affordable prices?"

Source: Gallup (2006, 2007) World Poll questionnaire.

Judging by their own perceptions of the quality of life, people in the region are not far from the worldwide average in their perceptions of the different dimensions of their personal lives. Based on the 2006 and 2007 Gallup World Polls, on a scale of 0 to 10, Latin Americans, on average, rate the quality of their own lives at 5.8, which is about the midpoint for all the world's regions (see panel (a) of Figure 2.1). When people in the region are asked if they are satisfied with all that they can do and buy, 68 percent respond in the affirmative—a figure that might seem surprisingly high, bearing in mind that 35 percent of all Latin Americans are officially rated as poor. It is, however, close to the midway point between Sub-Saharan Africa (39 percent) and Western Europe (86 percent) (see panel (b) of Figure 2.1). The vast majority of the region's population declare themselves to be satisfied with specific aspects of their lives: on average, nearly 80 percent are content with their health, work, or housing. Although such high levels of satisfaction might suggest blind optimism, even in the poorest regions of the planet, the average level of satisfaction with these life dimensions is above 50 percent, and in

Figure 2.1 Graphical Summary of Quality of Life Perceptions

a. Perceptions of Satisfaction with Own Life and of the Situation in the Country

b. Perceptions of Own Standard of Living and of the Economic Situation in the Country

c. Perceptions of Own Health and of National Medical System

d. Perceptions of Local Education System

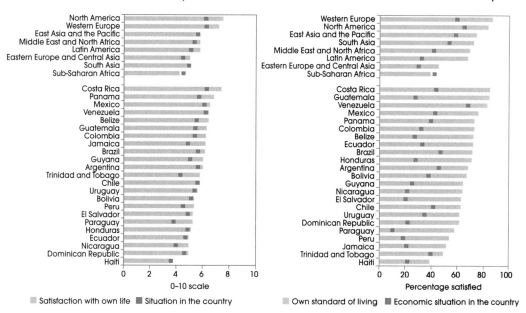

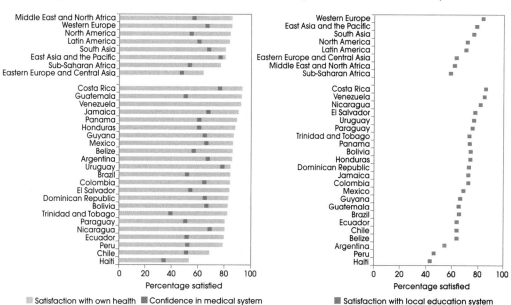

Note: No information is available on confidence in the medical system in Venezuela.

Figure 2.1 Graphical Summary of Quality of Life Perceptions (continued)

e. Perceptions of Own Work and of Government Policy on Job Creation

f. Perceptions of Own Housing and of the Housing Market

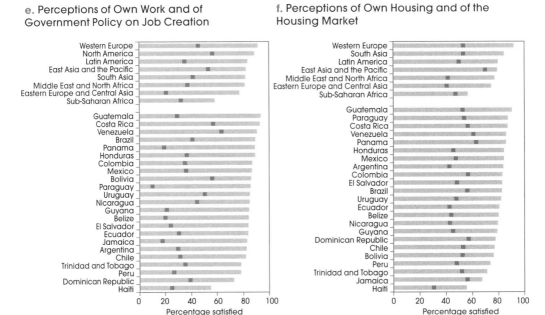

Source: Authors' calculations based on Gallup (2006, 2007).

the richer regions it rises to around 90 percent (see panels (c), (d), (e), and (f) of Figure 2.1).[2] Latin Americans do not differ greatly from the rest of the world in the way that they rate various dimensions of life *in their countries*, as demonstrated by points on the same panels of the figure.

In a region as diverse as Latin America, however, regional averages can be quite deceptive. Quality of life perceptions expressed by Venezuelans and Costa Ricans might come close to those expressed by North Americans and Europeans on various life dimensions. Surprisingly, though, given its low level of economic and social development, Guatemala appears in the list of countries with the highest satisfaction levels with various life dimensions. Guatemalans are the most satisfied with their jobs and their housing and, after Costa Ricans, are the ones who are the most content with their standard of living and state of health.

At the other end of the spectrum, various Caribbean countries declare very low levels of satisfaction, similar to the averages obtained in the poorest regions of the

---

[2] As will be shown in Chapter 3, it is not possible to affirm the existence of an optimistic bias for the region as a whole, when the influence exerted by income per capita on opinions on the quality of life in its diverse dimensions is isolated. The only exception is found in regard to satisfaction with employment, which turns out to be significantly higher in statistical terms than might be expected, given the levels of per capita income in the countries of Latin America.

world. It is no surprise to find Haiti near the bottom, as it is the poorest country in the region. Trinidad and Tobago, however, the richest country of not just the Caribbean but the region as a whole, appears to express some of the lowest levels of satisfaction with some aspects of life (see panels (a)–(f) of Figure 2.1). These apparent anomalies arise because a country's cultural traits wield great influence in regard to reported levels of satisfaction, as will be shown later.

Although country rankings may provide attractive newspaper headlines, the greatest wealth of information about quality of life perceptions is found elsewhere. A country ranking is merely the comparison of average values of a single variable, or of various variables reduced to a single dimension. Country rankings hide more than they reveal, given that, by considering a single variable, such rankings do not take into account the relationship between different dimensions of the phenomenon under investigation. In addition, because rankings average out the opinions of many individuals, they ignore the diversity of those opinions. Consequently, although country rankings might provide a good starting point, one must look further afield in order to explore the complexities of quality of life perceptions. First, it must be recognized that various behavioral traits can exert systematic influence upon opinions. Second, the variety of opinions existing within any group of individuals must always be taken into account.

Positive on Private Life, Negative on Public Life

In order to understand quality of life perceptions, one of the constants of human behavior must be borne in mind at all times: the marked tendency always to be more critical of society than of one's own situation.

When individuals assess different dimensions of the quality of life, they tend to be more positive in regard to their own conditions than they are in regard to their country, city, or community. In some respects, the differences are marked: whereas 83 percent of Latin Americans express satisfaction with their work, only 35 percent believe that governments are doing enough to "increase the number and quality of jobs available."

The systematic differences registered in favor of one's own circumstances are present as much in the more general aspects as in each of the more specific life dimensions shown in the panels of Figure 2.1. This observation is suggested by the fact that the points in the figure representing respondents' opinions on society are usually found inside the bars representing their opinions about themselves or about the conditions of their personal lives. This characteristic is not unique to Latin America: in all world regions, people in general hold a higher average opinion of their own personal situations than they do of the situations of others in all aspects of life. The differences are less noticeable in the more general aspects of the quality of life (panels (a) and (b) of the figure) than they are in more specific dimensions (panels (c)–(f)), but it is important to recognize that responses to questions about the condition of individuals are not strictly comparable to responses to questions about a country as a whole.

As noted in the epigraph at the beginning of this chapter, unrealistic optimism is a pervasive feature of human life and characterizes most people in the majority of social categories. For this reason, 90 percent of drivers believe that their driving skills are above average, and nearly everyone thinks that his or her sense of humor is better than everyone else's. Optimism affects aspects of life that are essential to well-being. For example, even though nearly half of marriages in the United States end in divorce, nearly all couples are certain that this will not happen to them, even if one of them has already experienced a divorce (Thaler and Sunstein, 2008). Although individuals judge their own situation more positively than that of society as a whole, this does not mean that the latter perceptions are more objective: both are influenced by cultural patterns.

The Influence of Culture

Individuals from different cultures appraise their own lives and the conditions of their countries in different ways. The importance of cultural factors in the formation of perceptions has been recognized by diverse authors.[3] The tendency to value personal satisfaction, for instance, is stronger in Western cultures than in Asian cultures. In the individualistic Western cultures, behavior is focused more upon the attainment of individual goals and achieving recognition for the positive consequences of decisions made, whereas in Asian cultures, consideration of the group as a whole results in behavior geared more towards avoiding losses and negative consequences. These differences contribute to the fact that Westerners express more satisfaction with their lives than do members of Asian societies. Perceptions expressed by individuals about themselves and their personal circumstances are also influenced by the importance that the individuals' culture places on happiness and personal satisfaction in relation to other values. In general, Latin American cultures assign more importance to these factors than do, for example, those of the countries of East Asia.

Within Latin America, Costa Rica, Guatemala, and Mexico stand out as optimistic cultures, with a tendency for individuals to express high levels of satisfaction in all aspects of their lives, whereas those who live in Chile, Paraguay, Peru, and Trinidad and Tobago are culturally more cautious in their judgments, as is demonstrated by statistical analysis of the Gallup World Polls (see Box 2.2). Measurements of cultural bias should always be treated with extreme caution, however, and cannot be considered either immutable factors or traits that can be applied equally to all aspects of people's lives or, obviously, to all individuals within a country. Nonetheless, given that the extent of cultural bias seems to be appreciable, these measurements suggest that all comparisons of opinions between one country and another must take the influence of culture into account.

Mainly as a result of the influence of cultural traits, a direct comparison between perceptions and objective social and economic indicators can be deceptive. In some quality of life dimensions, the national averages of people's opinions tend to reflect objective indicators quite well (see Table 2.2). Based on calculations for all countries in the world for which information is available, the correlation between general satisfaction with life in a particular country and its GDP per capita rises to 81 percent. Yet in other cases the correlation is lower: for example, the correlation between the opinion expressed about the general situation in a country and its GDP per capita is 59 percent. In others, it is startlingly low: there is a correlation of only 22 percent between the opinion about a country's economic situation and its GDP per capita, and of only 13 percent

---

[3] For a comprehensive literature review, see Diener, Oishi, and Lucas (2003).

Box 2.2 A Possible Measurement of Cultural Bias

Cultural bias is a recurring theme throughout this book. It might be expected that people's quality of life is determined as much by social advances and the objective problems experienced in each country as by the degree of conformity, tolerance, and optimism that characterizes each culture. If a high degree of this kind of cultural bias, which might be simplified under the general heading of "optimism," is clearly present, it follows that people might declare themselves to be satisfied with various aspects of their lives (health, employment, and housing, among others) irrespective of their objective individual condition or the problems faced by their country. Based on this simple concept, it is possible to construct ways of measuring optimism using information in the Gallup World Poll. The methodology employed in the calculation of cultural bias is based on techniques set forth in work carried out by van Praag and Ferrer-i-Carbonell (2007), designed to isolate the effect of individual psychological traits.

The measurement is the gap, for each individual in each country, between reported individual satisfaction and predicted satisfaction based on various objective characteristics of the individual and the country in which he or she lives. This measurement could yield drastically differing results, depending on the satisfaction variable employed and according to the objective variables selected to form the prediction. The metric presented in the figure shown in this box is the synthesis

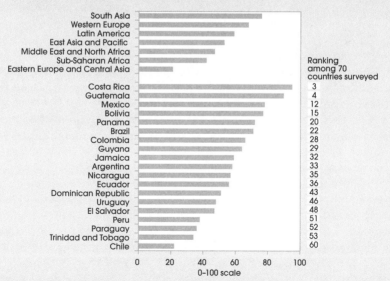

Indicator of Cultural Biases toward Optimism

Source: Authors' calculations based on Gallup (2006, 2007).

(continued on next page)

(continued)
of four different measurements, combining eight variables of personal satisfaction, four objective individual variables, and ten objective national variables.[a] The indicator of optimism has been calculated for 70 countries.

Variances in cultural biases toward optimism among the Latin American countries are similar in pattern to those existing between the different world regions. For example, Chile is nearly as pessimistic as the countries of Eastern Europe, whereas Paraguay, Peru, and Trinidad and Tobago are more pessimistic than the countries of Sub-Saharan Africa. At the other end of the spectrum, Costa Rica and Guatemala are among the countries with the highest optimism bias in the world.

These measurements should be considered with a high degree of caution. Their value resides solely in the fact that they demonstrate that cultural bias can be very pronounced and affect the perceptions that individuals have about themselves as much as the perceptions they have of society as a whole.

---

[a] The eight variables of personal satisfaction are satisfaction with the life that a person expects to lead in five years' time; personal economic satisfaction; satisfaction with health; satisfaction with housing; expectations held for the state of the country as a whole in five years' time; satisfaction with the national economic situation; confidence in the national medical system; and satisfaction with the education system. The four objective individual variables are gender, age, residential zone, and marital status. Finally, the ten objective national variables are GDP per capita, economic growth, inflation, levels of democracy, life expectancy at birth, infant mortality, school enrollment levels, political stability, government effectiveness, and the rule of law.

between perceptions of a country's economic situation and its annual rate of economic growth. In some cases, an unexpected relationship is observed between objective indicators and opinions: satisfaction with one's personal standard of living is *negatively* correlated with economic growth in one's country, constituting the "unhappy growth paradox" (discussed in Chapter 3). There are very low correlations when perceptions of personal health or national medical services are compared with life expectancy or rates of infant mortality, or when opinions on a country's education system are compared with a country's average years of schooling.

In certain dimensions of the situation of a country or its people, opinions are more a reflection of the country's cultural leanings than of traditional objective indicators. This is especially true in the case of collective dimensions. For example, as demonstrated in Table 2.2, the opinions (on average, per country) that people around the world have about the economic situations of their countries can be explained to a greater degree by the measurement of cultural bias (59 percent) than by levels of income per capita or by the countries' economic growth rates. In the same way, at least 60 percent of the differences between countries in confidence levels in the national medical system, the education system, or government policy on job creation can be explained by cultural differences between countries, and very little by traditional objective indicators. However, as will be shown from Chapter 5 onwards, this is also because these in-

Table 2.2 Correlation among Opinions, Objective Indicators, and Cultural Bias

	Correlation with objective indicators		Correlation with cultural bias
Satisfaction with own life	Per capita GDP	0.81	0.29
	Human Development Index	0.79	
Satisfaction with the situation in the country	Per capita GDP	0.59	0.44
	Human Development Index	0.60	
Satisfaction with own standard of living	Per capita GDP	0.65	0.51
	Annual economic growth rate	−0.30	
Satisfaction with the economic situation in the country	Per capita GDP	0.22	0.59
	Annual economic growth rate	0.13	
Satisfaction with own health	Life expectancy	0.21	0.39
	Infant mortality rate	−0.16	
Confidence in medical system	Life expectancy	0.29	0.60
	Infant mortality rate	−0.28	
Satisfaction with local education system	Years of schooling	0.38	0.68
	Scores on PISA test	0.42	
Satisfaction with own work	Unemployment rate	−0.26	0.36
Satisfaction with government policy on job creation	Unemployment rate	−0.44	0.66
Satisfaction with own housing	Coverage of basic services[a]	0.76	0.41
Availability of affordably priced good homes	Home ownership rate[b]	0.23	0.51
Subjective Human Development Index–Individual	Human Development Index	0.55	0.63
Subjective Human Development Index–Social	Human Development Index	0.41	0.73

Source: Authors' calculations based on Gallup (2006, 2007), World Bank (2007), and UNDP (2007). Countries are the unit of observation. Each correlation is calculated for all countries in the world for which information is available.
[a] Drinkable water, electricity, fixed telephone line (Gallup, 2006, 2007).
[b] Available only for Latin America and Sub-Saharan Africa.

dicators do not fully capture the quality of services or the aspects of those services that people value most.

Consequently, when perceptions of quality of life are being compared across countries, it is crucial not only to recognize the importance of cultural bias, but also to bear in mind that the same bias has a greater influence on the ways in which people judge their societies than on how they assess their own personal lives.

The "Aspirations Paradox": Poor People Express More Positive Opinions on Society

In addition to the importance of cultural differences between countries, the question must be asked whether there are also significant differences among diverse socioeconomic groups. The answer is no, although the similarity of the perceived quality of life among different income groups does seem surprising, especially considering the enormous inequalities in income between rich and poor people in Latin America.

As might be expected, individuals belonging to higher socioeconomic groups express more favorable perceptions of all aspects of their personal living conditions. However, perception curves are noticeably flat for differences of income or consumption. Based on the 2006 and 2007 Gallup World Polls, in Latin American countries, the quintile of highest income earners in each country receives an average of almost 57 percent of the country's total income, whereas the poorest quintile receives only 4 percent. Differences in perceptions between these quintiles, however, are very slight: the highest quintile rates its level of life satisfaction at 6.5 (on a 0–10 scale), whereas the lowest quintile rates its life satisfaction at 5.0. Similarly, 79 percent of individuals in the quintile of highest income earners in the country express satisfaction with material living standards, compared to 57 percent of those in the quintile of lowest income earners. The same can be said for each of the more specific dimensions of personal life (see panels (a)–(f) of Figure 2.2). This implies that the lowest-earning groups have a higher optimism bias than the higher-earning groups. As will be further discussed in Chapter 3, although higher levels of income are associated with greater satisfaction in all important dimensions, the relationship between income and satisfaction is tempered by expectations and by the points of reference whereby individuals compare themselves to one another.

When it comes to perceived living conditions and government policy in each country in the region, the poor tend to hold a similar opinion to—or even a more positive opinion than—the rich, which would seem to constitute a truly disturbing "aspirations paradox." For example, in Latin America, the lower quintiles express more confidence than the higher ones in both health services and government performance in implementing policies to create more and better employment. When more precise distinctions are drawn between the poor and the nonpoor, based on income and access to goods and services (according to criteria addressed in Chapter 3), the poor are found to have a more positive opinion of government policy aimed at combating poverty or creating employment than do the nonpoor.

The differences between the opinions of the poor and nonpoor with regard to such government policy are not insignificant, ranging from seven to ten percentage points (Gasparini et al., 2008). This variation could be attributed to the fact that government policy really does favor the poor. Then again, it could also be due to differences in information, either because the opinion of poor people is influenced by the image that the government or ruling politicians wish to promote or because the nonpoor have better information on the limitations of social policy—or because the nonpoor are less in agreement than the poor about the design or orientation of policy. This divergence could also reflect different expectations of what governments can or should do. Untangling all of these possible interpretations of the "aspirations paradox" is crucial in order to understand how opinions on government policy are formed and how they influence the process of public decision making. Chapter 3 will explore in detail the influence brought to bear upon opinion by so-called reference groups, whereby individuals compare themselves with each other. In the field of social policy, dissatisfaction among individuals increases as standards reached by the group to which the individuals belong rise. Complementary hypotheses will be examined in later chapters.

Figure 2.2 Comparing Perceptions on Public and Private Domains in Latin America
(averages by income quintile)

a. Satisfaction with Own Life and Evaluations of Situation in Country

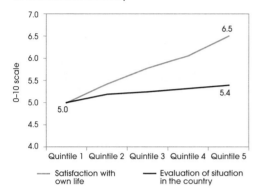

b. Satisfaction with Standard of Living and Evaluation of Country's Economic Situation

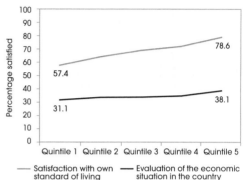

c. Satisfaction with Own Health and Confidence in National Medical System

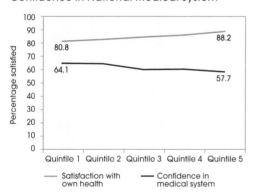

d. Satisfaction with Local Education System

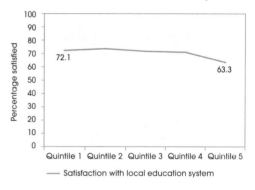

e. Satisfaction with Own Work and with Government Policy on Job Creation

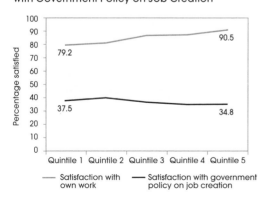

f. Satisfaction with Own Housing and with Housing Market

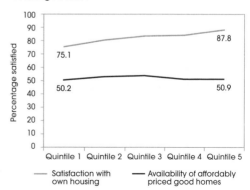

Source: Authors' calculations based on Gallup (2006, 2007). Respondents have been classified into income quintiles according to per capita household income in each country (not in the region as a whole).

The Divergence of Opinion

Given that the differences of opinion between income groups are slight, the conclusion could be drawn that the divergence of opinion between individuals is also small. Yet, nothing could be further from the truth. The source of the wealth of opinions on the quality of life is not to be found either in the differences between countries or the aforementioned income groups, but rather in differences between individuals. In the language of statistics, the variance of opinions *within* countries or income groups is substantially greater than the variance *between* (the averages of) countries or income groups. As the main part of this study is dedicated to the examination of these differences, only a brief outline of some general traits is given here to aid understanding of the dimensions of such variance. Subsequent chapters will deal with possible reasons for differences of opinion in diverse quality of life dimensions.

The Divergence of Opinions on Society Is as Great as the Divergence of Opinions Held by Individuals about Their Own Lives

It is not surprising that individuals hold a wide range of opinions on various aspects of their personal lives. Living conditions can be influenced by a multitude of factors pertaining to individuals, such as personality, abilities, or education, or factors external to them, but differentiated from each other, such as employment or housing conditions (consider the classification of variables in Table 1.1). Of all individual factors, personality traits perhaps exert the greatest influence over an individual's opinions on his or her own life.[4]

It is even more surprising that such a wide divergence of opinions exists among individuals with respect to society. If society is an object external to individuals and equally observable by all, it might be expected that opinions on it would show much less variance than people's opinions about their personal lives. Nonetheless, as the information on the "General" domain in Table 2.3 shows (with calculations based on individual-level information for 130 countries), the divergence of individuals' assessments of their own lives is only slightly higher than the divergence of their assessments of the situation of their country as a whole. (The standard deviations of the assessments on a scale of 0 to 10, meaning the typical distance between any individual's assessment and the average assessment of all the individuals, are 2.22 and 2.07, respectively.) In more specific life dimensions, such as economic situation, health, employment, and housing, the divergence of opinions on society is greater than, or at least equal to, the divergence of opinions on private life, as shown in the information for these domains found in the first column of Table 2.3. (For these domains, the standard deviations are measured on a scale of 0 to 1, given that they are taken from the responses of individuals to the question of whether they are satisfied in each of the dimensions.)

---

[4] Diener, Oishi, and Lucas (2003: 406–7) maintain that "demographic factors such as health, income, educational background, and marital status account for only a small amount of the variance in well-being measures." Key facets of personality, such as "agreeableness and conscientiousness, correlate approximately 0.20 with subjective well-being." Other psychological factors that seem to be closely related are "the way we approach our goals . . . and having a coherent sense of one's personality and acting in accordance."

Table 2.3 Analysis of Variance in Individual Perceptions

Domain	Perception	Diversity of opinions (standard deviation)	Diversity of opinions due to differences among countries (percentage)	Diversity of opinions due to differences within countries (percentage)	Correlation between perception of personal conditions and perception of conditions of society	Correlation after eliminating the average effect of each country
General	Satisfaction with own life	2.22	37.7	62.3	0.445	0.336
	Evaluation of the situation in the country	2.07	36.8	63.2		
Economic situation	Satisfaction with own standard of living	0.49	31.1	68.9	0.250	0.188
	Evaluation of the economic situation in the country	0.49	36.1	63.9		
Health	Satisfaction with own health	0.41	20.3	79.7	0.098	0.068
	Confidence in national medical system	0.49	25.9	74.1		
Employment	Satisfaction with own work	0.41	24.5	75.5	0.148	0.115
	Satisfaction with government policy on job creation	0.48	28.1	71.9		
Housing	Satisfaction with own housing	0.44	25.4	74.6	0.214	0.201
	Availability of affordably priced good homes	0.50	23.1	76.9		
Human development	Subjective Human Development Index–Individual	0.30	31.1	68.9	0.564	0.522
	Subjective Human Development Index–Social	0.34	33.8	66.2		

Source: Authors' calculations based on Gallup (2006, 2007). Calculations based on individual-level information for 130 countries.

Divergence of Opinion Is More a Reflection of the Diversity of Individual Points of View within a Country Than of Variations between Different Countries

In spite of great differences found between the richest and poorest countries in the world across all life dimensions, divergence of opinion on life dimensions is much greater among the individuals of a given country than among countries of the world. This holds true as much in private life dimensions as in collective life dimensions.

Differences between countries (i.e., between the average values for countries discussed previously in this chapter) account for only approximately a third of all divergence of opinion expressed by the world's individuals in any given dimension of the quality of life, whether private or collective. For example, in a private dimension such as the level of satisfaction with one's own life, only 37.7 percent of the variance is due to differences in average values between one country and another (see the second column of Table 2.3). The rest is made up of the differences among individuals within the same country. In a collective dimension such as the overall situation in one's home country, practically the same percentage (36.8 percent) is attributable to differences between countries. In other aspects of quality of life, differences between countries account for even lower percentages of difference in opinion, as much in private as in collective dimensions. In regard to satisfaction expressed with personal health, only a fifth of the variance is due to differences between countries, and in satisfaction with national medical systems, only a quarter.[5]

Divergence of Opinion Is Very High within Latin American Countries

In all countries of the world, divergence of opinion among individuals is high, but among the countries of Latin America it is even higher. For example, in assessments (on a scale of 0 to 10) made by Latin Americans about their own lives or about their country's situation, typical differences of more than two points are found within countries, more than in any other region of the world (see Figure 2.3). Contrary to what might be expected, though, this variance is not attributable to socioeconomic differences, as similar values are observed in each income quintile.

The wide variance in Latin America is partly a reflection of the fact that the region's countries occupy an intermediate position in the worldwide panorama. In the richest and poorest countries of the world, for example, there is less divergence of opinion, because objective conditions are more uniformly good or bad for the majority of the population. Beyond objective conditions, if in a given country the vast majority of people feel satisfied or dissatisfied—for cultural reasons, for example—with a particular life dimension, the divergence of opinion in that country will be, by definition, less than that in a country where half of the people declare themselves satisfied and the other half do not. Panel (a) of Figure 2.4 represents this relationship in regard to satisfaction with the medical system. In Costa Rica and Uruguay, divergence of opinion on the medical system is as low as in European countries, given that the levels of satisfaction are similar.

---

[5] The breakdown shown in Table 2.3 refers to all countries in the world in which interviews for the Gallup World Poll were conducted. However, the breakdown is similar when applied to the countries of Latin America. For example, 25.8 percent of the variance in responses concerning satisfaction with one's own life and 18.0 percent of the variance regarding satisfaction with personal health is attributable to differences between countries.

Figure 2.3 Variances of Individual Responses on Satisfaction with Own Life and on the Situation in the Country

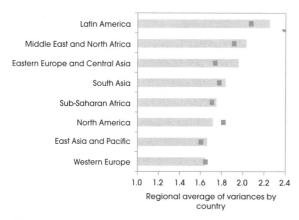

Regional average of variances by country

▨ Satisfaction with own life ■ Evaluation of the situation in the country

Source: Authors' calculations based on Gallup (2006, 2007).

In contrast, maximum variance is observed in the group of countries including Brazil, Chile, and Peru, because half of the people in those countries express satisfaction with the national medical systems, while the other half do not.

In the region as a whole, a higher divergence of opinion exists with regard to collective aspects than to private aspects of life. This ties in with the fact that, as discussed above, respondents express relatively positive opinions of private life dimensions and are more critical regarding public life dimensions (see panel (b) of Figure 2.4).

These are rather mechanical relationships between averages and variances, because they are based on questions that can be answered only "yes" or "no." However, when variance is measured in questions offering more response options, it becomes clear that divergence of opinion among people in Latin America is greater than that in other regions of the world. Figure 2.5 (in which every point represents a country) presents the averages of and deviations in the answers to the Gallup question concerning satisfaction with one's own life (on a scale of 0 to 10). As might be expected, in countries where average values of satisfaction are situated towards the middle of the scale, the divergence of opinion tends to be greater. The lower concave curve in the figure represents the relationship between the average and the deviation for all countries in the world. As can be observed, the relationship for Latin America (shown by the upper concave curve in the figure) is at a substantially higher level, representing a significant difference in statistical terms.

Consequently, in part because Latin America is largely made up of intermediate countries, and in part for other reasons, opinion on diverse dimensions of the quality of life diverges widely among individuals within countries in the region. Since this is expressed in regard to public as well as private life dimensions, it could be said that there is no such thing as a shared collective vision in the countries of the region. However, this variance is not attributable to socioeconomic differences, as similar results are obtained in all income quintiles.

Subjectivity Affects Opinions but Does Not Invalidate Them

The diversity of the opinions of individuals in Latin America on all aspects of life and society suggests that subjectivity has a bearing on these opinions. In effect, the combination of perceptions, on a personal level, of different quality of life dimensions can be explained to a degree of 28.5 percent by purely individual factors (after the influence

Figure 2.4 Relationship between Average Satisfaction and Its Dispersion

a. Confidence in the National Medical System, by Country or Region

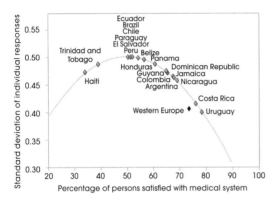

b. All Domains, Average for Latin America

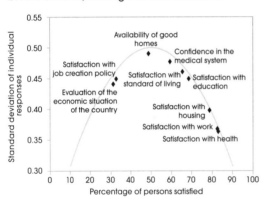

Source: Authors' calculations based on Gallup (2006, 2007).
Note: Standard deviations are the averages of the deviations calculated for each country.

exerted by all observable objective factors is taken into account).[6]

It can also be said that an individual's opinion on the quality of life in his or her country might be "contaminated" by that individual's assessment of his or her own particular standard of living. Consider, for instance, respondents' assessments of their own lives in general and of the general situation in their country, as shown in the first domain of Table 2.3. The correlation between the two assessments is not insignificant (44.5 percent) and declines relatively little (to 33.6 percent) when adjusted by extracting the portion of the correlation due to differences in average values by country for both types of opinion.[7] Similarly, if more specific life dimensions are examined, a certain degree of contamination from opinion on private matters to opinion on public matters is confirmed (between 10 percent and 25 percent).

Among the numerous factors that influence perceptions are ideological differences, varying ways of interpreting questions, and differences in tastes and life objectives. All of these could well be associated with personality traits. Furthermore, respondents might answer untruthfully for a wide variety of reasons, such as pride, status consciousness, or seeking public benefits.[8]

---

[6] This statistic was obtained by calculating the discrepancy between observed satisfaction and predicted satisfaction in 17 countries of the region, using six different variables of satisfaction. Predicted satisfaction was based on five objective individual variables. The six discrepancies were then combined using principal components analysis in order to obtain the share of the variance explaining the first principal component. Finally, this share was averaged for all 17 countries in question.

[7] These calculations refer to the full sample of individuals and countries included in the Gallup World Polls. When limited to just Latin America, the results are very similar: the correlation between assessments made about one's own life and about the general situation in the country is 33.7 percent, and is reduced to only 33.6 percent if the differences between countries are extracted.

[8] In a study carried out on Mexico by Martinelli and Parker (forthcoming), it was observed that, in order to save face, people claim to have assets that they do not in fact have, but that are desirable and possessed by other people, such as water, sanitation, and concrete-built housing. However, in order to claim advantages such as subsidies intended for the poor, they may also claim not to have goods such as household appliances that they do, in fact, possess.

Subjectivity is inherent in the more general perceptions of quality of life, but instead of being treated as a deficiency, it should be considered part of the wealth of this sort of information. The degree of satisfaction with their own lives that people express through opinion polls can help to identify the aspects of life that are of greater or lesser importance to them, as shown in Chapter 4. In the same way, when responses about satisfaction with housing are compared to objective information about housing characteristics, it is possible to deduce the aspects of housing that are most important to respondents. Similarly, when individuals' responses about satisfaction with their neighborhood are compared with information about the state of the roads, the diversity of available services, or levels of public safety, the relative importance that individuals assign to each of these aspects of urban life can be established (see Chapter 8).

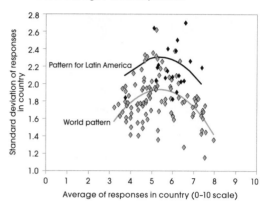

Figure 2.5 Satisfaction with Own Life: Relationship between Averages and Dispersion

Source: Authors' calculations based on Gallup (2006, 2007). *Note:* Each point represents a world country. Black points represent Latin American countries.

The majority of people in any given country might feel satisfied with their health, even though life expectancy is short, because they might not be aware of their own health limitations, or might compare their health to very modest models (see Chapter 5). People's opinions about the quality of the education system in their localities might not reflect traditional objective variables, such as school enrollment rates or the results achieved by students in internationally recognized academic examinations, because in their opinion as parents, the fact that their children are safe at school and are treated with respect might seem to be enough (see Chapter 6). The vast majority of Latin Americans might feel content with their work, in spite of high levels of employment informality and low levels of affiliation with the social security system, because many people place more value on their independence and flexibility than on the potential benefits of a health insurance policy or a pension plan (see Chapter 7).

A Subjective Human Development Index

It might be argued that the Human Development Index is the objective quality of life yardstick that exerts the greatest influence on governments and organizations promoting development around the world. In accordance with Sen's (1987) conceptual approach, this index does not seek to measure results achieved by individuals, but rather the capacities at their disposal to fully develop their lives according to their own preferences and decisions. By employing simple indicators that are available for virtually all countries in the world, on income, health, and education, and an elemental weighting system, the HDI can be used to draw up a worldwide country ranking of the basic human capital available in each country. How does this country ranking compare with the perceptions that individuals have of themselves and of their countries? What particular characteristics would a human development index have, if it were based not on objective data, but rather on perceptions?

In order to tackle these questions, Néri, Sacramento, and Carvalhaes (2008) propose the construction of a Subjective Human Development Index, the inspiration for the calculations presented in this section. Using econometric techniques, Néri and his team have developed an index combining diverse indicators of opinion. Here, a simpler method is adopted, allowing the creation of two subjective indicators of the HDI. The first of these indicators is the Subjective Human Development Index–*Individual* (SHDI-I), which synthesizes three measures of *individual* satisfaction in the same three dimensions that make up the original HDI (income, health, and education), using the same weighting system as the original HDI. The second indicator is the Subjective Human Development Index–*Social* (SHDI-S), which is differentiated from the SHDI-I by the use of measurements of satisfaction in the same three dimensions, but referring to the state of the *country or society*, rather than to individuals.[9]

Under the original HDI's methodology, a country would obtain a perfect score (i.e., a value of 1) if it fulfilled four prerequisites: an income per capita of at least US$40,000 (at purchasing power parity), an absence of adult illiteracy, full access to all three levels of the education system, and a life expectancy of 85 years. In the case of the SHDI-I, a country would obtain the maximum score if all persons in that country were satisfied with the things they could do or buy, satisfied with the education system in their town or city of residence,[10] and happy with their own state of health. In practice, no country attains a perfect score, either on the original HDI or on the proposed subjective index. The indices do, however, measure the discrepancy between the actual and the perfect score, and thereby permit comparisons both between different countries and between the different versions of the HDI.

Figure 2.6 shows country scores on the two versions of the SHDI: the individual version is represented in bars and the social version as points. Three Latin American countries (Costa Rica, Guatemala, and Venezuela) reach levels of subjective human development similar to those found on average in North America or Western Europe. The lowest positions in the region are occupied by Haiti and Peru, followed by Chile, Trinidad and Tobago, and Argentina. The position of several of these countries in regard to their scores on the SHDI-I contrasts with the position attained based on their scores on the traditional HDI, which is shown on the right. In spite of these discrepancies, the correlation between the HDI and the SHDI-I for all countries is 55 percent, and that between the HDI and SHDI-S is 41 percent. Consequently, the subjective versions of the HDI do not exactly reflect the original HDI based on objective indicators, although they are not far off the mark.

Given the information provided by the subjective indices, it is possible to determine whether a crossover exists between a country's objective achievements and the

---

[9] The questions considered in each case are to be found in Table 2.1. It should be pointed out that the question concerning satisfaction with education is the same for both indicators, given that there is no specific Gallup question for determining whether a person is satisfied with his or her own level of education.

[10] It should be remembered that owing to a lack of information, opinion expressed on education refers to its collective aspect and not its individual aspect.

perceptions people have regarding their own conditions. Using the statistical tool of cluster analysis, the 117 countries for which information is available can be sorted into seven different groups.[11] Panel (a) of Table 2.4 summarizes the objective HDI averages and the subjective HDI averages for the individual version for each of the seven groups and indicates to which group each Latin American country belongs. The majority of countries in the region are in the two groups in which a crossover exists between objective and subjective human development. The most interesting groups are those in which perceptions lag behind reality, which happens in the case of Argentina, Chile, Peru, and Trinidad and Tobago, countries where perceptions are very negative in the face of very real achievements in human development.

Similarly, panel (b) of Table 2.4 presents the results of the cluster analysis applied to the social version of the SHDI. All countries analyzed in Latin America belong to groups in which perceived human development is not equal to objective human development, which would seem to suggest a negative cultural bias in how collective aspects of human development are assessed. This discrepancy is particularly pronounced in two groups: the group in which Chile appears, alongside Trinidad and Tobago, and the group including Guatemala, Paraguay, and Peru.

As this analysis suggests, the subjective versions of the HDI do not reflect the objective HDI with any great precision, mainly because the former are heavily influenced by each country's cultural differences. In effect, the correlation between the aforementioned indicator of cultural bias and the individual version of the SHDI is 63 percent. The correlation with the social version of the SHDI is even higher (73 percent), which would seem to confirm that cultural leanings exert greater influence on opinions expressed about society than on opinions expressed about aspects of private life. Cultural bias explains 16 percent of the differences between the objective HDI and the SHDI-I, and accounts for 17 percent of the differences between the objective HDI and the social version of the SHDI.

Figure 2.6 Subjective and Objective Human Development Indices

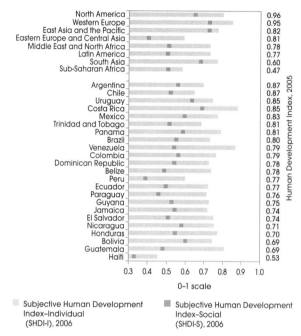

Subjective Human Development Index–Individual (SHDI-I), 2006

Subjective Human Development Index–Social (SHDI-S), 2006

Source: Authors' calculations based on Gallup (2006, 2007) and UNDP (2007).

---

[11] The total number of groups results from statistical analysis and is not determined a priori.

Table 2.4. Matches and Mismatches between the Objective HDI and the Two Versions of the Subjective HDI

a. Between the Objective HDI and the Subjective Human Development Index–Individual

Cluster	Human Development Index (HDI) 2005, average for cluster (a)	Subjective Human Development Index–Individual (SHDI-I) 2006, average for cluster (b)	Ratio of HDI to SHDI-I (b/a)	Number of countries in cluster	Countries of Latin America in cluster
A (countries with a very low level of both objective and subjective human development)	0.45	0.56	1.24	24	Haiti
B (countries with a very low level of objective human development but a medium level of subjective human development)	0.58	0.74	1.27	9	None
C (countries with a medium level of both objective and subjective human development)	0.73	0.72	0.99	17	Belize, Bolivia, Dominican Republic, Ecuador, El Salvador, Guatemala, Guyana, Honduras, Jamaica, Nicaragua, Paraguay
D (countries with a medium level of objective human development but a very low level of subjective human development)	0.77	0.56	0.72	17	Peru
E (countries with a medium-high level of both objective and subjective human development)	0.80	0.79	1.00	12	Brazil, Colombia, Mexico, Panama, Uruguay, Venezuela
F (countries with a high level of objective human development but a very low level of subjective human development)	0.89	0.67	0.75	13	Argentina, Chile, Trinidad and Tobago
G (countries with a high level of both objective and subjective human development)	0.93	0.84	0.90	25	Costa Rica
All countries	0.74	0.69	0.94	117	

Table 2.4. Matches and Mismatches between the Objective HDI and the Two Versions of the Subjective HDI (continued)

b. Between the Objective HDI and the Subjective Human Development Index–Social

Cluster	Human Development Index (HDI) 2005, average for cluster (a)	Subjective Human Development Index–Social (SHDI-S) 2006, average for cluster (b)	Ratio of HDI to SHDI-S (b/a)	Number of countries in cluster	Countries of Latin America in cluster
I (countries with a very low level of both objective and subjective human development)	0.46	0.44	0.97	22	Haiti
II (countries with a very low level of objective human development but a medium level of subjective human development)	0.55	0.70	1.28	11	None
III (countries with a medium level of objective human development but a very low level of subjective human development)	0.74	0.40	0.54	13	Guatemala, Paraguay, Peru
IV (countries with a medium level of objective human development but a low level of subjective human development)	0.75	0.56	0.75	19	Belize, Bolivia, Brazil, Colombia, Dominican Republic, Ecuador, El Salvador, Guyana, Honduras, Jamaica, Nicaragua, Panama
V (countries with a high level of objective human development but a medium level of subjective human development)	0.87	0.64	0.74	17	Argentina, Costa Rica, Mexico, Uruguay
VI (countries with a high level of objective human development but a very low level of subjective human development)	0.89	0.47	0.53	15	Chile, Trinidad and Tobago
VII (countries with a high level of both objective and subjective human development)	0.91	0.81	0.89	19	None
All countries	0.74	0.57	0.78	116	

Source: Authors' calculations based on Gallup (2006, 2007) and UNDP (2007).

As is often the case with perceptions, those that refer to individual dimensions tend to be more positive than those concerning society in general. In effect, the points representing the SHDI-S in Figure 2.6 are always situated within the bars that represent the SHDI-I.

Given that the SHDI is based on individual perceptions, it is possible to calculate the indices for different segments of the population. Figure 2.7 graphs average scores for Latin America on the two versions of the SHDI according to the income quintiles of individuals within a given country. The curve representing the individual version of the SHDI has the expected gradient, but it is noticeably flat for underlying income inequalities. For the social version of the SHDI, the gradient is negative, which confirms the "aspirations paradox," wherein poor people express more positive opinions on society as a whole than do rich people in the same country.

The SHDI further allows for the identification of the source of variance, given that it can be calculated for each individual according to his or her opinions. Returning to Table 2.3, the last two rows indicate that only a third of the divergence of opinions shown in the SHDI can be attributed to differences of opinion between countries, whereas most of the divergence of opinion derives from differences within the countries themselves. Table 2.2 demonstrates that divergence of opinion within the social version of the SHDI (73 percent) is higher than in the individual version (63 percent). Finally, Figure 2.8 shows that divergence of opinion within Latin America is rather high (consistent with the fact that many countries in the region occupy an intermediate position in the SHDI). In this way, the SHDI permits verification of all traits characterizing the formation of opinions on the quality of life, as summarized in the chapter conclusion, which follows.

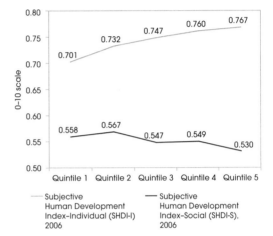

Figure 2.7 Subjective Human Development Index by Income Quintile, Latin America

Source: Authors' calculations based on Gallup (2006, 2007) and UNDP (2007). Respondents have been classified into income quintiles according to household per capita income in each country (not in the region as a whole).

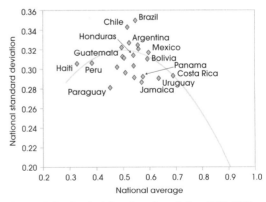

Figure 2.8 Dispersion and Average Level of Subjective Human Development Index–Social (SHDI–S), Latin America

Source: Authors' calculations based on Gallup (2006, 2007). *Note:* Each point in the figure represents a Latin American country; some points are labeled as examples.

Conclusion: The Personality Traits of Perception

This chapter has introduced the main actor in the rest of the book: public opinion, which turns out to be a surprising and truly versatile character.

Opinion is not merely a reflection of the objective reality that traditional economic and social indicators attempt to measure, although it is never divorced from these indicators. Opinion is greatly influenced by different cultures within different countries. Opinion is relatively positive in regard to private dimensions of life, and clearly more so than in regard to public dimensions. Contrary to what might be expected, in collective dimensions the opinions of the poor are generally more positive than the opinions expressed by the rich, giving rise to the so-called aspirations paradox discussed above.

Opinion, moreover, is not just a single character—it is numerous and diverse characters rolled into one. Although countries represent an important source of diversity, far greater variance flows from the diversity of individuals within a given country. One of the many intriguing traits of opinion is that divergence of opinion on collective life turns out to be at least equal to divergence of opinion about private life; in many cases it is even greater. While divergence of opinion within Latin American countries is greater than that found in other regions of the world, this diversity is not due, directly at least, to the stark economic inequalities found in those countries, but rather to other, more personal factors that will be identified in the rest of this volume. Now that the character traits of this new actor have been revealed, it is time to show how this actor relates with other, better-known characters, such as income.

3

The Conflictive Relationship between Income and Satisfaction

Men do not desire merely to be rich,
but to be richer than other men.—John Stuart Mill

Income is the most-revered variable in economics. At the aggregate level, the total income generated in a given country is a measure of the size of its economy. Per capita income reflects the conditions of productivity and the purchasing power of the population, and the growth rate of this variable is the yardstick by which the material progress of a country is most commonly measured. On an individual level, personal disposable income represents the various options open to individuals in order for them to achieve maximum satisfaction with life. In accordance with conventional economic theory, each increase in income gives rise to more satisfaction, albeit in ever-decreasing quantities as needs become increasingly satiated.

However, when these theoretical predictions are matched against the opinions of people all around the world, it becomes apparent that the relationship between income and satisfaction is more complex and less harmonious. It is true that satisfaction in nearly all dimensions tends towards a higher average in those countries enjoying higher levels of per capita income. This chapter, however, will demonstrate the existence of an "unhappy growth paradox": economic growth, instead of elevating, actually reduces the satisfaction experienced in various aspects of people's lives, especially in countries that have already reached a certain standard of income and consumption.

In a similar way, although higher earnings on an individual level tend to be reflected by higher levels of satisfaction, an increase in income for the social group to which an individual belongs produces the opposite effect, especially within the material dimensions of well-being. In this way, changes in expectations and aspirations can counteract the gains in satisfaction produced by increased income. This "aspiration treadmill" can lead to the paradoxical situation in which some of the most economically successful groups, with the highest aspirations, might have lower levels of satisfaction than economically and socially marginalized groups with lower aspirations.

Individual well-being does not depend exclusively on the consumption of private goods. Access to public goods and services and subjective models of evaluating one's own situation also affect well-being. Consequently, the distinction between those who are poor and those who are not can be made by combining these three dimensions of well-being in different ways. In Latin America and the Caribbean (hereafter "Latin America"), many individuals who are classified as poor according to objective indicators of private consumption and restricted access to certain public services do not consider themselves to be poor. Distinctions between poor and nonpoor according to objective and subjective criteria are relevant, because the relationship between income and satisfaction differs in each case.

The complex relationship between income and satisfaction poses multiple political conflicts. Is economic growth desirable, bearing in mind that it may decrease—at least temporarily—satisfaction and increase subjective poverty? Conversely, is it justifiable to maintain the ignorance of those who lack social aspirations in order to avoid a subsequent drop in satisfaction? Should efforts to improve the quality of life be concentrated on those considered poor according to objective criteria or upon those who consider themselves poor from their own subjective viewpoint? Given that political decisions in a democratic system are reached as a result of negotiations between groups with different visions and interests, the answers to these questions can result only from public debate on the conflictive relationship between income and satisfaction.

Satisfaction, Income, and Growth at the Aggregate Level

Tremendous efforts are made by governments to track the gross domestic product (GDP), the best-known measure of productive activity and of the size of an economy. Although GDP per capita is usually considered a good indicator of a society's standard of living, it was not initially conceived with this end in mind. GDP does not take into account a number of activities that generate well-being, such as leisure, whereas it does include others that might indeed even give rise to problems, such as narcotics production or the depletion of nonrenewable natural resources (see Box 3.1). In spite of these deficiencies, GDP does measure (after some accounting adjustments that need not be specified in this chapter)[1] the total income that people receive—and therefore has a bearing on satisfaction, because an individual's potential to consume is limited by income.

In the last few decades, the principal objective of economic policy in Latin America has been to accelerate the growth of GDP. After the "lost decade" of the 1980s, governments in the region embraced, to a greater or lesser extent, the tenets of the Washington Consensus, which promised to raise growth rates in a sustainable manner through a combination of policies aimed at ensuring macroeconomic stability while freeing up markets to augment efficiency. Since then, growth has indeed improved, but the gains have been modest in comparison with those experienced in other regions of the developing world, especially Southeast Asia. In the present decade, per capita income in the region has grown somewhat more quickly than that in the developed world, but it is still a long way from recovering from the gap accumulated in previous decades. Whereas in the 1970s and 1980s per capita income in Latin American countries was equal

---

[1] Personal disposable income is obtained by deducting from GDP the costs of capital depreciation, earnings withheld by companies, government income from its own properties and enterprises, net transfers of income from families to the government, and net transfers of income to the rest of the world.

Box 3.1 Is GDP an Indicator of Well-Being?

The idea of creating an accounting system dealing with national income and production arose as a result of the Great Depression of the 1930s, as a way to monitor the productive activity level. The idea was first put into practice in the United States in 1942, to monitor potential wartime production levels.

From its inception, GDP was thought of as a measure of productive activity or, more accurately, of the market value of the production of goods and services. Goods such as leisure or services carried out by people in their own homes are not included in GDP, although they contribute to well-being. On the other hand, all production arising from the marketplace, such as manufacturing of arms and production of narcotics, is included regardless of whether it increases well-being.

As GDP takes into account only production and income flows, but not variations in reserves and stocks, oil production is included, whereas a reduction in oil reserves is not. Additional forms of depletion of natural or other resources are also ignored. Therefore, a country suffering a natural catastrophe might even see an increase in its GDP due to reconstruction activities, in spite of deaths and loss of capital resulting from the catastrophe.

These shortcomings hamper comparison of GDP between countries that conserve natural resources and those that deplete them, or between countries obliged to dedicate a substantial part of their resources towards combating crime and those enjoying relative security. There are also difficulties in establishing international comparisons because of differences between currencies and relative prices, although such difficulties can be overcome by valuing goods and services at a common price (that is, in U.S. dollars, based on purchasing power parity).

In view of these limitations, various proposals have been introduced to adjust the way that GDP is calculated. James Tobin (Nobel Prize for Economics in 1981) and William Nordhaus suggested in the 1970s that the value of household and leisure services should be included in GDP, while certain "evils," such as pollution, should be discounted, as well as other activities, such as police services, which are aimed at correcting social problems rather than generating goods. Similarly inspired, other measurements have also emerged, such as the Genuine Progress Indicator (GPI), calculated by Redefining Progress, a private organization in the United States, and the Measure of Domestic Progress (MDP), produced by the New Economics Foundation in the United Kingdom. In both cases, the traditional aggregates are tempered by the value of environmental and social costs.

The United Nations, which since the 1950s has set international standards for GDP calculation, has expanded the original national accounting system with the aim of measuring various forms of capital stocks and their variations. Although these modifications provide an enhanced description of a country's economic system, they do not provide a good indicator of well-being. The quality of health care and education in a country, the general conditions of personal safety, and political stability are important dimensions of quality of life in that country that cannot be fully captured by national accounting alone.

Figure 3.1 Comparisons of GDP per Capita by Region and Decade, 1981–2006

a. Average annual real GDP per capita growth *(percent)*

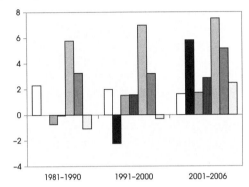

b. GDP per Capita
($US at 2005 purchasing power parity)

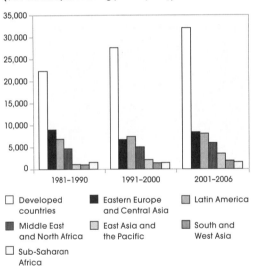

☐ Developed countries   ■ Eastern Europe and Central Asia   ▨ Latin America

■ Middle East and North Africa   ▨ East Asia and the Pacific   ■ South and West Asia

☐ Sub-Saharan Africa

Source: Authors' calculations based on World Bank (2007).
Note: In panel (a), data for Eastern Europe and Central Asia are unavailable for the decade 1981–1990.

to 33 percent of income in developed countries, today it represents barely 25 percent (see panel (b) of Figure 3.1).

It is important to remember, however, that Latin America is a highly heterogeneous region in regard to both economic growth and per capita income. During the current decade, the richest country in the region, Trinidad and Tobago, has also experienced the highest growth, with rates comparable to those of India or China. Trinidad and Tobago is followed in income by Chile, whose recent performance, although not matching that of previous decades, is still respectable given the standards of the region. In contrast, Mexico ranks high in terms of income but has achieved only a modest growth rate. It is further troubling to note that the countries achieving the lowest growth rates are also among the poorest in the region, such as Haiti, Guatemala, and Paraguay, where income per capita is comparable to average incomes in the poorest regions of the world (see Figure 3.2).

If all the world's countries were classified into two groups according to levels of per capita income, then the majority of Latin American countries would belong in the high-income category. The only exceptions would be (in descending order of income) Guatemala, Paraguay, Bolivia, Guyana, Honduras, Nicaragua, and Haiti. But if the world were divided into two groups based on the rate of growth of per capita income during the period 2001–2006, then the majority of the region's countries would belong to the group of countries experiencing slow growth. Only the following countries (in descending order) would appear in the group achieving rapid growth—Trinidad and Tobago, Ecuador, Peru, Chile, Panama, the Dominican Republic, and Costa Rica—and even some of those countries would be only temporary members of that group.

Satisfaction and Per Capita Income

In line with the principles of economic theory, the satisfaction expressed by individuals with various aspects of their lives and with their societies is higher in countries enjoying higher levels of per capita income. Figure 3.3, based on data from the 2006 and 2007 Gallup World Polls and World Bank (2007), shows that the link between general satisfaction with life and per capita income is strong. Statistical analysis confirms that the relationship with income is significant in all dimensions of personal satisfaction, and in several of the collective dimensions considered in Chapter 2 (see Table 3.1).

Owing to the logarithmic method used in calculating per capita income, the results imply that increased income does contribute to the enhancement of various aspects of satisfaction, but with diminishing returns. In order to increase average life satisfaction by one point on a 0–10 scale, in a country with an annual per capita income of US$2,000—the average annual income of Latin American countries—per capita income would need to be increased to US$7,500. To obtain the same increase of one point in life satisfaction in a developed country with a per capita income of US$10,000, a per capita income of US$36,000 would have to be achieved. Similarly, an increment from US$2,000 to US$5,000 would be needed to increase by 10 percent the proportion of the population declaring itself satisfied with its material living

Figure 3.2 Comparisons of GDP per Capita, World Regions and Latin American Countries, 2001–2006

a. Average annual real GDP per capita growth *(Percent)*

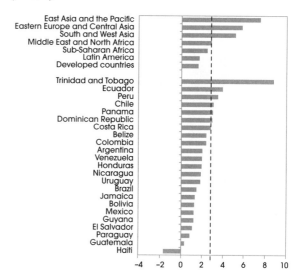

b. Average GDP per capita *($US at 2005 purchasing power parity)*

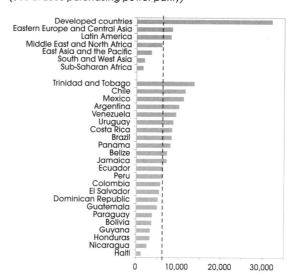

Source: Authors' calculations based on World Bank (2007).
Note: Dotted lines represent median value of growth per capita: in panel (a), median world economic growth between 2001 and 2006 for 122 countries (2.65 percent); in panel (b), median per capita GDP for 2001–2006 for 122 countries (US$5,089 in constant 2005 dollars at purchasing power parity).

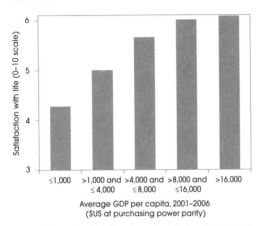

Figure 3.3 Higher Income, More Satisfaction: Relationship between GDP per Capita and Satisfaction with Life

Average GDP per capita, 2001–2006 ($US at purchasing power parity)

Source: Authors' calculations based on Gallup (2006, 2007) and World Bank (2007).
Note: Values for satisfaction with life are medians of the variable in 2006 and 2007. This figure is based on data from 122 countries.

standards in an average Latin American country, whereas in a developed country, an increase of per capita income from US$10,000 to US$25,000 would be necessary.

It should be noted that the coefficients on the variables of personal satisfaction in the table, except for those pertaining to the area of health, are higher than those on the variables that pertain to an individual's city or country of residence.[2] This implies that when opinions about different aspects of human life are compared, greater differences between rich and poor countries are found than when a comparison is made between rich and poor country opinions on society in general. This coincides with one of the constants of perception formation mentioned in Chapter 2.

Previous studies, carried out for a smaller number of countries than in the Gallup World Polls, on which these findings are based, have concluded that beyond a certain threshold, increased levels of per capita income do not translate into improved well-being (Diener and Diener, 1995). This conclusion can no longer be sustained, however, in light of the information provided in this chapter.[3] When the worldwide sample of countries is divided in two according to the level of per capita income, life satisfaction levels are observed to be slightly more sensitive to income level in those countries enjoying above-average income, even though the difference is not statistically significant. If, however, instead of satisfaction with life in general, opinions on the state of a country or its economic situation are canvassed, then this sensitivity is appreciably greater in those countries with an above-average level of income. In some specific dimensions of satisfaction with individual life aspects, such as work or housing, a lesser sensitivity is observed with respect to income in the countries in the above-average group, but in any case, significant and positive coefficients are obtained that are incompatible with the threshold hypothesis.

Consequently, at the aggregate level, the grounds for conventional economic theory regarding the relationship between per capita income and the diverse dimensions of satisfaction are confirmed.

---

[2] The coefficients on the variables of general satisfaction (i.e., satisfaction with life and with a country's general situation) are not comparable with the coefficients on the other variables because the first set of variables is measured on a 0–10 scale and the second set in percentages of satisfied individuals.

[3] As Stevenson and Wolfers (2008) demonstrate in their detailed study, this conclusion cannot be supported when analysis of the numerous existing databases covering many countries and periods is carried out. It is also important to mention that, in other studies, the relationship with income is stronger for the variable of life satisfaction, which is included in the Gallup World Poll, than for the happiness variable, which is not covered by the Gallup World Poll.

Table 3.1 Relationship between Average Satisfaction by Country and Per Capita Income and Economic Growth
(countries grouped by GDP per capita)

	Dependent variables	122 countries		Low-income countries: GDP per capita below world median		High-income countries: GDP per capita above world median	
		GDP per capita[a]	Economic growth[b]	GDP per capita[a]	Economic growth[b]	GDP per capita[a]	Economic growth[b]
General	Satisfaction with life	0.733***	-0.075***	0.629***	-0.034	0.843***	-0.140***
	General situation of the country	0.437***	-0.016	0.147	0.049	0.704***	-0.090
Economic situation	Personal economic situation	0.096***	-0.018***	0.129***	-0.007	0.125***	-0.039***
	Economic conditions of the country	0.032	0.012	-0.070	0.024**	0.184***	0.011
Health	Satisfaction with health	0.016**	-0.016***	0.029	-0.011**	-0.006	-0.029***
	Confidence in the medical system	0.032**	-0.011*	0.014	0.000	0.051	0.029***
Education	Satisfaction with local education system	0.045***	-0.004	0.035	0.001	0.080***	-0.008
Job	Job satisfaction	0.070***	-0.005	0.105***	-0.004	0.050***	-0.011***
	Policies to increase the quantity and quality of jobs	0.035**	-0.006	-0.014	0.003	0.121***	-0.011
Housing	Satisfaction with housing	0.078***	-0.004	0.111***	-0.002	0.065***	-0.012**
	Availability of good and affordably priced homes	0.018	-0.006	0.005	-0.002	0.027	-0.012

Source: Authors' calculations based on Gallup (2006, 2007). For further details, see Lora and Chaparro (2008).
Note: Satisfaction with life and *general situation of the country* are measured on a 0–10 scale. All other dependent variables are measured as percentages of satisfied people. The method of econometric estimation is ordinary least squares. Each regression uses GDP per capita and economic growth as explanatory variables.
[a]Figures in this column show how much two countries differ in average levels of satisfaction if one has twice the per capita income of the other.
[b]Figures in this column show how much average levels of satisfaction are affected by each additional percentage point of growth.
*Coefficient is statistically significant at the 10 percent level; **at the 5 percent level; ***at the 1 percent level; no asterisk means the coefficient is not different from zero with statistical significance.

The "Unhappy Growth Paradox"

In the relationship between income and satisfaction, however, not only the level but also the growth rate of per capita income intervenes. According to the simplest conventional economic theory, all things being equal, growth should not be expected to exert any additional influence on satisfaction levels, over and above that already exerted by commensurate increased income. The empirical results presented in the second column of Table 3.1 call this theoretical simplification into question, as various dimensions of satisfaction deteriorate in the face of economic growth. Similarly, Figure 3.4 suggests that general satisfaction with life and economic growth are inversely related.[4]

For each additional point in the average annual growth of per capita income during the five years preceding the 2006 Gallup World Poll, on a scale of 0 to 10, satisfaction with life in general drops on average 0.07 points. The percentage of the population that is satisfied with its living standards declines by 1.8 points, and the percentage of people who say they are happy with their state of health falls by 1.6 points. There are also negative coefficients in other dimensions of the perception of the quality of personal or community life, although they are statistically less significant.[5]

Although the "unhappy growth paradox" implies that the relationship between income and satisfaction is somewhat more complex than basic economic theory suggests, it does not entirely contradict the theory. One possible explanation for this is that satisfaction depends not only on income (to the extent that income limits purchasing power), but also on consumer expectations. The fact that growth is linked more strongly and negatively with perceptions of individual quality of life than with perceptions of a country's standard of living suggests that growth increases expectations and extends the parameters within which individuals assess their own situations. It is to be expected that if expectations and aspirations move in this direction, they will do so with more potency in societies in which the majority of the population has already surpassed those levels of consumption necessary to cover their basic needs and where spending power provides wider options for consumption and emulation.[6]

This is exactly what can be observed if a comparison is made between the coefficients of the growth variable of those countries that are above and those that are below the median level of per capita income. In the relatively richer countries, among which the majority of Latin American countries are numbered, growth is clearly and negatively associated with all personal aspects of life quality and even with some community aspects, such as the state of the nation or confidence in the health service. Among relatively poorer countries, however, growth is clearly and negatively associated only

---

[4] The conclusions are practically identical whether the effect on satisfaction of income per capita is controlled for or not, given that the correlation between economic growth and per capita income is practically nonexistent (more precisely, 0.05 for the growth in income per capita during the period 2001–2006 and the level of income per capita in 2006).

[5] These results are not greatly affected if, instead of growth in the period 2001–2006, a longer (1996–2006) or shorter (2005–2006) period is considered. Given that the Gallup World Poll dates back only to 2006, it is still impossible to tell which time length is the most adequate reference period.

[6] Alternatively, growth could generate dissatisfaction by demanding changes in working practices or in people's lifestyles, which could have a detrimental effect on their forms of economic organization and cultural traditions. This kind of dissatisfaction should be strongest among poorer societies to the extent that they become integrated into the market economy. This hypothesis, however, does not coincide with the results that are shown below. At the end of this section, alternative explanations are offered.

Figure 3.4 The Unhappy Growth Paradox: Relationship between GDP per Capita Growth and Satisfaction with Life

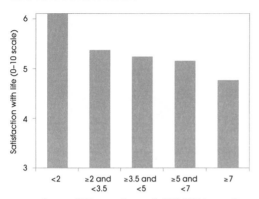

Source: Authors' calculations based on Gallup (2006, 2007) and World Bank (2007).
Note: Values of satisfaction with life are medians of the variable in 2006 and 2007. This figure is based on data from 120 countries.

with one personal life dimension, that of health. This link might be explained by changes in the standards by which individuals judge their own state of health or by a genuine deterioration in health associated with economic growth, due to the effects of pollution, stress, or obesity.[7]

If the negative effect of economic growth upon satisfaction is due to increased expectations, the "unhappy growth paradox" should be observable when growth rates are high, but not when they are low or negative. If an economy enters into recession, there is no reason to suppose that consumers are going to feel better, because they are not going to give up their expectations of material improvement. Calculations based on the 2006 and 2007 Gallup World Polls show that, indeed, if the sample is divided into two groups of countries with an average per capita income growth rate above and below the world median, then this inverse association between satisfaction and growth is maintained only in those countries with above-median income growth rates (seven of which are Latin American countries, as mentioned above). In these countries, the higher the growth rate, the lower the number of people who express satisfaction with their lives, with the things that they can do or buy, or with their state of health (Table 3.2). General confidence in the country's health system and in the government's housing policy is also significantly reduced. On the other hand, among countries with an average per capita growth rate below the world median, those with higher growth rates declare higher levels of satisfaction in all aspects of life, both public and private. These higher levels are significant (in the statistical sense) in regard to opinions expressed by people on the state of the nation, their own state of health, and the effectiveness of government policy in the creation of jobs.

In sum, although satisfaction and the *level* of income demonstrate the relationship supposed by basic economic theory, economic growth seems to have a negative effect on various dimensions of individuals' satisfaction with themselves and their personal conditions (and sometimes even their satisfaction with community conditions). The explanation behind the "unhappy growth paradox" is seemingly found in the increased expectations and aspirations generated by economic growth, especially in countries with relatively high income levels and countries experiencing high growth rates. This hypothesis will be examined later, at which point, instead of trying to explain the differ-

---

[7] In a study of causes of death in the United States, Ruhm (2000) found a procyclical pattern in mortality rates, in 8 out of 10 cases analyzed, in the incidences of tobacco consumption and of obesity. He also found that when the economy improves, physical activity drops and less-healthy foods are consumed.

Table 3.2 Relationship between Average Satisfaction by Country and Per Capita Income and Economic Growth
(countries grouped according to economic growth)

	Dependent variables	122 countries		Countries that grow slowly: economic growth below the median world rate		Countries that grow rapidly: economic growth above the median world rate	
		GDP per capita[a]	Economic growth[b]	GDP per capita[a]	Economic growth[b]	GDP per capita[a]	Economic growth[b]
General	Satisfaction with life	0.733***	-0.075***	0.846***	0.062	0.537***	-0.090**
	General situation of the country	0.437***	-0.016	0.522***	0.208**	0.254***	-0.065
Economic situation	Personal economic situation	0.096***	-0.018***	0.114***	0.024	0.059***	-0.025***
	Economic conditions of the country	0.032	0.012	0.056*	0.050	-0.013	0.006
Health	Satisfaction with health	0.016**	-0.016***	0.020**	0.016*	0.001	-0.023***
	Confidence in the medical system	0.032**	-0.011*	0.053***	0.016	-0.004	-0.020**
Education	Satisfaction with local education system	0.045***	-0.004	0.057***	0.017	0.022	-0.005
Job	Job satisfaction	0.070***	-0.005	0.072***	0.018	0.059***	-0.007
	Policies to increase the quantity and quality of jobs	0.035**	-0.006	0.049**	0.037*	0.001	-0.010
Housing	Satisfaction with housing	0.078***	-0.004	0.083***	0.018	0.064***	-0.009
	Availability of good and affordably priced homes	0.018	-0.006	0.013	0.025	0.014	-0.015*

Source: Authors' calculations based on Gallup (2006, 2007). For further details see Lora and Chaparro (2008).
Note: Satisfaction with life and general situation of the country are measured on a 0–10 scale. All other dependent variables are measured as percentages of satisfied people. The method of econometric estimation is ordinary least squares. Each regression uses GDP per capita and economic growth as explanatory variables.
[a] Figures in this column show much two countries differ in average levels of satisfaction if one has twice the per capita income of the other.
[b] Figures in this column show how much average levels of satisfaction are affected by each additional percentage point of growth.
*Coefficient is statiscally significant at the 10 percent level; **at the 5 percent level; ***at the 1 percent level; no asterisk means the coefficient is not different from zero with statistical significance.

ences *between* countries, emphasis will be placed on accounting for differences *within* countries, and it will be demonstrated that an individual's satisfaction depends not only on his or her income, but also on the income levels of others. It should be pointed out, however, that the hypothesis of expectations does not rule out the existence of other factors that might contribute to an explanation of the negative effects of growth upon some aspects of satisfaction, which will be discussed later herein.

Figure 3.5 illustrates how satisfaction levels in various countries are influenced by income levels and growth rates according to the previous discussion. Each curve in the figure represents a level of "isosatisfaction" that might be achieved using different combinations of per capita income and economic growth. There are equal differences between the selected countries in average satisfaction levels (approximately 0.6 points between each country and the one it follows), but the curves tend to move further away from each other, because greater and greater increases in income are needed to keep increasing satisfaction. The populations of Kenya and Honduras report relatively low average levels of life satisfaction (4.4 and 5.1, respectively, on a scale of 0 to 10) and are furthermore insensitive to changes in

Figure 3.5 Relationship among Economic Growth, GDP, and Satisfaction with Life *(isosatisfaction curves)*

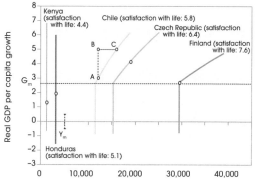

Source: Authors' calculations based on Gallup (2006, 2007) and World Bank (2007).
Note: The figure in each box represents the national average. Y_m is world median GDP per capita (US$5,089). G_m is world median economic growth per capita (2.65 percent).

the economic growth rate. The countries found on the right of the figure, Chile, the Czech Republic, and Finland, display higher satisfaction levels, but they are more sensitive to changes in growth when it exceeds a certain critical level (G_m).

When a country finds itself with a low level of income per capita, any growth rate can result in increased satisfaction levels (that is, moving gradually towards higher positions of satisfaction). However, after a certain income level has been reached (Y_m), acceleration in growth above the critical point (G_m) will lead initially to a reduction in satisfaction. For example, an increased rate of per capita income growth for Chile from 3 percent to 5 percent would take the country from point A to point B in the figure. A period of time would ensue in which satisfaction would be lower than it was before the acceleration in growth had taken place. Only after income had reached the level corresponding to point C would Chile regain its initial level of satisfaction. From then on, satisfaction levels would be higher as production levels per inhabitant keep on growing. This simple conceptual framework coincides with popular opinion on the effects of structural reforms in accelerating growth. Initially the reforms, although they stimulate economic growth, provoke feelings of unease that, in this conceptual framework, are caused by expectations as well as the possible costs faced by individuals forced to change their employment or adapt to new conditions of production designed to increase efficiency.[8] By their very nature, some structural reforms, such as opening up to international trade, generate a redistribution of income between labor and capital and also between different forms of labor, which has repercussions for satisfaction levels. (As a result of aversion to losing money, well-being subsequently declines more for individuals who lose income than it increases for those who gain income.)[9] If the reforms are reversed, the country may return to its initial position and thus avoid loss of satisfaction, but it will thereby sacrifice the possibility of achieving a faster increase in future satisfaction rates following the initial period of loss.

Hedonism, Jealousy, or Solidarity?

The relationship between levels of per capita income and the various dimensions of satisfaction holds true not only when separate countries, but also individuals within a country, are compared. This clearly requires the use of information about individual income levels that is not always accurately reported in opinion polls. In the Gallup World Polls, those interviewed are asked only to indicate their own and their family's income brackets, which generally range widely (and are not always easy to compare across countries). However, the income medians for Latin American countries that can be deduced using this information[10] hold up very well in comparison to figures obtained from more reliable sources, such as the household surveys carried out by national statistics institutions. There are other differences in the distributions of income between one source and another: distributions resulting from the Gallup World Polls can undervalue the income shares of the highest and lowest quintiles in the majority of Latin American countries (Gasparini et al., 2008).

Because individual income levels are not precisely measured in the Gallup World Polls, it is difficult to know exactly what influence they have on quality of life perceptions. It is likely that the econometrically estimated coefficients are skewed downwards (because of the "attenuation effect") and that the sensitivity of satisfaction with respect to individual income is therefore greater. However, as shown in Table 3.3, income has a positive, considerable and significant effect on all dimensions of satisfaction that relate to personal conditions. It is not surprising to find that its greatest influence is found in those aspects of people's lives that have most to do with their ability to generate income and consume material goods, such as employment, standard of living, or housing. Nonetheless, income also seems to have an important influence on satisfaction with health and life satisfaction in general. As might be expected, there is a looser relationship between individual income and satisfaction with community aspects of life.

---

[8] This is a plausible hypothesis, given that the phenomenon occurs only in countries experiencing relatively rapid growth and where the effort required of people to adapt to boost production levels is arguably greater. This would coincide with the strongly negative influence of economic growth on health in this group of countries. But, if this were the explanation, why should satisfaction with the standard of living deteriorate?

[9] The reforms can also cause disquiet for ideological reasons, or because the implementation process is not transparent or democratic. For a synthesis of public opinion on the structural reforms in Latin America and the effects of the reforms on production and growth, see Lora and Panizza (2001). For a discussion of their political and electoral effects, see Lora and Olivera (2005).

[10] In order to assign values to individual incomes, Gasparini et al. (2008) randomly give each individual an amount of income within the range of incomes declared in the survey. In this section, the individual income values are used, just as they were assigned by Gasparini.

Table 3.3 Relationship between Individual Satisfaction and Personal Income and Income of Others

	Dependent variables	Monthly household per capita income, $US at PPP, natural logarithm	Average monthly per capita income of reference group, $US at PPP, natural logarithm	Number of observations
General	Satisfaction with life	0.410 ***	0.254 *	8,593
	General situation of the country	0.131 ***	−0.077	8,496
Economic situation	Personal economic situation	0.370 ***	−0.217 *	8,525
	Economic conditions of the country	0.116 ***	−0.109	8,131
Health	Satisfaction with health	0.196 ***	0.003	8,588
	Confidence in the medical system	−0.035	−0.348 **	7,912
Education	Satisfaction with local education system	−0.048	−0.390 ***	8,345
Job	Job satisfaction	0.379 ***	−0.429 *	3,449
	Policies to increase the quantity and quality of jobs	0.005	−0.397 ***	8,405
Housing	Satisfaction with housing	0.261 ***	−0.236 **	8,592
	Availability of good and affordably priced homes	0.056	−0.278 *	8,095

Source: Authors' calculations based on Gallup (2006, 2007). For further details see Lora and Chaparro (2008).
Note: Each individual considered in the regressions belongs to a reference group that is made up of all persons of the same gender, within the same country and age range, and with similar levels of education. The regressions for *satisfaction with life* and *general situation of the country* are ordered logit, and the remaining regressions are logit. Each row in the table represents a separate regression that includes the following control variables: *age, age squared, marital status, religion is important,* and *has friends to count on. Satisfaction with life* and *general situation of the country* are measured on a 0–10 scale. All other dependent variables are measured as population percentages. PPP = purchasing power parity.
*Coefficient is statistically significant at the 10 percent level; **at the 5 percent level; ***at the 1 percent level; no asterisk means the coefficient is not different from zero with statistical significance.

That relationship is positive and significant only in relation to opinions expressed about a country's economic situation, which suggests that an individual's personal economic situation might color judgments he or she makes about the national situation.[11] However, with regard to other collective aspects, income is not commonly associated directly with satisfaction (for example, with government policy on job creation or housing provision), and when it is, the association is inverse. This confirms the "aspirations paradox" discussed in Chapter 2, which implies that individuals with higher incomes are more demanding of public policy (for example, in terms of confidence in state health and education systems).

Consequently, people's opinions about personal aspects of their lives are congruent with the basic tenets of neoclassical economic theory, which predicts that greater individual income will lead to higher utility derived from the consumption of a combination of diverse goods and services. But it is possible that, apart from having this effect,

[11] Since the regression analyses on which these conclusions are based include country dummies, the impact of the average income of all people in each country has already been isolated.

Sociologists have long accepted that people's behaviors, evaluations, and aspirations are not individualistically determined; rather, they depend on comparisons. Available literature concerning reference groups examines whom individuals compare themselves with and the types of comparisons they make (Merton, 1957; Hyman, 1960; Felson and Reed, 1986). Michalos (1985) has developed his Multiple Discrepancy Theory, which states that subjective well-being assessments are based on comparisons made in many aspects of life (economic situations, health, families, work, etc.). Michalos believes that these associations lead to discrepancies between what a person has in his or her present life and what he or she had at one time (historical discrepancies), what others have (group comparison), and what he or she would like to have (aspirational discrepancies). According to Michalos, a person's assessment of his or her situation depends on these discrepancies.

Source: Rojas (2008).

income might also exert influence on satisfaction, depending on the extent to which tastes and aspirations change.

Under the individualist approach of neoclassical economics, a person's well-being is influenced neither by the situation of other individuals, nor by their relative positions in society. This point of view contrasts with sociological theories, which have always held that behavior, assessments, and aspirations arise as the result of interaction with society (see Box 3.2). Although some economists as influential as Adam Smith, John Stuart Mill (quoted in the epigraph to this chapter), and Karl Marx have emphasized the importance of the relative positions of individuals and social groups, until recently the subject has been largely ignored by the profession.[12] However, in recent decades the topic has resurged, thanks mainly to the pioneering studies of Richard Easterlin (1974), which demonstrate that relative income is the explanation for the apparent paradox that differences in per capita income *between countries* are closely linked to the average satisfaction levels in those countries, whereas increases in income *over time* in a given country do little to improve the average levels of satisfaction enjoyed by its inhabitants.[13]

The explanation, according to Easterlin, is that individual satisfaction improves only when an individual moves into a better position relative to his or her social group as a result of an an increase in income. Other authors have verified that, in effect, relative income does influence satisfaction (van Praag and Ferrer-i-Carbonell, 2007; Ball and

---

[12] Two important exceptions are Veblen (1899), who emphasizes the role of conspicuous consumption, and Duesenberry (1949), who demonstrates that patterns of consumption and saving are significantly influenced by relative income.

[13] The United States clearly exemplifies this paradox. However, it is important to point out that Easterlin's paradox has become rather blurred with the appearance of data covering more countries and longer periods of time. An exhaustive analysis of the available polls, carried out recently by Stevenson and Wolfers (2008), has come to the conclusion that no such paradox exists: not only is satisfaction with life in general higher in richer countries, but the slope of that relationship is very similar to that resulting from analysis over time or in comparisons between individuals within the same country.

Chernova, 2008; Luttmer, 2005). It has also been observed that satisfaction depends on "aspirational discrepancy," meaning the difference between an individual's current income and the income that he or she considers necessary to satisfy his or her needs, which tends to increase at the same rate as his or her current income. This "aspiration treadmill" means that a higher level of income (usually double an individual's current salary) is always deemed necessary and, consequently, satisfaction does not increase (or increases much less than proportionally) with increased income (Stutzer, 2004; McBride, 2005).

In practice, it is difficult to determine the social group that each individual compares him- or herself with in order to judge his or her own economic situation. According to some studies, the pertinent comparison is made with people living in the same region (e.g., Stutzer, 2004); others maintain it is with the country as a whole (e.g., Ball and Chernova, 2008); and a third group of studies conclude that the most relevant comparison is with individuals in the same profession or of a similar ethnic background (e.g., Senik, 2004; Gandhi Kingdon and Knight, 2004).[14] These conclusions arise more from the limited availability of information than from theoretical considerations.[15] According to Ferrer-i-Carbonell (2005), the most useful method for defining reference groups involves splitting up samples by age ranges, education, gender, and country.[16]

When the influence of the average income of a reference group, defined in this way, is taken into account, it becomes clear that in the material aspects of private life, there is an effect of comparison—or jealousy—that reduces satisfaction. This occurs in satisfaction with standards of living, with employment, and with housing (as shown by the negative and significant coefficients in the "Average monthly per capita income of reference group" column in Table 3.3). In these aspects of life, the satisfaction of individuals greatly depends on what they see others do and consume. In the words of Dan Ariely, a prominent researcher in behavioral economics: "We are always looking at the things around us in relation to others" (Ariely, 2008: 7).

When the income of an individual's reference group increases at the same rate as the individual's, the improvement in satisfaction with standard of living that would normally accompany greater individual income is strongly counteracted by the comparison effect (see Box 3.3), and improvements in satisfaction with employment or housing disappear completely. Accordingly, it could be said that employment and housing behave like positional goods in the sense that they generate satisfaction only to the extent that they are better than those possessed by the people with whom one compares oneself (see Box 3.4). This does not happen with other aspects of personal life that are more difficult to display or compare, such as health, or with satisfaction expressed with

---

[14] For an extensive discussion of the specialized literature on this subject, see Rojas (2008).

[15] In a study of the population of Santiago, Chile, based on theoretical models of perception formation in regard to income distribution, Núñez (2007) observes that although the majority of people tend to describe themselves as middle class, the higher a person's income, the higher the income he or she believes a middle-class person receives. This suggests that individuals' reference groups depend on the economic stratum to which the individuals belong.

[16] More precisely, the following results are based on information from 19 Latin American countries. Within each country, they distinguish six age groups for each gender (from 15 to 75 years, with 10-year intervals), which are split into four education groups (primary incomplete, primary completed, secondary incomplete, and secondary completed). A reference group is considered to have a sufficient number of observations to allow statistical deductions when it has at least 20 individual members. As such, between 182 and 258 reference groups are formed, depending on the regression. Each individual can belong to only one reference group.

Box 3.3 Income of the Reference Group and Satisfaction

In the material aspects of people's lives, reaching a satisfied state tends to be a race in which the pace of others becomes important. The figure below clearly illustrates this phenomenon. Based on the case of a 30-year-old Argentinean male who has completed secondary education, the figure indicates the probability that he is satisfied with his economic situation in terms of two variables: his personal income and the average income of other similarly placed Argentineans. If this person receives a monthly salary of roughly US$150 and the average income of his peers is the same, then the probability that he will be satisfied with his income is approximately 65 percent. This situation corresponds to point A in the figure. If this person manages to increase his income to US$400 and, at the same time, there is no commensurate increase in his peers' incomes, the probability that he will be satisfied increases to 75 percent (point B). Here, attention should be drawn to what takes place when other people's incomes increase to match his (point C). Accordingly, the probability that this individual will express satisfaction with his economic situation decreases to approximately 70 percent. Although income and economic satisfaction are directly related, the situations of other people can affect economic satisfaction in the opposite direction.

Conflictive Relationship among Economic Satisfaction, Personal Income, and the Income of Others

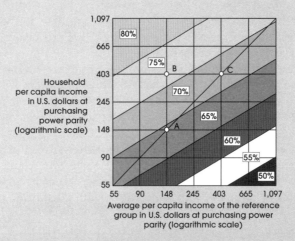

Source: Authors' calculations based on Gallup (2007).
Note: The areas in the figure represent the probability that a person is satisfied with his economic situation as a function of personal income and the average income of his reference group. Along the main diagonal, personal income is equal to the average income of the reference group. The calculations of probability were undertaken for married Argentinean men between 25 and 30 years of age who have completed secondary education. The reference group is made up of all persons of the same gender, within the same country and age range, and with similar levels of education. The question on economic satisfaction is the following: "Are you satisfied or dissatisfied with your standard of living, that is, with all the things you can buy and do?"

Similarly, the figure below helps illustrate the joint effects of personal income and the reference group's average income on satisfaction levels with housing. In this case, the negative effect of other people's incomes counteracts the positive effects of an individual's own income. Thus, the probability of satisfaction does not depend on personal income, but on the gap between that income and the average income of one's reference group. It should be noted that all the points situated on the principal diagonal, which represent cases of individuals earning personal income in parity with the average income, correspond to people with equal probability of being satisfied with their housing, approximately 83 percent.

However, not all aspects of life function similarly. There is a favorable effect on levels of satisfaction with life in general when others are doing well, whereas opinions expressed about the country's general economic situation are not affected by other people's well-being. Important differences also exist between various groups of people: men and women, or the wealthy and poor, react differently to the success or failure of their respective reference groups.

Conflictive Relationship among Satisfaction with Housing, Personal Income, and the Income of Others

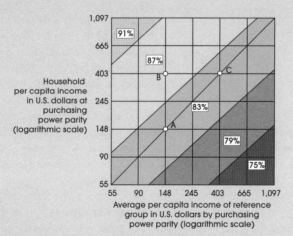

Source: Authors' calculations based on Gallup (2007).
Note: The areas in the figure represent the probability that a person is satisfied with his housing as a function of personal income and the average income of his reference group. Along the main diagonal, personal income is equal to the average income of the reference group. The calculations of probability were undertaken for married Argentinean men between 25 and 30 years of age who have completed secondary education. The reference group is made up of all persons of the same gender, within the same country and age range, and with similar levels of education. The question on satisfaction with housing is the following: "Are you satisfied or dissatisfied with your housing or the place where you are presently living?"

Box 3.4 Positional Goods

In a positional society, a concept introduced by Hirsch (1976), one's status depends on one's relative situation, rather than one's absolute situation. De Botton (2004) popularized the importance of status in his book *Status Anxiety*. Alpízar, Carlsson, and Johansson-Stenman (2005) and Carlsson, Gupta, and Johansson-Stenman (2005) show that some consumer goods play a greater positional role in status than others; for example, televisions are highly positional, whereas vacation lengths are not. Satisfaction arising from a positional good depends on its relative consumption, and thus the utility gained from purchasing a larger television might therefore be nullified if everybody in the neighborhood were to do the same, whereas the satisfaction value of an extra week of vacation does not depend on whether other people take longer or shorter vacations.

Source: Rojas (2008).

life in general. On the contrary, in the last case the effect is one of solidarity rather than jealousy: satisfaction with life in general is greater to the extent to which the members of one's reference group have a higher average income.

Note that the effect of solidarity on life satisfaction at an individual level does not correspond to the result at a national level, where those in countries that experience more growth declare less satisfaction, especially those in rich countries. This suggests that if expectations play a role in life satisfaction, they are not based on comparisons with the successes reached by others, but possibly they respond to economic growth through other channels. Such channels do not correspond to any of the private or collective dimensions of satisfaction analyzed in this chapter, since within all of them there is a negative effect of the comparison with (the income of) others. This establishes a "paradox of life satisfaction" that echoes the paradox of Easterlin, and for which there is no clear answer.

These results confirm that individual well-being depends not only on personal economic conditions, but also on the conditions experienced by others. In the more materialistic dimensions of personal well-being, there is an urge to compete with others, whereas in a more general assessment of personal life, there is a sense of empathy with the economic situation of other members of one's social group.

What can now be said about opinions held about society in general? Do other people's incomes have an influence here too? With respect to satisfaction with communal aspects of life, such as confidence in the health or education systems, satisfaction with government policy on job creation, or the availability of housing, the average income of the group to which each person belongs always has a significant and negative influence. However, in this case the negative influence is not due to the competitive effect caused by comparison of personal income with the average income of the reference group. In fact, personal income has no bearing whatsoever on these opinions (once the influence of the average income of the group has been taken into account). On the other hand, the negative influence of group income coincides with the fact (discussed in Chapter 2) that social groups with greater incomes are more demanding with respect to public policy and collective results. Instead of an individualized mechanism of increasing aspirations along with each person's income, in this situation there seems to be a group mechanism of aspirations that increases along with the average income of all the members of the reference group. Consequently, opinions on collective aspects of life are influenced as much by the individual's personal conditions (at least the economic ones) as by those conditions experienced by the group to which the individual belongs.

Nevertheless, the assessment made by individuals of their countries in general and of the economic situation of their countries in particular seems to follow a different logic. In contrast with material aspects of personal life, one's evaluation of one's country is influenced neither by a competitive mechanism nor by a sense of solidarity, as is the case with satisfaction with life in general. In contrast with other collective aspects of life, this evaluation is not affected by a mechanism of growing aspirations within a social group. Assessment by Latin Americans of their particular national situation seems to depend more on their personal income than on the income of others. It might be stated that people judge their country's situation with their own pockets. In that case, any opinion expressed about the collective situation is heavily conditioned by personal considerations.

These conclusions are generalizations that presume that all sociodemographic groups behave in a similar manner. But men and women, rich and poor, city dwellers and people living in the country might all shape their terms of reference and expectations differently. Men are more susceptible than women to competition with their peers with respect to material living standards, whereas women are more susceptible than men to the accomplishments of their peers in terms of their satisfaction with employment and housing (Table 3.4). In comparison with the poor, rich people worry more when people from their own economic and sociodemographic group earn a higher income than they do, which affects their satisfaction levels with material goods, with their employment, and even with the general situation in their country. However, as the reference group of poor people begins to earn greater income, the poor will become more demanding in regard to issues concerning their own health, with the health system in general, and with government policy on job creation.

In urban areas, people have more opportunities to consume and consequently more opportunities to compare their consumption standards with those of others. In cities, consequently, increased average income in one's reference group means a reduction in satisfaction with standards of living and employment, something that does not occur in rural areas. In cities, higher average earnings are usually associated with greater demands for better education and effective policies for job creation.

Changing Social Mobility and Expectations

As discussed, when opinions are compared *between countries*, it is apparent that economic growth has a negative effect on the satisfaction that people feel with their standards of living, and that when information is used concerning individuals *within countries*, it appears that an individual's satisfaction with standards of living heavily depends on his or her income level when compared to the average earnings of his or her reference group (with reactions differing between some groups and others). These results suggest that individual aspirations depend on the economic context in which an

Table 3.4 Relationship between Individual Satisfaction and the Income of Others
(differences based on gender, relative income, and area of residence)

		Men	Women	Estimated coefficients of the variable monthly household per capita income of reference group, $US at PPP, natural logarithm			
				Individuals with income above the regional median	Individuals with income below the regional median	Individuals living in cities	Individuals living in rural areas
General	Satisfaction with life	0.287*	0.259*	-0.129	0.549	0.149	0.500
	General situation of the country	-0.103	-0.039	-0.482**	-0.040	0.011	0.019
Economic situation	Personal economic situation	-0.330**	-0.174	-0.933***	-0.578***	-0.328*	0.044
	Economic conditions of the country	-0.157	-0.133	-0.163	0.101	0.088	0.050
Health	Satisfaction with health	-0.005	0.018	0.306	-0.921**	-0.014	-0.007
	Confidence in the medical system	-0.372**	-0.341**	-0.218	-0.847***	-0.262	-0.336
Education	Satisfaction with local education system	-0.418*	-0.370***	-0.585	-0.419	-0.409**	0.144
Job	Job satisfaction	-0.361	-0.506***	-1.810***	-0.142	-0.847***	-0.609
	Policies to increase quantity and quality of jobs	-0.394***	-0.397**	-0.377	-1.031**	-0.142	0.308
Housing	Satisfaction with housing	-0.121	-0.232*	-0.970*	-0.697**	-0.251	0.092
	Availability of good and affordably priced homes	-0.473**	-0.164	-1.232***	0.079	-0.436**	0.348

Source: Authors' calculations based on Gallup (2007). For more details see Lora and Chaparro (2008).
Note: Each individual considered in the regressions belongs to a reference group that is made up of all persons of the same gender, within the same country and age range, and with similar levels of education. Each coefficient is the result of a separate regression. All regressions include the following control variables: *age, age squared, marital status, religion is important, has friends to count on,* and *personal income. Satisfaction with life and general situation of the country* are measured on a 0–10 scale, and the method used is ordered logit regression. All other dependent variables are measured as population percentages, and the method used is logit regression.
*Coefficient is statistically significant at the 10 percent level; **at the 5 percent level; ***at the 1 percent level; no asterisk means the coefficient is not different from zero with statistical significance.

individual lives and works. These approaches might also suggest, although incorrectly, that patterns of comparison used by individuals are always the same (the country as a whole in the first case, and the sociodemographic group in the second). Various studies have demonstrated that comparison patterns can change—sometimes drastically—along with people's economic situation and may also be different across various dimensions of an individual's personal life.[17]

In a study on Peru, Graham and Pettinato (2002a) observe many cases of "frustrated achievers." These are people whose income has increased substantially as a consequence of economic reforms but who have evaluated their economic performance as poor and who, as a consequence, are unlikely to be in favor of the reforms that have (in absolute terms) benefited them. The authors conclude that frustration could be the result of comparison effects, as achievers tend to compare their income to that of people in higher income groups (who could have experienced skyrocketing wage increases in the wake of the reforms). This suggests that a person's reference group may change along with rising income. The authors also conclude that the relative income effect is larger for people in high income deciles and smaller for people in lower income deciles. This finding is probably related to differences in the positional content of the basket of goods purchased by people with a high or a low income (that is, the rich are more prone to consume goods that represent status).

An interesting study from Gandhi Kingdon and Knight (2004) highlights the importance of distinguishing between a person's relative income with respect to people of his or her own ethnic or racial group and with respect to people of other ethnic or racial groups. They conclude that, while increased income for those that belong to the same ethnic or racial group is seen as beneficial, increases in income for people from other groups diminish satisfaction.

The influence of relative income can also vary between the long and short term, as originally suggested by Hirschman (1973). When other people's incomes begin to increase, it may give rise to the hope that one's own income will increase. But if, after some time, one remains permanently behind one's peers, that same hope will turn into frustration.

Political attitudes can also respond differently to measures that benefit everyone versus those that benefit just a few people. In the most-fragmented societies, policies that favor only selected groups can provoke tremendous opposition. Attitudes towards inequality might differ according to whether the inequality is found within the social group to which an individual belongs, or between the groups themselves as a whole. It is to be expected that there will be greater opposition towards this latter form of inequality. However, attitudes towards inequality can also be determined by the breadth of opportunities that society offers. As demonstrated by Alesina, Di Tella, and MacCulloch (2004), in an interesting comparative study of Europe and the United States, there is a higher degree of tolerance towards inequality in the latter as a result of the commonly held perception that the opportunities for economic advancement are greater.[18]

---

[17] The survey that follows is based on Rojas (2008).

[18] In Graham and Felton (2005a) attitudes towards redistribution policies are discussed, while in Graham and Sukhtankar (2004) people's attitudes towards the market economy are analyzed, taking into account the role of relative incomes and inequality in subjective well-being.

Do Poverty Lines Make Sense?

Given that satisfaction depends not only on personal income, but also on the income of others and, generally speaking, the social and economic context in which people live and work, it is only fair to ask if it makes sense to separate so sharply those who are deemed poor from those who are not on the basis of income alone.[19] It has long been argued that deprivation goes beyond the income dimension. Amartya Sen (1987), for instance, has convincingly argued in favor of extending the measurement of deprivation to the dimension of functionings and capabilities. The Human Development Index of the United Nations Development Programme is perhaps the most well-known measure that follows the spirit of Sen's approach.

There is also growing interest in Latin America in going beyond the income paradigm in the measurement of poverty.[20] Several Latin American countries routinely compute indicators of multidimensional poverty, usually based on access to housing, water, sanitation, and education (from which the indicators of unsatisfied basic needs are developed). The measurement of multidimensional deprivation has been the subject of numerous studies aimed at developing and applying techniques to reduce (through a system of weights) to a single poverty line the diversity of variables that may be relevant for the well-being of the poor.[21]

Given that data on income, consumption, and economic activity are much more reliable and readily available than information concerning people's opinions, studies of multidimensional poverty rarely take into account subjective variables, which might offer valuable information on factors affecting the situation of poor people. By taking advantage of the fact that the Gallup World Polls gather data on a wide range of variables, both objective and subjective, Gasparini et al. (2008) have constructed diverse indicators of well-being or deprivation based on information from these polls; some of the indicators include subjective information.

The most simple poverty indicator that Gasparini and colleagues have constructed is that which is based on a conventional income poverty line. Using the poverty line of US$2 per capita daily income (adjusted to allow for differences in purchasing power), national poverty rates obtained are on average 16 points higher than those calculated on the basis of surveys by national statistics institutes (which would seem to imply a pronounced tendency to underreport earnings in the Gallup World Polls). However, the correlation between the two sources' poverty rates is high, especially if the Caribbean countries (0.86) and Venezuela (0.92) are omitted.[22] It is also evident that the profile of poor people is rather similar in the two surveys, based on the variables that bear reasonable comparison.[23]

---

[19] This section is based entirely on Gasparini et al. (2008).

[20] See a review of the literature and applications in Attanasio and Székely (1999).

[21] For a technical discussion, see Bourguignon (2003), Bourguignon and Chakravarty (2003), Duclos, Sahn, and Younger (2006), and Silber (2007).

[22] For all countries, the correlation is 0.59.

[23] There are, however, serious problems with some of the variables in various countries, and the representativeness of the samples is questionable in some countries.

The second poverty indicator that Gasparini et al. have devised takes into account the combination of services to the home and durable assets considered by the 2006 Gallup World Poll (water, electricity, telephone, television, computer and Internet). By applying conventional methods of factorial analysis in order to reduce this combination of variables to a single dimension, an index of assets can be formulated. Then a threshold on this index is defined so that 37.2 percent of all the population falls below it (since 37.2 percent is the poverty rate by income for the whole region). According to this multidimensional poverty indicator (by assets), Argentina, Chile, Colombia, Costa Rica, Jamaica, and Uruguay have poverty rates below 20 percent, whereas Bolivia, Haiti, Honduras, Nicaragua, Paraguay, and Peru have poverty rates above 50 percent. The correlation between these poverty rates and those obtained by respective national household surveys is high, although it is far from perfect.[24]

Finally, Gasparini and colleagues have also constructed a subjective poverty indicator that combines (using the same method of factorial analysis) responses on the following five items involving people's quality of life: satisfaction with life at present, with life five years ago, and with life five years in the future (using the "ladder" question in each case, based on a 0–10 scale), as well as satisfaction with the standard of living (yes/no) and whether money has been unavailable to purchase food (yes/no).[25] Once again, a threshold is established in order to separate the poor from the nonpoor in such a way as to classify 37.2 percent of the total population of the region as being poor.

As might be expected, Gasparini et al.'s three indicators of poverty correlate positively. However, the correlations are moderate, which indicates that poverty cannot be reduced to one single measure capable of portraying each and every one of its aspects. The correlation (for individual observations) between the income and assets indices is 0.46, that between the income and subjective indices is only 0.28, and that between the assets and subjective indices is 0.35. The correlations are also significant, although moderately so, when computed not for the values of the three indicators, but for how consistently they classify the population between poor and nonpoor. In each of the three methods, 37.2 percent of the population is classified as being poor. But the classification according to incomes coincides in only 42.8 percent of cases with the classification by assets and in only 43.3 percent of cases with the classification based on subjective opinions (between the classification based on assets and that based on subjective opinions, the coincidence is 48.6 percent).

It follows that poverty lines based on incomes are clearly insufficient to portray poverty. This does not mean, however, that they are irrelevant. Gasparini et al. have found two persuasive ways to demonstrate this. The first consists of letting the statistics speak for themselves to answer the question of whether information about incomes is relevant. The second consists in testing whether the income threshold on

---

[24] Paraguay and Mexico, for example, score very high levels of poverty on this indicator (due to very low rates of access to water in Paraguay and very low rates of telephone coverage and computing in Mexico) in comparison with official surveys.

[25] In Table 2.1, the text of the "ladder question" and of the question involving satisfaction with the standard of living can be found. Regarding the lack of money to buy food, those interviewed were asked the following question: "During the last 12 months, has there been a time when you or your family had insufficient money to purchase all the food you need?"

the poverty line is near the critical level of income at which a Latin American becomes indifferent to the question of whether he or she is satisfied or unsatisfied with his or her own life. The two tests are so technically complex that only an intuitive explanation can be offered here.

In the first of these tests, in order to determine whether information on incomes is relevant for an accurate portrayal of poverty, a statistical procedure (the so-called factorization of principal components) is employed, which places the income variable in competition with other variables that, a priori, would seem to be relevant to well-being. The variable (or combination of variables) that wins the competition is the one that manages to explain to the greatest extent the behavior of all the other variables (and the losing variables are those that are explained by other variables and therefore have nothing extra to contribute). This procedure generates an interesting result: the winning variable is a combination of income and goods and services that can be purchased with income (Internet, computer, and land-based and mobile telephones). In second place comes the combination of the five variables of opinion used in the subjective poverty indicator mentioned above, and in third place, a combination of domestic services. The most surprising aspect of the result is that all the variables can be grouped together into these three families, which indicates that each of the three dimensions must have a bearing on well-being. In other words, although income is important, it is not all-important; well-being really does have a multidimensional nature.

Gasparini et al. additionally test the relevance of income—or more accurately, the poverty line based on income—by calculating the level of income at which people become indifferent to the idea of whether they are satisfied or dissatisfied about some aspect of their lives, and then determining the relationship of that level with the poverty line. In order to put this approach into practice, the researchers use the answers given to Gallup World Poll questions regarding satisfaction with the standard of living and a lack of money to buy food. Their results show that, with monthly earnings of US$37, a Latin American (average in all other respects) has the same probability of having responded yes or no in the survey that he or she, or his or her family, has on occasion lacked sufficient money to eat. This sum of money comes very close to the income threshold of US$1 per day commonly used to define extreme poverty (or indigence). This poverty line, therefore, makes sense. The researchers do not find similar justification for the poverty line of US$2 per day, although they do for a somewhat higher line, close to US$5. In effect, with a monthly income of US$163, the probability of not having enough money to eat is reduced to 34 percent, and with US$177, the probability of a person's declaring him- or herself satisfied with his or her standard of living increases to 64 percent.

The Implications of Expectations for Political Economy

One of the central questions of modern political economy is why so many democratic governments maintain policies that are contrary to economic growth and limit the incomes of the majority of the population. The adoption by many countries of the Washington Consensus reforms prompted this question. During the 1990s, various theories attempted to explain why those reforms (which comprised monetary and fiscal discipline measures, market liberalization, and privatizations) had not been adopted before, and why they were adopted at different times and with varying intensity by each country. The explanations revolved around the distributive struggles that blocked progress on the adoption of reforms until one group could force others to accept the costs of those reforms. In order to speed up the reform process, it was thought convenient to implement at the same time various reforms that offered cross-compensations to those groups holding veto power, given that promises to compensate the future losers from a single reform lacked credibility.[26]

The evidence presented in this chapter suggests an alternative explanation of the political obstruction of progrowth policies that has received very little attention in theoretical or empirical studies of political economy. The explanation is the loss of satisfaction that arises from an increase in expectations and aspirations and is produced during economic growth by improvements in the incomes of individuals' reference groups. The most marked loss of satisfaction occurs in the material dimension of people's lives and tends to be strongest in the richest and most-urbanized societies, as well as in the countries with the highest growth rates. It could be that the expansion of communications media and publicity might also contribute to raising expectations, and there is some evidence to suggest that the societies that are the most culturally and ethnically fragmented are the ones most likely to suffer the negative effects that competition has on satisfaction. The inverse association between satisfaction and reference group income levels is not limited to the private aspects of people's lives: for example, individuals in Latin American societies with the highest income levels often feel less satisfied with the results of government policies on health, education, job creation, or housing provision than more needy people do.

In light of this evidence, any government strategy that focuses exclusively on improving efficiency and achieving economic growth may fall victim to its own success. This is especially true if, as occurred with the Washington Consensus, proponents exaggerate potential benefits, which tends to raise expectations. It is more feasible to garner political support via strategies that combine policies favoring growth with strategies aimed at social and economic inclusion and reforms in the areas of health, education, employment, and housing. The majority of Latin American governments learned this lesson the hard way during the 1990s. One visible consequence has been the notable increase in social expenditure, from 8.8 percent to 11.3 percent of GDP and from US$264 per capita in 1990 to US$418 per capita in 2005 (measured in year 2000 constant dollars), according to ECLAC (2007).

However, strategies that are aimed at economic inclusion and the provision of social services, and that achieve the widest political support, are not necessarily the ones that produce the greatest improvements in the living conditions of poor people. One policy aimed at avoiding loss of satisfaction might consist of reducing the income of some families or individuals who are the visible role models for those social groups that are most vulnerable to changes in expectations (in particular, the upwardly mobile urban middle class). In the same way, a social policy that is effective from a political point of view could be based on concentrating improvements in the quality and extent of services provided to the upwardly mobile middle and upper classes, whose

---

[26] For an introduction to these debates, see the brief summary and bibliographical references contained in the entry "Washington Consensus" in Reinert et al. (forthcoming).

demands tend to increase along with their growing income, while keeping the lower social groups, whose expectations from social policy are more modest, misinformed.

In democratic societies, it is healthy to air in a public debate these inconsistencies between what is politically effective and what truly contributes to the economic and social progress of the population. This debate would be more fruitful if opinion leaders, government economic advisors, and political organizations abandoned their simplistic thesis that increased income always leads to increased satisfaction (and thereby, political support), and in its place, accepted that the relationship between income and satisfaction is inherently conflictive.

4

Satisfaction beyond Income

Happiness . . . is the best, noblest, and
most pleasant thing . . . yet evidently . . .
it needs the external goods as well.—Aristotle

A broadened understanding of satisfaction challenges the traditional economic theory that assumes that individuals maximize their well-being based on decisions that correctly predict basic well-being derived from consumption and from other key decisions, such as the allocation of time between work and leisure activities. In reality, human behavior does not adhere to such simple propositions.[1] The motivations that intervene in decisions are diverse and include momentary impulses, commitments, or simple routines that give rise to decisions that do not necessarily lead to achieving maximum satisfaction. A paradoxical conclusion of satisfaction studies is that the explicit pursuit of happiness can be counterproductive, because it affects individual aspirations and because people make systematic misjudgments about what produces happiness. In general, people fail to predict future utility or welfare effectively; thus they overestimate the effect of extrinsic attributes (particularly, the value of consumer goods) and underestimate the benefits of intrinsic attributes (friends, family, hobbies). In analyzing the factors that influence levels of satisfaction, it is apparent that beyond income and what can be obtained with it, other aspects of life have a greater impact on maintaining them.

Since satisfaction depends on income, as well as other factors, the following mental experiment is pertinent: if a person undergoes a sudden critical change in some aspect of life, how much would his or her income have to be increased to maintain the same level of satisfaction? Although this concerns a completely hypothetical experiment, it is enlightening; it shows that greater income can hardly substitute for many of the most important facets of life, such as friendships or health. For example, for a Latin American, the average "value" of friendship is nearly seven times his or her income, which argues, as many people have stated, that a good friendship is priceless.

---

[1] The challenges that the "science of happiness" presents to economic theory are surveyed by Frey and Stutzer (2002); many of them were identified in the 1970s by the Leyden school (see van Praag, 1985) and by Brickman and Campbell (1971).

Previous chapters have analyzed various domains of individual satisfaction in parallel. With a different focus, this chapter concentrates on life satisfaction in general to explore how it is affected by diverse factors, beyond income, and how the different dimensions of people's lives are reflected synthetically in their level of satisfaction. Life satisfaction in the Gallup World Polls—which are the source of information for this chapter—is measured according to the life satisfaction "ladder" question, which asks respondents, "On what step of the ladder do you feel you are currently, with the highest step [10] representing the best possible life for you and the lowest step [0] representing the worst for you?"[2] This is one of a number of methods of investigating life satisfaction and measuring its subjective utility (see Box 4.1).

Individual Factors and Life Satisfaction

In surveys that use the "ladder" scale from 0 to 10 to determine a respondent's level of life satisfaction, the answers are concentrated mainly at the midpoint, but this does not mean the gradation lacks importance. Simply comparing the way in which answers are distributed in wealthy countries to their distribution in poor countries makes it clear that wealthier countries have a greater level of life satisfaction (as analyzed in Chapter 3). Using this scale, a little more than 80 percent of the people surveyed in the poorest countries rate the quality of their current life between 0 and 5, whereas in the richest countries barely 25 percent of respondents give scores in this range (see Figure 4.1). This would suggest that in order to understand life satisfaction, one must explain the differences *between* countries. Nonetheless, this route does not stretch very far; beyond the income per capita of the countries and the growth rate in past years, no other "national" variable makes a significant contribution to explaining the differences. Even if it did, it would not lead very far, since only a fraction (37 percent, to be exact) of the differences in levels of life satisfaction between some individuals and others is due to diversity among countries. The most effective gauges in analyzing life satisfaction are individuals, not countries. Individual satisfaction levels differ according to age, sex, and employment status. Within these characteristics and many other differences among individuals (many of them impossible to measure) lies the great diversity that reveals satisfaction levels.

Age and Gender

In general, Latin Americans experience a slight reduction in their satisfaction level in the first years of their adult lives, and an increase in the later years of their lives. The critical point seems to be reached at around age 56 for men and 60 for women, following a very stable trend, in spite of other factors that influence their satisfaction. Based on the Latinobarometer surveys, Graham and Pettinato (2000) have calculated that the lowest level of life satisfaction is reached at age 46. Many studies have found a U-shaped relation between age and satisfaction (e.g., Clark and Oswald, 1994; Oswald, 1997; van Praag, Frijters, and Ferrer-i-Carbonell, 2003). Both static studies (also called cross-sectional studies), like this one, and longitudinal studies (which evaluate infor-

---

[2] The complete text of the question appears in Table 2.1 (general domain of self-perception).

Box 4.1 Measurements of Subjective Well-Being

In recent years, the use of surveys that investigate sample individual opinions on diverse aspects of life, including life satisfaction in general, has resurged. In Latin America, the annual Latinobarometer surveys, which cover 17 countries, have included this type of question since 1996. The World Poll of the Gallup Organization, applied in 23 Latin American countries and in more than 130 countries since 2006, includes numerous questions regarding life satisfaction. The World Value Surveys (WVS), which currently cover 80 countries, also explore life satisfaction. Based on diverse sources, for 11 developed countries, these surveys have gathered data concerning life satisfaction for 25 years or more.

In order to measure life satisfaction, respondents are asked to answer questions such as "Generally speaking, how happy are you with your life?" or "How satisfied are you with your life?" with answer options that range from four different levels to a scale of 0 to 10. Though psychologists usually prefer the question of "satisfaction" to that of "happiness," both are narrowly correlated. According to Blanchflower and Oswald (2004) and Graham and Pettinato (2002b), the correlation coefficient between answers to both questions varies between 0.5 and 0.6. The "ladder" question employed in the Gallup World Poll is unusual in that it asks respondents to frame their evaluation of life satisfaction supposing "that the highest step represents the best possible life . . . and the lowest step the worst possible life," which imposes a certain comparative structure that does not exist in other life satisfaction measurement strategies.

Although these surveys are the best-known source of information on subjective welfare, there are other methods. The *experience sampling method* collects real-time data several times per day with regard to the respondents' feelings of well-being in their routine activities. This method has already been applied to representative populations in the United States, and studies have concluded that the most satisfactory daily activities include interactions with others and diverse leisure aspects, while some of the least satisfactory take place in work environments.

The *day reconstruction method* asks respondents how satisfied they are at different moments of the day. The U-index (for "unpleasant") of displeasure is equal to the portion of the day that an individual has unpleasant feelings. The *brain imaging method* measures brain activity associated with negative and positive feelings. These two last methods are quite costly and to date have been applied only in experimental form.

The broad consensus among academics is that subjective well-being is measurable to a certain degree of precision, moderately stable, and sensitive to changes in living conditions. The measurements are well correlated with diverse aspects of behavior associated with happiness, such as frequency of laughter in moments of social interaction. People who are happy according to such measure-

(continued on next page)

(continued)
ments are also considered happy by their friends and family; such individuals express positive emotions more frequently and are more optimistic, sociable, and extroverted. They also sleep better and are less likely to commit suicide.

Recently, a group of 50 notable academics proposed a system of *National Indicators of Subjective Well-Being and Ill-Being* (Diener, 2005; Kahneman et al., 2004).

Such new ideas and methods for measuring subjective well-being have revived the old dream of maximizing well-being, considered the final objective of public policies by economists since the eighteenth century, such as Bentham (1781), and some as modern as Tinbergen (1956) and Theil (1964). In the past, this dream was considered unattainable because of obstacles in measuring well-being on a cardinal scale that allowed for comparisons between individuals and the difficulties in building a consistent social function starting with individual preferences and involving diverse outcome variables (Arrow's famous Impossibility Theorem).

Today, measurements of subjective well-being provide the cardinal scale and comparability among individuals that were lacking, and consequently, in principle they permit the construction of social well-being functions. For instance, the sum of happiness scores for individuals (i.e., on a scale of 0–10) can be adopted as a simple and intuitive social welfare function, yet there are many objections to this hypothesis.

Sources: Frey and Stutzer (2007) and Veenhoven (2007).

mation on people over time) have come to this same conclusion. Such studies do not account for differentiation among generations; thus they cannot predict how the level of satisfaction of the youngest generations surveyed will be affected when they reach more advanced ages. Nevertheless, studies in the United States indicate that in recent decades all new generations have lower levels of satisfaction than previous ones.

Following a universal trend, Latin American women have declared themselves to be more satisfied with their lives, on average, than men, but the gender gap is more profound than a simple comparison of answers reveals; in fact, based on equivalent levels of income and other influential factors, which will be analyzed herein, women have indicated substantially higher levels of life satisfaction. For example, whereas a woman living under normal conditions has a 15 percent probability of giving a score of 8 (on a scale of 0 to 10) in terms of life satisfaction, this can reach 18 percent if the woman is in socioeconomic conditions similar to those of the average man. That said, although men usually have more favorable financial circumstances, it is women who feel more satisfied overall. This suggests that possibly their positive experiences are more intense or lasting (Diener et al., 1999).

Beyond these demographic trends, there are numerous individual factors, which can be considered objective (in other words, externally observable), that are associated with life satisfaction. It is expedient to begin with the capacities of individuals and gradually expand the focus to encompass the environment that surrounds them.[3]

The Importance of Capabilities

Good health is the basis of all capabilities. It is important to recognize that there is no universally accepted objective measurement of individual health. Some known variables related to health, at least in the population (not for each individual separately) are height and body mass. The Gallup World Polls include a set of quasi-objective questions on basic individual health conditions (known as EQ-5D and described in further detail in Chapter 5). Based on an indicator com-

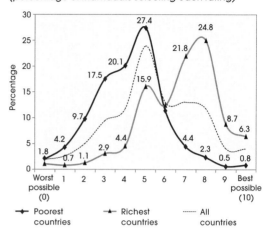

Figure 4.1 Life Satisfaction in Rich and Poor Countries
(percentage of individuals selecting each rating)

Source: Authors' calculations based on Gallup (2007) and World Bank (2007).
Note: Income groups were constructed using 2005 GDP per capita at purchasing power parity (PPP). The total sample was split into four different groups with the same number of people. Poorest countries are those with GDP per capita at PPP below US$2,077. Richest countries have a GDP per capita at PPP above US$13,977.

posed on the basis of answers to those questions,[4] it is apparent that those people with better health have, effectively, greater possibilities of declaring themselves more satisfied with life. The effect is very strong and statistically very solid (Table 4.1). Take, for example, a Mexican woman who in all aspects apart from health is considered at the midpoint within her country's population; in other words, she is a "median" person (in a statistical sense)[5] who has median income and education levels and a median amount of material comforts. If this woman does not have any health deficiencies, she will most likely rate herself a 7 on the scale of satisfaction. If her state of health corresponds to

---

[3] Throughout this discussion, the direct impact of income has been kept isolated, as it has already been discussed in the previous chapter. There, the influence of the principal individual variables (gender, age, marital status, education, the significance of religion and friendships), which are discussed in the present chapter, is also controlled for. This approach is necessary because otherwise, the impact of other variables that are correlated with income, which may have their own influence on life satisfaction (such as education), may be attributed to income.

[4] The responses to the set of EQ-5D questions are converted into a single index using a formula that attaches a weight to each of the possible health states. The scoring algorithm is taken from Shaw, Johnson, and Coons (2005). For further details, see Lora (2008).

[5] An explanation may be in order for those not versed in statistics: *median* and *average* are not the same thing. The *median* of a set of values is the value of the variable at the midpoint of all the values in the set, so that exactly half the values are above the median and half below, whereas the *average* is the sum of all the values divided by the number of values. Where the variable involved is "income," the *median* income is typically much less than the *average* income because the rich, though comparatively few in number, earn disproportionately large amounts, which distorts the average, inflating it well above the median value. (To give a crude example, consider a population of five individuals whose incomes are $100, $200, $300, $400, and $1,000,000; the median income for the population is $300, whereas the average income is a whopping $200,200.) Thus the median, rather than the average, individual is used to refer to the most typical or characteristic person within a particular population.

Table 4.1 Factors Related to Life Satisfaction

Dependent variable: life satisfaction (0–10)	Independent variables	Latin America		World	
		1	2	3	4
Demographic characterisics	Male	-0.1690***	-0.2409***	-0.1567***	-0.1614***
	Age (years)	-0.0489***	-0.0569***	-0.0331***	-0.0364***
	Age-squared	0.0004***	0.0005***	0.0003***	0.0003***
Human capital	Health score (EQ-5D)[a]	1.2702***	0.9735***	n.d.	n.d.
	Complete primary education	0.0052	0.0425	n.d.	n.d.
	Complete secondary education	0.0766	0.1566	n.d.	n.d.
	Complete superior education	0.2541**	0.3954***	n.d.	n.d.
Relational goods	Married	-0.0216	0.0562	0.0768**	0.0792*
	Divorced	-0.0650	-0.0478	-0.2737***	-0.2633***
	Widowed	0.0651	0.1456	-0.2655***	-0.2545***
	Have one child	0.0043	-0.0255	0.0405	-0.0163
	Have two or more children	-0.0117	0.0084	0.0159	-0.0167
	Consider religion to be important	0.2536***	0.1783**	0.0589*	0.0811*
	Have friends	0.4325***	0.3613***	0.6495***	0.5117***
	Have employment	0.1046**	0.0583	0.2025***	0.1849***
Material life conditions	Household income (monthly per capita in PPP US$)	0.2225***	0.2209***	n.d.	n.d.
	Live in the city	-0.0273	0.0368	0.1877***	0.1853***
	Access to running water service	0.0497	0.0821	n.d.	n.d.
	Access to electricity service	0.3551	0.1013	n.d.	n.d.
	Access to telephone service	0.1597**	0.1422**	n.d.	n.d.
	Asset index	0.1368***	0.1539***	n.d.	n.d.
	Does not have shortage of income to cover food costs	0.4919***	0.4229***	0.7334***	0.6645***
	Does not have shortage of income to cover household costs	0.2232***	0.1499*	0.2840***	0.2236***
Personality traits	Individual optimism score		0.3069***		0.2953***
Number of individuals		11,990	7,923	87,959	28,878
Number of countries		19	17	97	51
Fixed effects per country		Yes	Yes	Yes	Yes
Pseudo–R^2		6%	7%	8%	9%

Source: Authors' calculations based on Gallup (2007).

Note: Coefficients indicate the effect of the independent variable on the life satisfaction of a median individual, which is rated on a 0–10 scale. The method of estimation is ordered logit. Columns 2 and 4 include a variable that controls for personality traits. n.d. = no data.

[a] EQ-5D health score is a quantitative measure of health conditions based on five questions. A higher score indicates a better health status.

*Coefficient is statistically significant at the 10 percent level; **at the 5 percent level; ***at the 1 percent level; no asterisk means the coefficient is not different from zero with statistical significance.

that of a median woman, her level of satisfaction will probably be reduced to a 5, and if her health status corresponds to that of the 25 percent of Mexican women with the worst health conditions, her level could feasibly be a 4.

It is well-established that one's health status has a major impact on one's life satisfaction; in fact, the investigations of Dolan (2006) and Graham, Eggers, and Sukhtankar (2004) conclude that it is the *most* important determinant. Among the countries of the Organisation for Economic Co-operation and Development (OECD), where arterial hypertension is most common, it has been observed that average happiness levels are lower (Blanchflower and Oswald, 2007). Likewise, being obese increases the probability of leading a life with which one is less satisfied (Graham and Felton, 2005b; Graham, 2008).

Consequently, individuals with known health problems declare less satisfaction with their lives than healthy individuals. Probably there are causality relations in both directions, a question discussed in Chapter 5. However, stronger than the link between life satisfaction and individuals' objective health indicators is the relation between life satisfaction and health satisfaction, since both are influenced by traits of the individuals' personalities (van Praag, Frijters, and Ferrer-i-Carbonell, 2003; Argyle, 1999; Diener and Seligman, 2004).

The self-development capacity of any individual depends essentially not only on his or her health status, but also on his or her education level. Chapter 6 discusses the limitations of conventional methods of measuring education based on the level of formal schooling attained or the overall years of education completed, especially in a region such as Latin America and the Caribbean (referred to herein simply as "Latin America") in which deficiencies in the quality of schooling are so pronounced. Regardless of these limitations, surveys clearly show that the most-educated individuals tend to have greater life satisfaction levels. In the Gallup World Polls, respondents are asked only what level of education they have reached, and not the number of years spent in formal schooling. Nevertheless, the results clearly show that those individuals who have reached the tertiary level are more satisfied with their lives than those who have completed only secondary education, while at the same time, the latter individuals declare greater life satisfaction than those who have finished only primary school or have no formal education.

Since this statistical analysis accounts for the relation between income and satisfaction separately, the significance of education in life satisfaction levels is implicit for other reasons. It is difficult to interpret the many reasons why individuals with higher levels of scholastic attainment feel better. In part, the root may be an inverse causality: those individuals with more positive attitudes and greater self-assurance achieve higher levels of education. Nevertheless, this explanation does not go far in countries such as those in Latin America, where educational opportunities are so poorly distributed. There, it is more probable that the most-educated individuals enjoy a higher social status and can seek jobs and activities that offer them enhanced personal enrichment opportunities. Also, it is likely that such individuals have a greater potential to appreciate the nonmaterial aspects of life, including their interpersonal relations (Diener et al., 1999). In other words, more-educated people have more options not only to satisfy their consumption needs (although perhaps subject to greater aspirations, as observed in the previous chapter), but also to feel more autonomous, capable, and connected.

Interpersonal Conditions

Family conditions, friendships, and other interpersonal relations constitute part of the objective foundations of people's lives on which their self-development possibilities also depend (recall Box 1.1). Happiness studies regularly conclude that, when compared with single adults, married people feel better and divorcees and widows and widowers feel worse (Argyle, 1999; Oswald, 1997). Nevertheless, the dominating influence is unclear: whether having a stable partner enhances well-being or whether those individuals with a greater sense of life satisfaction have more possibilities in finding a partner and maintaining a stable relationship (Diener et al., 2000). The estimates included in Table 4.1 give partial support to these conclusions. In Latin America, only divorce seems to affect life satisfaction (and only once the influence of personality traits is isolated, as is discussed later in the chapter). Other marital statuses have no impact (in comparison to being single), whereas they do in the rest of the world.

Since having children is one of the most important decisions for any individual, it is conceivable that children contribute to life satisfaction; however, this is not what comes out of opinion surveys in Latin America or other parts of the world. Perhaps this sounds surprising, but diverse studies (though not the present one) have found that, based on the number of offspring per family, children can have a negative, although modest, effect on life satisfaction (Argyle, 1999; Clark and Oswald, 1994; Frey and Stutzer, 1999; van Praag, Frijters, and Ferrer-i-Carbonell, 2003). Nevertheless, no universal verdict exists on this subject. For example, whereas in western Germany children seem to diminish the level of life satisfaction, the opposite is found on the other side of the country (Frijters, Haisken-DeNew, and Shields, 2004a, 2004b). Those who have conducted in-depth studies into the channels through which having children may affect life satisfaction have concluded that children can create dissatisfaction, as they can augment levels of anxiety, stress, and depression, above all in the case of single parents. When such feelings manifest themselves, they have a stronger influence on the life satisfaction of men than women (Kohler, Behrman, and Skytthe, 2005; Ferrer-i-Carbonell and Frijters, 2004). The impact children have on life satisfaction seems to depend on diverse conditions. The first child (and, in certain cultures, especially when it is male) produces greater satisfaction when the couple to whom it is born has a stable relationship than when that relationship is not stable. Teenage pregnancies or unwanted children tend to result in diminished satisfaction.

Beyond family structure, life satisfaction seems to depend mainly on the potential to interact with others and on spiritual beliefs (Ellison, 1991). Analysis of the Gallup World Polls confirms that people feel more satisfied when they consider friends and religion important factors. Compared to the rest of the world, for Latin Americans, being religious has a greater influence on life satisfaction, and having support from friends has a smaller impact. One's work environment provides an outlet for interpersonal development, and worldwide it plays a critical role in life satisfaction. In Latin America, the effect is less pronounced, but this does not mean that the noneconomic dimensions of employment have less importance for Latin American populations; on the contrary, Chapter 7 shows that Latin Americans with paid employment especially value recognition and respect in the workplace, which confirms the importance of the relational dimension of the work environment. Nevertheless, many Latin Americans show a preference for self-employment because of the autonomy and flexibility it offers them.

It is important to keep in mind that when people express satisfaction with their lives and assert that religion or friendships are important factors, this may be a simple reflection of their personality and may not necessarily indicate that they dedicate more time or attention to activities that incorporate such factors. A method of testing whether personality is actually behind this correlation is to determine whether the level of satisfaction is maintained when a variable that synthesizes certain personality traits of each individual is considered.[6] As can be observed in Table 4.1, the majority of the results are maintained; in particular, those people who consider religion and friendship important continue to express higher satisfaction with their lives when the personality traits variable is taken into account. On the other hand, the positive effect of being employed diminishes, which suggests that the association between life satisfaction and having a job is more complex: perhaps those who feel more satisfied with life have a predisposition toward having a job, or perhaps being employed contributes to a more favorable opinion overall.

Material Life Conditions

For most people, having access to a variety of goods and basic services is a prerequisite for life satisfaction, as pointed out clearly by Aristotle in the epigraph of this chapter. The conditions of material life have been the focus of numerous studies and one of the main concerns of international development agencies since 1970. The most recent studies on happiness or life satisfaction support this position.

Clearly, income is the most obvious measure of people's economic capacity to satisfy their needs. However, even after income is accounted for, having access to specific goods and services contributes independently to life satisfaction. This could be the result of fluctuating income and the fact that some individuals lack access to credit or other financial assistance to satisfy their needs when their income is temporarily reduced, or because certain goods hold a value for people that surpasses their purchase price (or, more specifically, that such goods can surpass the satisfaction value that can be derived from other similarly priced goods).

From the Gallup World Polls, it has been observed that currently the life satisfaction levels of many people in Latin America are limited by their inability to cover their basic needs in regard to food or housing (occasionally or permanently). Some countries have reported alarming figures: 64 percent of those polled in Haiti declared that on some occasion in the preceding 12 months they lacked sufficient funds to buy food (see Figure 4.2). In El Salvador, 27 percent of respondents reported that in the preceding 12 months they had gone through periods in which they could not afford to pay for their homes. Food deprivation rates in various Latin American countries are abnormally high based on the income levels per capita in the region.

However, those goods traditionally considered essential (beyond individual income) are not the only ones that can affect life satisfaction. The statistical analyses summarized in Table 4.1 indicate that life satisfaction for the average Latin American

---

[6] This variable was introduced in Chapter 2, so no additional explanation of it is offered here.

Figure 4.2 Food Insecurity and GDP per Capita

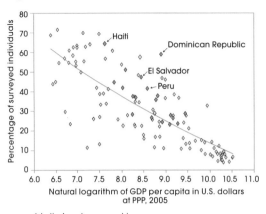

♦ Latin American countries

Source: Authors' calculations based on Gallup (2007) and World Bank (2007).
Note: Percentage of surveyed individuals refers to those who declared encountering some type of economic restriction in buying food for their families at some point in the preceding 12 months.

currently depends on having access to telephone service (fixed or mobile) and possessing a variety of durable assets, including a television, computer, automobile, washing machine, refrigerator, and DVD player. It is impossible to obtain precise estimates as to which of these durable goods are the most essential, although it is clear that the more of these assets inviduals have, the greater level of satisfaction they assert. (Table 4.2 shows the possession rates for the services and goods mentioned in this analysis and the synthetic index constructed to summarize them.)

Based on the impact of individual aspirations and comparisons of people regarding the satisfaction derived from consumption (see Chapter 3), it could be presumed that life satisfaction depends not only on, or not greatly on, one's own possessions, but rather more on the goods possessed by those around one. Based on data from the Gallup World Polls, there is no evidence to support this hypothesis. Nevertheless, Chapters 6 and 8 include analyses of the diverse aspects of the effect of the conditions of others on life satisfaction in certain realms. For example, in Santiago, Chile, spatial segregation has an impact on the poor population's ambitions and levels of satisfaction with education: the most segregated have decreased ambitions and do not demand that education for their children meet the same standards as those who live near families with higher education levels. In La Paz, Bolivia, homes located where there is a greater concentration of indigenous people have lower values, probably because this factor reduces the satisfaction that nonindigenous people have with their dwellings and neighborhoods.

How Much Are Certain Sources of Satisfaction Worth?

An interesting digression is to recall previously discussed results in regard to "valuing" those personal capacities, interpersonal conditions, or goods that contribute to life satisfaction—for example, the value of friendship. Perhaps it is crass and ill-mannered to ask how much friendship is worth in monetary or other material terms, since the satisfaction derived from having friends is a value on its own. It is not necessary for friendships to generate material benefits or to be considered good business in order for them to be important in the lives of many people. Nevertheless, because of the satisfaction it offers, it is possible to compare friendship with income, which also produces satisfaction (directly or indirectly). In view of this, a typical (or "median" in the statistical sense) Latin American woman "values" her friendships at 6.6 times her income (see Figure 4.3).

Table 4.2 Asset Index and Its Components, by Country, 2007

Country (ranked according to asset index)	Television	Computer	Vehicle	Washing machine	Refrigerator	DVD player	Asset index, national average[a] Range: −3 (own no asset) to 3 (own all assets)
			Percentage of people owning asset				
Chile	98.5	44.2	35.9	91.3	89.4	64.2	1.15
Mexico	95.2	25.2	40.5	72.6	87.9	67.5	0.82
Panama	96.0	17.9	29.0	82.2	84.9	67.9	0.71
Costa Rica	97.3	31.9	34.8	62.1	90.7	57.8	0.70
Argentina	97.6	29.7	36.4	61.0	67.9	47.7	0.39
Colombia	95.7	24.0	13.4	49.3	84.0	45.4	0.13
Dominican Republic	88.7	17.6	23.6	77.3	77.9	28.5	0.13
Uruguay	96.7	29.5	30.1	61.1	50.7	39.8	0.10
Ecuador	94.4	23.1	17.3	30.7	83.2	53.7	0.04
Brazil	94.0	21.8	31.0	38.4	30.8	60.6	−0.21
Guatemala	92.7	28.7	26.2	19.2	59.6	45.2	−0.23
Paraguay	88.0	10.6	20.3	51.2	61.1	28.1	−0.37
Peru	90.3	21.0	10.8	20.0	49.8	52.7	−0.50
El Salvador	89.3	14.2	14.3	13.6	63.4	46.3	−0.53
Bolivia	85.9	19.2	19.3	6.8	43.9	42.8	−0.74
Nicaragua	80.6	11.4	14.0	6.2	42.9	38.1	−0.98
Honduras	69.6	13.1	16.0	7.0	44.0	23.5	−1.18

Source: Authors' calculations based on Gallup (2007).

[a] The asset index is the country average of individual-level asset scores, and the score is constructed using the principal components statistical technique.

Note: Countries that appear in the table are those that had enough information in Gallup (2007) to permit calculation of the asset index at the individual level.

Now consider this result from a different angle. This median woman receives an income equivalent to US$163 per month and in all other aspects of her life, she is a typical person: she is 30 years old, lives in a city, has a secondary education, is married (her spouse has more or less the same income), has no children, considers her friends and religion important factors in her life, and lives in a modest home with all the basic services and an amount of household goods similar to that of other married women. She is in good health and does not suffer any serious economic limitations on her ability to pay for her housing or food.[7] If this woman lost her friendships, her life satisfaction level would crash, to a point at which if someone wanted to compensate her monetarily for this loss and make her feel the same level of life satisfaction again, that person would have to increase her income to US$1,246 per month. At that level, she would have the same probability of declaring the same level of life satisfaction as before.[8] This, of course, is a completely hypothetical exercise, but it reliably demonstrates that life satisfaction involves more fundamental factors than income.

Figure 4.3 Amount of Income Needed to Maintain Individual's Initial Level of Satisfaction When Faced with Change
(U.S. dollars)

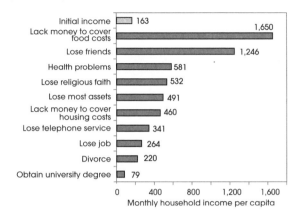

Source: Authors' calculations based on Gallup (2007).
Note: Individual depicted in this figure is a married 30-year-old Mexican woman with no children and secondary education, employed, with friends and religious beliefs, who lives in a modest house with all public utilities. Each bar represents the income this woman would need to receive in order to keep her level of life satisfaction constant given the occurrence of the event described in the label at the left of the bar.

This same method of appraisal is appropriate for other variables that have an impact on life satisfaction.[9] Health problems can also have a very large effect on satisfaction. If the health status of the "average" Latin American woman described herein were to deteriorate to the point that 25 percent of the overall population was in worse health, her income would have to increase to US$581 per month for her to report an equivalent level of life satisfaction. In other words, her good health status is worth US$418 per month (the difference between US$581 and her actual income). Figure 4.3 illustrates the valuation of other hypothetical life changes in this Latin American

---

[7] As attentive readers will have detected, these are all the significant variables that help explain life satisfaction for Latin Americans.

[8] On a scale of 0 to 10, we have supposed that this woman's level of life satisfaction was originally rated a 6, the most probable level given her personal conditions. Conceptually, the calculation is very simple: it considers the income level required to equal the probability of reaching the same level of life satisfaction after another explanatory variable (in this case the dummy variable that says she has friends that she can rely on) is changed.

[9] Note that the valuations herein measure the willingness to pay, not the ability to pay. In fact, several of these appraisals surpass the individuals' incomes and consequently are more than they would be able to pay. However, as a result of the attenuation bias (resulting from the measurement error) in the income coefficient, the valuations may be biased upwards.

woman's life, such as facing divorce and losing her religious beliefs, her durable assets, or her job. It is important to remember that because one's assets and occupation are important factors in life satisfaction, in addition to income, this implies that their values surpass their effect directly related to income.[10] If this hypothetical woman were to lose her job, her income would have to increase to US$264 per month, a level almost US$100 over her current income, for her to report an equivalent level of life satisfaction, because her job is not only a source of income, but possibly a valuable source of inter-personal relationships and personal achievements. Similarly, if this hypothetical woman, a secondary school graduate, completed university studies, she could feel equally sat-isfied with life with a lesser income. Nevertheless, in this case it is important to bear in mind that this hypothetical exercise does not consider the possible effects of additional education on income and consumption aspirations. As discussed in Chapter 3, shifts in aspirations can have a considerable impact on satisfaction.[11]

Life Satisfaction as a Synthesis of Different Life Dimensions

The previous section explored the relationship between life satisfaction and the diverse individual characteristics and conditions that can be observed externally or that respon-dents can presumably report with *some* objectivity. It is important to emphasize the word "some," because an individual can only judge, for example, whether he or she is experiencing pain or anguish, and whether its intensity is moderate or not (these are some of the health questions that form part of the EQ-5D survey mentioned previously), both of which imply subjective judgments, as well as to use personal judgment to decide whether friendships or religion are important.

In this section, an opposing approach is adopted; instead of trying to explain life as a function of variables that are—to a certain point—objective, the approach here is to determine the importance that *subjective appreciations* of different aspects of individuals' lives have on life satisfaction. This assumes that when people evaluate their lives in responding to the "ladder" question, they implicitly assign a certain importance to each aspect of their lives. It is not necessary to ask the respondents directly how much importance they attribute to each dimension; it is sufficient to evaluate the corre-lation (quantified in Table 4.3) between the answers to the "ladder" question and those regarding satisfaction with different realms. (According to some surveys that request explicit answers regarding the importance of the different realms, there is ample agreement between the two methods.)

Table 4.3 indicates that Latin Americans assign the greatest importance to sat-isfaction with their standard of living, more specifically, everything they can buy or do with their income. After this, the important factors are friendship, job and health satis-faction, and finally, satisfaction with their homes. (For those who are unemployed, job satisfaction is obviously not relevant, but the others are ranked similarly.) It is important

---

[10] If the price paid for some good corresponds to the equivalent satisfaction of the same amount spent on other things, then the good would not appear as an additional source of satisfaction in the regressions presented in Table 4.1, as the entire effect would be captured by income. For a technical discussion, see van Praag and Ferrer-i-Carbonell (2007), Chapter 11.

[11] Here, comparison effects with the reference groups have not been considered because of the limitations im-posed by group sizes in the estimations (see Chapter 3).

Table 4.3 How Life Satisfaction Is Related to Satisfaction with Different Life Aspects

Dependent variable:
life satisfaction (0–10)

Independent variables	Latin America		World		Latin America: Employed only	
	Employed people	Employed and unemployed people	Employed people	Employed and unemployed people	With income above regional median	With income below regional median
Economic satisfaction	0.7061***	0.7138***	0.7070***	0.7022***	0.6405***	0.4970***
Importance attached to friendships	0.6532***	0.6219***	0.3885***	0.4549***	0.2573	0.7674***
Job satisfaction	0.3355***	n.a.	0.2853***	n.a.	0.2693*	0.2124
Health satisfaction	0.3183**	0.4216***	0.2898***	0.3468***	0.5520***	0.0941
Household satisfaction	0.1477*	0.2000**	0.0830*	0.1393***	-0.0623	0.1988
Personal freedom satisfaction	-0.0499	-0.0482	0.0837	0.0828*	-0.0269	-0.0766
Importance attached to religion	0.0585	-0.0187	0.0735	0.0003	0.1063	0.1060
National economic conditions	0.0429	0.0244	0.1072*	0.0743*	-0.0470	0.1033
Confidence in medical system	-0.1057	-0.0784	-0.0390	-0.0050	-0.1254	-0.0064
Satisfaction with public labor policies	-0.1232	-0.0476	-0.0426	-0.0168	-0.1382	-0.0559
Confidence in education system	-0.2380**	-0.2524***	-0.0608	-0.0369	-0.2695***	-0.1751
Satisfaction with city conditions	-0.2018*	-0.1155*	-0.0251	0.0085	0.0546	-0.3817**
Individual optimism score	0.2315***	0.2381***	0.1579***	0.1480***	0.2047***	0.2788***
Number of observations	4,669	10,941	23,075	52,218	2,232	1,485

Source: Authors' calculations based on Gallup (2007).

Note: Coefficients indicate the effect of independent variable on the life satisfaction (rated on a 0–10 scale) of a median individual. The method of estimation is ordered logit. The independent variables, with the exception of optimism, are binary (yes = 1, no = 0). n.a. = not applicable.
*Coefficient is statistically significant at the 10 percent level; **at the 5 persent level; ***at the 1 percent level; no asterisk means the coefficient is not different from zero with statistical significance.

to bear in mind that these are the topics of personal life covered in the Gallup World Polls.[12] Other private domains include satisfaction with individual autonomy and the importance of religion in one's personal life, but these two fields do not seem to have much weight for Latin Americans in evaluating their personal happiness. It is possible that other personal domains exist in which being or not being satisfied affects overall life satisfaction.

In contrast with the importance of the personal life aspects, most social or collective dimensions do not seem to have significant weight in the subjective appraisals of well-being. For example, no association has been found between satisfaction with a country's economic situation, its health system, or its job creation policies and the residents' evaluation of life. Moreover, in the cases of satisfaction levels with the education system and city of residence, there is an inverse association with levels of well-being, possibly because as people satisfy their personal needs, they begin to worry about what surrounds them and their society and therefore become more critical about the deficiencies of certain policies (this assumes that in reality, the inverse association reflects a causality in the opposite direction—in other words, from life satisfaction to satisfaction with these public domains).

Perhaps what is stated above is not surprising, as it is to be expected that the appreciation each person has for his or her own life reflects, above all, his or her valuation of his or her personal conditions and interpersonal relations, more than a valuation of the environment where he or she lives. This is a significant conclusion that reveals that there are few individual motivations to influence public policies if they have no direct effect on personal conditions.

The relative importance that people of other regions assign to various private domains is similar to that which Latin Americans assign to those domains. Also, the conclusion that people attach little significance to public aspects in the valuation of their own lives is valid worldwide. In this sense, the only difference is that elsewhere in the world the level of satisfaction with the national economy seems to have a significant, although modest, importance (statistically) in the appreciation of life.

Where more profound differences can be noted is among Latin Americans who earn above and those who earn below the average income for the region (US$157 in monthly income per capita per household in terms of purchasing power parity).[13] When these two groups of workers are compared, it is clear that, in regard to private aspects of life, the wealthier groups consider health and job satisfaction more important than those with less income, for whom well-being depends solely on their satisfaction with their living standards and friendships. This difference suggests that in the case of the most affluent people, perhaps satisfactory employment supplies some of the needs otherwise supplied by interpersonal relations, whereas for those with less resources, friendships provide part of the economic security and protection mechanisms that employment provides for others.

---

[12] Actually, friendship is not a domain that can be judged in terms of satisfaction, but rather in terms of importance. This is equally true of religion.

[13] Here, this way of partitioning the sample is preferred to dividing the population based on the poverty lines discussed in the previous chapter, to maintain more-balanced samples between the two groups, which facilitates the estimations.

In reference to the collective aspects of life, Latin Americans above the midpoint in terms of income level also function distinctly from those below. The inverse relation between life satisfaction and satisfaction with one's city of residence holds only among the poorest segment of the population, and the inverse relation between life satisfaction and satisfaction with the education system arises only among the wealthiest. The interpretation given herein to such inverse associations suggests that the poorest tend to be conscious of deficiencies of the cities in which they live in direct relation to the level to which they have met their personal needs, while for the wealthiest, something similar occurs, but in relation to the education system.

A brief additional explanation with regard to the method employed in arriving at these conclusions may be useful for the more technically inclined reader. When correlation is sought between levels of life satisfaction and each of its domains, without consideration of the personality traits of individuals, many domains appear important. Clearly, this is because individuals' personality traits are reflected in their opinions on all aspects of life. Consequently, the estimations isolate this influence. If information were available for all domains, the estimations should simply try to explain life satisfaction as a function of satisfaction with all domains and the variable that captures the personality traits, without including objective variables in the regression. Nevertheless, when information is lacking in some domains, there are debates over methods for capturing this information adequately to avoid biasing the other results. In the results documented in this chapter, consideration has been given to other variables for which there is some subjective information regarding overlooked domains (friendships, religion, security). It could be argued that one must also consider objective variables related to disregarded domains—for example, education variables, given that there is no information on people's satisfaction with their own education. The problem is that the education variables can be correlated with many other things that are included (such as living standard satisfaction). In any case, the coefficients obtained for the domains with information are stable in terms of these options.[14]

The subsequent chapters explore some fundamental dimensions of the lives of individuals: health, education, employment, and housing situation and urban environment (as much in their physical dimensions as in terms of security). Throughout this chapter, it has been clear that subjective quality of life is associated with these dimensions, whether objective indicators are considered or an attempt is made to evaluate the weight that individuals subjectively assign to their satisfaction level with these domains. Nevertheless, the dimensions that are examined in the chapters that make up the remainder of the volume have not been selected because they are the most important for quality of life. In fact, it could be argued that friendships or religious beliefs have a more powerful influence on the subjective welfare of many people than the dimensions chosen for study here. However, these are not areas in which the government is able to, or should, intervene; rather they belong to a personal realm that should remain out of the public arena. On the other hand, health, education, employment, housing, urban infrastructure, and personal security are amenable to government intervention. These

---

[14] For a detailed technical discussion, please see van Praag and Ferrer-i-Carbonell (2007), Chapter 4.

are central areas for public policy, because what national and local governments do or do not do in these areas can affect quality of life.

Nevertheless, this does not mean that the objective of public policies in these or other areas should be to maximize satisfaction with life in general or with specific life domains. The final chapter of this volume revisits this discussion and underscores the possible conflicts between individual happiness and collective welfare. Clearly, public policies have a role to fulfill. Understanding people's opinions can contribute to improving the public debate, as well as to optimizing the design and implementation of public policies, but generating more positive opinions cannot be the determining criterion in making public decisions.

FACTS AND PERCEPTIONS IN ACTION

5

Getting a Pulse on Health Quality

With health, everything is a source of pleasure;
without it, nothing else, whatever it may be,
is enjoyable.—Arthur Schopenhauer

The health of people in Latin America and the Caribbean has improved tremendously over the last 50 years along most dimensions and for almost every definable class or group, yet surveys show that people are sometimes dissatisfied with their health and chances for leading healthy lives. This chapter describes how objective health measures have evolved over time, explores how popular perceptions sometimes reflect and sometimes diverge from these objective measures, and considers the implications of these findings for public health policies.

No effort to understand personal and social well-being can ignore health. It strongly influences people's chances for happiness, improves their ability to participate in social and economic life, and affects the way they experience their lives. Nevertheless, health is not an isolated feature of life. Health is, itself, strongly influenced by other aspects of a person's social and physical environment—education, employment status, social networks, safe water, and sanitation, to name just a few.

Health gains in Latin America and the Caribbean (hereafter "Latin America") over the last century are unprecedented in the region's history. People are living 10 years longer today than they were in 1960. Consider, for example, that average life expectancy for children born in Bolivia today is 64 years, which is higher than average life expectancy was in the United States in 1940 (62 years), when the United States already had a much higher level of income.

While these gains should be recognized and celebrated, large differences in health status that have persisted or increased over this same time frame cannot be neglected. In addition, personal access to the kinds of health care services and environmental conditions that are conducive to maintaining good health are not universally enjoyed. Complicating this picture further, medical technology is continually expanding the range of adverse health conditions that can be prevented or cured, while the population's epidemiological profile—the kinds of diseases commonly experienced—

continues to shift away from a preponderance of infectious diseases toward noncommunicable and chronic illness.

Because of all these factors, the way people in Latin America perceive their health and chances of living a healthy life is not a direct reflection of objective measures of health and access to services. People in the region are generally satisfied with their health, but this varies across countries in ways that are weakly related to health status, health care systems, and income, suggesting that cultural factors play a significant role. People appear to be more tolerant of ill health in some countries than in others, and within countries different socioeconomic groups experience health and health care services differently.

Therefore, political efforts to mobilize support for changing public health policies must contend with at least two ways in which popular views diverge from objective indicators. In countries where individuals have a high tolerance for ill health or weak health care services, it may be difficult to mobilize support for improving health care systems. In countries where individuals have low tolerance for ill health and tend to view public health policies negatively, simply maintaining support for well-functioning health care programs may be difficult.

Healthier Than Ever

People in Latin America are healthier than ever, and this is true for almost every social group. Unlike in other aspects of development, such as education and economic growth, Latin America has done quite well in terms of health outcomes. Today, the region has the greatest longevity and lowest child mortality rates among all developing regions (see Figures 5.1 and 5.2).

Life expectancy around the world has increased more rapidly in the last 50 years than ever, and Latin America has been at the forefront of this trend. The average country in Latin America had a life expectancy of only 56.2 years in 1960, yet by 2005 this average had increased to 72.7 years (see Table 5.1). This average, however, masks important differences across the region. Haitians born today can expect to live 17 years longer than those born in 1960, yet their life expectancy is still only 59.8 years. At the other extreme, citizens of Chile and Costa Rica have life expectancies above 78 years, representing gains of 20.9 and 16.6 years, respectively. Eight countries experienced gains in life expectancy of more than 20 years over this period: Bolivia, Chile, Ecuador, El Salvador, Guatemala, Honduras, Nicaragua, and Peru.

Life expectancy in the region appears to have improved in almost every social group; however, large differences remain, and in some cases, may have widened. For example, in 2000, life expectancy at birth was 71 years for the Brazilian population as a whole, but only 65.7 years for people of African descent (Borges Martins, 2004). In Honduras, life expectancy at birth for indigenous men was only 36 years compared to 65 years for all men, and only 43 years for indigenous women compared to 70 years for all women (PAHO, 1998). In Mexico, the nonindigenous population has a life expectancy of 74 years, about 5 years longer than that for the indigenous population (PAHO, 2002).

Historically, declines in infant and child mortality have been the main sources of rising life expectancy. In Latin America, infant mortality rates have declined fairly steadily from the end of the nineteenth century right into the present. The average child mortality rate (deaths for those below five years of age) in Latin America was about 150 deaths per 1,000 children in 1960—about one in every seventh child. By 2005, the average child mortality rate was only 28 per 1,000—less than one child out of 30 (see Table 5.2).

As with life expectancy, child mortality varies across regions and social groups. For example, in 1998, the mortality rate for children born alive in Ecuador to indigenous mothers was twice that for children of nonindigenous mothers (10.5 percent and 5.1 percent, respectively) (Hall and Patrinos, 2005). In 1997, indigenous Mexicans experienced a child mortality rate of 120 per 1,000 live births, while the national average was only 59 per 1,000 live births (PAHO, 2002).

Declining Fertility Has Contributed to Better Health

Greater longevity and declining infant and child mortality are tied to a massive demographic shift, which has revolutionized family structure, transformed economies, and altered perspectives on well-being. As mortality rates fell in the nineteenth and twentieth centuries, populations started to grow. For a variety of reasons, fertility rates subsequently declined as well. Fertility rates in Latin America were among the world's highest in 1960 at 5.9 births per woman, while today they are lower than the world average at 2.4 births per woman (ECLAC, 2004). Chile, Costa Rica, and Uruguay have the lowest fertility rates of about 2.0 births per woman, while Bolivia, Paraguay, Haiti, and Guatemala have the highest (3.7, 3.7, 3.8, and 4.3, respectively).

Figure 5.1 Life Expectancy at Birth

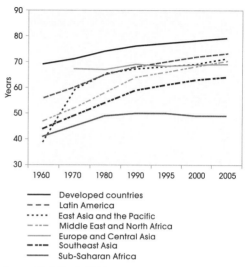

Developed countries
Latin America
East Asia and the Pacific
Middle East and North Africa
Europe and Central Asia
Southeast Asia
Sub-Saharan Africa

Source: World Bank (2007).

Figure 5.2 Child Mortality Rate

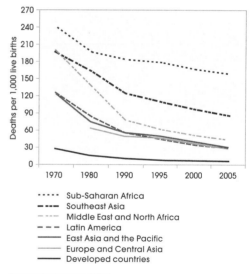

Sub-Saharan Africa
Southeast Asia
Middle East and North Africa
Latin America
East Asia and the Pacific
Europe and Central Asia
Developed countries

Source: World Bank (2007).

An important consequence of reduced fertility is improved maternal and child health. Short intervals between births deplete a mother's nutritional reserves and increase the risks of infant mortality and maternal complications (Merchant and Martorell, 1988; Curtis, Diamond, and McDonald, 1993; Pebley and Stupp, 1987). In addition, with

Table 5.1 Life Expectancy at Birth by Country, 1960–2005
(years)

Country	1960	2005	Difference 2005–1960
Haiti	42.4	59.8	17.4
Bolivia	42.8	64.8	22.0
Guyana	56.3	65.6	9.3
Trinidad and Tobago	63.7	69.4	5.7
Honduras	46.7	69.6	22.9
Guatemala	45.9	69.7	23.8
Suriname	59.8	69.8	10.0
Peru	48.0	70.8	22.8
Jamaica	64.4	70.9	6.5
El Salvador	50.8	71.3	20.5
Paraguay	63.9	71.4	7.5
Belize	61.7	71.8	10.1
Brazil	54.8	71.8	17.0
Dominican Republic	52.1	71.8	19.7
Nicaragua	47.3	72.1	24.8
Bahamas	63.3	72.4	9.1
Colombia	56.8	72.4	15.6
Venezuela	59.8	74.2	14.4
Mexico	57.3	74.4	17.1
Ecuador	53.4	74.7	21.3
Argentina	65.2	74.8	9.6
Panama	60.9	75.2	14.3
Uruguay	68.0	75.6	7.6
Barbados	64.5	76.5	12.0
Cuba	64.2	77.8	13.6
Chile	57.3	78.2	20.9
Costa Rica	61.9	78.5	16.6
Average	56.2	72.7	16.5

Source: World Bank (2008).

fewer children, parents are able to invest more in the education and physical nourishment of each of their children. Furthermore, undesired pregnancies are related to low birth weight, preterm delivery, and less healthy maternal behaviors—such as late seeking of prenatal care, smoking and alcohol consumption during pregnancy, and lower propensity to breast-feed (Eggleston, Tsui, and Kotelchuck, 2001; Pulley et al., 2002; Joyce, Kaestner, and Korenman, 2000). For these interrelated reasons, the trend toward lower fertility rates has made important contributions to the overall decline in mortality and morbidity.

Longer Lives Are Also Healthier Lives

Greater longevity is a broad measure of a population's health, but a longer life could be miserable if it is an unhealthy one. Fortunately, increasing life expectancy has been accompanied by large declines in morbidity as well. One of the best summary measures available for this improvement in health is the rising average height of the adult population.

After genetic differences are adjusted for, environmental conditions explain a considerable proportion of the difference in body size between populations. Nourishment, in particular, is strongly associated with growing taller, particularly in sensitive periods—prenatal, neonatal, early childhood, and adolescence (Eveleth and Tanner, 1976). Other inputs consumed by individuals, such as shelter and clothing, contribute to an individual's physical growth. Protection from illness increases the probability that individuals will fully achieve their potential for such growth as well.

In fact, children who are raised in optimal conditions show similar growth rates regardless of their race or location. Growth curves for children under 24 months of age are nearly overlapping in some countries, with children in India and Brazil reaching the same height for age as children in Norway and the United States. These similarities persist in children up to five years of age, and are so close across countries that it has led the World Health Organization (WHO) to establish a single global standard for assessing a child's health with height-for-age measurements. Thus, nutrition, health care, and environmental conditions appear to be more important for determining average growth patterns in a population than genetics or ethnicity (WHO Multicenter Growth Reference Study Group, 2006).

A population's average adult height is a good measure for summarizing health status. This average is correlated with other widely used measures of health status, such as life expectancy, is inversely associated with morbidity, and is associated with greater functionality (see Box 5.1). In Brazil and Colombia, average population height increased by more than 0.5 centimeters per decade during the twentieth century (Ribero and Núñez, 2000; Strauss and Thomas, 1998). Demographic and Health Surveys (DHS) in seven Latin American countries showed similar height gains of about 0.5 centimeters per decade for women, with most height gains occurring between 1955 and 1970 (Piras and Savedoff, 1999). Evidence from specific populations sometimes shows even greater gains; for example, girls born in Pelotas, Brazil, in 1982, whose mothers measured between 152 and 160 centimeters, were on average about 5 centimeters taller than their mothers when they were measured at age 19 (Gigante et al., 2006).

Table 5.2 Child Mortality Rates by Country, 1960–2005
(deaths per 1,000 live births)

Country	1960	2005	Difference 2005–1960
Cuba	54	7	–47
Chile	155	10	–145
Costa Rica	123	12	–111
Uruguay	61	13	–48
Argentina	73	16	–57
Brazil	176	21	–155
Colombia	122	21	–101
Venezuela	79	21	–58
Paraguay	94	23	–71
Panama	88	24	–64
Ecuador	178	25	–153
El Salvador	191	27	–164
Peru	239	27	–212
Honduras	204	29	–175
Jamaica	75	31	–44
Mexico	133	36	–97
Nicaragua	193	37	–156
Guatemala	202	43	–159
Bolivia	255	65	–190
Haiti	247	84	–163
Average	154	28	–126

Source: World Bank (2008).

A Changing Disease Profile

As the population's health has improved, the kinds of illnesses and conditions that it faces—its "disease burden"—have changed as well. The disease burden is a more comprehensive measure of population health because it includes all forms of illness and injury, not just those that are fatal. The most common measure for estimating the disease burden is the disability-adjusted life year (DALY), which measures how many years of "good health" are lost to each disease or condition and sums them across the population.

Using this measure of the disease burden, the major causes of death and disability in Latin America in 1950 were infectious and communicable diseases, while today the most common threats to good health are from noncommunicable conditions such as diabetes, heart disease, and cancers. By 2005, vaccine-preventable diseases were no longer among the top 10 leading causes of child deaths in the region, remaining significant only in Central America, Haiti, and the Dominican Republic (PAHO, 2007). Between 1970 and 2000, the disease burden fell in all major categories; the burden of communicable

Figure 5.3 The Changing Burden of Disease: Deaths by Cause, 1970–2000

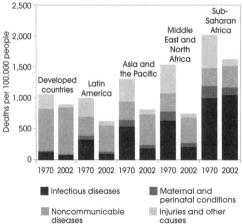

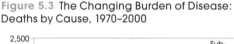

Sources: Bulatao and Stephens (1992) and WHO (2004).
Note: Deaths classified by causes due to infectious diseases, maternal and perinatal conditions, noncommunicable diseases, and injuries and other causes, using WHO's system of international classifications.

diseases fell by half, while that for noncommunicable conditions fell by about 6 percent (see Figure 5.3). Between 1990 and 2002, it appears that the share of deaths due to communicable illnesses fell from 42 percent to about 18 percent, while the share due to noncommunicable causes rose from about 43 percent to about 67 percent. The share attributed to injuries remained roughly the same at 15 percent (Bulatao and Stephens, 1992; WHO, 2004).

This epidemiological shift to noncommunicable diseases changes the kinds of health care services needed by the population. While age, sex, and genetic predisposition contribute to the burden of noncommunicable disease, many risk factors for these diseases can be reduced. Such risks include behavioral factors (e.g., diet, physical activity, smoking); biological factors (e.g., hypertension, obesity); environmental factors (e.g., exposure to toxins); and social factors (e.g., workplace stress). For most of the region's countries,[1] the three highest risk factors, measured by their contribution to the loss of disability-adjusted life years, are alcohol (6.2 percent), high blood pressure (5.0 percent), and tobacco use (4.0 percent) (WHO, 2002). Fortunately, a number of very effective interventions are available to address these risks (see Box 5.2).

While these trends in risk factors for noncommunicable disease are worrisome, it is important to remember that, on the whole, the burden of most of these diseases has actually declined. The mortality rate among adults in Latin America in 2000 was 173 per 1,000—about 35 percent lower than in 1960 (see Table 5.3). The concern with non-communicable illness is due largely to the latter's rising share within the overall disease burden. However, for particular conditions—notably tobacco-related cancers, diabetes, and cardiovascular disease—even the mortality rates are rising.

In sum, people in Latin America are now healthier than ever. Overall, they are leading longer lives with fewer risks of contracting the infectious diseases that were leading causes of mortality in the last century. Yet, these very successes mean that people are living long enough to succumb to noncommunicable diseases and chronic conditions, including strokes, diabetes, and cancers. Moreover, alcohol abuse, tobacco, hypertension, and obesity have become pervasive, leading to heart disease, diabetes, and cancers among poor and rich alike (see Box 5.3). Nevertheless, vaccine-preventable illnesses and other infectious diseases, malnutrition, and disability associated with re-productive health continue to be serious problems among the region's poor populations, indigenous groups, and people of African descent.

Many Factors Have Contributed to Improved Health

While rising agricultural productivity and improved nutrition contributed to health gains in the nineteenth and early twentieth centuries, evidence suggests that these have not been the major contributors to longevity in the last 50 years. For example, among countries with the lowest caloric intake, life expectancy at birth rose by almost eight years above the gain that could have been expected from nutrition alone (Soares, 2007). Rising income and material wealth have also played a role in improving health, but their contribution, too, is relatively modest (Palloni and Hill, 1997).

The story of why health has improved is difficult to tell, because so many social factors have played a role and changed over the same period. Increased female labor force participation, women's empowerment, and reductions in fertility over recent decades have all contributed to improvements in health. Urbanization was possible, in part, because of investments in infrastructure to preserve health, but urbanization also accelerated the dissemination of improved hygiene, nutrition, and shelter. More widespread education promoted women's autonomy, with positive effects on political and economic participation, reproductive health, and children's growth. Education also helped disseminate knowledge of how disease can be spread through microbes and an

---

[1] This ranking applies to a group that includes all of the IDB's borrowing member countries with the exception of Bolivia, Ecuador, Guatemala, Haiti, Nicaragua, and Peru. These latter countries face larger health risks from malnourishment, unsafe sex, and unsafe water. This is a reminder that each country's specific profile should be addressed when setting priorities, rather than relying on broad group averages.

Box 5.2   Effective Ways to Reduce Noncommunicable Disease

Chronic and noncommunicable diseases are increasing as a share of the overall disease burden in Latin America. Some of these conditions are expensive and difficult to address, but cost-effective approaches are available for others. While many of these approaches involve improvements in health care services, others involve public policies outside the health sector.

Alcohol abuse in the region contributes to an estimated 3 percent of all DALYs lost through intentional and unintentional injuries; neuropsychiatric disorders represent another 3 percent; and an additional 2 percent comes from cardiovascular and other noncommunicable diseases. As much as one-half of the 89,000 annual road traffic fatalities may be attributable to alcohol abuse alone. Among the most cost-effective interventions are raising excise taxes by 50 percent, reducing hours of sale at retail establishments, and comprehensive bans on advertising. One study estimates that the total cost to the region of these three programs would be fairly modest: US$110 million, US$85.2 million, and US$76.7 million, respectively (Rehm et al., 2006).

Tobacco use significantly increases the risk of death and disability from a wide range of cardiovascular diseases and cancers, and is responsible for about 260,000 deaths in Latin America each year. Among those who were smoking in 2000, tobacco will cause premature deaths for 40 million, reducing each lifetime by an average of 20 to 25 years. A number of cost-effective policies could significantly reduce this loss of life, including bans on advertising, raising cigarette taxes, and providing counseling and assistance in quitting. For example, the projected 40 million premature deaths could be reduced by an estimated 2.3 to 6.7 million if countries were to introduce a 30 percent increase in cigarette taxes (Jha et al., 2006).

High blood pressure is the leading risk for developing cardiovascular diseases, including strokes, infarctions, and hypertensive illness. Heart disease and strokes account for about 500,000 deaths each year in Latin America. High blood pressure, considered the leading risk, as well as high cholesterol levels and obesity contribute to this disease burden. Promising approaches to reducing blood pressure include community and personal interventions to encourage changes in diet and physical activity, as well as medications such as beta blockers and aspirin. Some studies, such as Wald and Law (2003), suggest that cardiovascular risk from hypertension could be reduced by as much as 50 percent through treatments that include aspirin and statins.

Sources: Rehm et al. (2006), Jha et al. (2006), Wald and Law (2003), and Savedoff (2007).

Table **5.3** Age-Specific Mortality Rates, World Regions

Regions	Mortality rate, infant (per 1,000 live births)		Mortality rate, under-5 (per 1,000 live births)		Mortality rate, adult (per 1,000 adults)	
	1960	2000	1960	2000	1960	2000
Europe and Central Asia	45	16	56	20	160	165
East Asia and the Pacific	130	30	195	39	560	150
Latin America	97	27	149	33	269	173
Middle East and North Africa	157	41	252	50	299	165
North America	26	7	30	8	177	111
South Asia	145	70	243	96	425	228
Sub-Saharan Africa	149	102	247	165	498	492

Source: Soares (2007).

understanding of what conditions modern medicine can prevent and treat. In places where social safety nets have been introduced and become effective, they have helped workers to survive unemployment, families to weather economic hardship, and elderly people to avoid impoverishment.

Broader social characteristics, most notably socioeconomic inequalities, have also been shown to affect population health through a variety of channels. Socioeconomic inequalities influence the distribution of power in a society and, consequently, influence the distribution of resources. They also influence social norms, behavioral patterns, and stress in ways that contribute to health inequities (Marmot and Wilkinson, 2006). While these inequalities are likely to be significant factors in explaining health inequities in Latin America, there has been no major reduction in socioeconomic inequalities across the region that could account for the health gains experienced across the entire population.

While environmental and social changes are significant factors in health improvements, health care services also need to be recognized—both for their past role and for their increasing importance. In Latin America, public investments in sanitation, vaccination, education, and combating disease vectors made significant inroads against vaccine-preventable illnesses, like measles and tetanus (see Box 5.4); respiratory illnesses, like pneumonia, bronchitis, and influenza; and other widespread diseases, like malaria (Palloni and Hill, 1997; Palloni and Wyrick, 1981). The availability of new medications has reduced the number of infections and deaths attributable to tuberculosis and respiratory infections. New treatments, such as organ transplants, chemotherapy, and angioplasty have reduced deaths from conditions which were invariably fatal 50 years ago.

More Access to Health Care Than Ever

The increasing access to health care services is remarkable when contrasted with the pace at which the demand for such services has grown. The region's population has increased threefold over the last 50 years, from about 180 million to 569 million today, and the physical resources available to provide health care have expanded even more rapidly. Between the censuses of 1960 and 2000, the ratio of doctors per 1,000 people increased from an average of 0.33 to 0.90 in five Latin American countries. The number

Box 5.3 The Puzzle of Rising Obesity and Persistent Stunting

Malnourishment has always been an important factor in Latin America's disease burden. Stunting persists as a serious problem, with about 16 percent of children in the region suffering from some degree of malnutrition, mostly among poor and socially excluded populations. For example, in Guatemala in 2000, the prevalence of stunting among nonindigenous children was high (33 percent); however, indigenous children had a rate almost twice that (60 percent) (Marini and Gragnolati, 2003).

With rising income in most of the region, malnourishment and stunting have declined, only to be replaced by a growing share of people who are overweight, and therefore at risk for a variety of noncommunicable illnesses, including diabetes and cardiovascular disease. In fact, abdominal obesity appears to be more strongly associated with heart attack risk in Latin America than in other parts of the world (Smith, 2007).

Obesity has spread quite rapidly; for example, in Chile in the 1950s, some 70 percent of children less than six years old suffered some degree of malnutrition, while today fewer than 2 percent are malnourished. Over the same period, however, the share of overweight adults has increased dramatically: today more than half of Chilean adults are considered overweight (i.e., a body mass index higher than 25 kilograms per square meter) (Uauy, Albala, and Kain, 2001).

In most countries, the share of adults who were overweight in the early 1980s was below 20 percent; today the share is close to or above 50 percent owing to a combination of social and economic changes that have led people to increase their consumption of energy-dense foods at the same time as they have reduced their physical activity. For example, in Mexico, fat as a share of total energy intake increased from 24 percent to 30 percent between 1988 and 1999. Between 1984 and 1998, household purchases of fruits and vegetables declined by 29 percent, while soft drink purchases increased by 37 percent. As a result, the share of overweight Mexicans rose from 28 percent in 1987 to 55 percent in 1999 and reached 70 percent in 2005. Today, about 41 percent of Mexicans are overweight and 29 percent are considered obese (i.e., a body mass index higher than 30 kilograms per square meter) (Rivera et al., 2004).

Sources: Smith (2007), Rivera et al. (2004), Marini and Gragnolati (2003), and Uauy, Albala, and Kain (2001).

of medical schools, hospitals, and health facilities has also grown dramatically through most of the region over the course of the last century. The expansion has continued in recent years. For example, between 1990 and 2005, the number of hospital beds in Mexico's public sector alone increased from 63,122 to 78,643 (SSS, 2008). Since 1995, the share of the Costa Rican population living farther than 25 kilometers from a hospital has declined from 30 percent to 22 percent (Rosero-Bixby, 2004).

Box 5.4 Progress in Immunization

Immunization programs are among the more remarkable successes of public health in the second half of the twentieth century (Levine and the What Works Working Group, 2006), having contributed to dramatic reductions in infectious diseases around the world. In the Americas, these successes have included eradication of smallpox and polio, along with steep declines in the prevalence of diphtheria, tetanus, and measles.

These successes are largely due to the increase in coverage of immunization programs. In 1970, fewer than 10 percent of children in Latin America were vaccinated for DPT (diphtheria, pertussis, and tetanus), whereas in 2001, more than 90 percent received this vaccine (see figure).

_____

Sources: de Quadros (2004) and WHO (2008).

Percentage of Children Receiving Third Dose of DPT Vaccine, 1980–2006

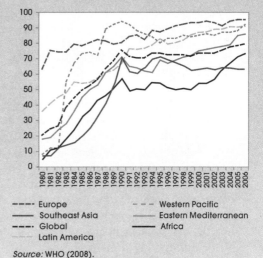

- - - - Europe
──── Southeast Asia
- - - · Global
········ Latin America

- - - Western Pacific
──── Eastern Mediterranean
──── Africa

Source: WHO (2008).
Note: Regional averages have been calculated using the estimated coverage rates together with estimates of the target population size from the Population Division of the United Nations. For all regions except Latin America, the size of the target population is the national annual number of infants surviving their first year of life. For Latin America, the size of the target population is the number of births each year.

This rapid expansion of health care service resources does not necessarily mean that more services were available to everyone, since the increase could have been highly concentrated in major metropolitan regions. However, census data for five countries in the region—Brazil, Chile, Costa Rica, Ecuador, and Mexico—show that the opposite is the case. For example, in Brazil, of the 15 states for which there are comparable census data between 1960 and 2000, the number of doctors per person grew slowest in São Paulo and fastest in Rio Grande do Norte. By 2000, São Paulo still had the highest ratio of doctors to 1,000 people (1.58), about double the rate in 1960 (0.76), but the ratio in poorer rural states tripled or quadrupled (Savedoff, 2008).

These increases are almost certainly associated with a surge in the number and quality of health care services provided to the population, because productivity has probably increased as well. Even though it is unclear whether the management of health care services has become more or less efficient, advances in medical technology have certainly increased the productivity of health care professionals. It is reasonable to believe that the rapid expansion of the health care workforce, above the rate of population growth, reflects greater availability of health care services in most of the region.

More People Have Financial Coverage

Access to health care services also appears to have increased when measured by enrollment in public insurance. For example, Chile and Costa Rica have effectively reached
universal health insurance enrollment. When those two countries created Social Security Institutes, in 1924 and 1941, respectively, very few people were covered. Yet, today,
almost everyone in those countries has health insurance coverage, whether through
public insurance in Costa Rica, or through mandatory health insurance in Chile, where a
little more than 80 percent are enrolled with public insurance and the remainder with
private insurers. Other countries in the region have been less successful with this strategy. For example, the Instituto Ecuatoriano de Seguridad Social (IESS, Ecuadorian Social
Security Institute) covers only 20 percent of the Ecuadorian population, 70 years after
its predecessor, the Instituto Nacional de Previsión (National Social Security Institute),
began to offer medical services to its affiliates.

Of course, social security is only one form of public financial support for the use
of health care services. Many governments directly provide free or low-cost medical care
in government facilities or subsidize services for particular populations through payments to providers. Some people also purchase private health insurance.

Although historical data are lacking, the low levels of financial coverage for
health care services in the 1950s have almost certainly been surpassed in the region;
nevertheless, the population share with financial coverage varies significantly across
countries. In the 2007 Gallup World
Poll, only 8.8 percent of Uruguayans
responded that they would have to
pay for hospitalization out of pocket,
and more than 91 percent said they
were financially covered, whether
by public programs, private health
insurance, or the social security system. More than 80 percent of those
polled in Brazil and Costa Rica also
reported that they had some form of
financial protection against hospital
costs for an accident or illness, while
by contrast, less than 30 percent of
those in Bolivia, Ecuador, Honduras,
Paraguay, and Peru felt that they had
recourse to some form of financial
coverage (see Figure 5.4).

Access to many health care
services is also easier today than it
was 50 years ago because costs have
actually declined in real terms; this is
the case, for example, with the real
cost of childhood vaccines, aspirin,
and off-patent antibiotics. The dra-

Figure 5.4 "If you had to go to a hospital because
of an accident or illness, who would take care of
the cost of your assistance?"
(percentage of respondents by country)

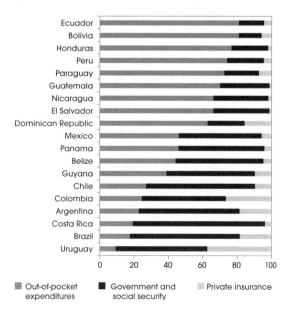

Source: Authors' calculations using Gallup (2007).

matic decline in the unit cost of anti-retrovirals in the last decade is only the latest example of how prices for similar drugs usually decline over time, especially after patents expire. A literature review found no information specific to Latin America, but studies in the United States have also documented declines in the costs of certain treatments (Griliches and Cockburn, 1994; Cutler and McClellan, 2001).

Declining unit costs for health treatments seem to contradict the common perception that health care is increasingly expensive; however, it is the newest and most expensive treatments that tend to be foremost in people's minds. Technological advances in medicine affect health spending in two directions. For certain interventions, the same amount of health gain can be achieved at lower cost, particularly for treatments that become routine or for which patent protections expire. For other interventions, costs for treating a particular illness may be higher, but the increased cost is more than compensated for by the resulting increase in health—that is, the price for each unit of health gain, whether an additional year of life or reduced disability, is lowered. The net impact is greater access to effective health care as existing interventions become relatively cheaper and new, more effective interventions become available.

More People Use Health Care Services

Utilization of health care services is a practical, but imperfect, measure of health care access. Although it has increased throughout the region, in most countries it remains inequitable. For example, in Peru the utilization of health care services ranges from 25 percent for the poorest fifth of the population to 48 percent for the richest fifth (Valdivia, 2002). The share of people in the richest income quintile seeking care when they are ill is about twice as high on average in Latin American countries as for the poorest income quintile (Dachs et al., 2002). The exceptions are countries like Argentina and Chile, where the differences are relatively small. For example, in Chile, despite an income difference of 20 to 1 between the richest and poorest quintiles, the share of the population that uses health care services differs modestly across income groups: between 8.8 percent and 9.7 percent of each income group use preventive health care, and between 2.8 percent and 3.7 percent utilize emergency care (Sapelli and Vial, 1998).

Another indicator of access to health care services is the coverage of skilled birth attendance, which is high in the Latin American region relative to other developing regions. Based on United Nations data, in South Asia only 37 percent of births are attended by a trained professional, compared to an average of 82 percent of births in Latin America—rates that are closer to those of the East Asian and Pacific region. Thirteen out of 21 Latin American countries with comparable data since 2000 report that skilled personnel attend 90 percent or more of births (see Figure 5.5).

In some countries, access to these services may be widespread and equitable. For example, despite its relatively low income, the Dominican Republic has a remarkably high rate of utilization of these services—over 90 percent for all income quintiles (Gwatkin et al., 2007). However, in many countries, skilled birth attendance is not widespread or equitably distributed. Data from 2000 to 2003 for Bolivia, Guatemala, Haiti, and Peru show that fewer than half the pregnant women in the poorest quintile have professional birth attendance, despite rates of over 90 percent among pregnant women in the richest quintile.

Figure 5.5 Percentage of Births Attended by Skilled Professionals in Selected Countries

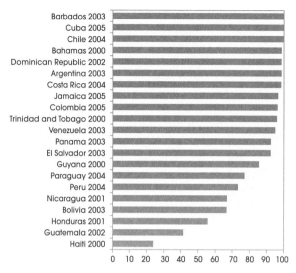

Source: UN (2008a).
Note: Countries selected for inclusion in the figure are those for which the United Nations reports comparable data after 1999.

Nevertheless, in recent years gains have been made. The coverage of skilled birth attendance for women in the poorest quintiles rose from 61 percent to 72 percent in Colombia between 1995 and 2005, from 20 percent to 26 percent in Bolivia between 1998 and 2003, from 89 percent to 94 percent in the Dominican Republic between 1996 and 2002, and from 33 percent to 78 percent in Nicaragua between 1997 and 2001 (Gwatkin et al., 2007).

In sum, environmental conditions and cultural factors have made enormous contributions to health gains in the region, but access to health care services has also played an important role. The region has been particularly successful at reducing the burden of vaccine-preventable illnesses, and has also made substantial progress in expanding the reach of critical health care services related to reproductive health. Whether the region's health care systems will meet the growing challenges posed by noncommunicable diseases and chronic conditions remains to be seen.

Health Really Does Make Life Better

Objective measures of health and the factors that contribute to better health show enormous gains over the last 50 years. But do these gains mean that people are better off? While good health is desirable in and of itself, it also contributes substantially to an individual's life chances and can play a direct role in overall life satisfaction.

In Latin America, health is the third most important factor contributing to life satisfaction—ranked below food security and having friends, but above employment, housing, and several other factors (see Chapter 4). Better physical health has been shown to be associated with greater life satisfaction in the United States, Latin America, and Russia (Graham, 2008), and increased longevity represents a significant part of the welfare gains experienced during the twentieth century (Soares, 2007).

Health affects well-being in many ways, but principally because some level of physical and mental functioning is necessary to engage in the individual and social activities of which a life is made. Health is essential to an individual's ability to live with autonomy, which is a universal prerequisite to well-being (Doyal and Gough, 1991). Healthy individuals have a wide range of capabilities that contribute substantively to their "positive freedoms" and consequently their chances of living a longer life with autonomy, material comfort, and meaning. The importance of health for those capabilities implies that social arrangements to ensure that individuals can become educated and have access to necessary medical care and healthy living conditions are an essential part of progress and development (Sen, 1999).

Good health enhances a person's ability to be productive and earn a living. Though income is certainly a factor that can improve and maintain health, the reverse has also been demonstrated. For example, agricultural workers are more productive when they have healthy iron levels in their blood; people in better health miss fewer days of work; and children's cognitive abilities improve when they are well-nourished (Thomas and Frankenberg, 2002). Healthier people, as measured by height and body mass index, also tend to earn more in the labor market (Strauss and Thomas, 1998).

Reproductive health plays a unique role in affecting life satisfaction. Women declare greater happiness when they have the number of children that they desire.[2] Both men and women are happier with the birth of a first child, although women's life satisfaction may decline with additional children (Kohler, Behrman, and Skytthe, 2005). It is known from many studies that autonomy, individual self-determination, and a sense of control in a person's life all have positive influences on life satisfaction. To the extent that the number and timing of children have profound effects on an individual's life, autonomy in making these choices fundamentally contributes to well-being.

In sum, improved health and access to health care services in Latin America has improved life in many ways. First and foremost, increased longevity and lower rates of morbidity represent direct improvements in well-being. Secondly, improved health has probably increased the population's ability to engage in individual and social activities in ways that increase their positive freedoms. Third, better health has contributed to greater material wealth, giving people resources with which to pursue their personal, family, and social goals. Finally, improved health may have contributed directly to greater general satisfaction with life, particularly as it improves the individual's capacity to exercise self-determination and autonomy in many spheres of social life and in choices about family size.

Feeling Healthy Is Not the Same as Being Healthy

Objective measures of health outcomes (e.g., longevity) and opportunities for preserving health (e.g., access to health care services) clearly have improved over recent decades in the Latin American region. Following Veenhoven's multidimensional framework proposed in Chapter 1, though, well-being also encompasses a range of subjective dimensions. How do people experience and interpret these large gains in health and access to care?

While happiness, or satifaction with life, is clearly related to health, the relationship between how people perceive their health and their objective health status is less obvious. There are at least four reasons that a person's perceptions of his or her own health might diverge from objective measures.

---

[2] Alfonso, Duryea, and Rodríguez-Pombo (2007) examine the links between the reproductive and psychosocial health of Bolivian women and find that unwanted pregnancies are significantly associated with decreased life satisfaction.

First, certain health conditions are *not physically or visually perceptible.* For example, people with high blood pressure, diabetes, or many internal cancers may not be aware of their condition until the illness reaches a very advanced stage, especially if they do not undergo routine medical exams.

Second, a person's *mental processes* filter and interpret his or her health condition. Thus, a health condition that might cause an individual with a generally negative attitude to feel very sick might, in another person with a more positive outlook, be considered minor or unimportant.[3]

Third, a person's health perception may be influenced by *how he or she feels relative to others.* For example, elderly people may report themselves to be in good health despite an illness or disability if they are comparing themselves only to others their same age (Groot, 2000; Parker, 2000). In general, however, health is not a positional good like housing or employment, for which satisfaction depends on a person's relative ranking (see Chapter 3). People's satisfaction with their own health is not higher when people in their reference group experience poorer health.

Finally, health perceptions are influenced by a person's *culture and language.* For example, a physical experience considered to be an illness by Western medicine, such as epilepsy, may not be considered a health problem at all in some communities, but may be interpreted instead as a spiritual experience. In more subtle ways, culture and language can encourage or discourage self-reflection on, and verbal expression of, one's health and health problems.

Despite these caveats, self-rated health is an important measure in its own right. For some health conditions, like pain and suffering, subjective responses are the only valid source of information. In other cases, self-rated health provides information that is complementary and additional to objective health measures. For example, after objective health indicators are controlled for, a person's self-rated health provides additional information about his or her risk of mortality (Mossey and Shapiro, 1982; Idler and Angel, 1990; Idler and Benyamini, 1997). In fact, in some studies self-rated health has been found to be a better predictor of subsequent death than objective health measures. In other cases, self-rated health is associated with objective measures of morbidity (Lora, 2008).

Satisfaction with Health Is High

People in Latin America tend to report relatively high levels of satisfaction with various aspects of life. The 2006 and 2007 Gallup World Polls confirm this finding: 85 percent of Latin American respondents report they are satisfied with their health, a rate that is comparable to that in most other regions but somewhat higher than that in Eastern Europe and Central Asia. While health satisfaction is certainly related to health status, the relationship is weaker than expected, and the two measures diverge in important ways. This can be seen both across countries and across individuals. The rest of this sec-

---

[3] Of course, mental processes are themselves a feature of health, and it could be argued that a person with a negative, perhaps even depressive, outlook should be considered more unhealthy than a person with a positive outlook. The point here is that the perception of a particular health condition (e.g., paralysis, cancer, shortness of breath) would not be the same in people with different mental states.

tion will discuss the diverse factors that influence health satisfaction, as reported in Lora (2008).

To explore this relationship, a health status measure is needed. Researchers have found that health status can be measured quite reliably with a parsimonious set of questions, referred to as EQ-5D, which inquire about people's ability to move around, to take care of themselves, and to undertake normal activities, and whether they experience pain or feel anxious and depressed. When this tool is used, people in Latin America report generally good health, but they still experience a range of ailments: about 25 percent report that they live with some pain; 18.5 percent live with anxiety; 10 percent report that they have limited mobility; 9.5 percent report having physical limitations that affect their daily activities; and 3.8 percent report that they have difficulties caring for themselves.

Health Status and Health Satisfaction Strongly Related

The relationship between health status and how people feel about their health is surprisingly weak when country averages are examined. Though people in countries with higher life expectancy are more likely to say they are satisfied with their health (hereafter referred to as "health satisfaction"), the effect is small and conceals wide variation (see Figure 5.6).

When the units of analysis are the individuals, not the countries, it is found that health satisfaction and health status (according to the questions of EQ-5D) are highly correlated. Extreme pain, moderate pain, extreme anxiety, and extreme limitations on daily activities are significantly associated with a person's reporting lower health satisfaction. Moderate limitations on daily activities, moderate problems with anxiety, and moderate difficulties with mobility also have some influence. By contrast, other conditions—such as extreme difficulties with mobility and limitations on self-care—do not show statistically strong relationships with health satisfaction, either because they are less frequent or because individuals more readily learn to adapt to or compensate for these conditions.

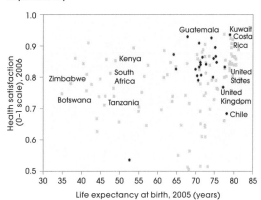

Figure 5.6 Health Satisfaction and Life Expectancy

Source: Authors' calculations using Gallup (2006).
Note: Black dots represent Latin American countries. Selected data points are labeled for illustrative purposes.

Health Satisfaction Varies by Age and Gender

Among other factors, a person's age and gender have some impact on health satisfaction. Older people are generally less satisfied with their health than the young. For men,

this decline in health satisfaction is fairly steady over time, while for women health satisfaction declines rapidly until 50–55 years of age, and then declines more slowly thereaf-
ter. Overall, men are more likely to report that they are satisfied with their health than
women. Nevertheless, men and women do not demonstrate significant differences in
their tolerance for ill health. Their responses to questions about health satisfaction are
equally sensitive to their actual health status.

More Income, More Satisfied—but More Growth, Less Satisfied

A country's income level has a relatively weak and complicated effect on health satisfaction. As might be expected, people in countries with higher income per capita tend to
report greater health satisfaction, but
the effect is small—doubling per capita income adds only a few percentage
points to the share of the population
reporting that they are satisfied with
their health (see Figure 5.7).

Figure 5.7 Health Satisfaction and GDP
per Capita

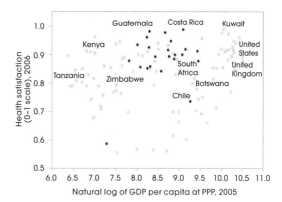

Source: Authors' calculations using Gallup (2006).
Note: Black dots represent Latin American countries. Selected
data points are labeled for illustrative purposes.

     Surprisingly, health satisfaction
is lower in countries experiencing economic growth.[4] A similar finding has
been documented with longitudinal
data in the United States, where mortality rates for eight out of 10 causes
rise during periods of economic growth
compared to periods of recession. Risk
factors like tobacco consumption,
weight gain, physical inactivity, and
unhealthy eating also increase during
economic upturns (Ruhm, 2000).
    This pattern is but one dimen-
sion of the "unhappy growth paradox"
discussed in Chapter 3. As with life sat-
isfaction and several other satisfaction domains, health satisfaction is positively related
to income levels and negatively related to income growth. More income allows people
to consume goods and services that improve their health, but it can have adverse effects
on some aspects of health, and may even raise expectations more rapidly than objective
health conditions can improve.

Whose Satisfaction Is Affected More: The Rich or the Poor?

Health satisfaction also varies across income groups within Latin American and Caribbean countries. Higher-income individuals are more likely to report that they are satisfied
with their health than poorer individuals in all but three of these countries (see Table
5.4). On average, the gap between health satisfaction among those in the richest and

---

[4] Deaton (2007) reaches the same conclusion on the basis of the 2006 wave of the Gallup World Poll.

Table 5.4 Percentage of Respondents Who Are Satisfied with Their Health

Countries	Income quintile					Difference
	(1)	(2)	(3)	(4)	(5)	(5)–(1)
Chile	58	59	65	72	79	21
Colombia	77	82	81	90	90	13
El Salvador	80	83	84	85	93	13
Nicaragua	73	77	85	78	86	13
Peru	71	72	79	83	84	13
Bolivia	76	85	87	85	88	12
Paraguay	74	78	80	87	85	11
Ecuador	73	83	77	85	83	10
Venezuela	88	92	98	91	96	8
Argentina	85	84	83	83	92	7
Costa Rica	91	90	91	98	98	7
Dominican Republic	85	79	83	84	89	4
Panama	88	90	89	94	92	4
Brazil	82	87	89	81	85	3
Guatemala	92	95	92	96	95	3
Mexico	86	83	85	86	89	3
Uruguay	82	79	86	85	84	2
Belize	94	95	95	72	93	–1
Guyana	90	79	86	90	85	–5
Honduras	92	91	86	91	87	–5
Average	82	83	85	86	89	7

Source: Authors' calculations from Gallup (2007).

poorest income quintiles is 7 percent. The gap is highest in Chile (21 percent), Colombia, El Salvador, Nicaragua, and Peru (each 13 percent). It is less than 3 percent in Brazil, Guatemala, Mexico, and Uruguay (and negative in Belize, Guyana, and Honduras).[5]

The difference in health satisfaction across income groups is driven largely by real differences in health status. For example, moderate difficulties with mobility, self-care, daily activities of living, pain, and anxiety affect more people in the lowest than in the highest income quintile (by as much as 8.7 percent in the case of pain). Extreme difficulties with these same conditions differ less among income quintiles, and in the cases of extreme difficulties with mobility and self-care, the relationship is actually reversed. Because extreme conditions are relatively rare, it may be that these latter differences are less precisely measured, or that they arise from conditions that are more evenly distributed across the population.

The poor do not tolerate ill health better than the rich. To the contrary, certain conditions—extreme difficulties with mobility and moderate difficulties with daily activities—reduce reported health status among the poor more than among those in higher income quintiles. By contrast, moderate difficulties with self-care and extreme difficulties with anxiety have less of an impact on reported health status among the richest quintile than in the rest of the population.

---

[5] Sampling problems may be behind these anomalous results, especially in Belize and Guyana, where sample sizes are just 500 individuals.

This disaggregation suggests that differences in cultural outlook do not explain differences between how the rich and poor regard their health. Rather, it suggests that the poor are more sensitive to particular ailments because they rely more on physical labor and/or because they have fewer resources with which to compensate for ill health. The wealthy, on the other hand, do have resources with which to purchase support services and physical aids that may diminish the impact of ill health on their self-reported health status and, thereby, on their health satisfaction.

Cultural Differences Are Significant

Health status, age, gender, income, and income growth all affect health satisfaction, but their impact is small relative to that of variables associated with cultural and social differences between countries and regions of the world. Knowing a country's religious composition, or its distance from the equator, is a better predictor of the population's health satisfaction than its national income, economic growth, public health spending, life expectancy, or infant mortality. For example, countries as different as Costa Rica and Guatemala have higher than average health satisfaction, while countries in the Southern Cone, such as Chile and Paraguay, report lower than average health satisfaction. The share of Guatemalans who report that they are satisfied with their health is very high, despite mortality indicators and health inequality measures that are worse than elsewhere. Chileans are the least satisfied with their health among Latin Americans, despite enjoying longer lives with fewer diseases and impairments.

One way of thinking about this divergence between health perceptions and health is to ask how likely it is that people will report they are satisfied with their health for any particular level of health. When such a measure is used for Latin American countries, Chileans appear to be the least tolerant of poor health status, while Guatemalans, Costa Ricans, Hondurans, and Panamanians are the most tolerant (see Box 5.5). For example, for any given health state, on a scale of 1 to 10, Guatemalans are much more likely than Chileans to state they are satisfied with their health (see Figure 5.8).

These cross-country differences in tolerating ill health are difficult to explain without reference to specific historical and social features that distinguish cultures. Explaining why people in certain countries take a more stoic attitude toward their health, while in other countries people tend to experience ill health more keenly and/or express their dissatisfaction more readily, is beyond the scope of this study. Nevertheless, regardless of its cause, this variation in tolerance for

Figure 5.8 Relation between Self-Reported Health Satisfaction and Health Status, Chile and Guatemala

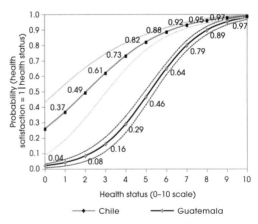

Source: Authors' calculations using Gallup (2007).
Note: Dotted lines are 95 percent confidence intervals. The vertical axis predicts the effect of a person's self-reported health status on the likelihood that he or she will report that he or she is satisfied with his or her health.

Getting a Pulse on Health Quality   **107**

Box 5.5 Tolerating Poor Health

The measure of health tolerance uses information from two health indicators extracted from the Gallup 2007 World Poll. The first indicator comes from asking, "Are you satisfied or dissatisfied with your health?" The second is the response to "Using a scale from 0 to 10, in which the best state you can imagine is marked 10 and the worst state you can imagine is marked 0, indicate how good or bad your own health is today."

By comparing the points in different countries at which the probability of reporting health satisfaction changes most sharply relative to a person's reported health state, it is possible to measure how countries differ with regard to the way poor health affects the population's perceptions of its health status. This measure shows that among Latin American countries surveyed, for a given level of reported health, Chileans are the least likely and Hondurans are the most likely to express satisfaction with their health.

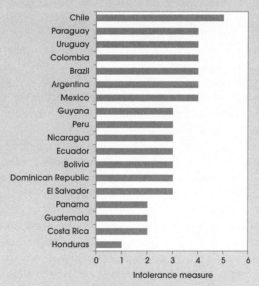

National Measures of Intolerance of Poor Health

Source: Authors' calculations using Gallup (2007).
Note: The intolerance measure is the interval in which the slope of the relation between one's self-evaluation of one's health status (on a scale of 0–10) and satisfaction with health status reaches a maximum.

Source: Lora (2008).

poor health has important implications for public policy. In countries with poor health conditions, high tolerance for ill health may make it difficult to mobilize support for funding and implementing public health interventions, or reforming poor-performing health care services. By contrast, in countries with good health conditions, low tolerance for ill health might undermine support for relatively well-functioning systems.

In sum, while a person's health satisfaction is clearly related to his or her health, perceptions of health and objective measures of health diverge systematically. Men tend to rate their health satisfaction higher than women, and younger people are generally more satisfied with their health than the elderly. In most countries, richer people are more satisfied with their health than poorer people, and their subjective experience of health is less sensitive to impairments. Contrary to expectations, the range across gender, age, and income is quite small, while differences across countries are quite large. Recognizing how sensitive different populations are to ill health is important both for choosing and for promoting good public health policies.

Are Health Systems Perceived to Be Adequate?

One of the factors that may make people feel differently about a health problem is whether they have access to health care services or social support to treat or alleviate their condition. Moderate difficulties with self-care may be less problematic, and therefore reduce satisfaction less, if other people are available to interact and assist. Treatments, physical aids, or constructing community buildings according to standards that assure accessibility can play a part in overcoming difficulties with mobility.

In general, the environmental conditions and availability of health care services have improved considerably in Latin America over the last 50 years. Yet, as with health satisfaction, personal perceptions of these conditions and services may diverge dramatically from objective indicators of the same.

Perceptions of health care access have been influenced by dramatic changes over the last 50 years in population, technology, education, income, and culture. A threefold population increase has driven rising demand for health care services. As the population's epidemiological profile has changed, the kinds of services that are demanded have also changed.

People demand access to more health care services today than ever for several reasons. Rising income and rising educational attainment increase the demand for health care services by increasing the population's purchasing power and by socializing individuals to seek care more readily. Social trends have also contributed to this increasing demand—with modernization and urbanization, the tendency to seek treatment from Western medical practitioners, rather than traditional healers, has grown. Wider dissemination of ideas through electronic media makes people aware of medical services to treat conditions that might otherwise have been ignored, remained unrecognized, or been accommodated. Finally, the political process itself often raises expectations, and expedience may lead politicians to promise more than government can deliver.

Health care service systems differ in their ability to meet these demands and, not surprisingly, satisfaction with the availability and quality of health care varies considerably across Latin American countries (see Table 5.5). Based on the 2007 Gallup World Poll, more than 70 percent of people in Costa Rica, Uruguay, and Venezuela report that

Table 5.5 **Percentage of Respondents Who Are Satisfied with the Availability of Quality Health Care in the City or Area Where They Live, by Income Quintile**

Country	Income quintile 1	2	3	4	5	All
Argentina	59.7	65.5	61.4	57.9	54.5	59.8
Belize	37.5	58.8	52.9	35.3	52.9	47.6
Bolivia	59.8	55.6	54.9	57.1	60.2	57.5
Brazil	43.9	47.1	48.3	44.8	46.6	46.1
Chile	50.3	46.8	43.0	45.6	37.8	44.7
Colombia	54.0	60.3	56.7	54.3	58.9	56.8
Costa Rica	78.6	80.9	73.5	77.1	74.2	76.9
Dominican Republic	50.7	63.3	55.6	51.3	56.3	55.5
Ecuador	42.2	58.5	54.7	50.8	50.8	51.4
El Salvador	60.7	62.1	62.8	55.2	62.1	60.6
Guatemala	53.0	47.0	51.0	58.0	57.0	53.2
Guyana	55.0	72.5	68.3	62.5	63.4	64.4
Honduras	61.9	55.9	50.8	57.6	54.2	56.1
Mexico	56.9	58.1	58.9	52.7	59.5	57.2
Nicaragua	49.7	56.1	57.2	61.1	55.6	56.0
Panama	60.8	57.0	63.5	61.4	63.5	61.2
Paraguay	43.3	46.1	48.8	45.5	51.5	47.0
Peru	46.3	35.2	43.0	50.3	45.5	44.1
Uruguay	84.4	78.9	74.8	73.2	79.7	78.2
Venezuela	75.2	69.3	79.7	71.9	68.2	72.8
Average	56.2	57.7	57.4	56.3	56.9	56.9

Source: Authors' calculations from Gallup (2007).

they are satisfied with health care services in their city or area, in contrast to less than half of those in Belize, Brazil, Chile, Paraguay, and Peru.

Men and women do not have significantly different perceptions when it comes to their confidence in the health care system or their satisfaction with the health care services available in their community. The only significant difference in perceptions across demographic groups is by age. Based on the same Gallup poll, after other factors are controlled for, Latin Americans in their fifties and sixties express greater satisfaction with health care services than those in their twenties (see Table 5.6).

Perceptions of health care services are also largely unrelated to income, despite evidence that poorer individuals have less access to health care services when they are sick and that the services they receive tend to be of poorer quality. This suggests that poorer people are more tolerant of poor-quality health care services than those who are wealthier, perhaps because their health care service aspirations are lower, consistent with the "aspirations paradox" discussed in Chapter 2. Because poorer people in the Latin American region who receive health care services are often beneficiaries of public programs, it may be that they are less demanding and more grateful for access to care that higher income groups might consider inferior in quality. In fact, people who report that they would use public health care services—a group that is disproportionately from lower income groups—express confidence in the health care system as much as those who are covered by social security or private insurance. Only people who expect to pay out of pocket for major health expenditures express significantly lower

Table 5.6 Percentage of Respondents Who Are Satisfied with the Availability of Quality Health Care in the City or Area Where They Live, by Age

Country	15–19	20–29	30–39	40–49	50–59	Over 60	All
			Age Groups				
Argentina	70.5	66.8	68.1	65.0	66.2	69.6	67.5
Belize	57.7	57.6	62.8	55.8	55.1	38.9	57.8
Bolivia	73.8	66.4	61.5	63.5	61.3	73.6	66.4
Brazil	56.3	45.9	40.9	51.5	59.9	61.0	51.7
Chile	50.7	39.4	45.2	50.6	51.0	62.7	51.3
Colombia	61.8	61.2	65.7	60.6	74.0	75.2	65.6
Costa Rica	78.3	72.8	69.1	78.3	82.3	87.5	76.6
Dominican Republic	72.9	62.9	57.1	65.6	68.0	77.9	65.9
Ecuador	61.4	50.0	50.6	51.2	55.5	39.7	51.3
El Salvador	63.1	55.0	51.6	51.7	46.9	59.1	54.5
Guatemala	64.5	49.0	51.0	47.9	51.2	38.0	52.0
Guyana	70.2	63.9	65.4	67.9	61.9	62.2	65.7
Honduras	70.1	60.2	60.4	54.3	60.2	61.7	61.4
Mexico	64.8	66.9	68.4	62.1	69.0	72.7	66.5
Nicaragua	70.0	67.4	65.3	77.5	66.7	80.3	69.8
Panama	57.0	57.3	60.7	64.8	62.4	62.4	60.5
Paraguay	52.3	53.1	45.0	52.6	50.0	50.0	50.4
Peru	59.9	55.5	44.4	51.4	51.5	51.5	52.4
Uruguay	77.2	81.6	73.0	77.6	71.4	85.3	78.9
Average	65.3	59.8	58.0	60.5	61.4	65.3	61.3

Source: Authors' calculations from Gallup (2007).

Figure 5.9 Percentage of Respondents Who Have Confidence in Health Care and Medical Systems, by Income Quintile and Financial Coverage

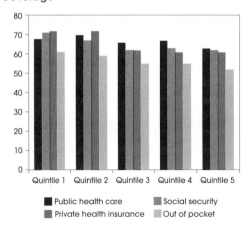

Source: Authors' calculations using Gallup (2007).
Note: Financial coverage is based on the likely source to pay for medical expenses if the respondent were to require hospital care.

confidence in the availability of quality health care (see Figure 5.9).

People who think health care services are available and good also tend to be more satisfied with their own health. In particular, individuals who answer affirmatively that they are "satisfied with the availability of quality health care" are more likely to express satisfaction with their health and rank themselves to be in better health. However, the direction and mechanisms of causality between perceptions of health and health care services are complex. The strong association mentioned above could indicate either that better health care services make people healthier, or that healthier people feel more optimistic about the availability of health care services.

What to Do When Perceptions and Objective Measures Diverge

Improvements in health and health care services over the last 50 years have been extraordinary and unprecedented in Latin America. People are living longer, healthier lives than ever, yet many feel dissatisfied with their health. Access to the conditions necessary to preserve health and health care services has also reached larger shares of the population than ever; nevertheless, the percentage that is satisfied with the availability of health care is relatively low.

Perceptions diverge from objective measures of health and health care service coverage for many reasons, but social and cultural factors appear to be particularly important. The greater tolerance for poor health exhibited by people in Honduras, Guatemala, Panama, and El Salvador contrasts strongly with that in countries that, by objective measures, enjoy better health, such as Chile, Uruguay, and Colombia. Within countries, the poor tolerate ill health less, probably because relative to wealthier people they lack resources with which to compensate or adapt. On the other hand, the poor report similar or higher levels of satisfaction with health care services, despite having access to poorer-quality care than those who are wealthier.

Effective public policies have to take all of these factors into account—objective measures of health as well as subjective ones, public interventions to directly improve health outcomes, and access to resources that improve a population's chances of leading healthy lives.

Pursue the Policies That Improve Health Outcomes

In terms of health outcomes, a large number of people still unnecessarily suffer from diseases and conditions that have been eliminated or significantly reduced among society's affluent. Addressing this tragic burden requires that countries implement programs that have been proven and implemented around the world—increasing immunization coverage, controlling disease vectors, expanding access to safe water and sanitation, ensuring adequate maternal care and family planning, and providing basic education.

Another set of health outcomes, related to chronic and noncommunicable illness, is more challenging because these outcomes often require behavioral changes and/or more complex health care services. Nevertheless, effective public policies—including taxes, building codes, community programs, and reorganizing medical care—are available to address many of these problems.

Public policies to address these health problems are of two kinds. The first are interventions that are "public health services," that is, services that are public goods or have large externalities and which, therefore, are most effectively provided through government action or other collective social institutions. The second are interventions that are "personal health services," that is, health care services delivered to a particular individual or family.

Public Health Initiatives Can Make a Difference

Among public health initiatives, immunization campaigns, disease vector control, and basic education are among the best known. The challenge facing governments that wish to expand the coverage of such services is to modernize public administration, addressing whatever obstacles to effective public action are most problematic. In some countries, this may require a move toward contracting-out services to nonprofits or for-profit firms, while in others it may involve negotiating contract provisions that provide public servants with intrinsic or extrinsic rewards for good performance, or introducing new forms of public accountability.

Many public policy actions outside the health sector can lead to health improvements in much the same way as these "public health services." Taxes on tobacco, reducing store hours for alcohol sales, and regulating additives that encourage weight gain, like trans fats, are all cost-effective public measures for improving health by reducing exposure to harmful substances (see Box 5.2). Changes to the urban environment in the form of safer roads, separating pedestrians and vehicular traffic, lighting streets at night, and reducing vehicle emissions also reduce injuries and illnesses. Education can teach children to adopt healthy lifestyles and empower girls to exercise greater autonomy and participate more fully in political and economic life—all to the benefit of their own health and the health of their children. Redistributive programs, like pensions for the elderly, conditional cash transfers, and unemployment benefits, also improve health (see Box 5.6). The challenge for public action in these areas is often one of political negotiation, dialogue between interest groups, and public debate over priorities and trade-offs.

Promising Strategies for Improving Personal Health Services

The second kind of intervention encompasses personal health services (e.g., prenatal care and professional birth attendance, growth screening for children, treatments for infections, surgery, and chemotherapy). Access to these kinds of health care services is often guaranteed by law, but missing in practice. The challenge facing governments in this regard is how to make universal access to health care services a reality for the poor as well as the rich.

A number of strategies are available and have been tried with differing degrees of success throughout the region. Countries have tried consolidating different health insurers into a single institution or into a regulated market, creating a public single-payer institution, affiliating the poor with new forms of health insurance, contracting private health care providers, decentralizing public services, and modernizing existing public health care services. There is little evidence to demonstrate that one strategy is superior to another, not only because of a lack of studies, but also because health care services are highly complex, interconnected systems that interact extensively with their political, social, and economic context, making conclusive analytical work difficult.

Promising strategies, though, seem to share a few common characteristics. For example, in countries where access to health care services has been extended to all or most of the population, public funding has been central. In the 2007 Gallup World Poll, fewer than 30 percent of those in Argentina, Brazil, Chile, Colombia, Costa Rica, and Uruguay report that they would have to pay out of pocket for major hospital expenses—all countries in which public funding plays a significant role in the health care system (see Figure 5.4).

Second, rapid expansions of access to health care services in recent years have generally utilized some form of financial incentives for health care providers. Guatemala

Box 5.6 Public Policy and Elderly Health in Brazil

Between 1998 and 2003, Brazil enacted a series of laws and implemented policy changes that had a demonstrable effect on the health of the elderly population. During this period, Brazil reduced the age requirement from 70 to 67 years for poor people to be eligible for the Benefício de Prestação Continuada (Continuing Service Benefit), which gave them an income supplement of one minimum salary per month. Changes in rural pensions and social security benefits also contributed to a significant change in the incomes of elderly people, which rose from 8 percent of national income in 1998 to 10 percent in 2003. At the same time, Brazil enacted a National Policy for Elderly Health to promote preventive and chronic health care, as well as the Elderly Statute, which expanded protections and rights for the aged.

These programs appear to have improved the health of Brazil's elderly. Those reporting that their health was "very good" increased from 37 percent before the reforms to 41 percent after, during a period with no significant change in self-reported health for the rest of the Brazilian population (see table). The elderly also increased their utilization of health care services, which seems to reflect not a larger need for health care, but an increased use of services that contributed to improvements in health. The increase in pensions had a demonstrable effect on the health of the aged, but did not appear to generate externalities, as the health of people living in the same household as an elderly person eligible for such pensions did not improve.

Self-Reported Health in Brazil
(percentage of responses)

	Elderly		Others	
	1998	2003	1998	2003
Very good self-reported health	37	41	82	81
Bed rest in last 15 days	10	9	4	4
Sought health care in last 15 days	26	30	12	14

Source: FGV (2008).

Source: FGV (2008).

has contracted nonprofit organizations to provide a basic package of health care services on a per capita basis to populations that previously lacked most services and to contract-in services for managing public facilities (IDB, 2006b). Colombia has developed a fund to subsidize health insurance premiums for lower-income citizens (Giedion et al., 2007). Brazil has created financial incentives for municipalities and doctors to participate in the national Programa da Saúde da Família (Family Health Program). In each case, the exact nature of financial incentives is different and, despite such incentives' being an element of many reforms, few studies have been able to demonstrate that introducing financial incentives improves performance over more traditional forms of public provision (IDB, 2006b).

Third, improved access is generally accompanied by complementary efforts to improve the quality of both public and private health care services. In Mexico, this took the form of a Cruzada de Calidad (Quality Crusade) at the same time that the government was extending its Seguro Popular (People's Insurance). In Chile, the Régimen General de Garantías en Salud (Regime of Explicit Health Guarantees), known as AUGE, has promoted better access to care by explicitly listing, and publicly disseminating, the services that are guaranteed to be available to every citizen.

Finally, many strategies have sought to consolidate otherwise fragmented systems. In Argentina, where individuals were affiliated with Obras Sociales (social support institutions that provide health insurance) on the basis of their employment, reforms allowed people instead to choose between them. Colombia's 1993 health reform also eliminated the segregation of individuals into different funds on the basis of where they worked. Chile's health sector regulations have gradually incorporated private health insurers (Instituciones de Salud Previsional, or ISAPREs) under the same regulatory authority and requirements as the national public health insurance fund. In Mexico, divisions between the Mexican Institute of Social Security (Instituto Mexicano de Seguro Social, IMSS), and services of the Ministry of Health have been blurred; for example, IMSS manages a program financed by general revenues to enroll and cover noncontributing individuals (IMSS-Oportunidades). Reforms under Brazil's 1988 constitution created a national health care system, Sistema Unica da Saúde (SUS), integrating all public services into a single system.

Experiences with health reforms and cross-country analyses also suggest some cautionary lessons. Research on health system financing suggests that systems with third-party payers, particularly those with competition among health insurance entities, tend to be more costly than systems that rely on single payers or direct public provision. This finding also seems to apply to Latin America, where countries like Argentina, Chile, and Colombia spend much larger shares of GDP on health than countries like Costa Rica or Mexico.

Secondly, in countries that expand public services without ensuring quality, the private sector usually expands, while the opposite is true in countries with effective public provision. For example, between 1986 and 1996, dissatisfaction with the quality of public health care in Brazil contributed to an increase in the number of privately insured people from 4 million to over 44 million (Medici, 1999). The opposite occurred in Chile where, between 1995 and 2005, investments in the public health care system helped the Fondo Nacional de Salud (FONASA, National Health Fund) expand its share of the health insurance market at the expense of private insurers (Bitrán et al., 2008).

Finally, dividing responsibility for health care service funding or provision between different levels of government has had mixed results (IDB, 2006b). On the positive side, some decentralization reforms have mobilized additional local resources for health care (e.g., those in Brazil, Chile, and Colombia) and reduced regional inequities (e.g., those in Chile and Colombia). On the other hand, decentralization may have exacerbated regional inequities in some countries (e.g., Bolivia); studies have not been able to show efficiency gains from decentralization, and, in some cases, problems in implementing decentralization appear to have adversely affected primary health care delivery (IDB, 2006b).

Address the Perceptions That Influence Policy

The foregoing recommendations are part of current health policy debates. However, the role of perceptions and subjective experience as they influence public policy is not commonly considered. If governments are to implement reforms, they need active public support. Yet, public support is influenced as much by perceptions of health and access to health care services as it is by objective measures.

People's perceptions of health status and of health care services differ systematically from objective indicators, and this divergence leads to trade-offs between policies aimed at providing what is good and those aimed at providing what people want. These trade-offs are well-known among public health professionals who are comfortable advocating for policies that are at odds with existing social preferences whenever those policies can make a significant difference in improving the population's health. However, many other people are not comfortable with such an approach, whether they put greater value on current norms or on individual autonomy.

Policy Trade-Offs When Health Status Is Not Accurately Perceived

Trade-offs for public policy emerge as a result of the divergence between perceptions of health status and actual health status. First, in many situations, people may feel healthy even when they have a condition that requires treatment, or are at risk for a preventable illness. For example, in a 2002 survey in Mexico, 3 percent of those surveyed had hypertension and knew it, but 13 percent had hypertension and did not. In the same survey, 4 percent were diagnosed with diabetes and were aware of their condition, but 7 percent had diabetes and were not (Parker, Rubalcava, and Teruel, 2008a). Similar problems occur when people start taking medications to treat infectious diseases (e.g., antibiotics) and think they are cured when they feel better, but actually need to continue the full course of treatment to ensure recovery (and avoid developing drug resistance).

One approach to this gap is to use persuasion and, in extreme cases, coercion to have people tested, informed, counseled, and offered treatments. In most cases, incentives are combined with public campaigns to encourage people to learn about their conditions. Taking advantage of the ways people are organized in the health care system—whether through insurance programs, provider networks, or public health services—it is possible to promote an appropriate pattern of checkups to detect conditions early and prevent them. Success in this area requires that public policy confront the balance between individuals' interest in remaining healthy and their perceptions that such programs are either unnecessary for them or too bothersome and intrusive.

A second trade-off emerges because most people consider themselves to be in good health (85 percent in Latin America) and tend to underestimate their likelihood of requiring health care services. This tendency undermines support for collective solutions to health care services, whether through public financing or public health services. This is similar to the way people fail to save sufficiently for retirement—a tendency which has led most countries to establish "forced" savings for pension programs. A key justification for introducing single-payer systems, national health services, or mandatory health insurance systems is precisely to address this tendency for people to undervalue health care services—until it is too late.

A third trade-off emerges whenever public policies succeed at increasing economic growth. For the same levels of health status, people in countries that grow faster feel that they are less healthy. Thus, as many countries learned in the 1990s, promoting economic reforms without concomitantly promoting improvements in health is likely to lead to dissatisfaction with health and to undermine support for such reforms.

Policy Trade-Offs When Health Care Services Are Not Accurately Perceived

The trade-off between what is good and what is wanted also emerges with respect to perceptions of health care services. For a number of reasons, expectations regarding adequate access to health care tend to rise faster than a country's ability to respond. As medical technology advances, wealthier groups get access first, such that the best predictor of inequitable access in health care services is a country's income level (Wagstaff, 2002). In fortunate countries, these advances are gradually extended to the rest of the population until the poor get access to these services at rates that are comparable to those for the rich. But by the time they catch up, new services and new standards of what constitutes "adequate" health care develop. In this way, success may breed discontent and undermine support for otherwise successful health programs.

Other factors that contribute to rapidly growing expectations are rising incomes and political competition. With higher incomes, people demand more health care services. If these are not provided with good quality in public sector programs, people will express this demand by purchasing private insurance or private medical care. This, in turn, tends to drive up wages and prices in the market for health professionals, medical supplies, and pharmaceuticals. Politicians may also raise expectations by promising entitlements or improvements in access to health care that cannot be attained or, at least, cannot be achieved quickly. Once expectations are raised, even a well-functioning health care service system can lose popular support.

Differences between socioeconomic groups also generate trade-offs. The most cost-effective way to improve the population's health may be to extend good-quality health care services to poor people. Nevertheless, politicians are more likely to allocate public resources to services demanded by wealthier groups that are better organized to pursue their interests. This analysis shows that differences in perceptions may exacerbate this imbalance, since poorer groups seem to tolerate lower-quality health care services, reducing further their likelihood of demanding change.

Finally, people generally perceive a need for personal health care services in the form of advanced technologies and hospital services and fail to see the value of public health programs—like vaccines, environmental protection, food safety, and epidemiological surveillance—that contribute much more to a population's health. Politicians frequently respond to this gap between demands and effectiveness by promising new hospitals or expanded personal health care, which, in a context of scarce resources, may detract from other more cost-effective investments.

Inform and Improve

In essence, two strategies are available to address these inevitable trade-offs. The first is to use information, policy debates, and communication to reduce the distance between what is good and what is wanted. The second is to improve the effectiveness and capacity of public health and the health care service system to address both the needs and the desires of the population. These two strategies will be complementary to the extent that informed public debate reinforces policies that increase the effectiveness of health care services, and contradictory otherwise. In this regard, the contrast between Chile and Guatemala is quite instructive. Chile's health care system and high health status are accompanied by popular discontent, while Guatemala's relatively weak health care system and poorer health status are accompanied by widespread satisfaction. The right mix of policies for addressing the balance between information, mobilization, managing expectations, and improving health care services will vary across such different contexts, but the key issue—addressing how perceptions influence policy and politics—remains central.

Conclusion

As a consequence of rising access to health care services and continuing discontent, public policy is often driven by factors that are least likely to improve the population's health status. Building impressive hospitals is more visible and rewarding to most politicians than distributing bed nets. Guaranteeing everyone access to the same services, on paper, is also more attractive than trying to deal with the difficult task of improving the efficiency of reimbursement systems, or managing health care provision to improve quality.

Two patterns can be discerned in the evidence on perceptions of health and health care services. First, people in a number of countries exhibit higher levels of tolerance for poor health and for poor health care. In such countries, better information about the population's health, the levels of health that are possible, and access to health care may be needed to mobilize popular support for the public policies that can ultimately improve health and well-being. Second, people in a few countries exhibit very low levels of tolerance for deficiencies in health and health care. In such countries, better information may be necessary to help the population recognize their relatively good fortune and avoid agitating for changes that could undermine effective public policies.

The full implications for public policy are not entirely clear because society's objectives with regard to health care access are by no means self-evident. Responding directly to people's demands—for example, acting on preferences for treatment instead of prevention or interventions that are less cost-effective but more desired—may address perceived needs, but at a cost of other health gains foregone. In fact, responding to perceptions is often a losing game—the expectation of what health care should provide to everyone is a constantly evolving target. Ultimately, the quest for improving access to health care services in democratic societies must rely on a public dialogue, in which popular perceptions are confronted by as much objective information as possible, inputs from experts inform the discussion with regard to cost-effective ways to improve health, and serious efforts are made by all concerned to increase the productivity of health care services through advances in public policy, governance, management, and technology.

6

Learning about Education Quality and Perceptions

*To be conscious that you are ignorant
is a great step to knowledge.*—Benjamin Disraeli

The notion that having an education is a prerequisite for a good life is intuitively appealing and hardly a new one. It can be traced as far back as Aristotle, who believed that the ideal life was the philosopher's life, understood not as a purely contemplative state, but as a reflective practical life, one in which consequential action was guided by self-knowledge and enlightened judgment or "eudaimonia."

In contemporary societies, it is widely recognized that education can affect an individual's quality of life through several avenues:

- It has the potential to enhance overall life opportunities, particularly in the labor market, leading to better jobs, higher wages, and reduced unemployment risks.
- It can open up opportunities to enjoy cultural experiences and interpersonal relations in ways that are not available to individuals who lack education.
- It can reduce risks stemming from ignorance of health or environmental information and principles, and generate positive externalities that benefit the individual's community as a whole.
- It can improve overall life satisfaction by enhancing a sense of self-worth and easing concerns about future opportunities for descendants.

Thus, it is no coincidence that for at least the last two centuries a powerful universal drive to spread education around the globe has led to a world in which having at least a primary education is now considered a basic human right, a major developmental goal—indeed, reachable within a short time frame—and a widespread social responsibility. Within societies worldwide, education has become an acknowledged and widely accepted core component of living standards and a cornerstone of growth and human development potential.

Over the last decade, the general push to expand education has received an additional stimulus prompted by the realization that the new global economy is largely a knowledge-based economy. In this kind of economy, the production and circulation of information and ideas—and their original applications—are central for sustained economic growth and competitiveness of national and local economies. The most dynamic economic sectors are the knowledge-intensive industries, and having highly qualified workforces in place has become a major competitive advantage. Naturally, this has led to growing skills requirements, and secondary education is now commonly referred to as the primary education of the twenty-first century, conveying the notion that a given worker has little chance of finding employment and a good salary in the absence of at least 11 to 12 years of basic education.

This chapter explores the relationship between the long-term evolution of education and quality of life in Latin America and the Caribbean (hereafter "Latin America"). It begins with a review of the quantitative expansion of education across all countries of the region, emphasizing that such a significant change has had beneficial impacts on many spheres central to the enhancement of the quality of life. Then, the analysis turns to why the gains from quantitative expansion have been considerably less than expected, given the experiences in other parts of the world, which leads naturally to a discussion of the general but serious shortcomings in the quality of education across the region—a well-known fact and source of debate in recent years. An in-depth exploration of the causes of poor education quality lies beyond the scope of this chapter. Nonetheless, its more direct consequences for quality of life in the region, such as lower productivity, lagging technological innovation, and lack of a well-educated labor force to meaningfully compete internationally, obviously constitute a primary concern in much of what follows.

Based on the assumption that quality of life is the product not only of "objective" conditions, but also of the way such conditions are individually experienced, the analysis moves on to explore the relationship between objective and subjective measures of education quality, highlighting the disconnect between these two dimensions in Latin America. The chapter closes with a discussion of the underlying causes of the gap between perceptions and more objective realities, and presents some policy implications.

The Quantitative Expansion of Education in Latin America

Latin America has been no exception to the worldwide trends mentioned above: education has been linked to high expectations of social progress and social mobility. In the twentieth century, one country after another expanded primary education, beginning with Argentina, Uruguay, and Chile, followed by Costa Rica, then most of the rest of South America in the 1950s and 1960s, and finally Brazil, Mexico, and Central America in the last quarter of the century. As a whole, basic literacy spread consistently in the region throughout the twentieth century, despite the volatile and disappointing records of economic growth in most countries (Table 6.1).

The impact of such general expansion in enrollment is evident (Figure 6.1) in the average years of schooling of the population 15 years and older in the region between 1960 and 2000, which increased from 3.5 to 7. In several of the region's countries, this indicator more than doubled during the same period.

Today, more children attend school than at any other time in the past. More importantly, these children represent all socioeconomic and ethnic backgrounds. They

Table 6.1 Evolution of Literacy Rates by Country in the Twentieth Century, Latin America

	Literacy Rates (Percentages)										
	1900	1910	1920	1930	1940	1950	1960	1970	1980	1990	2000
Argentina	51	60	68	75	82	88	91	93	94	96	97
Bolivia	19	20	23	25	28	32	44	58	69	78	86
Brazil	35	35	35	40	44	49	60	68	76	81	85
Chile	44	53	63	75	73	79	84	88	92	94	96
Colombia	34	39	44	52	57	62	70	78	84	89	92
Costa Rica	36	47	58	67	73	79	83	88	92	94	96
Dominican Republic	n.d.	n.d.	29	26	30	43	65	67	74	79	84
Ecuador	33	38	42	46	51	56	66	74	82	87	92
El Salvador	26	27	27	28	35	42	48	58	66	73	79
Guatemala	12	13	15	19	24	29	36	45	53	61	69
Haiti	8	8	8	9	9	11	16	22	31	40	50
Honduras	28	30	32	34	35	40	45	53	62	69	75
Mexico	24	30	35	36	46	61	65	75	82	88	91
Nicaragua	n.d.	n.d.	39	36	39	38	47	57	61	65	67
Panama	17	27	42	46	59	67	73	79	85	89	92
Paraguay	31	38	45	52	59	66	73	80	86	90	93
Peru	24	29	33	37	42	51	60	72	80	86	90
Uruguay	59	65	71	76	81	86	90	93	95	97	98
Venezuela	28	29	32	36	42	51	62	77	84	89	93
Average	30	35	39	43	48	54	62	70	76	81	86

Source: Astorga, Berges, and Fitzgerald (2005).
Note: n.d = No data.

enter school earlier and attend longer, completing higher levels of education than ever before. Rapid quantitative expansion has occurred from preschool to postsecondary education. Access to primary education has advanced considerably, allowing countries in Latin America, almost without exception, to reach the 2015 Millennium Development Goal of universal primary education completion.[1] It is worth mentioning a fact particular to the region: girls of recent cohorts have been incorporated into the education system on an equal footing with boys, with women on average exceeding men in completed years of schooling in all but a few countries in the region (Duryea et al., 2007).

Figure 6.1 Average Years of Education among the Population 15 and Older

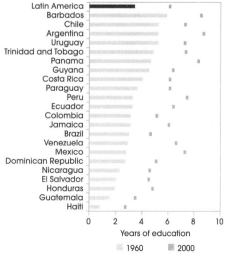

Source: IDB (2006a).

---

[1] The main exceptions are Haiti and countries with a high proportion of indigenous peoples (such as Guatemala and Bolivia). See also Marshall and Calderón (2006).

Preschool education coverage, widely believed to be key in developing the intellectual and emotional skills that influence lifelong learning, currently rivals levels reached in several developed economies, while secondary education has undergone an accelerated expansion in the past 20 years. In the meantime, higher education has gone through several waves of growth, advancing from a level reserved for elites at midcentury into a now-massive enterprise.

Such data underscore the fact that workers entering the labor force in the region today have completed more years of schooling than workers from previous generations; the average number of years of completed schooling has increased from under six for cohorts born in 1940 to over nine for those born in 1980 (see Table 6.2).

Education, bound at a maximum of about 25 years (unlike income, which has no upper limit), is more equally distributed than income and has played a moderating role in terms of the extreme inequalities that characterize Latin America. From generation to generation and country to country, in spite of the large differences in academic achievement observable between the top and bottom of the social scale, the distribution of education has been steadily equalizing. This is illustrated by Figure 6.2, which compares the education Gini coefficient between 1960 and 2000 for several countries in Latin America.

This achievement is more remarkable when viewed within the framework of the larger demographic trends that dictated high population growth rates in the region for most of the twentieth century.[2] In other words, Latin American education systems continued to expand coverage by including a growing proportion of children at any given age, while the number of new entrants grew at a fast pace. A paramount goal of education policies during the second half of the twentieth century was to accommodate these new students and make certain there were enough classrooms and teachers in place to receive them.

There clearly remain obstacles to be overcome in the process of expanding education coverage in the region: even though most children enter school at the right age, many leave prematurely; and most indigenous children do not achieve the same levels of education as the rest of the population, even if the gaps have been declining in Bolivia, Ecuador, Guatemala, Mexico, and Peru (Marshall and Calderón, 2006; Hall and Patrinos, 2006). Yet, it can hardly be argued that a quantitative expansion of education, such as the one noted above, can occur without producing some visible impact on the quality of life of a majority of individuals across Latin America. Access to education has broadened, enhancing the educational opportunities and achievements of the majority of the region's population.

---

[2] At the same time the population was growing in absolute size, its age structure was shifting in response to fertility and mortality declines. In many countries, the absolute cohort size started to diminish in the 1980s (Lam, 2006). The size of the youth population relative to the working-age population has also been lower in the past two decades in most countries, which is commonly referred to as a "demographic window of opportunity" for education systems in the region. Still, contingents reaching secondary and higher education levels, where the room for expansion is larger given previous limited coverage, are substantial. Also, political decisions have prompted a rapid expansion in age groups previously not served by public systems, such as preschool-aged children.

Table 6.2 **Average Years of Completed Schooling by Cohort, Latin America**

| Country | Year | Average years of schooling across age groups | | | | Average increase per decade |
		55–59	45–49	35–39	25–29	Total
Argentina	2002	9.19	10.11	10.90	11.19	0.50
Bolivia	2002	5.02	6.46	7.91	9.04	1.00
Brazil	2003	5.27	6.80	7.44	8.14	0.72
Chile	2003	8.38	10.30	10.92	12.02	0.91
Colombia	2003	5.70	7.08	7.76	9.08	0.84
Costa Rica	2004	7.00	8.61	8.82	9.24	0.56
El Salvador	2002	4.32	5.79	7.14	8.30	1.00
Guatemala	2002	2.64	3.38	4.51	5.74	0.78
Honduras	2003	3.52	4.50	5.57	6.08	0.64
Jamaica	2002	7.00	8.52	9.54	9.70	0.67
Mexico	2002	5.14	6.95	8.22	9.35	1.05
Nicaragua	2001	3.14	4.74	5.80	6.53	0.85
Panama	2003	7.57	9.51	9.76	10.22	0.66
Peru	2000	6.95	8.33	9.59	10.65	0.92
Paraguay	2003	5.67	6.83	7.93	8.76	0.77
Uruguay	2003	8.43	9.75	10.06	10.44	0.50
Venezuela	2004	6.59	7.98	8.69	9.22	0.66

Source: Authors' calculations based on household surveys.

Figure 6.2 Education Gini Coefficient for the Population 15 and Older, 1960–2000, Latin America

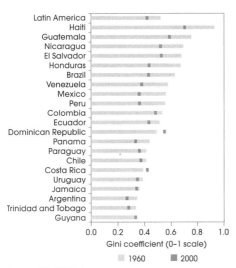

Source: IDB (2006a).

Not All Years of Education Are the Same

For the majority, access to the school system has brought about significant social benefits. The positive externalities believed to be associated with universal literacy and basic education include, at the very minimum, a moderation of population growth, a reduction in the obstacles presented by an illiterate population to market exchange, broad access to key information for public and individual health purposes, and an expansion of civic, cultural, and scientific horizons for the average citizen. In this sense, the education profile of the Latin American population has changed so drastically over the past half century that social interaction, economic activity, and both public and interpersonal communications have been visibly transformed for the better.

However, a set of well-established facts has generated serious concern in terms of the ultimate extent and depth of the progress achieved by enrollment growth in the region. A preliminary warning can be drawn from the stagnation of productivity in the region and the peculiar composition of relevant underlying factors. In contrast to Asia, Latin America shows a distinctive growth pattern, primarily supported by the accumulation of labor, combined with a remarkably minor contribution of human capital and technological knowledge, usually included as the main component of total factor productivity (TFP) in most estimates (IDB, 2001). At an aggregate level, this suggests that growth has been supported in the region by a consistently growing workforce, but not necessarily by a more productive one with the skills to generate, apply, and assimilate productivity-enhancing means, such as innovations in production, processes, and organizations (Figure 6.3).

These facts suggest that a rise in the number of years of education for an ever-increasing number of Latin American children does not necessarily translate into productivity growth, prosperity, and enhanced welfare. Latin Americans are not reaping the benefits they should expect from longer stays in the school system.

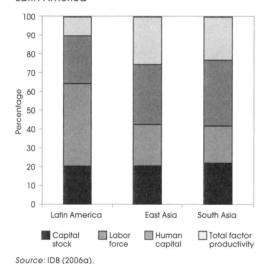

Figure 6.3 Economic Growth Decomposed by Contributing Factors, 1972–2000, Asia and Latin America

Source: IDB (2006a).

This macro perspective naturally links to the micro data gathered over the past decade regarding education quality in the region. In the last 15 years, there has been a major improvement in the collection and availability of data aimed at incorporating quality as a key dimension in the analysis of education in many parts of the world, making it possible to relate education quality within a particular school system, jurisdiction, or school to a set of variables, such as growth, income, or productivity (see Box 6.1). Most countries administer regular assessment tests to gather information regarding the extent to which children are learning in schools. In addition, the emergence of widely recognized international comparative tests, such as the Trends in International Mathematics and Science Study (TIMSS), the Programme for International Assessment (PISA), and the Progress in International Reading Literacy Study (PIRLS), has elevated awareness among national leaders and the public alike that an educated workforce is a critical component of developmental prospects in all nations.

Box 6.1 Education Quality and Economic Growth

For many years, a significant amount of research has confirmed a positive link between education, or investments in human capital, and economic growth. Countries do not become rich first and then buy education; rather, as skill levels increase, gains in productivity and growth follow. The quantity of education, measured through access to and years of education (e.g., enrollment rates), thus emerges as a basic education indicator associated with economic growth. The quantity of education has also been positively linked with other dimensions commonly associated with quality of life. For example, more years of education are associated with lower birthrates, better health outcomes, and lower crime statistics, as well as with social mobility.

Yet education has not always delivered on its promise to improve economic growth; particularly in the developing world, more extensive education has not produced commensurate gains in growth. Certain phenomena, such as the migration of qualified segments of the workforce as a result of economic hardship or political instability, may seriously decrease the developmental impact of education investments. In the end, the ability of a particular society to use human capital is a key determinant of whether such investments are really valuable.

With this in mind, part of the difficulty in drawing a more general conclusion regarding the effect of education on growth is theoretical and reflects the limitations of traditional studies of human capital focused on the quantity, particularly average years of schooling attained, without consideration of education quality. Such omissions are serious, and even the casual observer could grasp the importance of education quality and agree that it differs significantly between countries, and even within schools.

Recent research that highlights such observations has started to bridge the gaps. Using literacy scores to measure cognitive skills and as a proxy gauge of quality, Hanushek and Woessmann (2007) estimate the contribution of education quality to individual income, income distribution, and economic growth, and find quality to be a more robust indicator of productivity than years of schooling, so much so that the significance of quantity disappears once quality measures are considered. The distribution of skills is closely related to income distribution, and most importantly, the population's skill levels are strongly tied to a nation's economic growth rate.

Latin America has not done well in such comparisons; the countries of the region that have participated in international testing consistently show poor learning outcomes when compared to countries of the Organisation for Economic Co-operation and Development (OECD) and, even more importantly, when compared to their competitors in the emerging Asian economies. In turn, national assessment systems exhibit a stub-

Table 6.3 Latin America and OECD Scores on PISA Assessment Tests

Country	Mean PISA Scores in Reading			Mean PISA Scores in Math			Mean PISA Scores in Science		
	2000	2003	2006	2000	2003	2006	2000	2003	2006
Argentina	418	n.d.	376	388	n.d.	381	396	n.d.	391
Brazil	396	403	393	334	356	370	375	390	390
Chile	410	n.d.	442	384	n.d.	411	415	n.d.	438
Colombia	n.d.	n.d.	385	n.d.	n.d.	370	n.d.	n.d.	388
Mexico	422	400	410	387	385	406	422	405	410
Peru	327	n.d.	n.d.	292	n.d.	n.d.	333	n.d.	n.d.
Uruguay	n.d.	434	413	n.d.	422	427	n.d.	438	428
OECD countries	500	500	500	500	500	500	500	500	500

Sources: OECD (2001, 2004, 2007).
Note: PISA scores are statistically normalized, with the score for OECD countries as a median (500). Results show deviations from that median; a country's score can be above or below the median, with a greater (lesser) difference from the median representing a greater (lesser) difference between the performance of that country's students and that of students in OECD countries. n.d. = no data.

born lack of progress, in spite of years of policy reforms and growing resources devoted to education.[3]

Table 6.3 shows the scores from students of the seven Latin American countries that have participated in at least one of the three rounds of PISA,[4] compared to the OECD average. It is easy to observe that Latin American students consistently underperform.

Beyond the general averages reported in the table, a more-detailed analysis of the comparative-performance PISA data would reveal that the average score of 15-year-old students in participating countries could be considered the equivalent of about one grade level below the one characteristic of the lowest 25 percent of OECD students tested. A similar comparison with leading countries such as Finland and Korea would give rise to further disappointing conclusions about the quality of education in Latin American countries.[5]

---

[3] Several important caveats are in order: first, many assessment tests do not capture important aspects of what most educators, and all reasonable definitions of education quality, would deem pertinent, since they are generally focused on two or three subjects and are hence of limited value in assessing less tangible abilities (creativity, initiative, complex thinking). Second, by themselves, they capture far more than what a particular school can deliver, since some determinants of learning that are not directly controlled by the school (family background, innate ability, previous educational history, and so on) can dramatically impact scores and can be monitored only through in-depth statistical analysis—albeit quite imperfectly. The most important factor is the amount of value added by a particular educational experience—what influences do particular systems, schools, teachers, or school types have on learning? These data are rarely available; nonetheless when effectively planned and executed, standardized tests offer a reasonable approximation to valuing education quality and constitute widely used tools to assess the performance of education systems worldwide.

[4] PISA is used to test 15-year-olds worldwide and evaluates factors related to education and employability skills. Six Latin American countries participated in the 2000 and/or 2003 PISA tests: Argentina, Brazil, Chile, Mexico, Peru (only in 2000), and Uruguay (starting in 2003). In the 2006 round, Argentina, Brazil, Chile, Colombia, Mexico, and Uruguay participated.

[5] For a benchmarking exercise involving comparisons between Latin America and leading performers in several education dimensions, see IDB (2006a).

PISA results for the OECD countries are reported not only in the form of average scores, but also as a distribution of test takers along a scale that represents reading ability (1 to 5) or math proficiency (1 to 6) levels. In the participating Latin American countries, between 20 and 40 percent of students scored below level 1 (the lowest performance level) in reading or math, which means that a considerable number of 15-year-olds lack basic literacy skills. The problems are not confined to the lower end of the distribution. In Uruguay, the region's top performer, merely 15 percent of students perform at internationally competitive levels in reading (levels 4 and 5), and only 10 percent do so in math (levels 4 through 6); the corresponding percentages for OECD members, Mexico and Turkey excluded, are close to double in reading and almost four times greater for math.[6]

It is important to bear in mind that PISA is targeted to 15-year-old students, regardless of their actual grade level, which has two implications. Between 20 and 50 percent of the student population in the region is enrolled at least one grade below their expected grade, because of the widespread problem of grade repetition; as such, any given country has between a half year and two years of average cumulative overage among students of this age (Urquiola and Calderón, 2005). Many pupils have been in the system long enough to reach ninth grade or beyond, yet they are grouped with younger children and receive inadequate curricular content for their age and developmental capabilities. In fact, when the tests are administered, the proportion of PISA test-takers in Latin America enrolled in the grade best corresponding to their age is typically about 85 percent, whereas the corresponding figure in developed economies usually exceeds 95 percent. Accordingly, since one grade level is roughly equivalent to 60 points on the PISA scales, if the effects of grade repetition were isolated (or, alternately, if only 15-year-olds enrolled in ninth grade were included in the sample), PISA scores for Latin American countries would improve between 10 and 30 points—allowing for some variations among participating countries—or between 10 percent and one-third of the existing Latin America–OECD gap in average scores. Learning achievement of on-grade-level students would still be poor, but significantly improved. A conclusion here is that repetition and overage seriously impede educational performance, affecting many students' achievement levels and influencing the dismal results of the region in internationally comparable tests of learning achievement. These failures are embedded in the systems, weaken their overall performance, and hinder their ability to deliver a good education to individuals.

More importantly, many Latin American children have dropped out of the system by the time they reach 15, and thus are excluded from the PISA study. Some children leave because they need to contribute to their family's financial support; others cannot continue because of the lack of secondary school education in their locality; and still others fail to stay engaged because they are bored with classes they deem irrelevant for them. The size and precise characteristics of the dropout group varies from one country to the next, yet it is reasonable to assume that the overwhelming majority of the children in this group come from low-income families and consequently have less family

---

[6] PISA levels 4 and up are widely considered to be international benchmarks, in the sense that they can be taken as indications of a level of skills solid enough for an individual to be up to the demanding standards of the contemporary global knowledge economy.

support for their education and a high probability of having attended low-performance primary schools. One of the few analyses available that compares test results from children in and out of school at age 15 fully corroborates this assumption and concludes that children in school have significantly higher test scores (Parker, Behrman, and Rubalcava, 2008).

Table 6.4 illustrates the significance of this fact. In this table, following Pritchett's (2004) suggestion, an index of "lack of education"—understood as "lack of preparedness"—has been estimated by adding up the proportion of the 15-year-old student population scoring at level 1 or below on the PISA Reading Scale, and the proportion of those between ages 15 and 19 who did not complete ninth grade (lower secondary education, approximately). This provides a rough but reasonable approximation of the proportion of the youth labor force that is ill equipped to find a good job in the contemporary world economy, shown in the last column of the table.

The findings of a recent in-depth study of PISA in Brazil were entirely consistent with these results in the case of mathematics: out of 3.62 million 15-year-olds in 2003, approximately 86.6 percent (more than 3 million people) were likely "functionally illiterate in mathematics" (Waltenberg, 2008: 24–25). This figure was calculated by adding the more than 1.5 million 15-year-old Brazilian children who had left school, presumably having minimal math skills, to the number of children in the enrolled population equivalent to the proportion of the PISA sample scoring at level 1 or below on the test. Estimates for several Latin American countries indicate that adjusting PISA scores for each education system's dropout and enrollment rates results in average scores that are between 15 and 50 points lower, depending on differences among countries in coverage at age 15 (Abt Associates, 2008: 28). This more than compensates for the upward adjustment suggested by the preceding analysis of the impact of testing only on-grade-level students. Consequently, an average Latin American ninth grader tends to possess cognitive skills equivalent to those of a primary school graduate (sixth grader) in leading countries such as Finland or Korea, and confirms, beyond a doubt, the seriousness of the problems that Latin America faces when it comes to education quality.

The Quality-Quantity Trade-Off

Such poor educational performance has often been attributed to a trade-off between quantity and quality. In most countries, demographic pressures have been strong enough to direct most of the resources and policymakers' attention to enrollment growth, with little left for quality improvement. At the same time, as more children enter the school system, presumably those included last are those with greater learning handicaps[7] and harder to reach through conventional delivery systems. An example is the challenge that Mexico has faced in extending postprimary education to the millions of children dispersed in isolated rural villages. Conventional education systems designed for the middle class, its teaching methods and curricula, are often inadequate when applied to children of different social, ethnic, and cultural backgrounds.

There is some merit to this view of the problem; for example, if standardized learning assessment internal to the Brazilian education system shows declining scores

---

[7] In Tedesco's (2005) terminology, these are students with particularly acute "educability" issues.

Table 6.4 Lack of Education among 15- to 19-Year-Olds

Country	Percentage not completing grade 9[a]	Average PISA Reading Scale score	Percentage with Reading Scale scores at or below level 1[b]	Percentage of cohort who either did not complete grade 9 or had Reading Scale scores at level 1 or below[c]
Argentina	16.8	418	43.9	53.3
Brazil	43.3	403	50.0	71.6
Chile	10.1	410	48.2	53.4
Mexico	27.9	400	52.0	65.4
Peru	24.8	327	79.6	84.7
Uruguay	31.4	434	40.0	58.8

Sources: IDB (2008) for percentages not completing grade 9; OECD (2001, 2007) for percentages below or at level 1 on the Reading Scale.
[a]Data are for 18- and 19-year-olds. Data are from 2000 for Peru, from 2002 for Argentina and Mexico, and from 2003 for Brazil, Chile, and Uruguay.
[b]Data are from 2000 for Argentina, Chile, and Peru and from 2003 for Brazil, Mexico, and Uruguay. Figures represent percentages scoring at or below 407, the maximum PISA score for level 1.
[c]Formula: Percentage who did not complete grade 9 + (Percentage who did complete grade 9 × Percentage with scores at or below level 1).

precisely during a decade of vigorous enrollment growth, as was indeed the case for secondary education in the 1990s, it is hard not to find an explanation in the quality-quantity trade-off.

Along the same lines, Auguste, Echart, and Franchetti (2008) have closely examined several countries, mainly in Eastern Europe, that dedicate a proportion of GDP to education similar to Argentina's and have comparable per capita income levels, but achieve far better results in PISA and other international testing programs. A basic finding is that Argentina, like other Latin American countries, has a population pyramid with a larger base (i.e., is a "younger" country). As a result, spending on education per capita is consistently lower than in such comparator countries. Accordingly, although Hungary, Poland, and Argentina spend almost the same proportion of GDP on education, Argentina's spending per student as a proportion of GDP per capita is 12.3 percent, compared with 19.2 percent for Hungary and 23.5 percent for Poland. This underscores a typical characteristic of Latin America: populations are younger, and consequently there is a heavier burden on the education system. In turn, as long as countries in the region have not reached more-advanced stages of the demographic transition, they pay some price in terms of education quality because they give priority to quantitative expansion and enrollment growth. A young country can have only so much education quality, or so it seems.

Yet, while a certain quality-quantity trade-off may be at work, there is ample evidence that it cannot account for the full disadvantage that Latin America exhibits in education quality:

- There are important exceptions, such as the Czech Republic, which spends approximately the same as the Latin American norm per student, with far better results in terms of test scores.
- Poor educational performance is not confined to students of low socioeconomic backgrounds. The approximately 100-point difference in the average

PISA score for Latin America relative to the OECD average holds in the case of the top 25 percent of Latin American students, when they are compared with the same segment of the OECD student population. Individual country data also support this conclusion.

- There has been an actual decline in quality over the long run, affecting countries going through different stages of education expansion. Auguste, Echart, and Franchetti (2008) compare the 2000 PISA results of 35 countries also included in the Bratsberg and Terrell (2002) database of education quality derived from comparisons of foreign-born employees in U.S. census data, and compute the change in the relative ranking of test scores from 1980 to 2000 for these countries. Countries such as South Korea and Japan have made significant improvements in their standings, while over a longer time frame dating back to the 1950s, the rankings of all Latin American countries, with the exception of Mexico, have fallen. Although some Latin American countries are not included in this analysis, these results suggest that the region as a whole is not making considerable progress in improving the quality of education over time.[8] Therefore, something else beyond the costs of expansion and educational inclusion must be at work in determining the failure of education systems to provide Latin Americans with appropriate life opportunities (see Figure 6.4).

Figure 6.4 Change in Relative Ranking of Education Performance, 1980 versus 2000

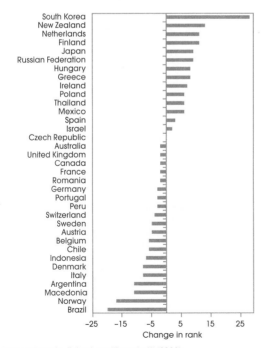

Change in rank

Source: Auguste, Echart, and Franchetti (2008).

Economic Inequality and the Distribution of Education

It is no surprise that the region's high level of socioeconomic inequality translates into a powerful factor behind inequality in education. Figure 6.5 shows the strong correlation between socioeconomic inequality and inequality in the quality of education offered to students in a given country.

Most Latin American countries exhibit a relationship between student performance in science and socioeconomic status that is stronger

[8] Even though, prima facie, this could be considered a fact lending further support to the quality-quantity trade-off argument, it instead reinforces the conclusion that other factors have a role in determining low education quality, since countries in different stages of demographic transition and enrollment expansion—such as Brazil and Argentina—have suffered comparable and simultaneous declines in education quality.

than the OECD average. Such a relationship is also found in the United States, France, Germany, New Zealand, and other countries, although in Latin America the relationship is more extreme and distinctive. In the region, an overwhelming number of schools concentrate low-income children, and in these schools the learning outcomes tend to be less favorable, with few but notable exceptions (Willms, 2006). One implication is that when it comes to acquiring human capital, education in Latin America provides relatively less support to the disadvantaged.

The impacts of the disparity in education quality on individual skills and, consequently, labor performance and life opportunities are cogently illustrated by recent research. For example, Curi and Menezes-Filho (2008) find that in Brazil, lower scores on proficiency exams (Sistema Nacional de Avaliação de Educação Básica, or SAEB) at an early age are related to lower future wages. Convergent conclusions come from a study using International Adult Literacy Survey (IALS) data from Chile (Manzi et al., 2008); after the effect of years of schooling and experience is controlled for, it is found that in Chile, adult literacy skills, which are strongly dependent on education quality, have a significant and positive effect on earnings along the life cycle. Interestingly, this relationship is stronger for people with eight years of schooling or less, which indicates that the effect of skills and, presumably, the quality of the education received is particularly relevant for workers with lower education levels. The same analysis establishes that better literacy skills reduce the probability of being classified as poor in the Chilean labor force, while improving labor participation. Schooling is the main determinant of literacy skills; yet, the actual acquisition of such skills—which varies according to the quality of instruction—has an independent and discernible effect on life chances, beyond the mere accumulation of schooling years by any given individual.

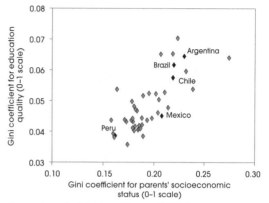

Figure 6.5 Relationship between Inequality in Education Quality and Inequality in Socioeconomic Status at Country Level *(PISA 2000)*

Source: Auguste, Echart, and Franchetti (2008).

Subjective Perceptions of Education

In education, as in other spheres of human activity, individual perceptions of given circumstances are relevant, and sometimes they present stark contrasts with what would otherwise seem unequivocal facts or situations that "speak for themselves." This psychological and social construction of reality has a powerful influence on well-being and behavior; therefore, no assessment of education quality from the perspective of how it affects the quality of life can avoid addressing the issue of how it is perceived. It can hardly be taken for granted that an individual's perception will be aligned, as a rule, with statistics based on "objective" data.

Indeed, while Latin America consistently performs very poorly in international student achievement tests, public opinion regarding education quality in the region is mostly positive. In fact, Latin Americans are more satisfied with their education quality than populations of other countries included in the 2007 Gallup World Poll (Flores and Herrera, 2008). How does the perception of education services vary with a measure of the quality of services? Figure 6.6 graphs the self-reported satisfaction level with education services in various countries according to the 2007 Gallup World Poll against a measure (the Quality Indicators of Human Capital, or QIHC) constructed by Altinok and Murseli (2007) of each country's performance on international achievement tests. Satisfaction in the majority of Latin American countries—Bolivia, Colombia, the Dominican Republic, Honduras, Mexico, Paraguay, Uruguay, and Venezuela—was above the predicted level. While satisfaction in Brazil and Chile was slightly below the predicted level, only Argentina had a considerably lower than expected satisfaction level given its test scores.

A further examination of the relationship between satisfaction with education and a few simple covariates at the personal (age, gender, urban area, and income category) and country (GDP per capita, and quantity and quality of education) levels suggests that Latin Americans have more favorable perceptions of their education systems than their peers in other developing and emerging regions. In fact they are approximately 10 percentage points more satisfied than would be expected from their standings in regard to other variables.[9] This "over-satisfaction" with education is robust to the inclusion of a control variable intended to capture any general tendency for a person to be more or less satisfied than on average.[10] Accordingly, it is possible that such higher satisfaction is driven by factors other than a tendency to respond more positively to questions or school quality at the national level.

Figure 6.6 Satisfaction with Education and QIHC Results

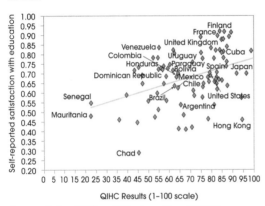

Sources: Gallup (2007) and Altinok and Murseli (2007).

Examining Satisfaction with Education

To examine how satisfaction fluctuates with individual-level variables, detailed household survey data have been collected in Belize, Chile, El Salvador, Guatemala, and Honduras through a special module focused on quality of life. Figure 6.7 shows the correlation

---

[9] Regression is based on Gallup World Poll data. The quantity of education is estimated by the net attendance rate for secondary school as reported in World Bank (2007). Altinok and Murseli's (2007) general index of human capital quality estimates the quality of education in various countries for the most recent year available.

[10] When the individual's satisfaction with health services is added as an explanatory variable, Latin America continues to display a significantly higher perception of education services, although the magnitude falls somewhat.

of an individual's level of education with his or her perceived satisfaction with public education services. Individuals with higher education levels (more than six years) are found to be significantly less satisfied with public education in all five countries, with the largest gaps observed in Chile and Guatemala, countries recognized for their high inequality levels.

In many cases, the education levels of respondents have a strong, nearly linear relationship with perceptions. As shown in Figure 6.8, affirmative responses to the question "Do you think the majority of children receive a good education?" drop off steeply with higher levels of education. The results indicate that those who presumably suffer more directly from the lack of quality education remain the most satisfied with the system, which implies an "aspirations paradox," compatible with findings in other sectors (see Chapter 2).

Therefore, a higher level of educational achievement is associated with a more critical view of the public education system for the full sample of respondents. However, regressions using the sample of parents have found that a higher level of education does not significantly decrease parents' satisfaction levels with their children's schools. These findings suggest that awareness of poor education quality increases with education levels, while at the same time tolerance for unequal conditions diminishes. Educated parents may be aware that their children attend better than average schools.

Figure 6.7 Satisfaction with Quality of Public Education Services by Education Level of Respondent

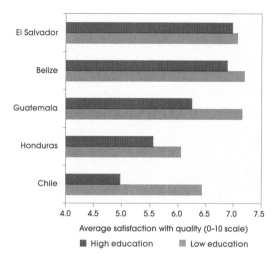

Average satisfaction with quality (0–10 scale)

■ High education   ■ Low education

Source: Authors' calculations based on Quality of Life Modules of household surveys.
Note: Sample consists of individuals 18 years old or older.

Figure 6.8 Satisfaction with Quality of Public Education Services by Years of Education

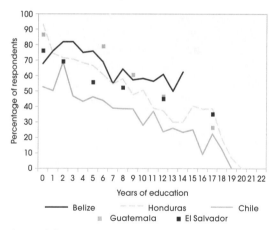

Source: Authors' calculations based on Quality of Life Modules of household surveys.
Note: Figure presents percentage of sample (those at least 18 years old) in each country who think the majority of the country's children receive a good education.

Thus, higher levels of education may still bring an awareness of the failures of the public education system, even if one's own children are somewhat protected by living in areas with better schools or by attending private schools. All this suggests that overall dissatisfaction with schools will rise as the population's overall level of education rises, but it is not clear if the demand for better schooling will be directed at public or private providers, and at schools in the same neighborhood or in other locations.[11]

To explore whether parents' level of satisfaction reflects a broader set of factors, parents of children under 16 were asked additional questions in reference to their oldest child attending school. This set included "Are you satisfied with the school your child is attending?" as well as specific questions characterizing the schools, including parents' perceptions in regard to safety, discipline, cleanliness, and teacher habits. Table 6.5 shows the responses to the full range of questions disaggregated by education level. Here again, the general picture in all countries—albeit slightly less so in Chile—is of parental satisfaction when it comes to the schools their own children attend.

In turn, Table 6.6 reports the effects of different factors on parental satisfaction with education. In all five countries represented, parents who were pleased with the level of in-school disciplinary action were significantly more satisfied with their children's school, with the magnitude of the additional satisfaction ranging from 7 to 15 percentage points. In all three Central American countries shown, parents' satisfaction levels were correlated with their perception of security in their children's school, as well as with whether teachers were complying with their teaching responsibilities by being present and active in the classroom.

Since the satisfaction regarding the factors reported in the table may reflect an overall propensity to respond positively to perception questions, to control for this unobserved tendency, regressions were performed including a variable measuring parents' perception of the health sector. The results are robust to the inclusion of this variable and suggest that parents may value a broader set of school characteristics than is typically reflected in reports of standardized test scores, especially when apprehension about security and behavior (of students and teachers) is of widespread concern. Moreover, the results resonate with those found in the value-added literature, which seeks to identify factors that affect children's performance in school. As an illustration, studies have found that absenteeism has a negative effect on test performance and that teachers' effective time in the classroom (rather than elsewhere in school) is critical for improving learning.

The way a person interacts with schools, students, or graduates may also influence his or her perceived level of satisfaction with the public education system. For example, employers may observe the increased skills and productivity of employees with certain levels of schooling, while parents, who have been shown to consider a broader set of factors when assessing school quality, observe how their children flourish in response to exposure to teachers and school materials. It is also possible to make explicit comparisons between parents' and employers' satisfaction levels with public education by comparing their responses to the same question. Regression analysis suggests that parents systematically report a higher level of satisfaction with public education ser-

---

[11] A related issue concerns the mainstream response to the perception of low-quality public schools, which has been a flight to privately managed schools, a phenomenon particularly typical among higher-income families. For instance, in recent years, a growing perception of the plummeting quality of the public education system in Argentina has led to a substantial growth in the market share of private schools (Auguste, Echart, and Franchetti, 2008). Judging from the Chilean experience, it is apparent that, if released from constraints on their ability to pay by a voucher-like system, as many as half the families with school-aged children could choose a private school, a fact easily interpreted within a voice-exit framework à la Hirschman (see Nelson, 2008). Yet, for reasons that will become clear later in this chapter, it is doubtful that parents make this decision based on conventional indicators of school quality, such as test scores.

Table 6.5 Full Range of Education Perception Variables Disaggregated by Education Level

	Belize		Guatemala		Honduras		El Salvador		Chile	
	Low education	High education	Low education	High education	Low education	High education	Low education	High education	Low education	High education
All respondents										
"There are good educational opportunities in this country."[a]	90.1	86.2	88.9	69.5	82.5	69.5	78.4	62.6	61.8	51.2
"Opportunities are equal for everybody."[a]	62.1	56.9	66.0	39.4	71.3	48.6	52.8	34.4	33.6	20.9
"Success in school depends basically on the skills and effort of each individual."[a]	86.4	83.4	92.7	92.9	95.7	92.4	91.5	83.6	86.8	76.8
"Do you think the majority of children receive a good education?"[b]	71.9	59.1	81.7	44.9	65.8	41.7	67.6	45.4	47.0	27.4
"In general, how would you rate the quality of public education services?"[c]	7.06	6.97	7.23	6.24	6.05	5.55	7.19	6.88	6.40	5.00
Parents										
"My child is safe at school."[a]	94.0	95.2	95.4	80.5	90.5	85.9	89.4	80.9	68.3	58.5
"The school is kept clean."[a]	95.8	94.3	94.5	94.6	96.6	96.2	98.1	95.7	81.3	76.7
"Discipline is applied fairly at the school."[a]	90.9	90.5	91.5	85.8	91.5	88.6	88.4	87.6	68.2	66.8
"Teachers are present and respect the school schedule."[a]	95.5	95.0	89.2	82.0	85.1	84.9	92.6	89.7	76.6	75.9
"The school tries to keep parents well informed about their children's education."[a]	92.4	95.8	94.9	92.0	90.4	88.9	97.3	95.7	83.7	75.2
"Are you satisfied with the school your child is attending?"[b]	97.3	95.4	94.8	85.8	90.5	88.9	96.1	91.4	76.9	80.8
"If you could change schools would you do so?"[b]	20.8	29.4	37.2	50.4	40.2	44.7	40.1	44.6	51.0	47.6

Source: Authors' calculations based on Quality of Life Modules of household surveys.

[a] Percentage agreeing with statement.

[b] Percentage responding affirmatively to the question.

[c] On a scale of 1 to 10, with 10 being the highest and 1 the lowest response.

Table 6.6 Effects of Different Factors on Parental Satisfaction with Education

	Effect of factor on the probability of being satisfied with school one's own child attends				
	Belize	Guatemala	Honduras	El Salvador	Chile
Male	0.005	0.015	−0.019	0.000	−0.006
Years of education	−0.000	0.002	−0.001	−0.008	0.002
Age	−0.005	−0.010*	0.000	−0.003	0.007
Age-squared	0.000	0.000*	−0.000	0.000	−0.000
Urban	0.000	0.003	0.015	0.005	0.005
Child at school is a boy	0.004	0.010	−0.001	0.003	−0.012
Child attends a public school	0.007	0.061*	0.002	0.004	−0.010
Child at school is in secondary school	0.002	0.006	0.001	0.010	0.010
Child is safe at school	−0.001	0.094**	0.126***	0.028*	0.033
Child's school is kept clean	0.004	−0.009	0.062**	−0.001	0.098*
Discipline is excercised fairly at child's school	0.084**	0.121***	0.129***	0.151***	0.072*
Teachers always teach their classes	0.002	0.168***	0.182***	0.073**	0.023
Satisfaction with health	−0.000	0.006*	0.005**	0.001	0.019

Source: Authors' calculations based on Quality of Life Modules of household surveys. The method of estimation is probit.
*Coefficient is statistically significant at the 10 percent level; **at the 5 percent level; ***at the 1 percent level; no asterisk means the coefficient is not different from zero with statistical significance.

vices than general respondents, after basic demographic characteristics, including age, gender, geographic area, and education level, are controlled for; however, employers are significantly less likely than the adult population in general to provide a positive assessment of the education system.[12] Cárdenas, Di Maro, and Mejía (2008) find similar results using Gallup World Poll data, which can be viewed as additional evidence that assessments of school quality are based on different criteria depending on the context of interactions.

Information and Parental Response

Great expectations have been placed on the potential role of information to help guide the decision making of parents and stimulate advances in quality. However, with the partial exception of decision making regarding higher education (see Box 6.2), available evidence tends to fall short of substantiating such expectations.

Flores and Herrera (2008) use a rich set of educational achievement data to explore how parental perceptions relate to isolation levels in Chilean communities, with their underlying model focused on the incomplete information available to isolated groups. Their study exploits national test data for children in the fourth grade in Santiago, as well as census data, to explore the effect of institutional and territorial factors on individual achievement. They calculate local socioeconomic segregation of neighborhoods to proxy for the social isolation encountered by residents. They find that in nonsegregated areas, parents of children attending schools with higher average test scores report significantly higher levels of satisfaction with their school than parents with children attending other schools in the same neighborhood. In nonsegregated areas, parents thus behave as expected: they report higher satisfaction with the quality

---

[12] Only the sample in Honduras included sufficient numbers of business owners to test the hypothesis.

Box 6.2 The Influence of Information on Higher Education Choices

Worldwide, and particularly in the United States, university rankings play a major role in influencing student and family decisions in choosing a tertiary education institution. Even though such rankings are not available in all Latin American countries, there are some national cases that strongly suggest that systematic collection and dissemination of information regarding the quality of higher education institutions and programs can influence parental and student choice, and even the overall quality of the supply of postsecondary education.

Brazil has long had widely disseminated university rankings produced by a variety of public and private sources. Based on work undertaken at the Instituto Nacional de Estudos e Pesquisas (INEP), the national institute in charge of education evaluation, in the 1990s, the country experimented with a standardized test for students approaching university graduation with the goal of assessing whether the skills acquired by members of a particular cohort of students were up to professional standards in a limited number of disciplines, such as engineering or law. As a result of the test, each university school or program received a score, which was made public, indicating how well its students as a group met the standards. Although the test, known as Provão, has been phased out, it produced observable shifts in the demand for particular programs; accordingly, institutions that received low scores in the first round moved proactively to enhance the quality of their programs, so as to prove to students that they had received the message (Guimarães Castro, 2002).

El Salvador, which emerged from its civil war with a number of tertiary education institutions altogether lacking in supervision or regulation, invested in developing a system of indicators dealing with basic proxies of institutional quality, such as library holdings, available infrastructure, and student-teacher ratios, and publicized the results, with noteworthy consequences. Several institutions were exposed as being so weak that they opted to close their doors, while others accepted the need for system-wide quality standards and regulation. Students and families adjusted their choices accordingly (Bernasconi, 2002).

of education when the proxy of that quality (average test scores) increases. However, in segregated neighborhoods with high poverty levels, residents are significantly less likely to report higher satisfaction if their schools' test scores are higher compared to other schools in the same neighborhood. Accordingly, in segregated areas, parental satisfaction with schools depends less on achievement levels than is the case in less-segregated neighborhoods. The authors posit that in socially isolated areas, parents lack complete information, which translates into weaker relationships between indicators of school quality and parental satisfaction.[13]

---

[13] A similar phenomenon occurs in segregated neighborhoods with high wealth levels; however, the effect in these areas was not measured to be significantly different statistically than that in nonsegregated areas.

These findings are consistent with recent studies in the United States by Hastings, Kane, and Staiger (2006, 2007), which find that low-income families place less weight on average test scores when choosing schools than higher-income families. They hypothesize that individuals in poor, isolated communities lack relevant information regarding public education that may affect their perceptions. For families in poor and isolated communities, this may reflect a lack of awareness that lower test scores may be an indication that school quality warrants more attention from local and national policymakers.

Chile has made tremendous efforts to implement national student testing and publicly disseminate the results. This was deemed particularly important given that Chilean parents have extraordinary latitude in choosing the schools their children attend. However, a recent study in Chile by Mizala and Urquiola (2007) finds that school test scores, adjusted for the students' socioeconomic characteristics, do not affect parental choices regarding schools. Neither enrollment levels nor the socioeconomic composition of its student body change when a given school receives an award for performance.[14] This is fully consistent with findings by Elacqua and Fábrega (2006), who conclude, based on the outcome of a survey of parents in the Santiago metropolitan region, that less than 50 percent of parents know the relative position of their children's school when compared to others in the same community, and less than 1 percent are aware of the precise average score attained by their schools in the Sistema de Medición de la Calidad de la Educación (SIMCE), the national standardized test; in contrast, parents reveal a keen awareness of the average level of education of other parents in the same school. This suggests that school selection is more influenced by social class and proximity to family homes than by test scores, understood as a metric focused on education quality.

Will a Better Alignment of Perceptions and Realities Make a Difference?

Narrowing the gap between perceptions and objective realities may ignite political mobilization, but there is little guarantee that resulting policy changes will effectively resolve underlying issues. There are many intermediate links between perceptions and policymaking, and most of them remain poorly understood. Are people reporting satisfaction with education reacting primarily to quantitative advances in education—such as those described at the beginning of this chapter—so that the considerable progress made in inclusion and universalization has left little room for concerns with quality? How long would this effect last? Or, in a possible interpretation of the instances of open discontent with education in recent memory (see Box 6.3), is inequality of opportunity— or, better, the perception of segmentation in education supply and, consequently, the unfairness of life chances—perhaps the springboard of political mobilization rather than poor quality alone?

Policies to improve education quality add their own complexities to the mix. Many of the proximate determinants of learning—parental education and family income, just to mention a few—remain outside the control of decision makers. Policies adopted in the name of improving quality often reflect the narrow interests of key actors, such as unions, are not evidence-based, or overwhelm available institutional capacity.

---

[14] Receipt of such an award means that the school has shown higher performance than expected given the students' characteristics.

Box 6.3 The Chilean Student Unrest of 2006

While studies have not necessarily found strong student and parental responses to information regarding local schools, Chilean youth and society at large seem to be responding to the widespread availability of information regarding the school system as a whole. Moving from complacency to action is a big step and perhaps is more likely to occur, at least on a theoretical level, when the gap between perceptions of reality and objective indicators of reality narrows. As the SIMCE results solidified the idea that most students in Chile receive a dismal education, secondary students led a series of protests and demonstrations between April and June of 2006. These were the largest demonstrations since the Pinochet era, with an estimated one million people joining in, and successfully catapulted education to the top of the nation's policy agenda. Among the students' short-term demands were free bus fare and the waiving of the university admissions test fee. Longer-term demands included the abolition of the Organic Constitutional Law on Teaching, which students saw as promoting the difference in achievement between public and private schools, and a quality education for everyone—defined by adequate financing and basic inputs, such as appropriate infrastructure. As a direct response to student protest and the widespread support it received across Chilean society, President Michelle Bachelet announced several significant reforms and validated them by convening an education council that included student participation.

The question remains whether the Chilean student and family political mobilization around education can be considered an isolated episode or rather a harbinger of similar movements in other Latin American countries. The experience fits the pattern described in Chapter 2, in which the demand for public policies, particularly for education, rises with income and levels of education, both at the country and individual levels. On one hand, it could be hypothesized that it is precisely the fact that Chile has passed through two decades of education reform—and has made a point of disseminating information about schools' performances as a key component—that has led to the movement; in other words, in a case of well-documented social dynamics, it is progress and not backwardness or stagnation that triggers social expectations and change. If this reading is correct, similar episodes could be prompted in other education systems in the region, many of which are going through significant education reforms. On the other hand, the particular institutional characteristics of the Chilean school system, which include high levels of social segregation between public and private schools, have distinguished this system as having the most-pronounced levels of social inequality between schools in the region. Accordingly, the student unrest could be interpreted as a response to extreme inequality in the opportunities offered by different schools, and in this sense the episode might be seen as rather idiosyncratic to the Chilean education system. The likelihood of similar episodes taking place in other national settings in which inequality among schools is less pronounced or less visible would consequently be lessened.

A recent comprehensive review of factors determining quality of education in Latin America (Vegas and Petrow, 2007) indicates the difficulty of finding effective policies to improve education quality (teacher incentives and institutional reforms, such as decentralization, conventional teacher training, etc.) New research on education quality points to the fact that, in producing effective policies, the "devil is in the details." In trying to distinguish the factors that are associated with enhanced learning, this research emphasizes factors that often escape the attention of politicians and parents; for example, whereas education reform policies may include new texts, research from Brazil (Menezes-Filho et al., 2008, based on data from Estudo da Geração Escolar [GERES]) shows that teachers' experience in using a particular text in the classroom is what improves learning. In Argentina, time on task appears to be an important consideration for improving learning, but it is how instructional time is allocated (e.g., towards reading) that seems to offer more promise (Auguste, Echart, and Franchetti, 2008); the same study encountered a contrast in the responses of Latin American education systems when dealing with young children with difficulties in reading (almost no attention given to the problem) and those of European systems (a major focus of effort and resources). A comparable study in Chile (Manzi et al., 2008) shows that putting emphasis on teachers can improve learning results, but that expanding only their level of training or qualification is insufficient.[15]

Thus, although in principle better dissemination of test results is unquestionably a desideratum of better education policies, expectations should be moderate regarding the probability that this alone will prove decisive in the constructive reform of the education deficits of Latin America. As with many other aspects of education policy, the distribution of information about outcomes is no "silver bullet," and, as stressed by Nelson (2008), many intermediate conditions have to hold for one to lead to the other.

However, once the wider issue of how education affects quality of life is considered, the facts and arguments discussed in this chapter suggest less negative conclusions. To some extent, positive perceptions of education in the region have been related to the "aspirations paradox": low expectations stemming from the relatively low level of educational achievement of the parents, directly associated with their socioeconomic status. As such, it is to be expected that as new cohorts with higher educational achievement replace the older ones, criticism of education systems is bound to increase, creating a medium-term opportunity for improvements and reform. The main policy challenge resulting from this conclusion is institutional in nature: education systems should immediately start to build the channels through which an eventual upsurge of criticism of education quality can be molded into a constructive force. The brunt of the pressure will be borne by the mainstream public systems, and it is there that the challenge of institution building will be inescapable.

It has also been documented that families make decisions and shape their perceptions of their children's schools by observing a wider set of school characteristics in which test scores—the most common measure of education quality—are just one of

---

[15] Chile was the only Latin American participant to improve its PISA ranking between 2000 and 2006, and the only country to institute regular performance- and standards-based evaluation of teachers, as well as the use of such results to guide policy. More-detailed findings on the determinants of education summarized here will appear in a forthcoming volume by the IDB.

many indicators, and often not the most important. Here it is worth mentioning a study that employs the Laboratorio Latinoamericano de Evaluación de la Calidad de la Educación (LLECE) approach in Peru, Paraguay, and Honduras, which found that infrastructure was the factor parents singled out most when asked why things had changed for the better within their children's schools. Moreover, it may be wrong to dismiss parents' disregard for test scores as the direct result of limited information or poor judgment, since, as has already been discussed, various factors are involved in a particular education output, many of which are beyond a school's reach. An important consequence is that a school's reputation built only on scores can be misleading: a pioneering study of value added by secondary schools in Brazil (Soares, Castro, and Comini Cesar, 2000) found a strikingly low correlation between a school's academic reputation and the actual value added for its students.

An important conclusion here, beyond the already stated need to modify expectations regarding the potential of school-level accountability as the basis for quality improvement, is that education systems should embrace a more explicit and expanded definition of quality. This definition should be better attuned to realistic decision-making criteria used by parents and have more potential to become an effective tool for overall school-level, and even policy-level, accountability.

Such an approach to education improvement does not imply a loss of focus concerning the centrality of academic achievement; it is hardly a coincidence that the most widely admired supervisory systems for schools in place in OECD countries incorporate a multifaceted view of quality assurance, understood as a key function of an education system.[16] Approaches to education quality embodied in institutions such as the British Office for Standards in Education, Children's Services, and Skills (OFSTED) or the Education Review Office in New Zealand are designed to keep a sharp focus on academic achievement, while paying consistent attention to the broader quality of services provided by enhanced school-parent relationships, the collegiality of the teaching staff, the leadership of the principal, the adequacy of the infrastructure, nondiscrimination policies in dealing with students, and so on. Such institutions are intended to gradually educate parents, teachers, and students about how to achieve a quality school experience. In certain approaches, an indicator of success is whether a school inspector can visit a school and ask its members—teachers, parents, or even students—where they are in terms of the learning process and what they need to do in the future, and subsequently receive a competent, individualized response.

How can the embracing of an expanded definition of education quality be translated into practice? Events may already be in motion in the region. It may not be a coincidence that Uruguay, whose education system has arguably made the most successful effort to use assessment testing information as a tool for detailed education decisions, is one of the best PISA performers in the region, or that in Chile, another top performer, the limitations of sample collection and dissemination (even through the press) of test-

---

[16] Hopkins (2007) reviews quality assurance systems in five OECD countries and reflects on possible adaptations to Latin American circumstances. A characteristic component of such systems includes a broad view of student achievement, defining it not exclusively as test results, but as comprehensive evidence regarding each student's personal development and well-being. See the guidebook *How Good Is Our School?* (HMIE, 2007), produced by Scottish education authorities, for a clear illustration of a multifaceted approach to good education. See also McKinsey and Company (2007).

ing results has led to the recent establishment of specialized institutions that embrace a wider definition of quality, such as the one discussed here.

For at least a decade, education researchers and policymakers have known that implementing assessment tests has limited value unless effective policies for the use of the data generated are in place. Adding to the considerable set of lessons learned from a recent study (Ferrer, 2006), the discussion herein highlights two additional challenges: first, the need to systematically collect information, probably at the school level of aggregation, on a richer set of indicators beyond test scores; and second, the need to focus on institution building, to the point that entirely new and highly specialized institutions in charge of quality assurance for the school system should be created.

This chapter has shown how the quantitative expansion of education in Latin America has generated a continual source of improvement in the quality of life of the majority of the region's population over the past century. Similarly, the promise of such educational progress has not been fully realized, given the severe quality shortcomings found in education systems throughout the region. At the same time, most Latin Americans seem to be reasonably satisfied with the quality of education they receive, so a gap between perceptions and realities has developed. An enlightened interpretation of this gap has policy implications that represent institutional and policy challenges that must be faced in the near future by all education stakeholders.

The open questions remain: Will the existing misalignment between perceptions and the hard realities exposed by internationally comparable and standardized tests diminish? Will this translate into the type of political mobilization recently experienced by Chile? And will school systems be prepared to channel such a reform-oriented mobilization into effective policy? The answers, when found, may have a powerful influence on the future of education and the overall quality of life in Latin America.

7

Rethinking Conventional Wisdom on Job Quality

Happiness is not doing what you like,
but liking what you do.—Anonymous

Most people work 40 or more hours per week. It is not surprising, therefore, that working conditions greatly impact people's lives and that high job satisfaction is identified as one of the most important aspects of a fulfilling, highly satisfying life. This chapter examines job quality in Latin America and the Caribbean (hereafter "Latin America") from two perspectives: a review of objective conditions commonly associated with good job quality, and a subjective assessment based on job satisfaction and the myriad factors that contribute to this satisfaction.

An analysis of objective conditions exposes the low—in many cases declining— quality of jobs in the region. However, new surveys strongly suggest that some widely accepted conventions about what constitutes a good or bad job can be misleading; for instance, evidence indicates that informal jobs—traditionally considered inferior, less desirable forms of employment—may be a sensible decision for some individuals who find more suitable niches for their skills, preferences, and conditions than those offered by formal jobs. Revealing empirical evidence indicates that, to a great extent, people who have salaried jobs would rather be self-employed, while there are considerably fewer people in the reverse situation. Salaried workers cite several reasons for preferring self-employment, including the possibility for higher earnings, greater flexibility, and the lack of a boss. This chapter identifies the job attributes most associated with job satisfaction and examines how jobs with such characteristics are distributed among different types of workers. Finally, the chapter explores the implications of the analysis of objective and subjective factors associated with job quality for the design of effective labor market policies and outlines an agenda for better job creation in Latin America.

In Search of Good Jobs

It is often said that countries in the region need more and better jobs. However, what constitutes a good job may be in the eye of the beholder. Analysts have resorted to two different approaches to measuring job quality: the first determines the quality of jobs based on objective criteria (number of hours, earnings, job category), while the second is based on the analysis of subjective valuations of job satisfaction.

Under the first approach, observers adopt certain objective criteria of what constitutes a good job. In developed countries, these criteria tend to be based on factors such as wages and working hours, while in developing countries, classifications are mainly based on what sector the jobs belong to, formal or informal. In relation to compensation, some analysts impose absolute targets that classify all jobs paying below a certain wage as low-quality jobs; others, mostly in OECD member countries, impose relative targets based on a given job's pay level relative to the median wage. Still other studies measure job quality based on the sector or occupation, which in turn is ranked according to whether that sector or occupation pays higher or lower than the average (Rex, 2006).

The length of the workweek, the share of workers working part-time, and whether the desired hours of work match those actually worked are other important factors for assessing job quality in OECD countries. Job security is another increasingly important factor, that is, whether jobs are permanent and, therefore, covered by employment protection legislation, or of a fixed-term nature, which means they are not protected.

In contrast, measures of job quality in developing countries tend to be based on which sector the job belongs to, formal or informal, although the definition of informal has shifted over time. The 1978 Regional Employment Program for Latin America and the Caribbean (PREALC) defines workers in firms with 10 or fewer employees, unpaid family workers, domestic workers, and the self-employed (except those in professional jobs) as informal. However, this excludes workers employed in large firms or public sector jobs that are not covered by labor laws. A newer definition includes all salaried workers whose jobs are outside the coverage of national labor laws and/or social protection systems.

An alternative and quite different approach to assessing job quality is to ask workers themselves how they perceive their jobs. While economists have been wary of relying on subjective data, burgeoning bodies of work in both economics and psychology examine how subjective measures of self-reported well-being (SRW) relate to individuals' economic behaviors. Additionally, it is useful to assess which job features (pay, hours of work, job security, and category) are most valued by workers. Based on these two criteria, the next section assesses job quality in the Latin American region over time and how it relates to that in other regions.

Job Quality In Latin America

Record Job Creation . . .

In terms of employment growth, countries in Latin America have outperformed most comparator countries (Pagés, Pierre, and Scarpetta, 2007). Between 1990 and 2004, the region created an average of 12 jobs per year for every thousand people of working age. Costa Rica, Honduras, and Venezuela had the most dynamic labor markets during the period analyzed, creating 18 jobs annually per thousand working-age people, and were closely followed by Ecuador, Guatemala, and Nicaragua, which averaged 17 jobs annually. In contrast, the Southern Cone countries (Argentina, Chile, and Uruguay), as well as Jamaica and Colombia, performed poorly, creating fewer than 10 jobs annually per each thousand working-age individuals (see Figure 7.1).[1] Compared to other countries, only Malaysia, Singapore, Spain, and the English-speaking countries of the OECD have kept pace with many Latin American countries in terms of job creation. In contrast, job creation in the Southern Cone countries has been more comparable to the lagging progress of continental Europe or Turkey.

. . . But of Low and Stagnant Quality by Most Objective Measures

In Latin America, job creation has increased in tandem with a growing labor supply fed by an upsurge in female participation and an expanding working-age population. Unfortunately, the boost in job creation has gone hand in hand with low productivity growth (see Figure 7.2); only Chile, the Dominican Republic, Trinidad and Tobago, and Uruguay sustained productivity growth above 1 percent per year during the 1990–2004 period. This pales in comparison with the rates in many countries, particularly in East Asia and the Pacific, such as China (7.2 percent), Korea (3.8 percent), and Malaysia (2.6 percent), as well as the United States (1.8 percent) and the European Union countries (EU15, 1.1 percent). Productivity is a main determinant of wages and other nonwage benefits; thus the combination of high employment and low productivity growth suggests that the quality of jobs created has been fairly low.

Figure 7.1 Distribution of Countries by Average Annual Job Creation, 1990–2004

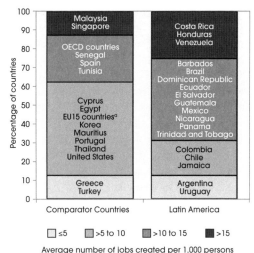

Source: Pagés, Pierre, and Scarpetta (2007).
[a] EU15 countries are Austria, Belgium, Denmark, Finland, France, Germany, Greece, Ireland, Italy, Luxembourg, Netherlands, Portugal, Spain, Sweden, and United Kingdom.

Figure 7.2 Labor Productivity Growth in Selected Countries, 1990–2004

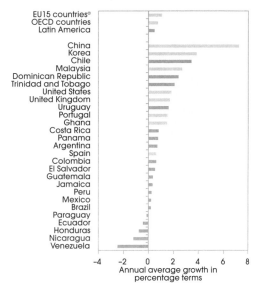

Source: Pagés, Pierre, and Scarpetta (2007).
[a] EU15 countries are Austria, Belgium, Denmark, Finland, France, Germany, Greece, Ireland, Italy, Luxembourg, Netherlands, Portugal, Spain, Sweden, and United Kingdom.

---

[1] Employment data for Uruguay cover only urban areas. The employment series was smoothed applying a Hodrick-Prescott filter.

Some commonly used job quality measurements, such as the share of informal jobs, point to a decline in quality of employment since the early 1990s. The proportions of self-employed workers, those employed by small firms, and those with unpaid jobs have increased in most countries (see Figure 7.3). Similarly, in all countries with available data aside from El Salvador, the number of workers without social security through their jobs—another commonly used measure of informality—has grown over the past 15 years (see Figure 7.4).

Likewise, poor-quality performance is found when job quality is assessed based on measures commonly used in richer countries. In terms of wages, weak productivity growth is associated with low wage growth. Between 1994 and 2004, Bolivia, Chile, and Nicaragua were the only countries, among the group for which such data for the overall economy could be collected, that experienced positive wage growth, and ended up with gains between 1 and 2.5 percent per year. The rest suffered declines in the purchasing power of workers' earnings; these declines were acute in some countries, namely, Mexico, Uruguay, and Venezuela (see Figure 7.5). In contrast, real earnings growth was positive in most OECD countries, except for Japan and Austria.[2] While in Latin America the average annual growth rate of real earnings was –0.1 percent, in OECD countries the average was around 0.6 percent per year. Moreover, among industrialized countries, the middle-income countries, such as Korea, experienced higher wage increases, close to 2 percent per year (see Figure 7.6).

Figure 7.3 Share of Workers in Informal Jobs *(percentage)*

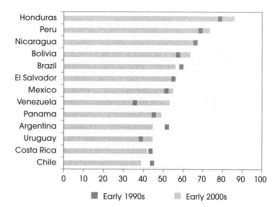

Source: CEDLAS and World Bank (2008).
Note: Informal status is defined as salaried workers in small firms and nonprofessional, self-employed and zero-income workers. The sample refers to adults from 25 to 64 years old. Data are for the following periods: Argentina (1992–1998), Bolivia (1993–2002), Brazil (1992–2003), Chile (1990–2003), Costa Rica (1990–2003), El Salvador (1991–2004), Honduras (1992–2005), Mexico (1996–2002), Nicaragua (1993–2001), Panama (1995–2004), Peru (1997–2003), Uruguay (1992–2004), Venezuela (1992–2004).

Figure 7.4 Share of Adult Salaried Workers Not Affiliated with Social Security through Their Jobs

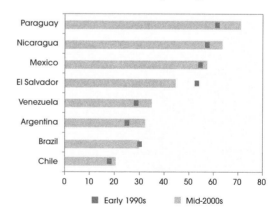

Source: CEDLAS and World Bank (2008).
Note: Data are for the following periods: Argentina (1992–1998), Brazil (1992–2003), Chile (1990–2003), El Salvador (1991–2004), Mexico (1990–2003), Nicaragua (1992–1998), Paraguay (1992–1998), Venezuela (1998–2004).

---

[2] Earnings are defined as the sum of wages, overtime payments, bonuses and gratuities regularly paid, remuneration for time not worked, bonuses and gratuities irregularly paid, and payments in kind.

For the least-privileged workers, the evolution of wages has fared no better than the average. IDB (2006c) shows that the percentage of workers receiving wages below an adequate threshold, one that would allow a worker to earn a per capita family income above the moderate-poverty floor of US$2 per day, increased in eight of 15 countries for which data were available. At the latest count, the ranks of the working poor varied considerably among countries, ranging from 4 to 8 percent in Argentina, Chile, and Costa Rica, to above 40 percent in Bolivia, Ecuador, and Honduras.[3] On average, a quarter of the region's working people do not earn enough to lift themselves and their families out of poverty, even when working. This cannot be blamed entirely on the low educational attainment of the labor force. Figures through 2005 showed that the ranks of the working poor also increased among those workers with higher educational attainment.

Other objective measures, such as working hours, are suggestive of low job quality; in Latin America, workers devote more hours to work than workers in industrialized economies. In Europe and the English-speaking countries of the OECD, workers spend an average of 38 hours per week on the job, compared to the average of 43.7 hours devoted by workers in Latin America (see Figure 7.7). Nonetheless, the average working time is still much higher in Korea than in Colombia, Guatemala, Bolivia, and Honduras, countries with the highest working hours in the region.

Another measure of employment quality relates to the stability of the work relationship. Based on the countries with

Figure 7.5 Evolution of Real Monthly Wages in Selected Latin American Countries
(index, 1994=100)

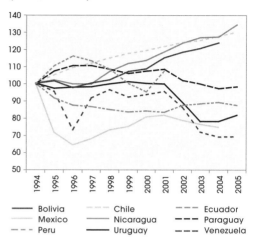

Sources: ECLAC (2008) data for 1994–2005, and authors' calculations based on 1994–2005 data from Central Bank of Mexico (2008a, 2008b) and Central Bank of Nicaragua (2008).
Note: For Bolivia, data refer to the private sector in La Paz; for Chile, data refer to the General Hourly Wage Index; for Ecuador, data exclude agricultural activities; for Mexico, data refer to the General Wage Index; for Nicaragua, data refer to the National Real Wage; for Paraguay, data refer to wages in Asunción; for Peru, data refer to average wages; for Uruguay, data refer to the private sector; and for Venezuela, data refer to the Earnings Per Hour Index.

Figure 7.6 Evolution of Hourly Real Earnings in Developed Countries
(index, 2000=100)

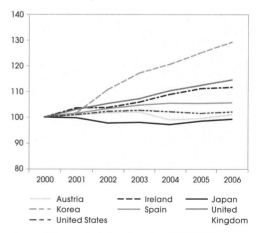

Source: Authors' calculations based on OECD (2008).

---

[3] Latest figures available during period 2001–2005.

Figure 7.7 Average Hours of Work, Selected Countries, 2002

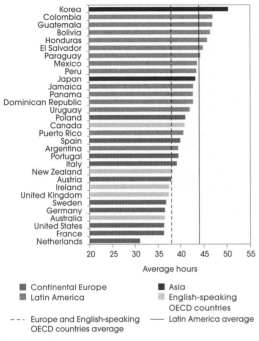

Average hours

■ Continental Europe   ■ Asia
■ Latin America   ▨ English-speaking
                                OECD countries
– – – Europe and English-speaking   —— Latin America average
        OECD countries average

Sources: IDB (2007) and ILO (2008b).

Figure 7.8 Temporary Workers in Total Salaried Employment

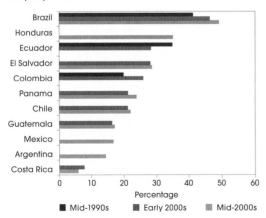

Percentage

■ Mid-1990s   ■ Early 2000s   ▨ Mid-2000s

Source: IDB (2007).
Note: Data for Brazil refer only to agriculture, silk production, farming, fishing, fish farming, and auxiliary services associated with these activities. Missing data are not available or not comparable between or within countries.

available data, it is apparent that a large share of salaried workers are employed in temporary jobs. In seven of the 11 countries for which data could be collected, more than 20 percent of the salaried workforce holds a fixed-term contract, with the highest percentages in Brazil, Honduras, Ecuador, and Colombia. While data are scattered, the share of workers in temporary employment increased in most countries studied, most notably in Brazil and Colombia, but also in Chile, Guatemala, and Panama (see Figure 7.8).[4]

But Job Satisfaction Is High

Given this dismal picture, it is remarkable that workers in Latin America report such high levels of job satisfaction. Information on job satisfaction for Latin American workers was drawn from the Gallup World Polls for 2006 and 2007, the Latin American Public Opinion Project (LAPOP) Survey for Chile, and some special modules that were added to regular household surveys in a smaller group of countries (Belize, Ecuador, El Salvador, Guatemala, and Honduras) and commissioned for this study (see Box 7.1).

Based on the 2006 Gallup World Poll, on average 81 percent of the workers in the region are satisfied with their jobs (see Figure 7.9).[5] The country with the highest job satisfaction is Venezuela, followed by Costa Rica and Guatemala, while the countries with the lowest job satisfaction are the Dominican Republic, Cuba, and Haiti. Interesting-

---

[4] The data in Brazil cover only agriculture, fishing, and services related to these activities; in Colombia and Ecuador, the data include only the urban population.

[5] The equivalent figure for 2007 is 85 percent.

ly, the average for the region is higher than that found in other countries with higher income per capita, such as Japan or South Korea (78 percent, both countries), although below the average for OECD countries (89 percent).

Worldwide, workers in richer countries tend to display higher levels of job satisfaction than those in poorer countries,[6] yet data also indicate that workers in the region report higher levels of job satisfaction than workers from other parts of the world with similar income per capita. Figure 7.10 illustrates the relation between job satisfaction and income per capita around the world based on the 2006 Gallup World Poll, excluding the Latin American region (the line in the figure), and shows that for almost all countries, job satisfaction in this region outperforms that in the rest of the world.

Who Knows Best?

How can the divergence between the low quality of jobs in the region—as measured by the level and evolution of wages, informal employment, or working hours—and the seemingly high levels of job satisfaction in the region be explained? One possibility is to dismiss the data on job satisfaction as misleading; after all, workers may have distorted views of their reality, perhaps due to their levels of exposure to or expectations of good-quality job conditions, which is consistent with the "aspirations paradox" identified in Chapter 2.

---

[6] Regressing job satisfaction against income per capita and income per capita squared yields a positive and statistically significant coefficient on income per capita, and a not statistically significant coefficient on income per capita squared.

Figure 7.9 Job Satisfaction in Selected Countries, 2006

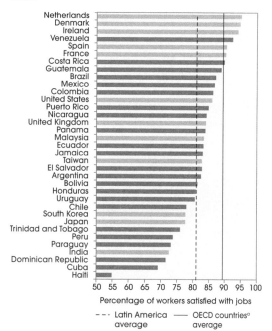

Source: Gallup (2006).
Note: Figure reflects affirmative responses to question "Are you satisfied with your job or the work you do?"
[a] OECD countries are Australia, Belgium, Canada, Denmark, Finland, France, Germany, Greece, Iceland, Italy, Japan, Netherlands, New Zealand, Norway, Portugal, Spain, Sweden, Switzerland, United Kingdom, and United States.

Figure 7.10 Job Satisfaction and Gross Domestic Product per Capita

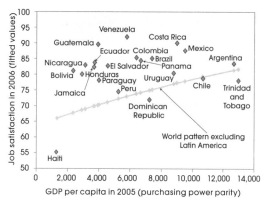

Source: Authors' calculations based on Gallup (2006).
Note: Line shows the fitted values of the ordinary least squares (OLS) regression of country's average job satisfaction on income per capita and income per capita squared for the world sample excluding Latin America.

Box 7.1 Information on Perceptions of Job Quality

Although work is a central aspect of people's lives, only recently have researchers begun to examine what Latin Americans think of their jobs. The Gallup World Polls (2006, 2007) are the source with the widest coverage of this subject presently available, offering comparable data for more than 100 countries, 22 of which are in Latin America. In each country the polls cover, 1,000 or more individuals are interviewed (except in Belize and Guyana, where the sample includes only 500 individuals).

Since the same questions are used for all countries, the polls allow for international comparison. Some of the most relevant questions are the following: "Are you satisfied with your job or the work you do?"; "In your job, do you have an opportunity to do your best every day, or not?"; "Is there someone at work who encourages your development, or not?" and "At work, do your opinions seem to count?" Respondents are also asked whether they make contributions to a retirement plan through their job and whether they believe that they could lose their job in the next six months. Given that the surveys include a multitude of questions on other (objective and subjective) aspects of people's lives, it is possible to explore which individual factors are related to perceptions of work.

Besides the Gallup World Poll, there is valuable complementary information, more detailed for some countries, that has been obtained through a special module on quality of life included in the regular household surveys for Belize, Ecuador, El Salvador, Guatemala, and Honduras, and in a special opinion poll for Chile (conducted by LAPOP). The sources provide much more complete information on various aspects of work, which makes it possible to study which characteristics of jobs are important for people.

Some additional technical information on these special surveys may be of use for specialists. The surveys were conducted in the second half of 2007, except those in Ecuador and Chile, which were conducted at the beginning of 2008. The surveys, which are representative at the national level, were conducted among persons over 18 years of age selected at random from each household. The exception is Ecuador, where information was gathered from all eligible family members, and where the survey encompassed only Quito, Guayaquil, and Cuenca, with 2,228 participants. Information on Belize is based on a random subsample of 1,594 respondents obtained two weeks after the national household survey. Data from El Salvador were collected 10 months after the household survey, with 1,082 participants. The survey in Guatemala, with 1,400 participants, was not a subsample of the household surveys; in the Honduras survey, with 8,282 participants, data were collected at the same time as in the national household survey. The LAPOP survey for Chile is also representative at the national level and was conducted among 1,500 persons over 18 years of age in selected households.

Alternatively, answers to the job satisfaction question may differ based on cultural norms. As discussed in Chapter 2, there is an optimism bias, which varies by individuals, countries, and regions and affects life or job satisfaction comparisons. In fact, there is a positive, although not very large, correlation between the degree of individual optimism and job satisfaction at the country level.[7] However, differences across countries in the degree of individual optimism do not explain the higher job satisfaction of Latin American workers relative to those in other countries with similar income levels. Thus, accounting for such differences does not change the results presented in Figure 7.10 in any significant way.

The former analysis indicates that cross-country, and possibly cross-individual, differences in job satisfaction perceptions are driven by a host of factors that go beyond cultural norms and optimism biases. This suggests that a promising avenue is to examine the determinants of this high job satisfaction. From what do workers derive high satisfaction? How do subjective measures of job satisfaction relate to aspects (such as wages, hours of work, benefits, job security, or formality status) that are generally associated with good-quality jobs? While the results are quite revealing, a note of caution is required in their interpretation given the small samples available and the fact that only a handful of countries have implemented this type of survey; nonetheless, they illustrate the benefits of such surveys for the analysis of labor issues in the region.

Learning from Workers' Views

Informal and Worse Off?

One tenet of development economics is that the informal sector is a marginal, less-advantaged sector in a segmented labor market. After all, formal employment implies access to an array of benefits and protection that informal workers lack. Implicit in this view is that all formal jobs offer protection, all benefits are desirable, and it is better to be an employee—particularly of a large firm—than self-employed.

In contrast, some studies postulate that workers may prefer to work in informal jobs for a number of reasons. They may prefer the autonomy of self-employment (Maloney, 2004), or to work in small firms rather than larger ones because they dislike the regimentation of larger firms (Idson, 1990). A related argument is that workers may find that informal jobs offer greater flexibility, which may suit individuals with competing time demands, such as students or parents of young children. Workers may also prefer not to pay taxes and social security contributions from which they derive little benefit (Maloney, 2004), which may be particularly relevant if governments provide free-of-charge social services targeted to informal workers (Levy, 2008).

Which view is more accurate? Most evidence of the marginal status of informality is based on studies showing that workers in the informal sector earn less than workers in the formal sector; however, this approach has been discredited for various reasons. First, formal and informal sector workers may greatly differ in their earnings potential.

---

[7] The correlation between the two measures is 0.31. Such a correlation can be used to estimate optimism. Optimism refers to a character trait or cultural norm of each respondent. Optimistic individuals tend to answer more favorably all questions across all quality of life dimensions. (For further details, see Box 2.2.)

Some of the differentials commonly attributed to the formality status may in fact be associated with differences in workers' ability, effort, or preferences. Secondly, and perhaps most relevantly, focusing on wage comparisons alone excludes an array of other job attributes that workers are likely to consider when comparing formal and informal jobs (Maloney, 2004). Lastly, earnings for informal workers, particularly for those who are self-employed, may not be well recorded; such workers may not properly account for operating costs when computing their earnings, and may also have far higher incentives to underreport their earnings.

Another line of inquiry focuses on uncovering workers' revealed preferences by studying their mobility patterns; if workers prefer formal employment, they should voluntarily move mainly from informal to formal sector jobs, while involuntary mobility should go in the opposite direction. Yet, studies find high rates in both directions, suggesting low barriers to entry in the formal sector. They also show that mobility is higher going from informal salaried to formal salaried jobs, consistent with a higher preference for formal salaried jobs. At the same time, the results indicate little mobility between formal salaried and self-employment jobs, consistent with either large barriers to entry, or high levels of self-sorting in the jobs in which workers have a comparative advantage (Bosch and Maloney, 2007a; Pagés and Stampini, 2007).

Mobility studies, however, face a fundamental challenge: the data do not make clear whether mobility is voluntary or involuntary, implying that even when workers move between the formal and informal sectors, it is difficult to know whether this is by necessity or by choice. Comparing workers' choices during normal and recession times can be helpful, as involuntary moves are expected to be more frequent during the latter (Bosch and Maloney, 2007b). An alternative, more straightforward way to assess preferences across types of jobs is to compare job satisfaction levels across formal and informal sectors, or even better, to ask workers which sector they prefer.

Prior to the analysis of the special modules on quality of life that concern the relation between work satisfaction and form of employment, and given the multiple interpretations of "informality," it is important to establish a precise definition of this term. Perry et al. (2007) distinguish between two alternative definitions. The first defines whether a job is informal based on the size of the firm. Under this definition, all employees of companies with 10 or fewer workers, including those who are self-employed, are considered informal. An alternative approach is based on whether workers enjoy the legal benefits established by labor laws. Since in most countries labor laws mostly refer to salaried workers, this approach does not readily apply to self-employed workers. Instead, it is probably best understood as making a useful distinction between salaried workers with and without mandatory protection.[8] The two definitions do not necessarily overlap. Importantly, while it is true that workers in large firms are more likely to have access to formal benefits, a considerable share of workers employed in such firms are without formal protection. On average in the Latin American region, more than one in four workers in firms with more than 10 employees do not have access to formal benefits.[9] The figure is one in two workers in 10 countries and even three

---

[8] In most countries, self-employed workers are not required to enroll in social security. Similarly, minimum wage or paid vacation laws do not apply to these workers.

[9] For some countries, the threshold is four workers or fewer, depending on data availability.

in four in Paraguay.[10] On the other hand, an average of one in four workers employed in small firms in the region has access to legal benefits, with figures close to 50 percent in Chile, which implies that firm size is only a rough proxy for legal benefits access. As such, it becomes important to separately identify the effects on job satisfaction of three job attributes: working in salaried versus nonsalaried jobs, being salaried in a small firm versus a larger one, and working with or without social security coverage.

Happy Microentrepreneurs

A comparison of job satisfaction between salaried and self-employed workers yields interesting and unexpected results. Gallup World Poll data for 20 Latin American countries suggest that business owners (large or small) do not have lower levels of job satisfaction than workers in other occupations such as professionals, company managers, clerks in private businesses or public agencies, sales workers, construction or mining workers, manufacturing or production workers, transportation workers, installation or repair workers, or farming, fishing, or forestry workers. This result is not driven by differences in optimism across individuals. In fact, controlling for this factor here and in the rest of this chapter, following the methodology in Chapter 2, does not affect the results.

It could also be argued that these results are driven by the fact that Gallup World Poll data do not distinguish between microentrepreneurs and owners of larger businesses; therefore similar comparisons are performed using more-detailed data from the Quality of Life (QOL) modules from Chile, Ecuador, El Salvador, Guatemala, and Honduras (see Box 7.1 for a description of these surveys). The results here suggest that, at least in some countries, being a microentrepreneur can yield higher job satisfaction than being a salaried worker. Comparing workers of similar characteristics in terms of age, education, gender, health, and civil status shows that workers in self-employment are equally or more likely to report job satisfaction than workers in salaried jobs. Controlling for hours worked and monthly earnings yields the same results in all countries, with the exception of Chile. The most extreme case is Guatemala, where results indicate much higher levels of job satisfaction among self-employed workers. In contrast, salaried workers in Chile are more likely to be satisfied with their job than the self-employed.

Could this simply reflect that self-employed workers are inherently a happier group, who, given these characteristics, voluntarily chose self-employment? If so, their higher levels of job satisfaction could reflect their sunnier disposition rather than their sense of job satisfaction. However, this does not seem to be the case; even after possible differences in personality are taken into account, the self-employed seem happier with their jobs. In addition, microentrepreneurs are less likely to want to switch jobs than salaried workers, suggesting that their higher levels of job satisfaction are genuinely linked to their jobs. In a 2007 QOL survey, quite starkly, almost 80 percent of salaried workers in Honduras reported a preference for self-employment. The corresponding numbers for surveys in Ecuador, El Salvador, and Guatemala were about 60 percent (see Table 7.1). In contrast, based on the same surveys, a minority of self-employed workers in these three countries would have preferred salaried positions. Still, a considerable number of self-

---

[10] Calculations here are based on Perry et al. (2007).

Table 7.1 Workers' Preferences in Selected Latin American Countries

Country	Salaried workers who would prefer being self-employed	Self-employed workers who would prefer being salaried
	Percentage	
Ecuador	59	41
El Salvador	67	48
Guatemala	57	32
Belize	45	23
Honduras	79	32

Source: Authors' calculations based on QOL surveys from Ecuador (2008), El Salvador (2007), Guatemala (2007), Belize (2007), and Honduras (2007).

employed workers reported a preference for changing jobs, most notably in Ecuador and El Salvador (over 40 percent).

According to the QOL surveys, salaried workers provide three main reasons why they would prefer to be self-employed: higher earnings, more flexibility, and not having a boss, in descending order. Conversely, workers who would prefer being in salaried jobs tend to report higher and/or more stable earnings as the reason. The importance of these job attributes for job satisfaction, as well as the different incidence of valued characteristics across different job categories, is assessed in more detail later in the chapter.

A relevant question is why so many workers are not employed in their first choice, that is, they wish to be self-employed but are in salaried jobs, or vice versa. The answer may be that many workers are waiting for the appropriate moment to make the transition; however, it may also be a reflection of insufficient access to credit or to other barriers to entry determined by red tape or discrimination. This suggests the need to further investigate if there are barriers that prevent workers from acting on their aspirations in future work.

Lastly, higher satisfaction for the self-employed could be associated with these workers' being more able workers, which in turn allows them to excel in their field and reach a higher level of job satisfaction. However, it should be noted that selection into self-employment based on workers' ability would not invalidate the observation that, at least in some countries, self-employed workers are on average happier at work.

Unhappy Small-Firm Employees

In contrast to microentrepreneurs, evidence indicates that workers in small firms are less satisfied with their jobs than either self-employed or salaried workers in larger firms, independently of whether they have access to social security benefits. Based on QOL and LAPOP surveys, Table 7.2 shows how likely salaried workers in either small or large firms are to declare job satisfaction relative to self-employed workers, once differences in personal characteristics and job attributes have been accounted for.[11] In Guatemala,

---

[11] The table reports the marginal effects obtained from a probit model estimating the effect of work category on job satisfaction, with individual characteristics and job attributes (objective and subjective, including hourly wages and hours of work) controlled for, except in the case of Chile, where data do not include wages. See Madrigal and Pagés (2008) for a complete description of the analysis.

Table 7.2 Job Satisfaction of Salaried Workers Relative to Self-Employed Workers, by Firm Size

Country	Firm size	Effect on probability of being satisfied at work relative to self-employed workers
Guatemala	Small	–0.25**
	Large	–0.12**
Honduras	Small	–0.04*
	Large	0
El Salvador	Small	–0.02
	Large	0.05
Chile	Small	0.04*
	Large	0.07*

Source: Authors' calculations based on QOL surveys from Guatemala (2007), Honduras (2007), and El Salvador (2007), and from the Latin American Public Opinion Project in Chile (2008).
Note: Coefficients in table refer to marginal effects of the probit estimation of probability of being satisfied at work on work category, with gender, education, urban and health status, hours of work, labor income, and job attributes controlled for. Estimates from Chile do not control for labor income. A positive (negative) sign implies that self-employed workers are more (less) satisfied with their jobs than salaried workers.
*Coefficient is statistically significant at the 10 percent level; ** at the 5 percent level; ***at the 1 percent level; no asterisk means the coefficient is not different from zero with statistical significance.

salaried workers in both types of firms are less likely to be satisfied with their job than self-employed workers. In Honduras, workers in small firms are less likely to be satisfied than the self-employed, while workers in larger firms are equally satisfied. Preferences in El Salvador conform to the expected pattern in a dual labor market: salaried workers in bigger firms are more likely to be satisfied than either the self-employed or salaried workers in smaller firms. Finally, in Chile, all salaried workers show a higher probability of job satisfaction than the self-employed, with higher satisfaction among larger-firm employees. These results suggest different rankings of job preferences among diverse types of workers worldwide, with an apparently higher preference for self-employment in poorer countries and a generalized lower preference for employment in small firms. It is unclear what drives the small-firm effect, which appears even after differences in wages and job amenities (such as job stability, ability to progress, schedule, and mandatory benefits) are controlled for. Accounting for differences in optimism across individuals does not affect these results.[12]

The Value of Social Security

Labor laws mandate that employers register workers for social security and offer workers a package of benefits. It is often assumed that workers value such benefits, that they are paid for fully by firms, and that, therefore, they constitute benefits above and beyond the monetary compensation received. Yet, such assumptions do not necessarily hold if the compensation package is determined by the interplay of labor demand and labor supply, as legislation designates only which portion of the compensation package

---

[12] However, for Chile the coefficient on being salaried in small firms is no longer statistically significant once differences in optimism are accounted for.

is paid in wages and which part is paid in kind. If that is the case, workers could end up paying for most of their benefits and giving up part of their wages. In addition, diversity in preferences for leisure versus work, or in valuation of present versus future consumption, means that individuals may have different valuations of the standard benefits package. Some individuals may be willing to trade benefits for higher pay. Others might prefer to contribute less towards their future pension in exchange for higher wages today. Still others may consider that paying for medical insurance is not a priority if they are healthy.

Thus, the relation of mandated benefits to job satisfaction is not that simple. Presumably, at least some workers try to avoid paying for the benefits they do not value by taking jobs in firms that, by virtue of their nature and size, can easily escape the notice of the authorities concerning such mandates. This is especially the case if workers have alternative protection against health shocks and old-age poverty risk, by means of, for example, other public programs not tied to individual contributions, or relying on offspring and relatives when needs arise. In that case, being employed in a job without benefits may not be a reflection of exclusion, but rather a deliberate decision of workers to exit the formal system (Perry et al., 2007).

The evidence on the relationship between job satisfaction and benefits differs across types of workers. In the Gallup World Poll sample for all of Latin America, being affiliated with a pension plan is associated with higher job satisfaction; however, an analysis by education level suggests that workers with either very low or very high levels of education show less preference for pensions—or, in other words, their job satisfaction does not increase significantly if they contribute to a pension plan through their job. Levy (2008) reaches similar conclusions with respect to the poorest workers in Mexico, as a result of the low quality of and difficult access to social security and medical and hospital services. For their part, workers at the top end of the distribution are likely to have better access to alternative mechanisms to save for retirement. In a related manner, analysis by age indicates that workers less than 25 years old, and those older than 50, derive less job satisfaction from being affiliated with social security.[13]

A more-detailed analysis using QOL surveys in Guatemala, Honduras, and El Salvador provides similar findings. Given that in Honduras, self-employed workers were not asked about their affiliation status, and that in these three countries most workers employed in small firms do not receive the benefits that are mandated, the analysis distinguishes between four possible labor market statuses: being self-employed, being salaried in a small firm, being employed in a large firm with benefits, and being employed in a large firm without benefits. The comparison of job satisfaction across these categories indicates that in Guatemala and Honduras, workers in large firms with access to social security are more likely to declare job satisfaction than workers in similarly large firms without benefits, even after the influence of individual characteristics and other job attributes is isolated (Table 7.3). In contrast, in El Salvador workers employed in large firms without benefits are more likely to be satisfied with their jobs than self-employed workers. It is also interesting that, even after social security benefits are factored in, only in

---

[13] Many workers close to retirement age who have contributed few years to social security know they will either not qualify for pensions or obtain a minimal amount from them. In such cases, paying into the system may be of low value to them.

Table 7.3 Job Satisfaction of Salaried Workers Relative to Self-Employed Workers, by Firm Size, Benefits, and Education Level

		Effect on probability of being satisfied at work		
Country		All	Less than primary completed	Primary or more completed
Guatemala	Salaried workers in small firms	−0.24***	−0.26***	−0.14
	Salaried workers in large firms with benefits	0.05	−0.21	0.051*
	Salaried workers in large firms without benefits	−0.16**	−0.24**	−0.075
El Salvador	Salaried workers in small firms	−0.01	−0.05	0.038
	Salaried workers in large firms with benefits	0.06	−0.62*	0.12*
	Salaried workers in large firms without benefits	0.09*	−0.31	0.12*

		All	Primary completed	High school completed	College completed
Honduras	Salaried workers in small firms	−0.04*	−0.03	−0.01	−0.02
	Salaried workers in large firms with benefits	0.06*	0.031	0.037**	−0.016
	Salaried workers in large firms without benefits	−0.01	0.004	0.025	−0.035

Source: Authors' calculations based on QOL surveys from Guatemala (2007), Honduras (2007), and El Salvador (2007).
Note: Coefficients in table refer to marginal effects on work category and benefit status of the probit estimation of probability of being satisfied at work, with gender, education, urban and health status, hours of work, labor income, and job attributes controlled for. A positive (negative) sign implies that workers are more (less) satisfied in self-employment than in salaried jobs in any category.
*Coefficient is statistically significant at the 10 percent level; ** at the 5 percent level; ***at the 1 percent level; no asterisk means the coefficient is not different from zero with statistical significance.

Honduras are salaried workers in large firms more likely to be satisfied with their jobs than self-employed workers; these results strongly suggest that the relation between job satisfaction, firm size, and access to benefits does not always correspond to the conventional wisdom, and that results can vary considerably from country to country. As reported above, workers in small firms tend to be less satisfied with their jobs than workers who are self-employed or employed by large firms without benefits.

Interestingly, performing the same exercise, but distinguishing between workers with different education levels, suggests again that the relationships between job satisfaction and work categories differ substantially across education levels, with a lower preference for benefits at the lower end and, possibly, at the higher end. In Honduras, for example, only workers who have completed high school exhibit a preference for being employed in large firms with benefits (Table 7.3). For workers with lower or higher educational attainment, access to benefits is not as relevant for job satisfaction. Similarly, even though in Guatemala and El Salvador the smaller number of observations does not allow for the same level of disaggregation, in these countries only workers who have completed primary education or more associate being employed in large firms with higher job satisfaction. For those with lower levels of education, being self-employed is as preferable as, or, as in El Salvador, more preferable than being in a large firm with benefits in terms of job satisfaction. These results do not change when differences in the degree of optimism across individuals are accounted for.

In sum, the assessment of the relationship between informality and welfare yields important conclusions. First, the analysis points to the lack of overlap between different, if often interchangeably used, dimensions of informality. Not all jobs in small firms are unprotected, nor does the law protect all workers employed in large firms. Second, some jobs commonly categorized as informal seem to be preferred over jobs traditionally labeled as "good jobs." This is particularly the case of self-employment, which seems to lure many workers under the expectation of higher income, more flexible schedules, and no bosses. Thus, there seems to be an abundance of good jobs (at least in the view of workers) in self-employment, and plenty of "bad jobs" in large firms, while preferences across categories vary substantially across countries. Third, evidence indicates that having access to a pension plan improves job satisfaction, but only for workers with education above a certain level, and possibly only for those with intermediate education levels. Low levels of willingness to forgo current income for future pension, because of myopia, or alternative arrangements for social protection—for example, relying on offspring and relatives in old age, or in the case of high-income workers, being enrolled in alternative private programs—may reduce the willingness of workers on both ends of the income spectrum to participate in mandatory social protection systems. This may partly explain why participation of workers with low levels of education is so low across countries, and why self-employed workers, who can voluntarily affiliate with the system, rarely do so (Auerbach, Genoni, and Pagés, 2007). Yet, even if individuals do not value certain benefits—such as social security—it does not necessarily follow that the state should not mandate them. While it may be individually optimal to trade off a higher wage today for a lower pension (or none) tomorrow, socially it may not be so if workers do not correctly anticipate their retirement needs. The implications of this friction between individual desires and societal needs will be considered later in this chapter.

Unemployment Risk and Job Insecurity

Objective indicators of mobility show that unemployment risk looms large in Latin America. Between 25 and 30 percent of jobs in formal manufacturing firms are either created or destroyed every year (see Figure 7.11). Job destruction occurs partly because some firms become unprofitable and exit the market, and partly because some firms downsize their labor force. Job destruction is likely to be even higher in the service sector or in the vast majority of small-scale establishments. Longitudinal data from household surveys, for the few countries in which such data are available, suggest that workers without access to social security (i.e., those unlikely to be covered by employment protection laws) tend to have higher exit rates to unemployment than those with access, although this association does not hold for Venezuela, where the exit rates to unemployment are lower for those without access. Exit rates to unemployment are higher in some cases for high-skilled workers (Venezuela), while in others (Argentina and Mexico) the less skilled bear the brunt (see Figure 7.12). While job destruction is also prevalent in industrial countries (see Figure 7.11), the corresponding figures for the Latin American region, for the few countries with available data, are among the highest of the group. In addition, it may be argued that there are more mechanisms in place to protect workers against unemployment risk in higher-income countries; therefore, it is likely that, unless workers have found alternative, better mechanisms to protect themselves against unemployment risk, job insecurity is higher in Latin America.

Figure 7.11 Job Creation and Destruction as Percentage of Total Employment in Manufacturing in Selected Countries, 1990–2000

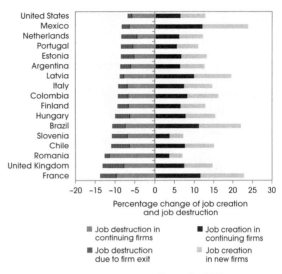

Source: Bartelsman, Haltiwanger, and Scarpetta (2004).

Job insecurity is clearly a concern for workers in the region, as perception data confirm. Based on the 2007 Gallup World Poll, on average, 20 percent of workers fear they could lose their jobs within six months. The highest perceived job insecurity is in Mexico, at 27.3 percent, and the lowest in Uruguay and Paraguay, at 12.5 and 10 percent, respectively (see Figure 7.13). Unfortunately, comparable information on job insecurity is not available for other countries outside the region, and therefore international comparisons on job insecurity cannot be performed.

How does job insecurity affect workers' welfare? The data suggest a strong negative relation between perceived job insecurity and job satisfaction. Table 7.4 illustrates this impact according to information from QOL surveys after worker characteristics and other work attributes are accounted for. In these surveys, job insecurity was measured based on workers' responses to the question of whether they might lose their jobs within six months. Answering that question affirmatively reduced the probability of job satisfaction between 8 and 15 percentage points, depending on the country. By way of comparison, it is possible to compute how much a worker's wages would have to increase to compensate for lost job satisfaction associated with job insecurity for at least one country: Honduras. The magnitude of such compensation is substantial, on the order of 300 percent. Similar results, albeit of somewhat smaller magnitude, were found when this analysis was performed using Gallup World Poll data for the entire Latin American region (see Table 7.5).

Table 7.4 also suggests a negative association between life satisfaction and job insecurity for salaried workers in Ecuador (see note to table). A recent study (Menezes-

Figure 7.12 Percentage of Workers Who Transit from Jobs with and without Social Security to Unemployment in a Year, by Education Level

a. From jobs without social security to unemployment

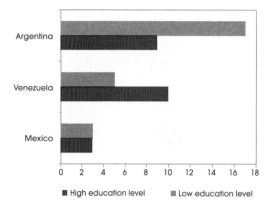

■ High education level ■ Low education level

b. From jobs with social security to unemployment

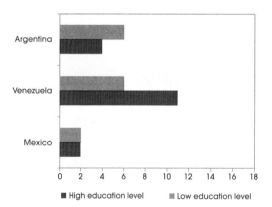

■ High education level ■ Low education level

Source: Pagés and Stampini (2007).
Note: Low level of education refers to those with no education and less than secondary education; high level of education refers to those with at least secondary education completed.

Filho, Corbi, and Curi, 2008) explores this issue using Gallup World Poll data for Latin America and finds a strong and robust relationship.[14] Moreover, being affiliated with social security, a proxy of whether employers are in compliance with labor regulations and, therefore, whether workers are eligible for severance pay and other employment protection, is not associated with higher employment security. If anything, affiliated workers seem to be more worried about losing their jobs than unaffiliated ones. Given that the data do not follow individuals over time, such findings could be driven by the fact that more risk-averse workers self-select into formal jobs; yet they could also reflect that current social protection institutions offer little protection against unemployment risk. The Menezes-Filho et al. analysis indicates that workers in good health, and/or with higher income or household assets, tend to feel more secure in their jobs.[15] But, less predictably, women suffer lower job insecurity than men. Despite these differences, the study finds no important variations in how job loss risk affects quality of life across different groups of workers.

An in-depth look at job insecurity perceptions using the QOL surveys confirms the negative relationship between education and perceived job insecurity, although that relationship is not statistically significant in all countries. Another interesting dimension is a quite-common U-shaped relationship between perceived job insecurity and age, which implies that job insecurity is higher in young workers, then declines with experience, and later increases as workers approach retirement age. In all countries, the perception of job insecurity is higher among salaried than self-employed workers, even

---

[14] Data for the question regarding job security are available only for this subsample of countries.

[15] The effect of these covariates holds after the effect of selection on employment is controlled for.

after individual and job characteristics are controlled for. It may well be that self-employed workers, as owners of their economic activity, feel more in control of their job situation than those who depend on third parties for their work. Among the salaried, workers in small firms tend to experience higher job insecurity than workers in firms with more than 10 employees, except in Guatemala, where even after a large set of individual and job characteristics are controlled for, job insecurity is higher among employees of larger firms. Finally, and unlike those based on Gallup data, estimates based on QOL surveys reveal no clear relationship between gender and job insecurity. In some countries (El Salvador, Guatemala), women experience more job insecurity, while in others (Chile) men experience more. In some countries, the difference is not statistically significant.

A relevant issue is whether perceived job insecurity is related to the actual probability of unemployment. Studying this issue would require longitudinal data to verify whether all those who reported job insecurity ended up losing their jobs, yet unfortunately, such data are hard to find for countries in the region. Menezes-Filho, Corbi, and Curi, (2008) attempt to study this issue, examining whether personal characteristics that predict the probability of unemployment are also correlated with perceived job insecurity, and find a positive, but not statistically significant, relation between predicted probability of unemployment and perceived job insecurity in Brazil. Again, it is hard to interpret such a lack of correlation without longitu-

Figure 7.13 Perception of Job Insecurity in Selected Latin American Countries, 2007

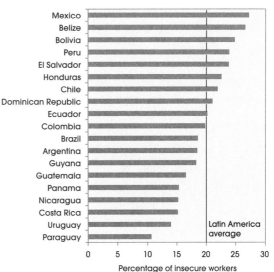

Percentage of insecure workers

Source: Gallup (2007).
Note: Figure reflects affirmative responses to question "Do you think you could lose your job in the next six months?"

Table 7.4 Impact of Job Insecurity on Job Satisfaction

Country	Effect of job insecurity on the probability of being satisfied at work
Ecuador	−0.03*
Guatemala	−0.09*
Honduras	−0.08***
Chile	−0.12***
El Salvador	−0.14**
Belize	−0.13***

Source: Authors' calculations based on the QOL surveys from Ecuador (2007), Guatemala (2007), Honduras (2007), El Salvador (2007), and Belize (2007) and from the Latin American Public Opinion Project in Chile (2008).
Note: Coefficients in table refer to marginal effects of the probit estimation of probability of being satisfied at work, with gender, education, urban and health status, hours of work, labor income, and job attributes controlled for. In Ecuador, the dependent variable is life satisfaction and refers only to salaried workers. Estimates from Chile do not control for wages. A negative (positive) sign implies that workers are less (more) satisfied if they think they could lose their job. Job insecurity is based on answers to the question "Do you think you may lose your job in the next six months?"
*Coefficient is statistically significant at the 10 percent level; ** at the 5 percent level; ***at the 1 percent level; no asterisk means the coefficient is not different from zero with statistical significance.

Table 7.5 Impact of Job Attributes on Job Satisfaction

Job attribute	Effect on probability of being satisfied at work
Do your opinions seem to count?[a]	0.10***
Are you able to do your best every day?[b]	0.21***
Does someone encourage your development?[c]	0.10***
Could you lose your job?[d]	−0.08***
Are you affiliated with a pension plan?[e]	0.02

Source: Authors' estimations based on Gallup (2007).
Note: Coefficients in table refer to marginal effects from a probit estimation of probability of being satisfied at work, with gender, education, marital, urban and health status, labor income, and job attributes controlled for. Country effects and an optimism variable, which captures the effects of personality, are also controlled for.
[a] Reflects answers to the question "At work, do your opinions seem to count, or not?
[b] Reflects answers to the question "In your work, do you have an opportunity to do your best every day?"
[c] Reflects answers to the question "Is there someone at work who encourages your development?"
[d] Reflects answers to the question "Do you think you could lose your job in the next six months?"
[e] Reflects answers to the question "Are you affiliated with a retirement plan to which you contributed last month?"
*Coefficient is statistically significant at the 10 percent level; ** at the 5 percent level; ***at the 1 percent level; no asterisk means the coefficient is not different from zero with statistical significance.

nal data. It may well be that those who are more likely to be unemployed at any given time are actually more employable, and can find a new job more easily than others and therefore do not perceive more job insecurity. On the other hand, perhaps those who have less secure jobs have adapted to shifting jobs or holding several at a time, and will not report more job insecurity.

Yet, whether or not correlated with actual unemployment risk, perceived job insecurity might have important negative consequences for workers' health outcomes. Such insecurity is positively associated with depression, whereas job satisfaction reduces the incidence of depression in the Gallup World Poll data (Parker, Rubalcava, and Teruel, 2008b). Since the causality can run both ways—depressed workers may feel more insecure while workers with their jobs at risk may feel more depressed—it is necessary to explore further sources of data to disentangle the causality. Parker, Rubalcava, and Teruel (2008b) use longitudinal data for Mexico, which follow individual workers over time, to shed further light on this issue. They find that workers who lost their job between the first and second wave of the survey had more mental health problems (such as problems sleeping, appetite loss, low concentration, or lack of confidence) than those who were employed in both periods; in contrast, people who moved from unemployment into jobs experienced fewer health problems. To assess causality, these authors examined whether health status in the initial period predicted employment status in the second period and found that it did not, suggesting that the causality runs from work status to mental health.

Being Well Paid and Feeling Well Paid

It is reassuring that subjective measures of job satisfaction relate to economic variables in expected ways. Previous chapters have documented a positive relationship between earnings and life satisfaction. In addition, most studies confirm a positive relationship between higher pay and higher job satisfaction (Clark, 2004), and the Latin American region is no exception.[16] Data available for Belize, Honduras, El Salvador, and Guatemala show that higher pay is associated with greater job satisfaction. In the latter two countries, however, wages cease to have a direct effect on job satisfaction when other job attributes are controlled for.

In fact, more important than being well paid is the perception of being well paid. In studies for the above-mentioned countries, workers who felt well paid declared higher levels of job satisfaction than workers who earned the same pay but felt less well paid, even after a large set of individual and job characteristics were controlled for. This implies that higher (subjective) relative income contributes to job satisfaction and that this contribution can be more important than the effect of actual pay. These results are not likely driven by some individuals' being more optimistic, and at the same time better paid, and therefore feeling more satisfied with their jobs, as results hold when such individual characteristics are taken into account.

Interestingly, perceptions of pay are more evenly spread than actual pay. While there is a well-documented gender and race gap in wages (see IDB, 2006c, and references therein), the evidence for Belize, Ecuador, El Salvador, and Guatemala indicates that women and people of indigenous origin do not feel significantly less well paid than males or nonindigenous people. Experimental evidence described in IDB (2006c) is consistent with the notion that women bargain less and demand lower starting wages. Accordingly, a first step towards wage equality may require changing workers' expectations, which paradoxically could lead to lower job satisfaction. The only exception is Honduras, where evidence suggests that females in the workforce do feel less well compensated than their male counterparts. Moreover, this gap is entirely attributable to differences in pay, as perceptions between men and women are similar when such pay variations are controlled for.

Chapter 3 documents that when life satisfaction is measured, relative earnings are as important as absolute earnings. An investigation of whether job satisfaction is related to relative earnings for Honduras, the only country where detailed wage data allow for the computing of reference wages—taken to be the average wage of workers of the same sex, age, and education—yields mixed results: the effect of higher wages for the reference group on job satisfaction, keeping individual earnings constant, is negative but not statistically significant.

Balancing Life and Work

Workers in Latin America put in longer hours than their industrial-country counterparts, while higher fertility rates mean these workers face greater family demands. How do they balance life and work?

Part of the answer to this age-old question resides in lower female participation rates and a more traditional division of labor within households: men work long hours while many women stay at home. Perhaps this traditional arrangement explains why in the five countries in which the relationship between hours of work and job satisfaction

---

[16] Studies also show that workers care not only about absolute wage levels, but also about relative wages. A lower than average wage increase may actually reduce job satisfaction. Chapter 2 presents a related discussion of the effect of absolute and relative incomes on life satisfaction.

is examined (Chile, Ecuador, El Salvador, Guatemala, and Honduras) there is no evidence that the number of hours worked negatively affects job satisfaction, even after wages are accounted for. In fact, in El Salvador and Honduras working longer hours is associated with higher levels of job satisfaction. Moreover, contrary to expectations, there is weak evidence that women have a preference for shorter working hours than men, although these results may be due to the small number of observations in these surveys, particularly of women, given their lower participation rates. Only in Honduras and Chile are the differences between men and women in relation to their preferences for working full or part time statistically significant. In both countries, men who work part time are less likely to feel satisfied with their jobs than those with full-time jobs, while women are equally satisfied working part time.

Data obtained from the household surveys indicate that 43 percent of women who work in the Latin American region work less than 40 hours per week (part time), and this figure is much lower for males (27 percent). The proportion of part-time work among women is highest in Argentina (60 percent) and lowest in El Salvador (29 percent). Across countries, part-time work is associated with higher participation by youth, women, and older workers in the labor force, which suggests that part-time work may be a successful instrument for combining paid work with other activities (see Figures 7.14 and 7.15) for which women sacrifice little in terms of job satisfaction.

Figure 7.14 Part-Time Workers in Latin American Countries by Gender, Early 2000s

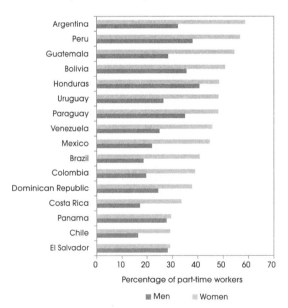

Percentage of part-time workers

■ Men ▨ Women

Source: IDB (2007).
Note: Part-time workers are defined as the percentage of total employed people working less than 40 hours a week.

High Pay and Stability Are Not Everything

A good-quality job consists of more than just good pay and job security. Other attributes generally not accounted for in objective measures of job quality carry considerable weight in determining job satisfaction. For example, based on Gallup World Poll data, job satisfaction is highly associated, in decreasing importance, with being able to perform at one's best, having someone at work that encourages one's development, and having one's opinions count at work. Interestingly, these factors matter more for job satisfaction than having access to a pension plan through work or having job security (see Table 7.5). This is particularly relevant once differences in optimism levels are taken into account, given that the effect of being affiliated with a pension plan remains of equal magnitude but ceases to be statistically significant. Such data lead to the conclusion that being listened to at work and having a mentor are particularly important for young workers, while being able to perform at one's best is equally important for workers of all ages. Also, it is possible to conclude that men derive more satisfaction from having their opinions count, while women are more satisfied when they are able to perform at their best.

Individual country QOL surveys provide additional information on work attributes that are highly valued by workers. In Honduras and El Salvador, after having a well-remunerated job and enjoying a good work schedule, being able to advance at work is the attribute that contributes the most to job satisfaction, along with having a secure job. In Guatemala, the highest contributors to job satisfaction, after having a well-paid job, include having a job that is not monotonous and having a job that allows for advancement. Similarly, in Chile, the greatest job satisfaction comes from being allowed to do one's best, followed by having a great deal of autonomy and the possibility of career advancement. For salaried workers, while the analysis is weakened by a lower number of observations, being treated with respect and having a fair employer are the most-prized job attributes. An important issue for health and risk policy is that negative attributes, such as a dangerous or stressful environment, do not seem to affect job satisfaction greatly.

How many workers have access to jobs with these valued attributes? Quite surprisingly, according to the 2006 Gallup World Poll, many workers have such access. On average, 87 percent of workers report being able to perform to the best of their ability

Figure 7.15 Labor Force Participation and Part-Time Work

a. Workers from 15 to 24 years old

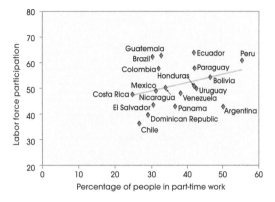

b. Workers from 50 to 64 years old

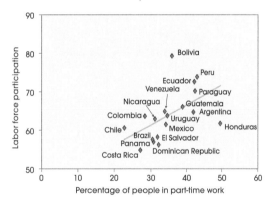

c. Female workers from 15 to 64 years old

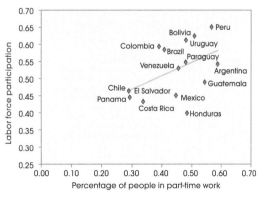

Source: IDB (2007).

Figure 7.16 Percentage of Workers Who Declare They Have the Opportunity to Do Their Best Every Day, 2006

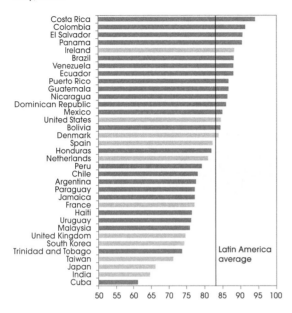

Source: Gallup (2006).

Figure 7.17 Percentage of Workers Who Declare There Is Someone at Work Encouraging Their Development, 2006

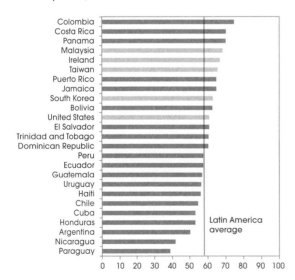

Source: Gallup (2006).

every day, 67 percent report having someone at work encouraging their development, and 81 percent feel their opinions count at work (see Figures 7.16, 7.17, and 7.18).[17] The QOL surveys also indicate that a large percentage of salaried workers report having a fair employer (above 70 percent in all countries and as high as 83 percent in El Salvador and Belize). On the other hand, these surveys indicate that a relatively lower percentage of workers are able to advance at work (Belize: 57 percent; Chile: 46 percent; Ecuador: 54 percent; El Salvador: 47 percent; Guatemala: 57 percent; and Honduras: 65 percent).

Who lands the jobs with the most-valued attributes? As in developed countries, workers with more education and higher wages have better chances of securing jobs with these attributes. The Gallup data indicate that in the Latin American region, urban, older, healthier, and more-educated workers are the most likely to hold jobs with the most-valued attributes. The QOL surveys confirm these patterns for Guatemala, Honduras, and El Salvador. For example, in these countries workers with higher wages and more education are more likely to report that their job offers greater opportunities for advancement. Quite notably, in all countries, self-employed workers are equally as likely as or, often, more likely than salaried workers to report advancement prospects.

This indicates that in addition to wages, hours, and job secu-

---

[17] These percentages are slightly lower in the 2006 data set.

rity (the usual job attributes that tend to be measured by objective indicators of job quality), there are a host of other job attributes that are as important, or even more important, for job satisfaction. In turn, judging from workers' own accounts, these attributes are more widespread than the ones on which analysts tend to focus. This may explain why, despite disappointing objective indicators, job satisfaction in Latin America is relatively high.

Summing Up

Job quality is often assessed using factors such as the incidence of formal or regular-indefinite employment, the evolution of wages, or the hours of work, aspects that commonly are considered directly related to welfare. According to most of these yardsticks, the quality

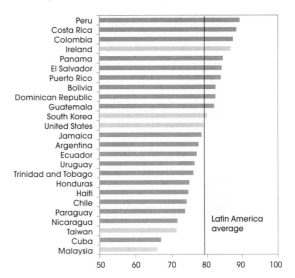

Figure 7.18 Percentage of Workers Who Declare Their Opinions Count at Work, 2006

Source: Gallup (2006, 2007).
Note: U.S. data are from 2007.

of jobs has declined in the past decade in Latin America. The share of informal workers and workers not covered by social security and the number of workers with low wages have increased in most countries, while wages have increased very slowly, if at all. At the same time, more workers have taken on temporary jobs and many are working more hours, while job turnover has substantially risen.

A look at the attitudes and preferences of workers in relation to their jobs complements the standard assessment of job quality in a number of ways. It reveals that self-employment may be a surprisingly attractive option for many workers, particularly in the low-income countries of the sample of countries analyzed, as it is perceived to provide, among other valued characteristics, better opportunities for advancement and higher earnings. Moreover, while being affiliated with social security through work may be an essential benefit for many workers, others may value it less. Although the reasons are unclear, a combination of a reliance on informal safety nets (such as leaning on offspring and relatives when old), a lower ability to save money for health and old-age poverty risks, and an increasing supply of government programs providing basic health and pensions to workers in the informal sector may reduce the value of being affiliated with social security for lower-income workers. These factors should be considered in policy design, particularly if governments seek to expand the reach of social protection mechanisms.

The results presented here suggest that the conventional wisdom that classifies formal jobs as "good" and informal jobs as "bad" is likely to be erroneous. In addition, the current practice of using the term "informality" in a generic way, lumping many different categories together without properly distinguishing which ones are used in the definition, may be misleading, as overlap between categories can be quite low and preferences across these categories can vary substantially across individuals and countries. Rather than using dualistic categories, it seems more appropriate to identify job quality based on a number of separate work attributes, of which job category, firm size, and enrollment in mandatory benefit programs are only a few. Perception data can help analysts to determine which job characteristics are valued the most.

One such valued attribute is job security, which also seems to have important implications for overall happiness and health and which can be tracked more regularly among workers and their families. In addition, being and feeling well paid are important components of job satisfaction, which suggests that tracking absolute and relative pay might be a much better indicator of job quality than job category. Finally, the analysis uncovers a number of very valued job attributes not regularly tracked by standard indicators of job quality, such as being able to do one's best, having one's opinion count, enjoying a nonmonotonous job, having someone promoting one's development at work, being presented with advancement opportunities, or having a fair employer. Some of these attributes seem to be widespread, while others are not. The fact that more than 40 percent of workers see no opportunities to progress in their job is a reason for concern, especially when having such opportunities is closely correlated with welfare at work. Improving the measurement of those characteristics that truly make for a good job according to workers is an important step towards achieving higher job quality in the Latin American region.

Yet, as discussed in previous chapters, the policy objective should not necessarily be to maximize job satisfaction, as there are a number of instances in which individual perceptions and societal goals may conflict. One such conflict arises when workers do not properly assess their needs when sick or aging. Another potential source of conflict arises from the fact that workers may have overly strong preferences for working. As such, an analysis of workers' self-reported preferences would indicate that most workers prefer working a relatively high number of hours, even with earnings adjusted for. If such preferences turn out to be incompatible with other societal goals, restricting hours of work may be justifiable. On the other hand, even if such a conflict arises, measuring reductions in work hours as an indicator of job quality may not be appropriate in middle- and lower-income countries. Another conflict could arise if workers excessively discount negative attributes, such as stress levels or unsafe workplace practices. The evidence presented here suggests that they may actually do so, since in the data analyzed, stress levels or performing a dangerous job does not carry much weight in regard to job satisfaction. If workers are not sufficiently aware about safety or healthy workplace practices, government may need to spend more resources on public outreach and education campaigns, even if this leads to lower job satisfaction.

Fostering Better Job Creation in the Region

The analysis of objective indicators of job quality suggests that most countries in the Latin American region do not have problems creating jobs, but rather struggle to create good-quality jobs. The analysis of perception-based data complements such research by suggesting that workers care about job security and pay, two aspects that, given recent wage and temporary-contract trends, have not improved recently in the region. Workers are also concerned about job attributes such as promotion opportunities or having one's opinions count, which are not routinely measured, and therefore it is difficult to know whether they have deteriorated over the years. Regarding the poor evolution of wages, low productivity growth and large labor supply growth have strained labor markets during the past 15 years. While demographic pressures will subside in the near future, the region needs to increase the pace of productivity growth in order to foster the creation of higher-paying jobs, which is particularly relevant in a context where skill-biased technological change may have increased the incidence of low pay in the region (IDB, 2007). Increasing the growth of labor productivity requires cultivating a better allocation of resources and spurring higher investment in equipment, technology, infrastructure, and human capital. It also requires enhancing the business climate in which firms operate. However, while labor productivity growth determines earnings growth, which is a key determinant of job quality, employment policies can, at least to some extent, foster higher job quality.

Smarter Regulation, Better Worker Protection

A common answer to the question of how to create better jobs is to promote labor regulation, for example, by enforcing higher minimum wages or ensuring greater job security (e.g., by restricting temporary-contracts use or increasing the cost of dismissal). Given the importance of high wages and job security in perceived job quality, what role should regulatory policy have in achieving those goals?

Labor regulations in Latin America cover a broad spectrum, including length of the workweek, types of contracts, minimum wages, and procedures to terminate work relationships. All countries regulate labor relations to a greater or lesser extent, and Latin America falls in the middle range when it comes to labor regulations (for example, concerning nonwage labor costs, the rigidity of hours, or the overall indicator of regulations—rigidity of employment index) (see Figure 7.19). In terms of terminating employment relationships, the region has a mixed position. It highly restricts hiring outside of regular, indefinite contracts (difficulty of hiring index) and mandates relatively high severance pay (firing costs index). Yet, administratively it is easy to terminate work relationships, as shown by the region's low position in the difficulty of firing index.

Latin American countries have also signed a large number of ILO conventions, placing the region third in terms of number of overall signed conventions and second in regard to the eight fundamental conventions (see Figure 7.20). Some conventions are not necessarily enforced, such as that involving child labor, which has not been eradicated from the region, but has been declining in recent years in some countries (see Figure 7.21).

There is an economic case for labor market regulation because free markets are unlikely to lead to outcomes that maximize social welfare. Yet, evidence suggests that current labor regulations may be partly at fault for creation of low-quality jobs. These findings are obtained from a host of recent studies assessing the impact of labor regulations on labor market outcomes. Unlike a first set of studies based on cross-country analysis, more recent studies analyze episodes of reform in depth, comparing economic sectors and workers who are affected and not affected by reforms.

Figure 7.19 Indicators of Labor Regulations across the World

a. Difficulty of hiring index
(0–100)

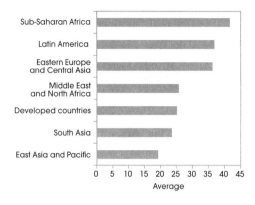

b. Rigidity of hours index
(0–100)

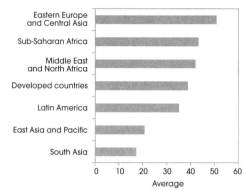

c. Difficulty of firing index
(0–100)

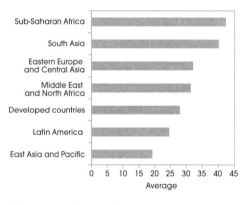

d. Rigidity of employment index
(0–100)

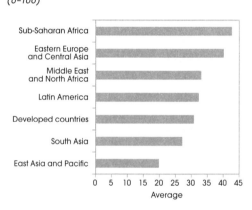

e. Nonwage labor cost

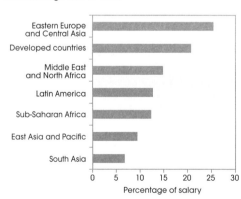

f. Firing costs

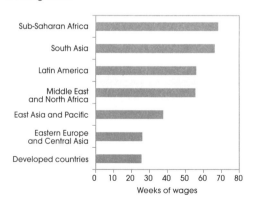

Source: World Bank (2008).
Note: Higher values on the indices and other measures indicate higher protection for workers.

In terms of minimum wage laws, studies in middle- and low-income countries find that minimum wages that are set far above the market price provide wage gains to those who keep their jobs, but can lead to employment losses among the most vulnerable. Studies for Indonesia (Rama, 2001), Hungary (Kertesi and Köllo, 2003), Colombia (Bell, 1997, and Maloney and Núñez, 2004), Costa Rica (Gindling and Terrell, 2007), and Chile (Cowan, Micco, and Pagés, 2004) find that minimum wage hikes have a negative impact on employment, and may also expand the proportion of workers in self-employment (Andalon and Pagés, 2008, for Kenya), although, as discussed above, this is not necessarily negative unless it is the result of workers' not finding the jobs they really want. Studies also find that employers may reduce average hours for workers earning close to the minimum wage (Gindling and Terrell, 2007), which, judging from the preferences of workers—particularly male workers—for long hours, would be associated with adverse outcomes for job satisfaction. Some studies, however, have not found negative employment effects (Lemos, 2004, for Brazil, and Bell, 1997, for Mexico), which suggests that effects may differ across countries and may depend on the minimum wage level. Nevertheless, most studies find that for each 10 percent increase in the minimum wage, some 1 to 2 percent of jobs are lost.

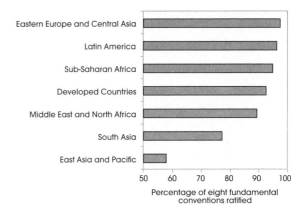

Figure 7.20 Ratification Rates for Eight Fundamental International Labour Organization Conventions, by Region

Source: ILO (2008a).
Note: Eight conventions have been identified by the International Labour Organization's governing body as being fundamental to the rights of people at work, irrespective of levels of development of individual member states: freedom of association (#87, #98), abolition of forced labor (#29, #105), equality (#100, #111), and elimination of child labor (#138, #182).

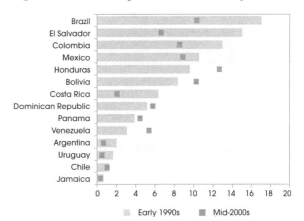

Figure 7.21 Percentage of Children Working

Source: CEDLAS and World Bank (2008), except for data for Argentina and Colombia, which are from IDB (2007).
Note: The term "children" refers to the population ages 10–14. Percentages over the population of children for the following periods: Argentina (1993–2000), Bolivia (1993–2002), Brazil (1992–2003), Chile (1992–2005), Colombia (1990–2004), Costa Rica (1996–2005), Dominican Republic (2001–2004), El Salvador (1993–2002), Honduras (1991–2003), Jamaica (1992–2004), Mexico (1990–2003), Panama (1992–2005), Uruguay (1995–2004), Venezuela (1990–2002).

Given these findings, minimum wage policies must be carefully monitored. This ideally entails access to longitudinal data, which allows workers to be followed over time and what happens to their employment status, earnings, and job satisfaction before and after the introduction or modification of wage floors to be assessed. If costs are deemed to be high, there are several policy alternatives to boost the earnings of low-income workers, some of which involve improving the productivity of workers through better education and training programs. Other policies imply fostering increases in productivity in the industries and sectors that pay lower wages. Finally, governments can consider direct income transfers to workers who are working but are poor (Cox Edwards, 2007), which can provide for redistribution without reducing employment opportunities for such workers.

Studies also provide insight into the economic impact of legislation that raises administrative or economic costs of dismissals. While in principle such regulations would appear to favor workers by enhancing job security, there are important trade-offs that must be considered. Thus, while turnover is found to decline with higher dismissal costs, employment can also be negatively affected, particularly in labor-intensive sectors or in sectors that face unstable demands (Autor, Donohue, and Schwab, 2004, 2006; Besley and Burgess, 2004; Micco and Pagés, 2006; Ahsan and Pagés, 2007). In addition, women, youth, and unskilled workers tend to lose in terms of employment and wages, while skilled male workers benefit (Montenegro and Pagés, 2004, 2007; Kahn, 2007). Employment protection has also been shown to push employers towards offering temporary jobs and outsourcing (Autor, 2003; Kahn, 2007), particularly for female, unskilled, and young workers (Kahn, 2007), as well as to condemn the jobless to longer periods of unemployment (Kugler, 2004). Finally, employment protection can alter workers' long-run prospects and job quality by lowering total factor productivity (Autor, Kerr, and Kugler, 2007).

Studies based on workers' perceptions also confirm that quite surprisingly, employment protection legislation does not seem to increase the perception of job security. Data for 12 European countries show that workers feel less secure in countries with stricter employment protection legislation (Clark and Postel-Vinay, 2005). Similarly, in Latin America, both formal workers—eligible for employment protection—and informal workers suffer the same degree of job insecurity (Menezes-Filho, Corbi, and Curi, 2008). While employment protection decreases the incidence of job loss, it also stunts workers' reemployment prospects in cases of unemployment. Temporary and outsourced workers are likely to face greater job insecurity as well.

It therefore appears that employment protection legislation (EPL) brings about important, undesired collateral effects in regard to the economy, while failing to protect workers against unemployment risk. This failure emerges from design and implementation shortcomings that must be remedied in order to create an effective protection mechanism. What explains this failure? First, EPL does not prevent job loss in the event of firm closure, an event that affects a large proportion of workers (see Figure 7.11). Second, in many cases firms are unlikely to meet their obligations towards workers when they are burdened by economic problems. Third, severance pay does not protect workers against the risk of extended unemployment (i.e., the severance pay is the same regardless of how long workers remain unemployed). Fourth, given high levels of employment rotation, severance pay may be quite low for many workers.

How is it possible to enhance unemployment risk protection, while at the same time minimize the aforementioned adverse side effects? The answer is country specific, depending on government administrative capacity, development of the financial system, and size of the government, among other things. Still, some general principles can be advanced, such as shifting from systems designed to protect jobs to systems designed to protect workers. This implies moving to some form of unemployment insurance mechanism geared to protect workers against income loss associated with unemployment. In industrial countries, higher unemployment benefits are associated with both higher national well-being (Di Tella, MacCulloch, and Oswald, 2003) and greater perceptions of job security (Clark and Postel-Vinay, 2005).

Yet, unemployment insurance mechanisms are difficult to implement in countries that suffer from poor administrative capacity and have large informal sectors; moreover, they may bring problems of their own. Unemployment insurance systems that provide benefits that either are too high or last too long discourage job search and foster extended unemployment unless costly monitoring and activation mechanisms are in place. On the other hand, despite such negative effects, unemployment insurance mechanisms that pool unemployment risk and provide resources to enable workers to look for a suitable job result in longer terms of employment in subsequent jobs (Tatsiramos, 2004). This positive effect is larger in countries with more generous unemployment insurance, as they allow better matches between workers and jobs. Clearly, then, there is a balance needed between sufficient and excessive insurance.

Some countries in the Latin American region already have some form of unemployment insurance, although its coverage tends to be low (Mazza, 2000). There is also an overlap between benefits and beneficiaries when countries have both severance pay and unemployment insurance. An effective reform should assist in shifting from one system to the other, rather than superimposing programs and benefits. Some countries, like Chile, already allow firms to subtract a portion of unemployment insurance contributions from severance pay obligations. Credits of this kind can constitute a promising way of shifting between systems without raising labor costs, and while unemployment insurance systems styled after those in industrial countries may be difficult to implement in middle- and low-income countries, unemployment insurance schemes based on a mixed system of individual accounts and government paid benefits, as in Chile, may be a feasible solution for some countries (Acevedo, Eskenazi, and Pagés, 2006).

Active Labor Market Policies: How and When

Another effective way to protect workers against unemployment risk is to revamp job intermediation (JI) services, which typically have low levels of effectiveness and coverage (Mazza, 2003), capture a small proportion of vacancies (Ramos, 2002, for Brazil), and show large within-country geographical disparities in terms of quality (Samaniego, 2002). Despite limited evidence on the performance of job intermediation services in the Latin American region, existing evidence suggests that JI can help workers find better jobs, although the effects may differ across groups of workers (Ramos, 2002, on Brazil; Flores Lima, 2006, on Mexico). JI needs to be improved by expanding registration of workers and vacancies, enhancing the quality of services, extending regional coverage, and reducing geographical quality disparities. It should also be linked with other active labor market programs and with the receipt of benefits in countries with unemployment insurance programs.

Public works programs can be useful devices to transfer resources temporarily to workers or households in need when other mechanisms are not available, although they are not permanent solutions to job creation failures and do not improve subsequent earnings or employment probabilities (Jalan and Ravallion, 2003, for Argentina; Betcherman, Olivas, and Dar, 2004). To ensure proper incentives, work requirements need to be enforced and payments should be below market to provide workers with an incentive to leave the program for better prospects. Similarly, wage/employment subsidies should be considered temporary solutions. The available evaluations, which have mostly been carried out in developed countries, show that in practice subsidies lead to substantive employment creation, but at the expense of large deadweight losses and substitution effects (Marx, 2005; Betcherman, Daysal, and Pagés, 2008), with little positive effect on future earnings (Galasso, Ravallion, and Salvia, 2004).

In turn, labor training, while not the end-all solution for labor market problems, can improve employment prospects of some workers, although the results differ across types of workers and countries (Betcherman, Olivas, and Dar, 2004). Ibarrarán and Rosas Shady (2008) compare the results of the evaluations of seven training programs in Latin America and find that employment effects range from none to about 5 percentage points, but are higher for some groups, such as women in Colombia and Panama— with impacts of 6 to 12 percentage points in the employment rate. They also find a significant impact on the probability of finding a job with a contract or health insurance. Evaluations suggest that the quality of training is important in explaining subsequent labor market outcomes. In the case of Peru, youth attending higher-quality courses have greater subsequent earnings after the program (Chong and Galdo, 2006).[18] Evaluations also suggest that involving employers and/or private providers in training improves outcomes for trainees.

Improving Social Security

Workers' valuation of social security mechanisms is a key parameter in the design of labor market policy, because a low valuation is a source of problems in the labor market. As stated above, workers, particularly those with lower incomes and educational attainment, may not be willing to pay for social security benefits, particularly pension plans, because of myopia, lack of understanding of the need to save for the future, or reliance on informal safety nets, or because they simply need the cash for basic consumption. Another important reason for not valuing social security relative to its costs is that benefits may be of poor quality, or simply not available, or perhaps workers do not have faith in the government's ability to manage the programs. This problem may be compounded by the emergence of new programs aimed at expanding health and medical insurance for workers not affiliated with social security. While the intentions of these programs are obviously good, subsidizing coverage for those not in the social security

---

[18] Quality is measured through quantitative and qualitative criteria that include class size, expenditures per trainee, eight teacher variables, six infrastructure and equipment characteristics, 19 curricular structure variables, and nine variables characterizing the link between the course content and the institution's knowledge in regard to workers and occupational analysis of labor demand. These variables are combined into a single quality index using principal components analysis (Chong and Galdo, 2006).

system is likely to reduce workers' incentives to pay into the system for services that they might otherwise obtain free, or at a very low cost if workers are informal (Levy, 2008). This implies that many workers' nonparticipation in social security is a matter of choice rather than exclusion (Auerbach, Genoni, and Pagés, 2007; Perry et al., 2007).

Low valuations are a problem, because accordingly social security contributions become a tax on employment. Studies suggest that on average workers pay for a substantive part of this tax in the form of lower wages (Heckman and Pagés, 2004; Betcherman and Pagés, 2007). However, evidence also implies larger adverse employment effects for low-income workers who are less willing to trade off protection for lower wages (Taymaz, 2006). The former suggests the need to monitor more closely workers' valuations of social security and other programs paid for through wage contributions. Surveys eliciting a combination of objective and subjective data on workers' preferences, in the spirit of the ones discussed in this chapter, can be useful in this regard.

If the low valuation of the programs is confirmed, and if governments consider it important to provide health and pension benefits to workers who do not pay into the programs individually, alternative ways of funding social security for low-income workers should be considered. One possibility would be to make social security contributions more progressive, reducing tax rates for workers with lower earnings and funding their benefits with broad-based taxes, such as value-added taxes. This, however, is not an easy matter in a region where tax collection is low. Other alternatives may imply implementing tax incentives to foster saving for retirement, which could be particularly relevant for self-employed workers with low participation in social security programs. One objective would be to reduce the proliferation of programs targeting formal and informal workers separately and ensure that all workers are guaranteed similar benefits regardless of their occupation.

Innovations Required

There is an urgent need to develop policy innovations that improve the current situation and are at the same time compatible with the needs and administrative capacities of the countries of the Latin American region. Implementing changes in the labor market is notoriously difficult, but the expected gains can be large. Reforms should be achieved in a consensual manner, creating a framework for social dialogue that incorporates all interested parties and achieves long-lasting consensus. A fruitful social dialogue remains a challenge in many countries, developed and developing alike; however, examples of successful dialogue between government, employers, and workers' representatives exist. Cases in the region include Barbados and Panama (Fashoyin, 2004) and Chile, leading up to the 2008 pension reform.

Lastly, as emphasized in this chapter, innovations in measurement could be of great help in achieving better labor market institutions and policies, which in turn could foster better job creation. Traditional measures of job quality based on formal/informal categories have shown only limited validity in policy design. To assume, for example, that all workers aspire to be salaried employees with benefits mandated by law may greatly disregard the complexity of the matter and prevent the design of labor regulations, policies, and safety nets that reconcile social and individual objectives. In order to steer policies in a better direction, it would help to have a better sense of which key work attributes affect workers' welfare, of how workers value different public programs and policies, and of their willingness to pay—in the form of lower wages—for mandatory programs or reforms. Gathering information on workers' preferences in regard to work and labor policy may also provide useful bargaining chips to governments when negotiating reforms that stand to benefit the majority but are blocked by minorities. Finally, it is important to be mindful that workers' preferences and experiences can vary substantially across gender, race, age, location, and other dimensions. Therefore, data that document such differences should be collected and taken into account in the design of policies. Such heterogeneity is difficult to reflect when working with surveys as small as the ones discussed in this chapter. These shortcomings notwithstanding, the analysis presented herein points to the many potential benefits of collecting this type of data.

Urban Quality of Life:
More Than Bricks and Mortar

Socrates, we have strong evidence that the city pleased you;
for you would never have stayed
if you had not been better pleased with it. — Plato

Cities in Latin America and the Caribbean have been powerful magnets for rural populations in search of economic opportunities. While in Asia less than 40 percent of the population lives in cities and towns, 77 percent of the population in Latin America and the Caribbean (hereafter "Latin America") is urban. Today, cities are home to nearly two-thirds of the region's 209 million poor people. Although urban expansion in Latin America has proceeded at the fastest pace of any region in the world, the region has nonetheless managed to democratize home ownership and to provide basic services to most homes. Two out of every three families own their homes, and even among poor families, the majority are owners of the places in which they live. Nearly 95 percent of the urban population has electricity, and over 85 percent has running water and even telephone service (thanks to the recent expansion of cellular service). Nonetheless, significant gaps remain in services (especially sanitation) in a number of countries and cities, and many homes have not been built with appropriate materials or to proper standards.

Improving the quality of life in cities is no longer a simple matter of bricks and mortar. Although four out of five people in Latin America express satisfaction with their homes and with the situation of their cities, most acknowledge that their satisfaction would increase if other problems were resolved. The most-pressing problem in the region is the climate of insecurity. Almost 60 percent of the people in Latin America feel unsafe walking alone at night in their neighborhoods. No other region of the world suffers from such a climate of insecurity.

Many of the needs that Latin American cities must address, such as transportation, quality of public spaces, or recreational opportunities, elude generalization because diversity is the essence of urban life. Different people seek different things in the same city, and every city, even every neighborhood, responds differently to the diversity of interests and needs of its residents.

Housing prices can be a good barometer for some of the things people need. In eight cities studied (Bogotá, Buenos Aires, La Paz, Lima, Medellín, Montevideo, San

José, Costa Rica, and Santa Cruz, Bolivia) it was found that home values clearly depend on neighborhood features, ranging from street lighting and cleaning to distance from the city's cultural sites (though in a different way in each city). Using this method (called hedonic pricing), it is possible to calculate the contribution that each city facility and service makes to the price of each home. However, not everything that affects the quality of life is accurately reflected in housing prices. An alternative method (known as the life satisfaction method) can be used to calculate the value of city facilities and services based on their contribution to the quality of life.

The combination of these two valuation methods makes it possible to identify which city or neighborhood problems tend be solved by the market, and which ones require the intervention of local governments. It also helps identify those problem areas for which it is possible to finance solutions with taxes tied to home values.

Because cities vary greatly, both methods require the establishment of detailed quality of life monitoring systems that can help local governments identify priorities for action and financing sources to respond to the diverse needs of urban populations. Such systems can also help identify problems of racial segregation, social exclusion, geographic marginalization, and absence of community values, whose solutions are crucial if cities are to be successful.

The Great Urban Expansion

Since the mid-twentieth century, the urbanization process in Latin America has progressed more rapidly than in any other region (see Figure 8.1). Squalid living conditions in the countryside due to the concentration of land ownership in the hands of a few families, and the low productivity of the work of campesinos and tenant farmers, sparked a process of migration from rural areas to cities that continues in many countries. The driving force of the great expansion of Bogotá, Caracas, Lima, and Mexico City since the 1960s has been rural migration, intensified by still-high fertility rates and by lower (and rapidly falling) infant mortality rates in the cities. In the 1960s and 1970s, a large number of foreigners, who were more educated and had more capital than destitute campesinos and rural workers, migrated to some large cities, such as São Paulo. But this was exceptional. Urban expansion has mostly been driven by internal migration, and the new city dwellers have tended to have little or no education or capital. Moreover, guerrillas and armed conflicts in rural areas in Peru in the 1980s, in Guatemala, El Salvador, and Nicaragua for several decades, and more recently in Colombia have speeded up the migration process to the large cities among the impoverished inhabitants of rural areas.

In this way, the migration process has led to the urbanization of poverty. Currently, although the poverty rate is higher in the countryside, the poor are concentrated in urban areas. Of the 190 million poor residents of Latin America in 2007 (representing 35 percent of the population), 130 million are estimated to live in urban areas (ECLAC, 2007). Because large cities are dominant in Latin America, the possibility of the urban poor escaping poverty and improving their quality of life is crucially dependent on the opportunities and conditions that those cities offer.

Latin America has four of the world's 20 cities that have over 10 million inhabitants, and 55 of the world's 414 cities that have over one million people. These 55 cities are home to a total of 183 million people, one-third of all Latin Americans. However, the larg-

est cities are no longer the fastest growing. In Argentina, Brazil, Chile, and Mexico, which urbanized more rapidly and
are more advanced in the demographic
transition process than most of the region's other countries, megacities are
growing more slowly and losing importance in relation to intermediate cities.
As expected, the cities that are growing
most rapidly at present are in countries
where population growth is still high and
urbanization rates are low. As a result of
this redistribution of urban growth, the
urban population throughout the region
has been gradually dispersing from large
to intermediate cities.[1]

Instability, both political and economic, also seems to have had an impact
on urban growth patterns in recent de-
cades. Migration processes are triggered not only by the conflicts in the countryside, but
also by irregular changes of power in the cities. There is an inconclusive debate about
the reasons, but it is possible that proximity to power is an attraction for relocating to
large cities when regular mechanisms for allocation of public resources weaken. The fact
that economic instability, and not only economic growth, contributes to accelerating
the growth of large cities suggests that they offer better opportunities for improving
income, as well as for coping with economic risks.[2]

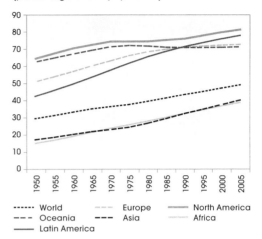

Figure 8.1 Urban Population by Continents
(percentage of total population)

Legend:
- ······ World
- − − − Oceania
- ——— Latin America
- − − − Europe
- − − − Asia
- ——— North America
- ········ Africa

Source: Cristini and Moya (2008), based on UN (2008b).

Home Ownership and Services

The expansion of Latin American cities in the second half of the twentieth century produced a democratization of home ownership at rates unprecedented in the region and
possibly in the world. Around 1950, roughly only one in four families in Buenos Aires,
Mexico City, or Santiago, Chile, owned their own home (see Table 8.1), but now about
two-thirds of families are home owners in those cities. Nevertheless, in Colombia home
ownership has stabilized at lower levels and has even decreased slightly according to
recent statistics. The most recent surveys of urban areas in 22 countries show average
ownership rates of 68.4 percent (Table 8.2). This rate is higher than that in other developing countries and very close to that of the United States (69 percent), which has very
developed mortgage markets and a long tradition of incentives for home ownership
(Fay and Wellenstein, 2005). In the region as a whole, the urban home ownership rate is
higher among families with higher incomes (71 percent versus 64 percent), but this average difference of 7 percent masks some more-marked cases. In Uruguay, for example,

---

[1] According to Cristini and Moya (2008), the Hirschman-Herfindahl concentration index of urban population decreased by half between 1950 and 2005.
[2] See the theoretical and empirical analysis of Ades and Glaeser (1995) and Gaviria and Stein (2000).

Table 8.1 **Home Ownership**
(percentage of families who own the houses in which they live)

	1947–1952	1970–1973	1990–1993	1998–2002
Bogotá	43	42	54	52
Buenos Aires	27	61	72	75
Guadalajara	29	43	68	62
Medellín	51	57	63	56
Mexico City	25	43	70	76
Rio de Janeiro	33	54	63	75
Santiago	26	57	71	73

Sources: Gilbert (2001), UN-Habitat (2003), and DANE (1998–2002).

home ownership is over 75 percent for higher-income families and just 44 percent for lower-income families.

The democratization of housing in cities in rapid expansion in the second half of the twentieth century occurred spontaneously, largely based on irregular acquisition of land by rural immigrants and the poor urban classes. Methods of acquisition ranged from the purchase of suburban land without subdivision permits to de facto occupation

Table 8.2 **Home Ownership Rates by Income**
(urban areas)

	Low income	High income	Average
Argentina	58.4	70.6	66.0
Bahamas	51.9	61.8	57.7
Bolivia	55.4	55.0	53.9
Brazil	65.3	73.1	69.9
Chile	59.8	69.2	65.9
Colombia	57.8	64.1	60.0
Costa Rica	69.1	74.2	72.2
Dominican Republic	59.3	58.3	59.3
Ecuador	70.6	69.5	69.4
El Salvador	56.3	71.0	66.0
Guatemala	71.1	70.0	70.0
Guyana	31.3	42.9	40.6
Haiti	47.3	45.2	46.0
Honduras	57.2	62.0	59.2
Jamaica	57.2	48.5	52.5
Mexico	67.3	71.8	69.5
Nicaragua	67.6	79.6	76.6
Paraguay	75.6	74.2	74.4
Peru	55.1	70.0	65.7
Suriname	65.4	67.1	63.7
Uruguay	43.9	75.5	64.0
Venezuela	77.2	74.3	75.3
Latin America (weighted average)	63.6	71.3	68.4

Sources: Cristini and Moya (2008), based on the Socio-Economic Database for Latin America and the Caribbean (SEDLAC) (http://www.depeco.econo.unlp.edu.ar/cedlas/sedlac/).
Note: "Low income" corresponds to the lowest two quintiles and "high income" to the highest two quintiles. The data are taken from household surveys, and they may differ from census data.

of privately or officially owned land. For example, most of the settlements of poor families in Peru originated through land occupations. The district of San Juan de Lurigancho in Lima, where over 830,000 people now live (representing over 10 percent of the population of the city), was formed in the 1960s as an irregular settlement area, like most of the districts in the three "cones" that extend toward the desert to the north, east, and south of Lima (Reid, 2007). Occasionally, occupations have been permitted by the government, as was the case in some Brazilian and Mexican cities in the 1970s and 1980s, in Santiago, Chile, before 1973, and in Lima during the administration of President Odría (1948–1950). However, not all irregular settlements in the region originated from illegal occupations. Currently, a large part of that illegality is only nominal, in the sense of non-compliance with planning regulations or the absence of relevant title deeds to confirm voluntary transfers of ownership. Many of the region's governments have implemented ownership title programs to solve this problem. For instance, the military government in Chile handed over more than half a million title deeds between 1979 and 1989, and the two democratic governments that followed distributed another 150,000 title deeds up to 1998 (Rugiero Pérez, 1998). In Peru, the Commission for Formalization of Informal Ownership recorded over one million titles between 1996 and 2000 (Calderón, 2001). But even today, about 20 percent of the home owners in low socioeconomic strata in Latin America lack deeds, and some countries exhibit much worse levels (see Figure 8.2).[3] The lack of title deeds has contributed to disorderly development of home building in large Latin American cities. For example, it has been calculated that in 1990, 60 percent of the population of Mexico City lived in self-built houses, and the situation was similar in Caracas (42 percent) and Lima (38 percent) (Gilbert, 2001).

Forty or fifty years after the great urban expansion, relatively high percentages of homes have now been built to acceptable standards of construction and have access to basic services. What does and does not constitute an acceptable home has been the subject of intense debate among economists, architects, urban planners, and sociologists in Latin America for several decades. All agree that no universal standard can be defined, because basic requirements depend on climate, building methods, customs and, in the last instance, individual needs and tastes. A simple standard, imposed more by available information than by conceptual rigor, consists of defining

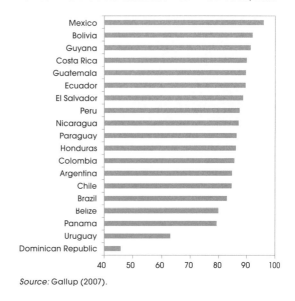

Figure 8.2 Percentage of Home Owners in the Lowest Two Income Quintiles with Title Deeds, 2007

Source: Gallup (2007).

---

[3] The statistics in Figure 8.2 have large margins of error because of the small size of the samples (approximately 1,000 households).

"unfit housing" as that built with low-quality materials according to the standards of each country. Using this criterion for a set of 65 cities in the region that account for over half of the urban population, an average of 18 percent of homes are unfit. However, this average hides a distribution with rates of unfit housing ranging from 5 percent to almost 20 percent in 17 of the 22 largest cities in the region. The rates are particularly alarming as well in intermediate cities of Bolivia, Mexico, and Brazil.

Apart from the quality of building materials, access to basic services of sanitation, water, electricity and, more debatably, telephone connection is considered a basic requirement for good-quality housing. Although there are notable disparities between countries, access to electricity is practically universal in the urban areas of the region (95 percent of homes have this service) and access to running water is high (86 percent). In contrast, a very high percentage of homes have no connection to sanitation networks (coverage is only 60 percent) and telephone service (average coverage of landline telephones is 61 percent, but coverage rises to 87 percent when mobile telephones are included).[4] These differences are reflected in access gaps by socioeconomic group, which tend to be moderated for electricity and water services, but are much more substantial for sanitation and telephone services. However, based on the Socio-Economic Database for Latin America and the Caribbean (SEDLAC), there are access gaps of over 20 percentage points in electricity in Haiti and water in El Salvador, Paraguay, and Peru. In sanitation, countries with relatively high income levels—such as Argentina, Brazil, Mexico, and Uruguay—have access gaps of over 30 points (see Table 8.3).

Democratization of access to services has advanced at a much more modest rate than democratization of ownership or improvement of home building materials. But each city is a different story. Of the five cities considered in Figures 8.3, 8.4, and 8.5 (Buenos Aires, Caracas, Lima, Mexico City, and São Paulo), Caracas is the city where access to public services is most extensive and equal. Still, even in Caracas, one out of three homes among the families in the three lowest income deciles suffers from basic deficiencies in building materials. In Buenos Aires and São Paulo, few homes are considered unfit, at least by official standards, but in Buenos Aires, four out of five homes of those in the lowest decile lack sanitation, water, or telephone, and in São Paulo, less than half the families in the three lowest deciles own their homes. In Lima and Mexico City, home ownership rates are not high, but there is not much difference between rates among the rich and poor. Both of these cities have made enormous efforts to provide basic services to all homes, but 15 percent of homes in the poorest decile in Mexico City and 33 percent in Lima are still without one of the basic services. The poorest families in these two cities will have to make a great effort to improve their homes: in Mexico City there is a 35-point difference between the highest and lowest deciles in percentage of unfit homes, and in Lima the difference is 27 points (Cristini and Moya, 2008).

Housing Deficits

How far are Latin American cities from solving the most basic deficiencies of home building and provision of water, sanitation, and electricity services? This has been a

---

[4] Figures for telephone coverage come from the Gallup World Polls, whose margins of error are substantially greater than those of official household surveys, from which the other figures are taken.

Table 8.3 Public Services Coverage in Urban Areas and the Coverage Gap between the Highest and Lowest Two Quintiles

	Year	Sanitation		Water		Electricity		Telephone		Telephone/Cellphone	
		Coverage	Gap	Coverage	Gap	Coverage	Gap	Coverage	Gap	Coverage	Gap
Argentina	2003	60.4	39.2	98.4	4.0	99.5	1.2	64.8	39.5	93.0	11.1
Bahamas	2001	12.8	-0.1	86.7	12.4	96.1	5.7	n.d.	n.d.	n.d.	n.d.
Belize	1999	n.d.	n.d.	n.d.	n.d.	n.d.	n.d.	62.7	38.9	93.3	n.d.
Bolivia	2003–04	61.2	-3.2	90.2	9.7	92.5	6.1	45.5	27.0	86.6	11.0
Brazil	2005	65.5	30.2	95.6	9.9	99.6	0.9	95.7	7.0	98.0	4.0
Chile	2003	91.8	11.2	99.3	1.3	99.7	0.6	69.8	24.9	93.1	13.0
Colombia	2004	87.6	10.4	89.9	5.2	90.4	4.6	76.2	13.7	94.9	4.8
Costa Rica	2005	43.4	5.8	98.9	0.6	99.9	0.2	74.1	15.0	87.8	14.2
Dominican Republic	2006	32.3	14.6	80.6	18.9	94.4	4.7	40.6	43.8	84.9	20.1
Ecuador	2003	67.4	28.7	91.1	9.7	99.3	1.2	49.3	39.2	77.9	31.5
El Salvador	2004	50.6	30.7	73.7	23.8	90.7	14.4	59.0	19.2	87.2	8.9
Guatemala	2004	66.7	23.9	77.9	0.8	96.0	11.0	42.9	25.1	84.3	14.0
Guyana	1992–93	1.6	-3.3	88.7	7.3	91.0	14.6	83.3	1.6	95.2	0.4
Haiti	2001	n.d.	n.d.	23.2	11.1	61.9	28.7	n.d.	n.d.	n.d.	n.d.
Honduras	2006	63.8	31.1	n.d.	n.d.	97.0	10.1	51.3	5.8	70.5	6.7
Jamaica	2002	32.9	1.3	65.3	12.0	92.3	6.3	n.d.	n.d.	n.d.	n.d.
Mexico	2005	69.5	37.1	94.9	8.9	99.6	1.0	68.4	20.3	81.4	23.3
Nicaragua	2005	36.4	23.8	89.5	13.4	95.5	12.8	37.1	32.4	79.5	18.8
Paraguay	2005	15.0	14.7	89.7	20.1	98.4	3.8	40.1	48.0	82.6	28.9
Peru	2006	77.6	34.3	83.4	23.8	96.3	12.6	58.2	50.5	82.2	29.1
Suriname	1999	97.8	0.1	87.3	7.4	99.3	0.2	n.d.	n.d.	n.d.	n.d.
Uruguay	2005	66.2	38.3	98.8	1.5	99.3	1.9	71.9	42.1	90.1	21.4
Venezuela	2002	95.1	5.7	93.9	6.7	99.1	0.9	69.2	24.5	89.8	12.6
Average		56.9	17.8	85.6	9.9	94.9	6.5	61.1	27.3	87.0	15.2

Source: Cristini and Moya (2008), based on SEDLAC (http://www.depeco.econo.unlp.edu.ar/cedlas/sedlac/). Data for telephone coverage are from Gallup (2007).
Note: n.d. = no data.

Figure 8.3 Percentage of Home Owners by Income Deciles

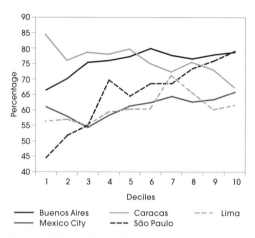

Source: Cristini and Moya (2008).

Figure 8.4 Percentage of Unfit Households by Income Deciles

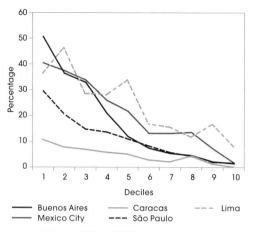

Source: Cristini and Moya (2008).

Figure 8.5 Percentage of Households Lacking Any Public Services by Income Deciles

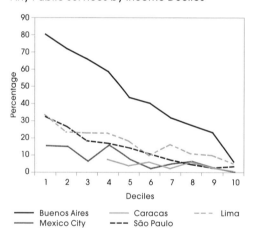

Source: Cristini and Moya (2008).

recurring question that is usually tackled on the basis of calculations of the "quantitative" and "qualitative" housing deficits. The former is the difference between the number of households and the number of homes, and the latter is a measure of the quality of housing based on quality of building materials, access to services, or other criteria. ECLAC and CELADE (1996) estimate that in 1995, the total (quantitative and qualitative) deficit in all countries in the region was 53 million homes, which was equivalent at that time to 54 percent of the housing stock. The quantitative deficit was calculated at 28 million homes, and the qualitative deficit (defined simply as lack of connection to running water) at 25 million homes. The most recent estimates, which have used more-refined criteria for calculating the deficit, reveal alarming total deficits: 64 percent of total housing in Bolivia and between 27 percent and 40 percent in Chile, Colombia, and Uruguay (Szalachman, 2000).

The main limitation of these calculations is their attempt to cover everything, which means imposing homogeneous criteria across countries, across rural and urban areas, and between cities, based on a very small number of variables. Because each city presents a different case, it can be more informative and more useful for policy purposes to analyze each city separately, based on the best information available in each instance. Another crucial limitation is that the deficit expressed as a number (or percentage) of homes does not convey the seriousness of the deficiencies or the cost of fixing them.

A recent study by Cristini and Moya (2008) is a step in the direction of quantifying housing deficits in a more-refined way. For 64 cities, they calculate quantitative deficits using the traditional definition (households less homes), and qualitative deficits according to the quality of materials (based on local standards) and access to water and sanitation services. They also calculate the costs of addressing the deficits, taking into account, city by city, housing prices at low levels (implicit in rental values), the possibility of refurbishing existing homes (using standard materials), and the cost of connecting to services. Table 8.4 summarizes the results for 17 of the largest cities included in this recent study. Eliminating the basic deficits of housing, water, and sanitation would require an investment equivalent to 8 percent, on average, of one year's GDP of the cities considered. About half of this cost relates to improving unfit homes built with deficient materials. Various Brazilian cities have considerable challenges in this area, with costs of over 10 percent of city GDP in the cases of Recife and Fortaleza, but for other large cities in the region—such as Mexico City, Greater Buenos Aires, or São Paulo—this represents less than 4 percent of their GDP. Correcting quantitative housing deficits would cost over 7 percent of local GDP in Bogotá and Recife, but in other cities the costs are modest and would represent only 3.3 percent, on average, of their GDP. The fixed cost of the investment in infrastructure needed to provide universal access to water and sanitation services would be equivalent to only 1 percent, on average, of the GDP of most cities (although in Greater Buenos Aires this cost would be 2.5 percent of GDP and in Fortaleza and Recife, over 5 percent). If spread through a period of, say, 10 years, these costs are modest, even after the additional requirements imposed by the expansion of the cities are included.[5]

However refined they may be, calculations of housing deficits and the cost of eliminating them are no more than an illustrative but hypothetical exercise, because they do not take into account the demand side. Who would be willing to pay for such improvements or connections to services? If the families cannot afford to pay these costs, would payment by national or local governments be justified? Moreover, if resources are not sufficient to remedy all deficits at once, which ones should get priority?

Housing deficits have another implicit limitation with respect to guiding policy decisions: they are based on only some aspects of housing and ignore the multitude of factors that affect the quality of urban life beyond the physical characteristics of housing. Provision of public spaces, quality of public transport, and public safety can be as important as, or more important than, the characteristics of housing, depending naturally on individual conditions and tastes.

Cross-Country Evidence on City and Home Satisfaction

An alternative approach is to consider people's opinions about their homes and living conditions in their cities to understand what their most important needs are. Based on results from the 2007 wave of the Gallup World Poll, the conclusion is that the great majority of Latin Americans claim they are satisfied with both their homes and their cities.

---

[5] Fay (2001) calculated the cost of addressing the growing requirements of water and sanitation in Latin America in 2000–2005 at 0.05 percent to 0.18 percent of GDP.

Table 8.4 Qualitative and Quantitative Housing Deficits and the Costs of Urban Infrastructure Improvement Policies

Country	City (ordered by population size)	Housing deficits		Unfit households		Households without sanitation or water	
		Quantitative deficit		Unfit households			
		Percentage of households	Cost to address (percentage of city's GDP)	Percentage of households	Cost to address (percentage of city's GDP)	Percentage of households	Cost to address (percentage of city's GDP)
Mexico	Mexico City	3.6	1.7	15.8	3.6	6.2	0.3
Brazil	São Paulo	4.8	3.0	12.4	2.5	13.7	0.7
Argentina	Greater Buenos Aires	3.7	2.6	13.5	4.0	41.2	2.5
Brazil	Rio de Janeiro	6.1	6.2	12.7	5.5	9.4	0.8
Colombia	Bogotá	12.1	7.5	n.d.	n.d.	n.d.	n.d.
Peru	Greater Lima	4.8	2.2	17.3	3.4	15.8	1.7
Brazil	Belo Horizonte	6.5	4.6	19.2	5.0	14.4	1.0
Mexico	Guadalajara	5.4	2.2	10.5	2.0	4.5	0.3
Brazil	Porto Alegre	5.3	4.6	10.9	3.5	15.3	1.3
Mexico	Monterrey	4.5	2.6	9.3	0.4	0.9	0.0
Brazil	Recife	10.3	8.7	50.6	18.5	56.0	5.2
Brazil	Brasília	3.3	1.5	10.3	2.0	17.1	1.0
Brazil	Salvador	9.2	6.3	20.5	6.0	14.6	1.0
Brazil	Fortaleza	10.2	6.6	41.7	11.6	49.2	5.1
Colombia	Medellín	4.1	2.8	n.d.	n.d.	n.d.	n.d.
Venezuela	Caracas	n.d.	n.d.	5.6	1.6	4.2	0.3
Brazil	Curitiba	4.9	3.8	17.6	5.8	20.5	1.3

Source: Cristini and Moya (2008), based on household surveys and national census data.
Note: n.d. = no data.

Table 8.5 Satisfaction with Homes and Cities
(percentage)

	Satisfied with own home	Satisfied with own city	Own city is improving
East Asia and Pacific	82.1	87.2	68.6
Eastern Europe and Central Asia	75.2	79.8	60.5
Latin America	79.7	79.5	52.9
Middle East and North Africa	80.0	79.4	72.5
North America	n.d.	88.0	57.9
South Asia	87.6	87.5	67.3
Sub-Saharan Africa	62.2	69.7	55.2
Western Europe	89.9	92.4	50.2

Source: Gallup (2007).
Note: n.d.= no data.

The percentage is almost identical, on average, for both questions (79.7 percent for hous-ing satisfaction, 79.5 percent for city satisfaction) and is also close to the answer obtained in other regions of the developed or developing world—with the exception of Sub-Saharan Africa, where the percentages are significantly lower (Table 8.5). In Latin Amer-ica, the highest satisfaction rates for both home and city are in Guatemala (90.6 percent and 92.5 percent, respectively). The lowest satisfaction rates with housing are found in Haiti and Trinidad and Tobago (57 percent and 66 percent), and in regard to satisfaction with the city, the lowest rates are found in Haiti and Peru (49 percent and 70 percent).

Opinions are more critical and rather more diverse on the question "Would you say that the city/area where you live is improving or worsening as a place to live?" Only 53 percent of Latin Americans answer affirmatively, ranging from a low 36.4 percent in Uruguay to 66.3 percent in Ecuador. But again, opinions of Latin Americans are not sub-stantially different from those in the rest of the world (the most favorable opinions are in the Middle East and North Africa at 72.5 percent, and the most pessimistic opinions are in Western Europe at 50.2 percent).

An analysis of the overall levels of satisfaction people have with their home and city (see Table 8.6) reveals that these levels do not, in general, correlate with objective conditions. Economic conditions of each country affect perceptions in ways that are not fully consistent with predictions of conventional economics. While higher levels of income per capita are associated (in a statistically significant way) with higher levels of satisfaction with housing and cities, in contrast, the growth rate of income per capita is *inversely* as-sociated with satisfaction with housing. (Income growth is also negatively associated with satisfaction with the city, but this result is not statistically significant.) The unconventional association between economic growth and satisfaction is present in many other dimen-sions of people's lives, giving origin to the so-called unhappy growth paradox, introduced in Chapter 3, which suggests that satisfaction is influenced by aspirations that increase with economic growth as individuals contrast their own consumption with that of others.

Evidence from Individual Surveys on Satisfaction with Housing

Individual data are often more informative than country-level data when describing satisfaction with housing. Housing quality and the provision of neighborhood services

Table 8.6 How Home and City Satisfaction Relates to Some National-Level Variables

Independent variables	Satisfaction with own home		Satisfaction with own city		Own city is improving	
			Dependent variables			
Natural logarithm, GDP per capita, 2005	0.0544***	0.0470***	0.0573***	0.0558***	0.0362*	0.0317
Real annual average GDP per capita growth, 2000–2005	–0.0084**	–0.0099*	–0.0003	–0.0009	0.0183**	0.0166*
Urban population growth, 1950–2000	0.0012	0.0049	0.0173*	0.0197*	0.0465***	0.0248
Constant	0.3499***	0.4448**	0.2765*	0.2579	0.0909	0.2225
Regional dummies	Yes	No	Yes	No	Yes	No
Number of observations	91	91	76	76	68	68
Pseudo-R^2	0.4356	0.5538	0.2798	0.4078	0.2365	0.3586

Source: Authors' calculations based on Gallup (2007).
Note: The calculations stem from ordinary least squares regressions.
*Coefficient is statistically significant at the 10 percent level; **at the 5 percent level; ***at the 1 percent level; no asterisk means the coefficient is not different from zero with statistical significance.

vary greatly within countries and even within cities. Individual opinions provide an interesting and at least complementary, if not superior, avenue for research. The results across individuals in many countries can be used to answer questions such as what basic characteristics of homes allow Latin Americans to be satisfied with their houses. One very important feature that stands out is access to services, which justifies why this characteristic is usually identified as one of the criteria for defining qualitative housing deficits. Based on Gallup (2007) data, access to running water increases the probability of people being satisfied with their homes by 34 percent, and having access to telephone service increases the probability by 22 percent, assuming that the other characteristics of the homes and the families that inhabit them are the same (see list of control variables in Table 8.7).

Possession of title deeds is also closely associated with satisfaction with the home: there is a 50 percent higher probability that family members will be satisfied with their homes if they have deeds, regardless of other basic characteristics of the home or household, including home ownership, which in itself does not seem to be an important factor. Indeed, having a title deed, and not simply being the owner of the home, raises the probability of being satisfied with the home. This is relevant because although home ownership rates are high even among families in the two poorest urban quintiles, about 20 percent of the homes owned by these families lack title deeds.

Hernando de Soto (2000) emphasizes the importance of title deeds for facilitating access to credit and releasing the productive potential of the capital of the poor. However, empirical studies do not support this hypothesis, possibly because access to credit for the poor can be restricted for other reasons. For instance, creditors may be hard pressed to take possession and recover the homes offered as collateral when debtors default on their obligations (IDB, 2004). An interesting study compares the behavior of families in Buenos Aires who have obtained title deeds with that of families identical in all other respects who have not had the good fortune to obtain deeds. Those with deeds tend to invest more in improving their homes and have fewer non–family members living with them, possibly because they feel less of a need to maintain ties of solidarity as a precaution against the risk of being left homeless (Galiani and Schargrodsky, 2007). Consequently, increased satisfaction with the home among those with title deeds may be reflected in physical improvements within the home and the space available for family members. It may also reflect a greater sense of security.

Many other characteristics of the home, apart from access to services and possession of title deeds, can influence satisfaction. Evidently, families with higher incomes can have homes that are suited more to their tastes, as confirmed by the analysis in the previous section. An individual in the richest quintile, for example, has a 16 percent higher probability of feeling satisfied with his or her home than someone from the next quintile (similar in all other basic aspects). But although income level contributes to satisfaction with housing, aspirations operate in the opposite direction, as discussed in Chapter 3.

Table 8.7 Factors Contributing to House Satisfaction

	How much does the probability of being satisfied with one's house increase when...
House characteristics	
House has water	34.082***
Someone in the house has a telephone	22.232**
House has electricity	–4.843
Family owns the house	26.179*
Family has a title deed	50.172***
Personal characteristics	
Woman	5.053
Age	–5.315***
Age-squared	0.061***
Family characteristics	
Children at school	–0.418
Number of household members	0.581
Number of children at home	–3.120
Income quintile	16.336***
Country fixed effects	Yes
Number of observations	6,371
R^2	0.056

Source: Authors' calculations based on Gallup (2007).
Note: The calculations regarding probabilities stem from logit regression coefficients.
*Coefficient is statistically significant at the 10 percent level; **at the 5 percent level; ***at the 1 percent level; no asterisk means the coefficient is not different from zero with statistical significance.

What Does Satisfaction with the City Depend On?

While satisfaction with the home is an important element of overall life satisfaction, satisfaction with the urban area where that home is located may be at least as important. Again, using the Gallup World Poll data across many countries, the way in which Latin Americans perceive aspects of their cities can be compared to that in other regions.

When urban areas of Latin America are compared with other regions of the world in various dimensions (Table 8.8), public safety appears as the weakest point of the region's cities, which is reflected in the low percentage of people in the region (41.6 percent in 2006) who feel safe walking alone at night in their cities or residential areas. This percentage is not far from that of the former communist countries of Europe and Asia or the countries of Sub-Saharan Africa, but is substantially lower than in other re-

Table 8.8 Regional Average Percentage of People...

	Satisfied with the following aspects of cities:							Who feel:
	Public transport	Roads	Education system	Health system	Quality and price of available housing	Air quality	Water quality	Safe walking alone at night
East Asia and Pacific	76.2	75.5	79.6	80.9	71.1	72.1	82.4	70.5
Eastern Europe and Central Asia	66.4	42.6	57.6	41.4	37.6	45.7	53.1	44.8
Latin America	59.4	54.1	68.0	59.2	48.8	68.7	74.1	41.6
Middle East and North Africa	65.6	61.0	63.4	62.5	46.8	53.6	59.1	69.7
North America	67.3	61.1	66.9	72.7	49.4	70.7	85.3	72.2
South Asia	78.1	69.6	83.0	75.2	52.6	76.2	72.8	69.8
Sub-Saharan Africa	47.2	40.1	58.2	49.0	43.5	63.4	60.8	47.5
Western Europe	75.5	75.8	81.3	81.2	39.8	70.2	87.8	68.2
By how much is Latin America above or below the world pattern?	4.6	1.5	1.6	0.7	-1.5	2.2	6.8***	-17.4***

Source: Gallup (2007).
Note: The table shows simple regional averages of country data, except the last row. In this row, each of the values is the coefficient of a dummy variable for Latin American countries in a country-level regression in which the dependent variable is the rate of satisfaction and the explanatory variables are income per capita and the dummy variable.
***Coefficient is statistically significant at the 1 percent level; no asterisk means the coefficient is not different from zero with statistical significance.

gions of the world. Latin Americans have one of the highest victimization rates in the world (based on the number of people who report having had money stolen from them or being mugged during the previous 12 months), second only to Sub-Saharan Africa.

Not a single Latin American country has managed to create a climate of real urban security. Safety perceptions and confidence in police are low in the region. The lowest safety perceptions are found in Brazil, Argentina, and Chile. However, confidence in police is high in some of the countries most affected by fears of insecurity, such as Chile (Figures 8.6 and 8.7). This contrast raises the question of the extent to which people's perceptions are shaped by the objective reality of their surroundings. Perceptions may not correctly reflect the real risks that people face: some of the countries where the population feels safest have very high homicide rates, even by regional standards.[6]

The relationship between crime, safety, and income is not straightfoward. In line with the findings of Gaviria and Pagés (2002), using data from the Latinobarometer, the Gallup World Poll data reveal higher reporting of crime victimization among people with higher incomes in Latin America, but not in the rest of the world (Figure 8.8). On the other hand, the perception of being unsafe at night differs very little from one social level to another, in both Latin America and the rest of the world, as Figure 8.9 shows.

---

[6] The 2007 homicide rate per 100,000 inhabitants was 59 in Jamaica and 30 in Trinidad and Tobago (*The Economist*, January 31, 2008).

Of the various aspects of the cities considered in the Gallup World Polls, only one gives people in Latin America significantly more satisfaction than would be expected given the income level of the countries: water quality (see Table 8.8). Three out of four Latin Americans say they are satisfied with this public service, with no appreciable differences by socioeconomic stratum; in contrast, there are differences by country (in the Dominican Republic, Guyana, and Haiti less than 60 percent of the population is satisfied with the quality of the service). In the other dimensions of the quality of urban life, the pattern in the region does not differ significantly from the world pattern associated with levels of income per capita.

The opinions of the public on various aspects of their cities can be used to deduce the priorities that people would assign to each of these aspects in order to feel better about their cities. There may be great dissatisfaction with specific aspects of the cities, but that does not mean that the problem should receive the highest priority, or that it has equal priority for all. Only 52 percent of Latin Americans say they are satisfied with the state of sidewalks or pedestrian walks, and only 55 percent express satisfaction with the availability of parks, plazas, and green areas, while 75 percent consider water quality to be satisfactory (a very high proportion by world standards). However, the problem of water could be a priority in relation to other problems for

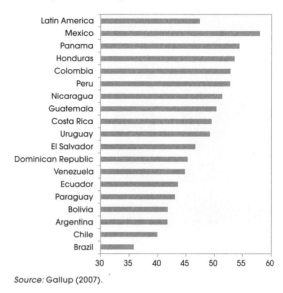

Figure 8.6 Percentage of People Who Feel Safe Walking Alone at Night

Source: Gallup (2007).

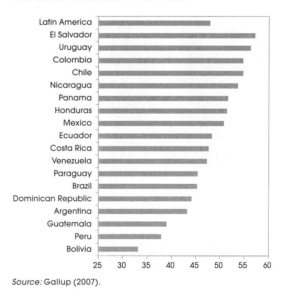

Figure 8.7 Percentage of People Who Have Confidence in Local Police Force

Source: Gallup (2007).

one of three reasons: because it can be more important for individual satisfaction (with one's city or, more generally, with one's own life); because water quality results in benefits for people and society that individuals do not consider in their subjective judgments; or because, compared with other problems to which the two previous criteria

Figure 8.8 Percentage of People Who Had Money Stolen or Were Mugged in the Preceding 12 Months, by Income Level

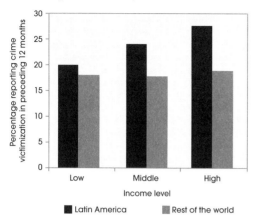

Source: Di Tella and Ñopo (2008), based on Gallup (2007).

Figure 8.9 Percentage of People Who Feel Safe Walking Alone at Night in City, by Income Level

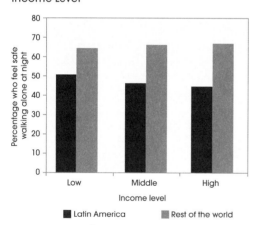

Source: Di Tella and Ñopo (2008), based on Gallup (2007).

may apply, solving the problem of water could be cheapest. This section is concerned only with the first of these criteria. The others require a discussion that is beyond the scope of this volume, but should be borne in mind when trying to draw policy implications from the analysis that follows.

Figure 8.10 shows the relative influence on the satisfaction of individuals of the various aspects of the quality of urban life covered by the Gallup World Polls, considering the *percentage of people affected* by these problems (according to the information presented) and their *impact on people's satisfaction* with the cities in which they live. To establish the impact on satisfaction, an econometric analysis is used that attempts to identify which aspects of the city contribute best to predicting who would say they are satisfied with their city and who would say they are not. The econometric analysis also considers the fact that satisfaction with the city can depend on an individual's own circumstances and possibilities (gender, age, whether the person works, socioeconomic stratum), his or her housing satisfaction, and any other common factors by country. Some of these controls weigh heavily on one's satisfaction level with one's city, particularly satisfaction with the home; a person who declares satisfaction with his or her home has a 19 percent higher probability of claiming satisfaction with his or her city than a person whose other conditions are identical, but who is not satisfied with his or her home.[7]

As mentioned, problems of safety are very frequent, and high percentages of Latin Americans say they feel unsafe walking alone at night, or that there are gangs or illegal drug trafficking in their residential areas. These three expressions of lack of safety also have a significant impact (statistically) on satisfaction with the city. The com-

---

[7] Gender has no influence on satisfaction with the city, while age has a positive, although not statistically significant, influence that declines with years. Those who have a job tend to feel better about their city, but likewise, this effect is not significant. Economic levels do not have a discernible influence, in one direction or another, on satisfaction with the city. National factors are important for several countries.

Figure 8.10 Importance of Various Urban Problems According to Perceptions

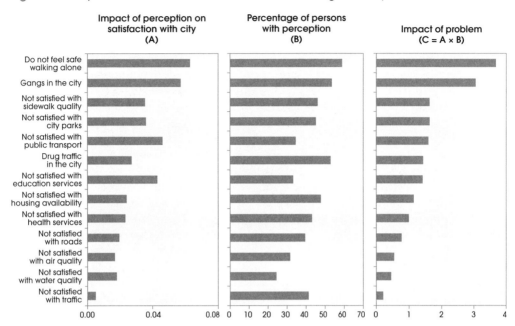

Source: Gallup (2007).
Note: The values in the first panel are the marginal probabilities, that is, how much each factor reduces the probability of being satisfied with one's city. These results come from a logit model for city satisfaction in which the independent variables are those shown in the figure and sex, age, income quintile, employment status, and house satisfaction.

bination of high frequency and impact suggests that safety is the problem that most affects the quality of life in Latin American cities. Naturally, the problem may be more acute in some cities relative to others, as is examined later in the chapter. While safety issues appear to affect all socioeconomic groups, there is evidence that the impact of feeling unsafe is stronger for women than for men (although reported victimization is higher for males). In general, problems of safety affect all age groups equally; however, the presence of illegal drug trafficking and lack of confidence in local police seem to affect the elderly much more.

These patterns of self-reported victimization and perceptions of insecurity have direct links with different aspects of individuals' perceptions of well-being, emotions, and beliefs. Di Tella and Ñopo (2008) point out that, in general, those who report being victimized and those who report the presence of gangs and drug dealing in their neighborhoods are less likely to have felt positive emotions (enjoyment and smiling/laughing a lot) and are more likely to have felt negative emotions (anger, physical pain, worry, sadness, boredom, or depression) the day before. The same results are recorded for those having higher perceptions of corruption in businesses and the government. Those who have not been victimized and have lower perceptions of corruption trust the local police more, feel safer walking alone at night, have better perceptions of the educational opportunities offered by their country to children and to those who want to get ahead through hard work, are more satisfied with the efforts of their country to deal with the poor, and are more likely to think that their country is a good place to start a new business.

Apart from issues of safety, other aspects of cities that affect the quality of life include the existence and quality of sidewalks and pedestrian areas, parks, and public transport. The quality of schools and the availability of housing at affordable prices are somewhat lower in order of importance, but these aspects still have a significant influence on satisfaction with the city. The other aspects considered (quality of health services; roads, highways, and freeways; air quality; water quality; and traffic flow) do not have a significant impact on satisfaction with the city. The fact that traffic appears as the least important of all the problems surveyed is at odds with the severity of the problem in some large cities (see Box 8.1), although this may reflect the fact that the Gallup World Polls are representative at the national level only.

Many dimensions of the quality of urban life tend to have the same effect on people of both high and low socioeconomic statuses, men and women, and individuals of different ages. There are some exceptions: for example, the state of sidewalks or pedestrian walks is more important for those with higher income levels but less important for elderly individuals, and the availability of good housing at affordable prices has less impact for those who are employed. However, this apparently general homogeneity of impacts could be the result of the aggregation into one single statistical exercise of a large number of urban centers, inside of which some dimensions of urban life can have differentiated impacts on different groups.

People Value Different Things in Different Places

The fact that cities exist suggests that the positive aspects of urban living outweigh the negative ones. This may be because cities offer better (or perhaps the only) sources of employment, better education or health facilities or, for the luckier ones that have the time and resources to enjoy them, better recreational and other amenities. Another great attraction of cities is variety. Different people can find the aspects of city life that they like or feel comfortable with. Moreover, as reviewed in the opening sections of this chapter, the cities of Latin America are quite varied. Indeed, given the variety of individual tastes and the differences between cities, using a single approach to consider satisfaction with houses and cities across countries may be too coarse a methodology. A more-detailed analysis at the level of city, or even better, at the level of a neighborhood of a city, is warranted.

Six Latin American countries were selected to be included in a unique pilot project aimed at exploring ways to monitor the quality of life in more detail in urban areas.[8] The cities selected within those six countries were La Paz and Santa Cruz, Bolivia; Buenos Aires, Argentina; Bogotá and Medellín, Colombia; San José, Costa Rica; Lima, Peru; and Montevideo, Uruguay. Although these cities cannot be considered a representative sample of all Latin American cities, they are certainly diverse in terms of their history and socioeconomic characteristics. In-depth surveys were used to gather opinions regarding a host of

---

[8] The documents from this project are available at www.iadb.org/res/network_study.cfm?st_id=91, and the methodology and results are summarized in Powell and Sanguinetti (2008). The papers are as follows: Ferre, Gandelman, and Piani (2008), Medina, Morales, and Núñez (2008), Alcázar and Andrade (2008), Cruces, Ham, and Tetaz (2008), Hernani-Limarino et al. (2008), and Hall, Madrigal, and Robalino (2008).

Box 8.1   What about the Traffic?

Traffic congestion is clearly a problem in many large Latin American cities.
According to the 2007 Gallup World Poll, more than 40 percent of Latin American
urban inhabitants state that they are dissatisfied with the traffic. In Mexico City and
Caracas, citizens rate the "ease of moving around the city" with scores of just 2.6
and 2.4, respectively, out of 5, according to the AméricaEconomía Intelligence
(AEI) surveys for 2007. Other large cities, such as Bogotá, Buenos Aires, Lima, and
Santiago, have only slightly higher scores (see figure).

As a result of the rapid growth in the number of vehicles in the cities and the
greater distances that people must travel because of urban sprawl, traffic problems are worsening. Of the 10 cities analyzed by AEI, only Guayaquil and Caracas
reported some improvement from 2006 to 2007, whereas in Monterrey and Santiago the situation worsened notably, according to those surveyed.

Bogotá has had a system for monitoring mobility since 1998 that provides
evidence of the difficult struggle against mounting traffic. Despite the success of
the Transmilenio (a bus system with lanes exclusively for use of buses), introduced
at the beginning of this decade, for most people the time used to move around the
city has remained the same or has increased year after year. For those who live at
the far ends of the city (Suba, Bosa, Ciudad Bolívar, and Usme), the average time
of each trip was 58 minutes in 2005, and has certainly increased since then.[a] This
represents enormous decreases in well-being and productivity.[b]

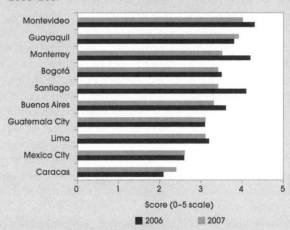

Evaluation of the Ease of Moving around the City,
2006–2007

Score (0–5 scale)

■ 2006   ■ 2007

Source: Bogotá Chamber of Commerce (2007).

---

[a] See Bogotá Chamber of Commerce (2007).
[b] For a journalistic analysis of the consequences of productivity, see "Colapso Total," *Dinero*,
February 29, 2008, 33–39.

(continued on next page)

(continued)

Given the seriousness of the traffic problem, one would expect that it would have a major impact on perceptions of quality of life. Nonetheless, of all the urban problems considered in the 2007 Gallup World Poll, it is the one that least affects satisfaction with cities (see Figure 8.10), and there is no evidence whatsoever that it changes citizens' evaluations of their own quality of life.

This is surprising, because numerous studies have shown that individuals who have been exposed to heavy traffic tend to suffer stress, irritability, and other behavioral deficiencies, and are more inclined to experience high blood pressure. Prolonged travel amidst heavy traffic is associated with lower immunological resistance and longevity, and with higher probabilities of certain forms of cancer and cardiovascular problems.[c] One could presume that subjective perceptions of well-being would be lower for those who are continuously subjected to heavy traffic, yet there is no evidence to show this. It may be due to simple adaptation, or to the consequences being manifested in other areas of satisfaction, such as health or family relations. Yet, even though the negative effects of heavy traffic are not manifested in individuals' perceptions, there are numerous reasons for trying to solve the mounting traffic problems that overwhelm large Latin American cities.

[c] For a summary, see Frank (2005).

aspects of houses and their surroundings in a selection of neighborhoods in each of these cities. Unlike the Gallup World Polls, which ask the same questions and intend to provide comparable results for the same satisfaction domains across countries, the surveys of this project were designed individually to focus on the most relevant aspects of each city. While this limits comparability, it makes the analysis more practical and offers multiple perspectives for assessing the quality of life of the Latin American urban dwellers.

Employing a methodology similar to that in Chapter 4, a set of housing and neighborhood characteristics are found to be important for each city. An overview of the results is provided in Table 8.9. The table indicates statistically significant coefficients in a regression of life satisfaction on a set of standard variables (age, sex, marital status, etc.) and then a set of house and neighborhood characteristics.[9] Several housing characteristics are found to be significant—consistent with the findings reported above. In poorer cities, such as La Paz, the basic quality of house construction (floors and walls) is important, while in richer cities, such as Bogotá and Medellín, the number of bathrooms and whether the house has a satellite dish come into play.

With respect to neighborhood characteristics, and perhaps not surprisingly given the previous results, security comes through as one of the most important issues in

---

[9] The distinction here between what is considered a house characteristic and what is considered a neighborhood characteristic is somewhat artificial, as the data are at the level of each household. In practice, the distinction may be drawn given the relative variation across individual houses in a subneighborhood. For example, in a (small) subneighborhood, most houses will have or will not have access to water; hence this is considered a neighborhood characteristic here.

Table 8.9 Housing and Neighborhood Characteristics That Contribute to Life Satisfaction
(significant factors from regressions)

	Bolivia (La Paz and Santa Cruz)	Colombia (Bogotá)	Colombia (Medellín)	Costa Rica (San José)	Peru (Lima)	Uruguay (Montevideo)
Housing characteristics						
	Condition of roof	Number of bathrooms	Number of bathrooms	Condition of floors	Condition of walls	Condition of walls
	Condition of floors	Condition of floors	Satellite TV services		Dwelling characteristics	
			Condition of floors			
Neighborhood characteristics						
	Running water	Quality of energy	Distance to main/connector street	Safety (presence of gangs)	Safety (robbery)	Running water
	Sewage	Quality of garbage collection	Distance to places of cultural value		Condition of street	Street lights
	Paved street	Quality of telephone services	Presence of prisons		Green areas in good condition	Safety (vandalism in neighborhood)
	Access to electricity network	Safety in neighborhood			Trust in neighbors	
		Robbery				
		Drug dealing				
		Recreation/sports centers				
		Average education in neighborhood				

Source: Authors' compilation based on the IDB Latin American Research Network project on Quality of Life in Urban Neighborhoods in Latin America and the Caribbean, available at http://www.iadb.org/res/network_study.cfm?st_id=91.

Note: All regressions also include the following control variables: household income per capita, age and marital status of respondent, and family size. Life satisfaction regressions in Argentina were conducted using a two-stage methodology and are not shown in the table. The neighborhood characteristics that were found to be significant include sidewalk conditions when raining, cultural and sports activities, amount and quality of green areas, security during the day, opinions that the respondent has about his or her neighbors, and traffic in the neighborhood.

virtually all cases. For example, in the case of San José, the presence of gangs negatively affects life satisfaction. In the cases of Bogotá, Lima, and Montevideo, safety is seen as an important neighborhood attribute. Access to basic services such as electricity, water and sewage, garbage collection, and telephone also comes through as an important neighborhood characteristic. For Bogotá, inefficiencies in the provision of certain infrastructure services like energy, garbage collection, and telephone services have a negative and significant impact on subjective well-being. In La Paz and Santa Cruz, access to sewage and running water networks improves self-reported utility.

Several neighborhood characteristics that might be considered important a priori do not seem to influence individuals' satisfaction. One such set of variables is transit and congestion issues, which is consistent with results from the Gallup World Polls reported earlier in this chapter. It is possible, however, that such issues, while very important for some cities with high levels of congestion in the region, are not as critical in the particular neighborhoods analyzed in this project, or in all urban areas, as covered in the Gallup World Polls. Interestingly, while traffic issues are generally found not to be significant, aspects of public transport are found to be important.

Apart from its role in assessing which housing and neighborhood characteristics are particularly important, the life satisfaction approach can also be used to place a value on living in a neighborhood or on a particular house or neighborhood characteristic.[10] As income influences life satisfaction along with certain characteristics (say, the condition of sidewalks), the trade-off between greater income and better sidewalks can be used to estimate the value of improving sidewalks. As mentioned in Chapter 4, where the same approach was used to value aspects of life as diverse as friendship, religion, and marital status, the value obtained through this method reflects only an implicit willingness to pay. At no point do interviewed people actually express how much they are willing to pay for these characteristics. The life satisfaction approach is particularly useful, as it can be implemented to value amenities that do not yet exist or for which there is no market price available.

In order to illustrate the life satisfaction approach in action, Table 8.10 presents the values for those neighborhood characteristics that turned out to be significant for three neighborhoods in Buenos Aires: Avellaneda, Caballito, and Palermo.[11] This table demonstrates how the approach can be used to place a value on neighborhoods as such, as well as their specific characteristics. For instance, living in Caballito or Palermo has an implicit value when compared to living in Avellaneda. This value goes beyond the differences in the set of neighborhood characteristics considered—in other words this value is in addition to any measured differences in neighborhood characteristics. Some neighborhood characteristics are objective, in the sense that they can be verified by an external observer, for instance, the presence of garbage in the streets or the availability of

---

[10] Frey, Luechinger, and Stutzer (2004) describe the theory and applications of these techniques in practice.

[11] These valuations stem from a two-stage technique, in which in a first step, overall life satisfaction is regressed on income and on a set of domains (including satisfaction with the neighborhood) and then in a second step, neighborhood satisfaction is regressed on a set of more objective neighborhood characteristics. The coefficient on income in the first regression and the coefficients on neighborhood satisfaction are then combined with the coefficients in the second step to determine the trade-off between income and, for example, improving security during the day. This trade-off implies how much someone would be willing to pay to obtain a little more security, and hence can be interpreted as the price of additional security.

pay phones (for this project, information on the variables classified as objective was reported by the interviewers). But many of the neighborhood characteristics that matter are subjective, in the sense that they come from people's own opinions. Among the subjective variables, good neighbors are found to be particularly valuable, as are the perceived conditions of sidewalks and security. The perceived availability of green areas in the neighborhoods is also highly valued.

The valuation of public goods is a critical area for public policy. If public goods can be valued, this helps national government and local authorities make rational decisions as to what goods should be offered to try to improve quality of life as much as possible, given the always-present budget constraints. The life satisfaction approach provides one promising route for doing this, as well as for monitoring valuations over time to determine whether they change depending on socioeconomic developments and alterations in the characteristics of cities.

Table 8.10 Valuing Neighborhood Characteristics in Buenos Aires Using the Life Satisfaction Approach
(implicit log change in income)

Neighborhood dummies	
Avellaneda	0.376
Caballito	1.404
Palermo	1.409

Housing characteristics	
Number of bedrooms	0.170
Garage	0.424

Neighborhood characteristics: Subjective	
Annoying noise during the day	−0.470
Sidewalk conditions when raining	0.492
Conditions of pavement/streets	0.550
Cultural and sports activities	0.300
Amount and quality of green areas	0.413
Traffic in neighborhood	0.315
Security during the day	0.405
Evaluation of neighbors	0.702

Neighborhood characteristics: Objective	
Garbage during the day	−0.279
Visual contamination	0.249
Pay phones	0.553

Source: Cruces, Ham, and Tetaz (2008).
Note: The values are the implicit log change in income that corresponds to the change in satisfaction due to each amenity, based on a regression analysis.

Using Housing Prices to Determine Amenity Values

The life satisfaction approach uses surveys and an implicit calculation to value housing and neighborhood characteristics. The so-called hedonic approach uses objective housing prices and rents to assess how much the market values those same (and many other) housing and neighborhood characteristics. Assuming housing prices are free to adjust and given a sufficient variation of housing and neighborhood characteristics in the sample available, housing values can be used to tease out the value of each characteristic.[12] The urban economics literature has usually assumed that city amenities affecting the quality of life are reflected not only in land or housing prices, but also in wages. However, when two same-city neighborhoods are considered, the assumption is that employment opportunities in both are the same. Hence, between such neighborhoods, it is housing prices that will, according to this theory, adjust to compensate for different levels and qualities of public good provision.

---

[12] For a good description of the microeconomic fundamentals behind hedonic pricing of characteristics of dwellings and cities, see Gyourko, Linneman, and Wachter (1999).

As part of the pilot project referred to above, information on housing prices and rents was collected in the same urban areas in the six countries. There is considerable variation across these urban areas in terms of features that affect house prices. For example, in the San José metropolitan area, the slope of the land in a neighborhood and the vulnerability to volcanoes negatively affects property values. On the other hand, in La Paz, the altitude of a neighborhood is found to be a significant factor. In Montevideo proximity to the coastal promenade (Las Ramblas) is an important feature of a neighborhood. In some cities, proximity to a main avenue or thoroughfare may be considered an asset, whereas in another context it may indicate congestion or pollution. Thus, while in Buenos Aires or in Medellín, proximity to a metro station contributes to higher house prices, in Bogotá proximity to the Transmilenio transport system does not affect house prices.

Other neighborhood variables that have proved to be important in several of the cities considered include proximity to schools, proximity to a park or green space and, consistent with results presented in previous sections, security (see Table 8.11 for a list of significant variables by city). In those cities where basic services coverage is still deficient in some areas, its influence on house prices can be gauged. Results indicate that access to running water, to sewage, and to piped gas are all associated with higher house prices.

Housing prices also depend strongly on the characteristics of the particular home that is being valued. Location is definitely not everything when it comes to housing prices or equivalent rents. Here, there is more homogeneity regarding the variables found to be significant. In particular, the number of rooms (total rooms or bedrooms), the number of bathrooms, and the condition of walls, roof, and floors are typically found to be significant. In Buenos Aires, the age of the house is found to be important (with a negative coefficient), and in some cities the presence of a garage and a private kitchen are found to be important.

Policymakers frequently need to know the relative importance of different variables, as they must make decisions about where to invest scarce resources. In the pilot project discussed here, the question was asked, should investments be made in the quality of housing construction or in providing neighborhood amenities? In the case of Bogotá, around 22 percent of the variance in housing prices is explained by identified neighborhood amenities, while 48 percent is explained by housing attributes. For Medellín, the numbers are 18 percent and 58 percent, respectively. In the metropolitan area of San José, neighborhood amenities explain 39 percent of the variation in rents. Neighborhood features, while not everything, are definitely significant.

In order to quantify this further, Table 8.12 presents an exercise considering San José that uses the coefficients from hedonic regressions to derive an implicit price (expressed in monthly terms) for different housing and neighborhood attributes. This price indicates how much the monthly rental of an average house would change with an additional unit of a particular amenity. The prices thus derived indicate that, for example, each degree of slope of land implies a lower housing cost of about 60 cents (US$0.60) per month, whereas an extra unit of safety (measured as reported crimes per week in the neighborhood) would imply a higher cost of housing of over US$20 per month.[13]

---

[13] Housing costs refer to "equivalent rents," which are either the rent itself or a calculation of the opportunity cost of owning the house that depends on the value of the house and prevailing interest rates. Any differences between renters and owners in relation to their preferences are ignored in this analysis.

Table 8.11 House and Neighborhood Characteristics Revealed in House Prices

	Argentina (Buenos Aires)	Bolivia (La Paz)	Bolivia (Santa Cruz)	Colombia (Bogotá)	Colombia (Medellín)	Costa Rica (San José)	Peru (Lima)	Uruguay (Montevideo)
Housing characteristics								
	Number of rooms	Number of rooms	Number of rooms	Number of rooms	Number of rooms	Number of rooms	Number of rooms	Number of rooms
	Garage	Bathrooms	Bathrooms	Garden	Bathrooms	Bathrooms	Bathrooms	Bathrooms
	Condition of walls	Condition of walls	Condition of walls	Garage	Fixed phone line	Condition of walls	Condition of walls	Condition of walls
	Lot size	Condition of floor	Condition of floor	Condition of floor	Internet or satellite TV	Condition of floor	Condition of floor	Condition of floor
	Age	Condition of roof	Condition of roof	Size of house	Garage	Condition of roof	Condition of roof	Condition of roof
	Number of bathrooms	Private kitchen	Private kitchen	Size of plot	Condition of floors	Private kitchen	Private kitchen	Private kitchen
	Parking place				Condition of walls			
Neighborhood characteristics								
	Distance to avenue	Running water	Running water	Running water	Running water	Safety	Condition of sidewalks	Access to running water
	Distance to freeway	Sewage	Sewage	Average education	Gas main	Slope		Access to sewage system
	Distance to metro	Paved street	Paved street	Distance to restaurants	Average education	Eruption vulnerability		Access to gas
	Distance to train	Altitude	Proportion of indigenous people	Schools per capita	Restaurants per capita	Distance to parks		Access to drainage
	Distance to green space	Proportion of indigenous people		Homicide rate	Environmental risks	Distance to fire station		Condition of street
	Drug dealing			No bus/train terminal	Distance to metro	Neighborhood road		Condition of sidewalk
				Education inequality	Distance to bus terminal	Primary road		Street lights
				Distance to universities	Distance to main/connector street			Presence of trees
				Lower unemployment	Distance to places of cultural value			Air pollution
					Distance to university			Satisfaction with parks
								Satisfaction with sports facilities

Source: Authors' compilation based on the IDB Latin American Research Network project on Quality of Life in Urban Neighborhoods in Latin America and the Caribbean, available at http://www.iadb.org/res/network_study.cfm?st_id=91.

Table 8.12 Hedonic Estimation of Implicit Prices for Housing and Neighborhood Amenities, Metropolitan Area of San José, Costa Rica

(price of amenities measured at mean prices in 2000 dollars, 308 colones= US$1)

	Estimated coefficient	Implicit price
Housing characteristics		
Number of bedrooms	0.55***	30.84
Number of rooms (excluding bedrooms)	0.33***	18.80
Floor in good condition	0.24***	13.63
Walls in good condition	0.44***	24.82
Cinder block walls	0.82***	45.72
Roof in good condition	0.32***	18.23
Ceiling in good condition	0.43***	24.46
Water source: community organization	−0.36***	−20.24
Water source: rain	−0.82**	−46.07
Water source: well	0.13	7.44
Water source: river	−0.89***	−49.63
Sewer (septic tank)	−0.10***	−6.03
Sewer (latrine)	−0.21*	−11.72
Sewer (other)	−0.33***	−18.60
No sewer	0.09	5.05
Private bathroom for the household	0.48***	27.07
Electricity not supplied by Instituto Costarricense de Electricidad	−0.24***	−13.66
No electricity supplied	−0.70**	−39.15
Total housing characteristics contribution	60.84%	
Neighborhood characteristics		
Safety index	0.46***	25.82
Slope degrees	−0.01***	−0.57
Precipitation (mm³)	−0.12**	−6.99
Risk of eruption	−0.13**	−7.52
Log distance to national parks (km)	−1.25***	−70.09
Log distance to clinics (km)	0.01	0.57
Log distance to secondary schools (km)	0.02	1.18
Log distance to primary schools (km)	0.00	0.19
Log distance to rivers (km)	0.06***	3.42
Log distance to fire departments (km)	0.05**	3.14
Log closeness to La Sabana Park	−0.54***	−30.58
Log distance to La Paz Park	1.35***	75.56
Length of primary roads (km)	−0.46***	−25.89
Length of secondary roads (km)	0.23***	13.31
Length of urban-neighborhood roads (km)	0.57***	31.77
Neighborhood classified as poor	−0.35***	−19.91
Total neighborhood characteristics contribution	39.15%	

Note: To obtain the values in the "Estimated coefficient" column, estimated prices were multiplied by quantities of the amenity. The price was calculated following Blomquist, Berger, and Hoehn (1988). *Coefficient is statistically significant at the 10 percent level; **at the 5 percent level; ***at the 1 percent level; no asterisk means the coefficient is not different from zero with statistical significance.

Using these implicit prices, an index of the overall value of neighborhood characteristics can be generated, and by combining this with the average value of housing characteristics, an overall neighborhood satisfaction index expressed in monetary terms can be calculated. Employing this technique, the average rental value of houses by district (including both housing and neighborhood characteristics across 51 districts)

Table 8.13 Using Hedonic Prices to Construct a Quality of Life Index by Neighborhood, Metropolitan San José
(ranking of districts by housing and neighborhood characteristics)

	District	Housing and neighborhood characteristics		Neighborhood characteristics		Housing characteristics	
		Ranking	Value ($US)	Ranking	Value ($US)	Ranking	Value ($US)
Top 10	Sánchez	1	370	1	27	1	343
	San Rafael	2	285	2	9	8	275
	Mata Redonda	3	275	10	−23	2	299
	Carmen	4	264	11	−24	3	287
	San Vicente	5	258	8	−20	6	277
	Anselmo Llorente	6	254	13	−28	4	281
	San Isidro	7	245	3	−5	23	250
	San Pedro	8	238	20	−32	10	271
	San Juán	9	237	16	−30	11	267
	Sabanilla	10	237	35	−39	7	276
Bottom 10	Alajuelita	42	172	48	−59	34	230
	Hospital	43	169	40	−42	42	211
	San Jocesito	44	166	46	−54	38	220
	San Felipe	45	165	36	−40	46	205
	Cinco Esquinas	46	164	28	−37	48	200
	Patarrá	47	154	15	−29	51	183
	San Juán de Dios	48	148	50	−62	45	210
	Tirrases	49	144	51	−67	43	211
	Concepción	50	143	49	−61	47	204
	Aserri	51	143	47	−57	49	199

Source: Hall, Madrigal, and Robalino (2008).

in San José ranges from US$143 to US$370 per month. Table 8.13 lists the top 10 and bottom 10 neighborhoods in San José according to this measure. The contribution to this rental value of the neighborhood amenities and other characteristics ranges from US$−67 to US$27—the contribution can take negative values as some neighborhood characteristics are "bads" (for example, the probability of a volcanic eruption) rather than goods. The contribution of housing characteristics ranges from US$183 to US$343, reflecting the different quality of housing construction across districts in San José.

As expected, the wealthier districts such as Sánchez and San Rafael have relatively high rental values attributable to neighborhood variables, while poorer areas such as Patarrá, San Juán de Dios, and Tirrases have lower values. Although this is not surprising, it illustrates how neighborhood characteristics may exacerbate income differentials in terms of the distribution of quality of life. These valuations also provide a guide to where scarce resources might be concentrated to improve that distribution the most. However, there are also some unexpected results. For example, Mata Redonda ranks very high in housing characteristics (third) but rather poorly in neighborhood amenities (10th), while Patarrá ranks poorly in housing characteristics (47th) but relatively high in neighborhood amenities (15th). Such discrepancies illustrate that there is indeed considerable room for action. Public policy has contributed to these results and may be used further to enhance the welfare of those living in districts where neighborhood valuations are currently at the lower end.

A similar exercise for Buenos Aires also ranks neighborhoods according to a monetary value that includes the valuation of neighborhood characteristics. Table 8.14 presents the top 10 and the bottom 10 neighborhoods based on the results of this exercise. Neighborhood characteristics include the distance to different urban infrastructures, such as avenues, schools, parks, freeways, train stations, and subways. Similar to the case of San José, in Buenos Aires the wealthier neighborhoods, such as Recoleta and Palermo, are included in the top 10, while poorer ones, such as Villa Lugano and Mataderos in the south of the city, are in the bottom 10. Interestingly, there are some relatively expensive neighborhoods at the bottom of the table (such as Villa Devoto), while some middle-income neighborhoods (such as Chacarita and Villa Crespo) are among the top 10. With respect to the 2006 average price per square meter of real estate in the city of about US$1,041, the implicit price differences given by this index range from US$219 to US$–127, with an average of US$72.50, or just under 7 percent of the average property value.

In Buenos Aires, the correlation between the price per square meter and the index is positive, but it is far below 1.0. This reflects a significant but imperfect relationship between the index and property prices (the price/index correlation is 0.43 and the price/rank correlation is 0.71), which again suggests that there are other factors that determine real estate prices other than basic housing features and neighborhood characteristics; fashion could be one possible explanation. In the case of Buenos Aires, the ordering developed in Table 8.14 can also be used as a guide for public investment to improve the distribution of quality of life.

On Segregation in Latin American Cities

Housing prices are clearly highly informative regarding the quantity and quality of the provision of public services and neighborhood characteristics more generally. This is precisely as predicted by theoretical accounts of the organization of cities, such as Tiebout (1956) and Vandell (1995). In Tiebout's classic paper, inhabitants organize themselves into different areas depending on their preferences in regard to public goods. Different preferences imply an economic rationale for segregation as subcity areas develop that are homogenous within their boundaries, but are exacerbating segregation. A prediction of the model, borne out by evidence from the United States, is that the more segregated an urban area is, the more local governments may sprout up to service the needs of each homogeneous subcity zone. The contribution by Vandell, in an extension of the same argument, is that the greater is the income inequality, the greater will be the segregation, as higher-income families will outbid lower-income ones for property with desirable characteristics.[14] The result is richer areas clustered close to desirable amenities. More generally, according to this view, market forces are likely to generate areas where residents have similar attributes, which may include neighborhood characteristics such as natural features or parks, but also the provision of higher-quality public services. As is well known, Latin America's income inequality remains very high, and hence it should

---

[14] Vandell (1995) divides these characteristics into four categories: (1) housing and lot characteristics, (2) neighborhood amenities, (3) accessibility characteristics, and (4) resident attributes—the last of these refers to attributes such as race, income, wealth, education, family composition, and occupation.

Table 8.14 Using Hedonic Prices to Construct a Quality of Life Index by Neighborhood, City of Buenos Aires
(ranking of districts by monetary value of amenities index)

	Neighborhood	Amenities index (value, US$)	Amenities index (–1 to 1 scale)	Ranking by amenities index	Average price per square meter (US$)	Ranking by price per square meter
Top 10	Chacarita	218.7	0.186	1	1,021	14
	Colegiales	214.0	0.166	2	1,174	7
	Puerto Madero	209.2	0.064	18	2,810	1
	San Nicolás	204.2	0.159	3	1,159	8
	Palermo	202.9	0.129	7	1,507	3
	Belgrano	184.7	0.136	5	1,269	5
	Villa Ortuzar	178.0	0.148	4	1,118	9
	Recoleta	158.2	0.105	10	1,453	4
	Retiro	154.3	0.091	14	1,721	2
	Villa Crespo	138.8	0.128	8	1,016	16
Bottom 10	Monte Castro	–42.8	–0.051	36	862	30
	Villa Devoto	–44.5	–0.056	38	960	22
	Villa Soldati	–44.9	–0.070	40	680	45
	Villa Lugano	–46.4	–0.081	43	605	47
	Mataderos	–60.4	–0.082	44	754	42
	Villa Luro	–63.1	–0.079	42	836	36
	Liniers	–63.6	–0.076	41	852	34
	Versalles	–89.0	–0.108	45	873	28
	Villa Riachuelo	–90.0	–0.124	46	760	41
	Villa Real	–126.6	–0.164	47	850	35

Source: Cruces, Ham, and Tetaz (2008).

come as no surprise that large cities in the region are also highly segregated.[15] Moreover, as reviewed in this chapter, these large cities have developed very rapidly over the last 50 years. These are the perfect conditions for the development of segregation. The urban economics literature also concludes that the rapid development of cities allows the demand for segregation to be more swiftly and deeply realized (Watson, 2005).

In the case of Montevideo (see Figure 8.11), the high-income strata are spatially concentrated in very few neighborhoods. In two of these neighborhoods, Carrasco and Pocitos, more than 90 percent of the population belongs to the highest socioeconomic stratum. For Metropolitan Lima (Figure 8.12), the spatial concentration of families by socioeconomic stratum runs along center-periphery lines. In general, districts in the periphery of Lima are poorer, and higher-income districts are located more towards the center of the metropolitan area.

Based on tendencies of neighborhoods to be segmented by income (socioeconomic strata) in large cities in the region, and given that housing prices reflect neighborhood characteristics, there is an implication that quality of life will also be highly segmented. In Bogotá, the spatial distribution of Índice de Calidad de Vida (ICV, a quality of life index) and the Necesidades Básicas Insatisfechas (NBI, Unsatisfied Basic Needs)

---

[15] Here we focus on economic rationales for segregation, but there may also be other rationales, such as religious or racial, discussed in the literature.

Figure 8.11 Neighborhoods in Montevideo According to Socioeconomic Strata

Socioeconomic stratum
- ☐ Low
- ☐ Medium-low
- ☐ Medium-high
- ■ High

Source: Ferre, Gandelman, and Piani (2008).

indicators (Figure 8.13) demonstrate that the poorest families with the lowest quality of life indicators are consistently located in the southern and western census sectors of the city, and those better off are located in the northern and eastern sectors, which correspond to the highest socioeconomic strata.

Segregation is also apparent considering other characteristics: for example, educational attainment. In the case of Greater Buenos Aires, within a limited geographical space, there are areas in which 25 to 50 percent of the populations hold a university degree adjacent to areas with significantly lower levels on the same indicator. Highly educated residents tend to concentrate in the northern half of the City of Buenos Aires and in the three municipalities north of it, which constitute the *corredor norte* (north corridor). The same pattern is apparent when the proportion of the population with at least one category of deficit in basic needs, a widely used measure of structural poverty captured with census data, is analyzed. In 2001, the outer area of Greater Buenos Aires had by far the highest concentration of population living under these conditions.

Greater Buenos Aires, although on average a wealthy city by Latin American standards, displays high levels of segregation of urban services.[16] Moreover, while access to

---

[16] The presence of potential externality effects will be dealt with in the following sections when some of the implications of segregation are discussed.

Figure 8.12 Distribution of Population by Socioeconomic Stratum, Metropolitan Lima

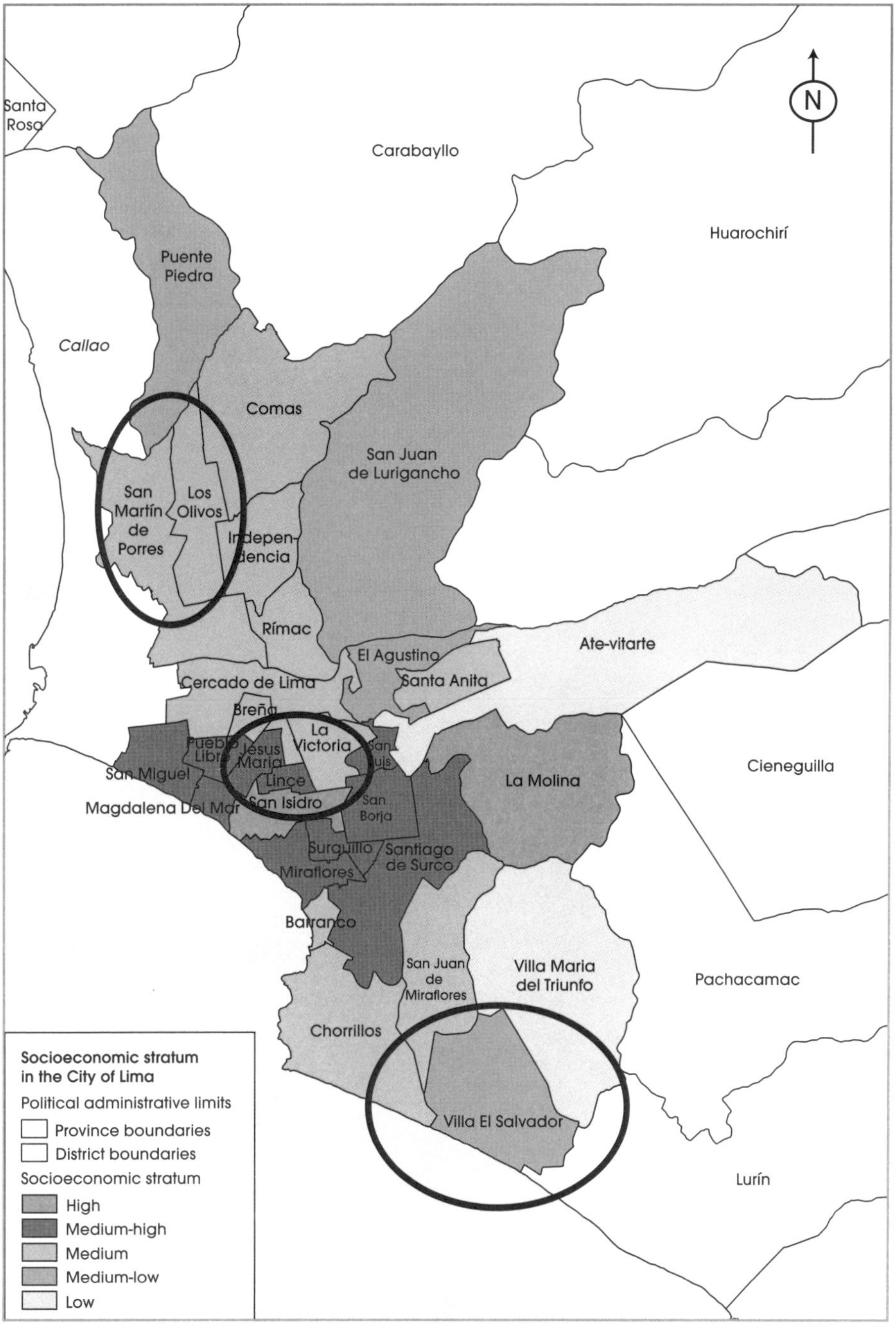

Santa
Rosa

Carabayllo

Huarochirí

Puente
Piedra

Callao

Comas

San Juan
de Lurigancho

San
Martín
de
Porres

Los
Olivos

Indepen-
dencia

Rímac

El Agustino

Ate-vitarte

Cercado de Lima

Santa Anita

Breña

La
Victoria

Pueblo
Libre

Jesus
Maria

San
Luis

San Miguel

Lince

Cieneguilla

Magdalena Del Mar

San Isidro

San
Borja

La Molina

Surquillo

Santiago
de Surco

Miraflores

Barranco

San Juan
de
Miraflores

Villa Maria
del Triunfo

Pachacamac

Chorrillos

Villa El Salvador

Lurín

**Socioeconomic stratum
in the City of Lima**

Political administrative limits

☐ Province boundaries
☐ District boundaries

Socioeconomic stratum

▨ High
▨ Medium-high
▨ Medium
▨ Medium-low
☐ Low

Source: Alcázar and Andrade (2008).

Figure 8.13 Spatial Socioeconomic Stratification of Population in Bogotá

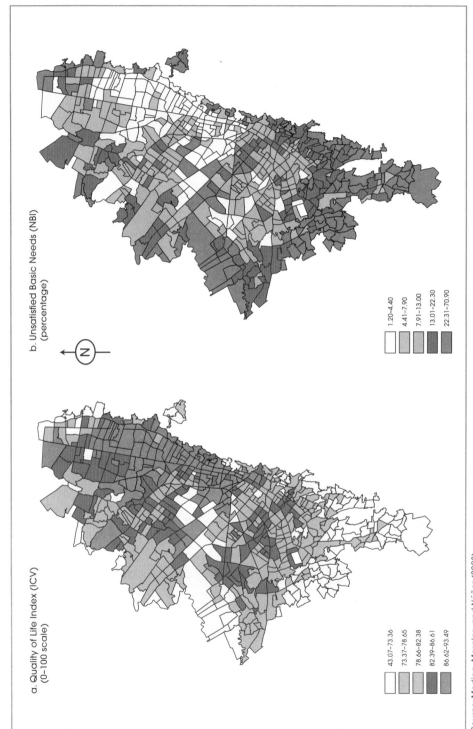

a. Quality of Life Index (ICV)
(0–100 scale)

43.07–73.36
73.37–78.65
78.66–82.38
82.39–86.61
86.62–93.49

b. Unsatisfied Basic Needs (NBI)
(percentage)

1.20–4.40
4.41–7.90
7.91–13.00
13.01–22.30
22.31–70.90

N

Table 8.15 Coverage of City Services for Selected Districts, Metropolitan Lima
(percentage)

	Los Olivos Outskirts Medium income	La Victoria City Center Medium-low income	Villa El Salvador Outskirts Low income
Households with water supply	93.0	81.0	78.0
Households with sewage connection	47.4	52.5	52.6
Children not attending school	4.1	3.3	4.5
Households with at least one unsatisfied basic need	28.4	21.9	48.4
Dwellings with infrastructure deficiencies	7.0	1.6	29.4

Source: Alcázar and Andrade (2008).

the public network for water is relatively high for all residents (84 to 100 percent), there are still several pockets, like Villa El Salvador, where 22 percent or more of households are not connected to this network,[17] especially in the urban outskirts. Moreover, there are also some poorly covered areas within the City of Buenos Aires, corresponding to some of the city's poorer areas (or *villas miseria*). To underline the segregation patterns in the city, the higher socioeconomic status neighborhoods (such as Palermo and Caballito) have a significantly higher number of leisure-related and educational facilities, more trees, and more garbage bins per block than areas with a greater number of lower socioeconomic status inhabitants, such as Avellaneda and San Cristóbal.

In the case of Montevideo, there is also significant variation in services across city areas. Dwellings in a neighborhood corresponding to a medium-high socioeconomic status have access on average to between 8 and 8.4 public services, while dwellings in a medium-low socioeconomic status neighborhood have access to only between 5.6 and 7.1 services. In general, in Montevideo there is a positive correlation between the socioeconomic status of the inhabitants of a neighborhood and the number of basic services that are offered: the higher the socioeconomic status, the more services are offered. In Metropolitan Lima the conclusion is a little more mixed (see Table 8.15). Neighborhoods such as La Victoria, which is considered a medium-low-income neighborhood and may be considered to be in the center of the urban area, have better access to public services (including transport, police officers and security, and hospitals and other health facilities), while neighborhoods such as Los Olivos, corresponding to a medium socioeconomic status, and Villa El Salvador, a low-income neighborhood, are located more in the city's periphery, and access to public resources there is more restricted.

For the cases of Bogotá and Medellín, the data show that the strong pattern of spatial segregation by socioeconomic stratum found for these cities is also observed when the allocation of some basic services is considered. For example, the distribution of piped gas is concentrated in a few neighborhoods within each city, and these areas coincide with the high-income neighborhoods. In summary, the evidence suggests that there are important disparities in access to local public services and urban amenities across neighborhoods in Latin American cities. The question then arises, what, if anything, should be done about it?

---

[17] As the rates of access vary considerably across the city, this is another indication of segregation.

Returning to the economic theory, there is an argument that the type of Tiebout segregation described above may actually be a good thing. If segregation does indeed reflect different preferences, then the variation across areas allows inhabitants to choose the area that corresponds most to their desires. This implies that subcity areas will be relatively homogeneous in their demands for public services, and voting mechanisms in the area would ensure less disappointment regarding taxation and service provision—as people would tend to vote for the same options given homogeneity. So if segregation produces a larger set of local governments offering different bundles of services according to inhabitants' tastes, then just as variety is important for consumers when shopping (for cars, for example), so segregation may also be desirable.

However, this positive side to segregation may easily be outweighed by a set of negatives, and indeed there are several reasons to be concerned about this strong pattern of socioeconomic spatial segregation. First, as the distribution of socioeconomic indicators is also reflected in the allotment of basic urban public services and neighborhood amenities, cities are not working as a compensating mechanism to moderate differences in quality of life across the urban population. Indeed, segregation in services and amenities implies that inequality in quality of life may be even deeper than inequality in income. There is also evidence that segregation extends racial divisions. For example, research in the United States suggests that blacks living in more highly segregated cities have significantly lower outcomes (education and future income) than blacks living in less-segregated areas, when current socioeconomic variables are controlled for (Cutler and Glaesser, 1997). Moreover, a highly segregated city population is less likely to be one that demands high-quality public services in general (Alesina, Baqir, and Easterly, 1999). The theory here is that a more-segregated population across a metropolitan area is one in which collective action is made more problematic, and hence the inhabitants are less likely to be able to effectively communicate demands.

Moreover, there are additional costs to creating separate areas of high and low income, particularly that crime and violence may flourish in the low-income areas and then spill over to all areas. Indeed, the efficiency of Tiebout-style sorting may turn negative if there are significant spillovers not contemplated in the original model. Given the major concerns with crime consistently discussed in this chapter, one view is that the high perceptions of serious crime in Latin America are a fairly direct function of highly segregated cities, which by itself surely constitutes an important reason to be concerned about such high levels of segregation in the region.

While in theory, then, there may be some positive aspects to segregation, in practice many find disparities in income and access to basic services morally intolerable and politically untenable. The moral position and existence of externalities across areas justify policies to diminish segregation. In particular, basic services in poorer areas may be subsidized and richer areas may be taxed, although this is unlikely to cover all of the costs. Another approach is to encourage movement of people between areas to diminish segregation. However, this is not easy to accomplish, as richer areas may tax their citizens more, and this would be a deterrent to lower-income families' moving into those areas. Again, schemes that allow mixing of social groups should be devised.[18]

---

[18] See Wassmer (2002) for an interesting discussion.

Deriving Policy Recommendations

Latin America is the most-urbanized region in the world. It is impossible to think about policies to improve the quality of life in the region without paying special attention to urban issues. Over the last 50 years, Latin America's great cities have grown haphazardly, driven largely by the internal migration of poorer families. Not surprisingly, this has led to many problems, ranging from poor quality of housing to limited access to services. However, according to objective measures, the quality of housing has improved significantly, although access to services has lagged, especially for the lower deciles of the income distribution. For example, 15 percent of homes in the poorest decile in Mexico City and 33 percent in Lima are still without one of the basic services of water, sanitation, and electricity.

There is, then, an urgent need to eliminate, or substantially reduce, the housing deficits identified in this chapter, which would imply investments equivalent to 8 percent on average of the cities' annual GDP. In turn, this would mean determining the source of financing for these investments and deciding what the home owners themselves will pay for and what public funds will cover, as well as establishing the mechanisms for doing so. Given the size of mortgage markets, a related and urgent task is to further deepen the financial markets with reasonable access criteria, while maintaining the safety and soundness of financial institutions. There is an important role for multilateral development banks such as the IDB in this process. However, while housing quality is important for life satisfaction, an interesting finding is that without the title deed to the property, a person's subjective satisfaction with his or her home is highly limited. Lack of title deeds, as reflected by the startling statistics on deed possession, may also restrict access to the required financing for home purchase. Using the life satisfaction and hedonic approaches, quantitative measures can be obtained of the value people and markets implicitly assign to specific features of housing quality, access to different services, and access to goods (such as parks or other city amenities) and bads (such as crime). This chapter illustrates how these techniques can be used in a general way across countries and also in a more specific way at the neighborhood level.

Apart from housing quality and access to services, the aspect of urban life that stands out as significantly affecting the quality of life in urban areas is safety. Interestingly, objective measures of crime do not always correlate with perceptions in this area. Creative policy thinking is required not only to reduce the actual incidence of crime, but also to ensure that urban populations feel safe. Unfortunately, not a single country in the region has been able to provide the perception of a safe environment for its urban population.

At a more local level, municipal governments should establish information systems for monitoring the variables affecting quality of life in urban neighborhoods. There are already important and interesting experiences in setting up these monitoring systems, including the City of London (London Sustainable Development Commission, 2005), Canadian cities (Canadian Treasury Board, 2005), and the Urban Audit Program of the European Union (European Communities, 2000). In Latin America, Bogotá and its "Bogotá, Cómo Vamos" scheme is another well-known example.

What variables and what questions should be included in these initiatives? The lessons learned from the analysis presented in this chapter suggest that they should cover both objective and subjective indicators. In particular, the questions and variables must employ secondary sources (censuses and household surveys) to gather quantitative information at a very disaggregated, census-track level of basic socioeconomic and housing indicators. These secondary sources of information should be complemented with surveys that have subcity representation, in which in addition to some objective socioeconomic and housing variables, responses to subjective questions regarding satisfaction with several dwelling and neighborhood characteristics (in addition to overall life satisfaction) are collected. One key objective of these subjective questions is to gauge the consistency between objective quality of life indicators and people's perceptions regarding these variables.

A second purpose of these subjective questions is to use them to extract an implicit value for certain public goods (or bads). In terms of this last objective, it is important to record and monitor a third very important data set: housing prices and rents. Secondary sources such as real estate quotations and surveys on these issues are useful methods for obtaining this information.

National statistical offices in some countries collect valuable information on many relevant variables. The focus, however, is typically at the national level with no regional or city-level discrimination. A lesson from the analysis in this chapter is that preferences depend on the context in which people live, so a more-detailed approach may be required. Moreover, data are not collected on all relevant variables, and subjective opinions are rarely sought—an exception is the Encuesta de Calidad de Vida (Quality of Life Survey) in Bogotá. An effort is needed to link the valuable information already available at the national level with other information sources, including subjective surveys, and to provide results that are useful at different levels of government (regional, city, and even lower levels if they exist).

The purpose of these local quality of life monitoring systems is not only to gather the information in an integrated and consistent way. To inform the policy process, the information provided by these systems must be part of the public debate and influence the policy agenda. This could be better achieved if there were public access to the information and the main results were presented to the public in a framework that ensured a certain level of independence with respect to the authorities.

The monitoring of quality of life indicators at the city level could both reveal existing overall disparities in quality of life across neighborhoods and identify the main drivers or factors causing them. The question, however, then arises of how to employ the diagnosis to guide policy interventions. In other words, which disparities should be given priority in terms of public investment and/or compensation schemes? The clearest case is when the survey determines that particular areas of a city lack certain basic services (say, running water) or are subject to a particular negative amenity (say, pollution) and people's perceptions are consistent with these facts. This evidence could clearly support a public program to take on these problems.

The issue of segregation as identified above is a further cause for concern. The rapid growth of cities, high levels of income inequality, and reasonably free markets for housing provide the conditions for deep segregation. Segregation may in part be fueling the general perceptions of lack of safety, as some typically low-income areas with poor public services may become a breeding ground for crime that in turn spills over to other areas. This in itself may justify public actions to decrease segregation and develop more mixed areas in terms of socioeconomic characteristics. Greater socioeconomic integration of cities can also contribute to raising the aspirations of the poorest individuals regarding the necessary quality of services (as shown in Chapter 6 in the case of education in Santiago, Chile) and to generating political pressure to improve services.

The analysis in this chapter indicates that housing prices yield important information about the quality of public services in Latin America. If all public goods or services were reflected in real estate prices, then it could be deduced that the market works in such a way as to establish a numerical value for these intangibles. Accordingly, if people wished to enjoy a certain feature or service, they could move to the neighborhood that offers it and pay for it through the price of or rent for the housing. And if the supply of these intangibles were increased, this improvement would be reflected in higher home values, which in turn could justify taxes on the home appreciation to finance the increased supply.

There are, however, aspects of cities and neighborhoods that affect the satisfaction of individuals that are not reflected in housing prices. The life satisfaction method makes it possible to identify these aspects. The differences in the results arising from the hedonic method and those emerging from the life satisfaction method can shed light on which aspects the market covers and which aspects it does not. It is important that local governments be able to establish which of these life satisfaction aspects fall into which category—that is, which are reflected in market prices and which are not—and monitor them on a continuous basis, not only because they affect the possibilities for financing city improvements, but also because they affect patterns of segregation and their impact on the most diverse aspects of urban life.

THE CURTAIN CALL

The People's Choice?
The Role of Opinions
in the Policymaking Process

In the naive public-interest view, democracy works
because it does what voters want.
In the view of most democracy skeptics,
it fails because it does not do what voters want.
In my view, democracy fails because
it does what voters want.—Bryan Caplan

This volume has revealed a number of surprises. The public's opinion of the quality of life among people in Latin America and the Caribbean (hereafter "Latin America") is often at odds with objective indicators. Examples abound. The correlation between the well-known Human Development Index and a subjective version of this index based on perceptions regarding the same issues—income, health, and education—among people in the region is not very high, around 0.55. In some countries with poor health profiles, people are more tolerant of poor health or low-quality services than in others where health services and outcomes are clearly far better. In a region where inadequate education has effectively stymied economic growth, people are relatively satisfied with the quality of education, which is judged by the public—particularly lower-income groups— in terms of discipline, security, and the physical appearance of the schools rather than on test results. When assessing the quality of their jobs, most workers value flexibility, autonomy, and development potential more than social security, stability, paid vacations, and other benefits, usually considered key tenets of public policy. People's satisfaction with their housing and cities depends not just on the provision of basic services and physical infrastructure but on a host of other factors ranging from security, to proximity to amenities, to disaster risks, to the skin color of their neighbors.

Clearly there is a disconnect between how people view the quality of their lives and how their lives stack up in terms of objective indicators. Yet policymakers often use these objective indicators as reference points for developing public policy. Not surprisingly, evidence from this volume, as well as from other literature on Latin America, shows that people are seldom happy with the public policies they receive. How should public opinion weigh into the public policy debate? Should public policy be guided by public opinion on satisfaction with life? Should policymakers aim to make people happier? Unfortunately, the drawbacks to this approach may be greater than the gains, and pursuing short-term happiness for individuals, whose opinions may be clouded for a myriad of reasons, may conflict with the goal of long-term welfare for society as a whole (Box 9.1).

This chapter examines how public opinion is formed and its impact on public policy, and also shows how policymakers' opinions may be affected by the information they receive and the way they process it. The chapter further argues that a reason why public policies do not maximize either happiness or welfare is that they are affected by the availability of information and the beliefs and perceptions of both people and policymakers. In this way, the viewpoint in this chapter distances itself from the more traditional and long-standing view that the gap between public satisfaction and public policy stems from governments' inability to provide what voters want, as suggested by the second sentence of the epigraph that opens this chapter.[1] The spirit of this chapter is reflected more by the third sentence. Public policies are the result of the interaction of voters, politicians, and interest groups who vie for what they believe would be best for them. Whether those policies are truly in their best interest is affected by how well they can infer what is best for them and society as a whole.[2]

The Demand for Policy: How People's Beliefs Affect Their Choices

In a perfect world, people's policy preferences and political choices reflect their unbiased evaluation of the benefits, costs, and trade-offs involved in choosing one policy over another. The assumption is that people have information on the true benefits and costs of each policy and that they can correctly estimate their impact on their welfare. In turn, the presumption is that each person will vote for the politicians who advocate the policies he or she judges most beneficial (or least harmful) to his or her own interests. But this is not necessarily the case. Often, people do not form their own opinions and enter the political arena without preconceived notions, and they are not always armed with complete, impartial information.[3]

People's opinions about their particular situation, the economy, and certain public goods and policies are determined by their preferences for outcomes, their beliefs

---

[1] The epigraph's second sentence is closely related to the social choice and "government failures" literature. For a thorough overview of the social choice literature, see Arrow, Sen, and Suzumura (2002). Government failures and the deviation of public policies from those that would maximize welfare have been carefully studied and reported in a major strand of literature in the public choice tradition, such as Mueller (2003), Drazen (2000), and Persson and Tabellini (2002).

[2] A companion working paper (Scartascini, 2008) offers a more careful treatment of these issues. Particularly, the working paper introduces these concepts—beliefs and perceptions—in terms of a specific decision-making mechanism and compares its results with those produced by the standard models in the literature.

[3] This chapter avoids describing the specific method used for aggregating preferences. For simplicity, Caplan (2007) and Scartascini (2008) use a median voter model. Mueller (2003) as well as numerous social choice books explains decision-making mechanisms and how voters' preferences are aggregated at the policy level in greater detail.

Box 9.1 Should Government Seek to Maximize Happiness?

The use of surveys to gather public opinion data and the expanding role that some analysts are assigning to the study of happiness raises an interesting question: should maximizing the public's happiness be the government's policy goal?[a] This question is not irrelevant for this volume, given the close relationship between happiness and satisfaction with life. While it may be enticing to think of a place where everyone is more satisfied with his or her life and happier, guiding government policy by aiming to increase a subjective happiness indicator has several drawbacks.[b]

To begin with, subjective opinions may be swayed by short-run events, making it difficult to determine from survey answers what truly makes people happy. Subjective assessments of happiness may be easily influenced in the short run by issues that have nothing to do with long-term happiness, such as the weather, a temporary health problem, or the outcome of a sporting event. Deeper determinants of happiness, such as long-term disabilities or the loss of a relative, also have a strong impact in the short run that tends to dissipate over time.[c] Changes in income also have an impact on satisfaction with life that tends to disappear rapidly. After a year, more than two-thirds of the improvement in satisfaction related to increases in income tends to disappear (Layard, 2003). Consequently, if the objective of policymakers were to influence satisfaction with life in the short run, they might have to endorse some policies that have no major impact on the long-term welfare of their citizens. By the same token, they would probably have to avoid policies that imply short-term sacrifices, even if they have a long-term positive impact on welfare.

Because most people are loss averse, their satisfaction is more negatively affected by a loss than positively affected by a gain. Therefore, policies that seek to maximize happiness may have a strong bias toward the status quo, as politicians avoid any policy that would reduce aggregate happiness, including redistributive policies. In this case, the search for subjective happiness could be at odds with other equally important objectives, such as justice or equity.

Policies to maximize happiness could also conspire against individual rights. If maximizing happiness were the main objective, where should policy intervention stop? Some of the factors that most influence happiness are marriage, friendship, and religion. Does the government have any place intervening in these areas?

(continued on next page)

---

[a] For example, in Bhutan, maximizing the Gross National Happiness Index is an explicit policy objective (Shrotrya, 2006).

[b] Coyne and Boettke (2006) and Frey (2008) are complementary sources that elaborate on many of these and related drawbacks.

[c] This phenomenon is known as the hedonic treadmill. Byrnes (2005) surveys the literature and evidence on the topic.

> *(continued)*
>
> Another problem with promotion of happiness as a policy goal is that a person's satisfaction with his or her life is affected not only by the actual state of affairs but also by the information available to him or her. People without information may not be able to evaluate their situation realistically. They may be content with their plight simply because they do not know that they could be doing better. By the same token, individuals who are bombarded with information about how well everyone else is doing may become frustrated, not because their situation is so dire, but because they feel they are lagging behind their peers.[d]
>
> Still, while there are many arguments as to why the government should not pursue maximizing life satisfaction as the main policy objective, public opinion polls that provide quantitative information on quality of life perceptions are useful. They can enrich the public debate, provide information (sometimes more accurate than what the experts have traditionally used) to experts and policymakers on what matters to people, and help explain certain policy outcomes, such as why certain reforms do not take place despite consensus among technocratic elites on their convenience. Whether or not they are well-founded and balanced, these opinions can help in deciphering the political attitudes, ideological preferences, and beliefs that condition the political process.
>
> _____
> [d] These victims of information (or the lack thereof) are known in the literature as "contented achievers" and "frustrated achievers." See Graham and Pettinato (2002a) for more on this subject.

about how the world works, and how they perceive reality.[4] Differences between the objective indicators for a sector (e.g., health or education), which tend to measure outcomes at a specific point in time, and people's opinions may reflect the greater insight of people, as compared to those objective indicators, into the dynamics of how the sector functions.[5] However, it may also be true that people lack the information needed to evaluate many aspects of their lives, especially those pertaining to societal or communal aspects. Their judgments may reflect this dearth of information, and how the little information they have is processed through a particular prism shaped by their own personality traits, their life circumstances, and historical and cultural factors.

The origin of many biases has to do with the way people make decisions based on the information available to them. Usually, people do not make reflexive and rational

_____

[4] This chapter tries to gauge the role of biases in perceptions and beliefs in the design and implementation of policies in Latin America. Traditional political economy and political science studies have already considered differences in preferences (i.e., some people prefer more of some goods than others) and information (e.g., some people make decisions with more information than others). When information is not complete, people rely on their beliefs for deciding on the best course of action (i.e., people make a logical connection between an action and an outcome) and rely on new information to update their beliefs. If their perceptions of reality are correct, they update their beliefs in a way compatible with reality. In the context of models developed in these studies, people make decisions to the best of their ability and choose those actions, policies, and candidates that would help maximize their long-term welfare.

[5] In this chapter we will refer to the difference between objective indicators and people's opinion as "biases."

choices, but use rules of thumb—or heuristics.[6] Some people start their reasoning from a reference point that is familiar to them, and then adjust it in the direction they think is appropriate, such as when people generalize based on events that have affected their family or surrounding community. For example, they may interpret a local employment crisis as a national crisis. Another decision-making approach is to use readily available examples and information in order to judge certain events. A person's assessment of the probability of a natural disaster, for example, may be affected by whether a recent natural disaster has taken place and whether the person has personally experienced a disaster.[7] Finally, people may depend on stereotypes to guide their opinions, particularly when they lack sufficient information. For instance, one stereotype is that poor people are more likely to commit crimes; thus people may cross the street to avoid a poorly dressed individual under the assumption that he or she is a criminal.

Results from one Latin American study show some of these heuristics at play. When people are asked about the state of affairs in their country, the employed tend to perceive the state of the national economy as stronger than those who are unemployed, and those who have been asked for and/or have paid a bribe tend to perceive public corruption in the country as more pervasive than those who have not been exposed to an act of corruption (Higueras and Scartascini, 2008).

In addition to the heuristics described above, other behavioral biases may affect how people evaluate external factors and influence their opinion on public matters. Optimism and overconfidence can make people overestimate their future performance beyond what would be statistically feasible. For example, most people would rate their performance on most issues, such as how well they will do in a business endeavor, in a casino, or how well they drive, among the top tier, even though relatively few of them actually belong to that category.

People are also generally loss averse: they suffer more from the loss of an object than they benefit from its acquisition. Loss aversion can be partly explained by individuals' preferences regarding risk. However, while it may be natural for people to prefer something with certainty over facing a lottery (or as the saying goes, "a bird in the hand is worth two in the bush"), it is less intuitive that somebody may be willing to pay less to acquire an object than what he or she would be willing to sell it for. Experiments have illustrated this point clearly; for example, one study shows that while people would pay a small amount for a coffee mug, they would not sell their mug for less than two or three times that amount (Thaler and Sunstein, 2008).

Loss aversion is one of the drivers of inertia. Also, many people are happy to stick with the status quo; such people usually hang on to default options or known alternatives. Marketing companies often bank on this behavior when they entice people to sign up for programs—such as a free first month's subscription to a magazine—because they know that most people will not cancel them.[8] This resistance to change is an obvious

---

[6] Heuristics are decisions that are intuitive and automatic instead of reflective and rational (reflective system). Three heuristics identified by Tversky and Kahneman (1974) are anchoring, availability, and representativeness. See also Kahneman and Tversky (2000) for an overview of their work and that of their coauthors.

[7] For example, the purchase of earthquake insurance increases sharply after an earthquake but then falls steadily as memory fades (Elster, 2007: 131).

[8] The status quo bias is highly correlated with procrastination: putting off doing something, especially out of habitual carelessness or laziness.

obstacle to policy reform.[9] Framing is also very important, as the same information presented in slightly different ways may generate completely different responses. People respond differently to positive and negative messages that provide the same information: the statement "The glass is half-empty" conveys the same literal information as the statement "The glass is half-full," but the reaction to the two statements is likely to be markedly different.

In addition to these largely behavioral or character traits, cultural factors are important in shaping biases; such factors influence how people evaluate outcomes, giving rise to several paradoxes. Contrary to expectations, while average satisfaction with life tends to be greater in higher-income countries, income growth actually leads to lower levels of happiness in countries with incomes above a certain threshold. What explains this "unhappy growth paradox"? First, as people's income grows, so do their aspirations; and as people's living standards rise, they often long for things they cannot reach. Second, people compare their living standards with those of a reference group; if other people fare better, people become dissatisfied. It's the age-old "keeping up with the Joneses" phenomenon.[10] Envy is powerful, particularly among those who are climbing the social ladder. Clearly, many people evaluate their happiness based not only on their own situation, but also on the situations of those around them, the source of income growth, and their beliefs about the justice of the outcomes.

This has very direct implications for people's opinions on policies, such as redistribution and other social welfare policies. Studies (e.g., Fong, 2006) show that people tend to oppose redistribution if they believe their society has few impediments to upward mobility. They tend to interpret the evidence to suggest that less well-off individuals have not made the effort to improve their standards of living, therefore they do not deserve government support (Fong, 2006). In Latin America, most people are pessimistic about their own mobility prospects, and those people who are worse off, or think that market outcomes are unfair, tend to support greater redistribution.[11]

Moreover, those who see their peers' incomes rising may demand greater redistribution than those at the same level of income who are not aware of these increases. As noted earlier in the chapter, while an increase in one's own income raises satisfaction, income increases among those in one's reference group produce the opposite effect. Furthermore, in the words of Richard Layard (2003: 5), if a person "earns an extra 10 percent and so does everyone else, he experiences only two-thirds of the extra happiness that would accrue if he alone had had the raise." In the end, "it's not the absolute level of income that matters most but rather one's position relative to other individuals" (Frey and Stutzer, 2002: 411), and "what people believe is as important as the objective

[9] This phenomenon might party explain the evidence regarding failed pension reforms in some European countries (Immergut, Anderson, and Schulze, 2007).

[10] It is important to note that the relevant aspect here is not the distribution of preferences within society, but how people use certain benchmarks to evaluate outcomes that are different than those the standard literature would suggest. While in the more traditional models more information would tend to resolve certain biases, here it could make them worse. For example, a person who receives a salary increase may be happier if he or she does not know that others have received more. In this example, less information generates more happiness.

[11] Gaviria (2007) presents the evidence for Latin America. Interestingly, the demand for redistribution depends on the degree of fractionalization of society. In those cases where fractionalization is higher, demand for redistribution is lower, showing that altruism is not necessarily the main driver, particularly when redistributing resources from one group to another is at stake (Wantchekon, 2003; Finseraas, 2006).

economic circumstances in explaining people's attitudes to political issues like redistribution" (Georgiadis and Manning, 2008). In this context, redistributive policies have to take into account their impact on the well-being not only of the groups that are directly targeted, but also of those whose status and incentives towards greater effort may be affected.[12]

The evidence from Latin America supports these hypotheses. While lower income groups tend to support redistributive social policies, they are usually less satisfied with poverty reduction policies when people in their same age and education group are doing better. Envy often clouds people's judgment of public policies, and this culture of envy can be a serious impediment to social progress. If the rich do not care about the poor and the poor resent the economic progress of their peers, the establishment of a social pact for growth with equity that implies, for example, a system of redistributive taxes and promotion of business activity seems very unlikely. Table 3.2 shows similar results for most public policies. As their reference group does better, people's satisfaction with most public policies drops consistently, especially among the poor.

Opinions and beliefs are not necessarily correlated with standard socioeconomic groups (not all rich or poor people think alike). Some biases may be correlated with the role of people in certain areas (e.g., beliefs about the fairness of a soccer game result are correlated among team fans regardless of age, income, and education), and some may be correlated with variables such as level of education and media exposure. People with less education may be more gullible and accept as universal truths certain facts that hold true only in very limited situations. Such individuals may also have lower expectations. A similar phenomenon may occur with people who have limited exposure to the media. Preliminary results show that media exposure helps explain people's assessments of their country's performance along several dimensions, ranging from the economic situation to the level of corruption. People with less exposure to the media tend to use their own reality as a benchmark to a greater extent than those with greater exposure (Higueras and Scartascini, 2008). Chapter 6 shows the impact of socioeconomic status on the evaluation of education policies: lower-income individuals who live in more-segregated neighborhoods have lower expectations; therefore, they tend to be less demanding than both those in higher income groups and the poor, who are more exposed to people with better education. Overall, the poor demonstrate a disturbing "aspirations paradox": their opinions about their standards of living and the policies of their country tend to be more favorable than the opinions of higher income classes. They have greater confidence in the government's health and job creation policies, even though they suffer the most from deficiencies in such policies.

Some biases may also have to do with cultural upbringing, religious beliefs, and geographical location. Most people use known benchmarks for estimating the impact of a particular policy when they are uncertain about the issue at hand. Therefore, those who live in former industrial communities where many jobs have been lost since trade liberalization may hold stronger beliefs against free trade, regardless of their personal

---

[12] If social status is determined according to the level of consumption of a conspicuous good, an increase in equality, through increases in the income of the lower class without a parallel increase in the income of the middle class, will tend to decrease the latter's welfare (Hopkins and Kornienko, 2008). Comparisons and expectations affect not only demand for public policies, but also decisions in everyday life. For example, they may affect employees' level of effort (Brown et al., 2005; Clark, Masclet, and Villeval, 2006).

situations, than those who live in areas that have been revitalized thanks to such policies. When estimating the impact of free trade, rarely will anyone take a position (and vote in a subsequent election) based on the impact of the free trade policy in the country as a whole, which they are unaware of. Instead, they will use known benchmarks for making their decisions, such as the impact of the policy on the surrounding community.[13]

Relative Power Determines Policy

Since biases differ across people, the policies chosen in a given society at a particular time will depend on the relative influence of different groups of the population in the policy process. Not every group in society has the same level of political clout.[14] Some groups may have better access to public officials; they may have the pivotal vote; they may have more capacity to organize themselves; and they may participate more.[15] Politicians and political parties have an incentive to cater to the policy wishes of those who are expected to vote, those who can provide campaign resources, and those who can mobilize the support of others. Consequently, the preferences of such groups will eventually weigh more heavily on policy than the preferences of others.

Moreover, preferences and beliefs are not necessarily uniformly distributed across groups. Therefore, if groups with stronger power have biased beliefs, those beliefs may translate more easily into biased policy demands.

Decision Making at Work: An Example from Labor Markets

An example from labor markets may help illustrate how not only preferences and relative power but also certain beliefs regarding how labor markets work may influence policy.[16] According to labor market theory (and the evidence gathered from the opinions of people in Argentina, Chile, and Venezuela), most workers decide whether to support labor regulations according to their best interest (preferences).[17] Those who expect to be positively affected, such as low-skilled workers with permanent contracts, tend to support labor regulations (minimum wage increases and firing restrictions) more than those who might be negatively affected (low-skilled workers whose job stability is subject to great uncertainty and who may be let go and who would have greater difficulties in accessing the job market if the restrictions were put in place). In addition, those who may be negatively affected (business owners) or who may have a better understanding of the costs of regulations for society (e.g., people with higher education) are also usually against labor regulations. One particular group, labor union members, may show greater support for labor regulations based on their beliefs about the workings of labor markets. They support labor regulations more than other people, regardless of their in-

---

[13] Of course, self-interest may be the first of these benchmarks. Here, it is assumed that the impact of the policy is neutral on the individual.

[14] For the logic of collective action and interest group formation, see Olson (1965). For the impact of interest groups in politics, see Grossman and Helpman (2001).

[15] "Pivotal vote" refers to the case when an election is determined by one vote. Here the definition is used broadly, in the sense that one group may be decisive for certain policies.

[16] This case is developed in detail in Rueda Robayo and Scartascini (2008a).

[17] See Saint-Paul (2000) for theoretical and empirical support for this claim.

come and education level; that is, their support seems to go beyond what the traditional models would suggest based only on expected costs and benefits.[18]

Labor union members are also known for their higher levels of participation in political contests through mobilizing people and providing campaign contributions to those candidates they support. If they therefore have more political clout, then given their strong feelings about the positive impact of labor regulations, there may be more and stricter labor regulations than society might otherwise have chosen based solely on the general benefits and costs of those regulations. In contrast, those who may be affected negatively by labor regulations (such as informal workers and the unemployed) tend to have a weaker presence in the political arena, and they may lose this presence altogether in the long run.[19] As regulations increase, it may become harder for displaced workers to return to the formal sector, making it more difficult for them to regain political clout in labor policy discussions.

However, not everything is lost for those who do not have political clout in one market. If those displaced workers find that working in the informal sector is appealing (which Chapter 7 determines is a distinct possibility), they may have even fewer incentives to organize themselves to protest and participate in changing the formal labor market policy equilibrium. They may, however, organize themselves to gain benefits related to their new role in the economy as informal workers, a hypothesis that is partially confirmed by the data. According to public opinion surveys conducted in Latin America, self-employed individuals are more likely to demand that the government support independent workers and microenterprises than to argue against traditional labor market regulations, such as firing restrictions and minimum wages, which may have contributed to their departure from the formal labor market in the first place.

Ultimately, the economy in question may end up with a set of suboptimal policies. Those with strong positions in favor of labor regulations and power in the labor market may achieve those policies that favor their situation, while those who are hurt in the labor market and move toward self-employment and informality may solve their problems in a different market, asking for social and redistributive policies. Hence, instead of discussions about the right degree of labor regulation being held between those who benefit and those who lose, each group hastily demands policies in different political arenas, and those policies turn out to be inefficient.[20] Such a case is very similar to what arguably has occurred with public policies in Mexico (Levy, 2008).

Thus, voters' biased beliefs may affect the demand for policy, and the final outcome depends on the relative power of different groups of voters. If those voters who have stronger biases also have the greatest power (i.e., they participate more and have more money or other resources to offer), policy demand will usually deviate even further from what society might have otherwise chosen.

---

[18] On the one hand, they may receive benefits that are difficult to capture in the data. On the other, those who decide to join labor unions may do so because they believe in certain values that are traditionally supported by those organizations. The latter explanation is widely supported in the literature on labor union membership.

[19] Rueda Robayo and Scartascini (2008b) show that union membership is significant for explaining labor regulation in a cross-section of countries.

[20] This argument is similar in spirit to that in Spiller and Liao (2006). People tend to approach the "window" that would provide them with the highest chance of obtaining the rent they are seeking.

The Supply of Policy: Biases among Politicians

Just as voters may hold biased beliefs about how the world works, thereby affecting the demand for public policies, policymakers may have biases that affect the supply of public policies. Potentially, biases could stem from the fact that politicians are not selected at random from the population. Instead, they belong to a particular group in society, either before being elected (e.g., leaders come from the elite), or after being elected (i.e., their job is different than that of the average citizen). This difference may have positive implications: it may mean that policymakers are more educated, more interested in the issues that people care about, more altruistic, or better able to choose advisors and distinguish between good and bad recommendations. However, it may also have negative implications.[21] Policymakers may not understand the needs of the people, they may pay closer attention to certain interest groups, and they may be easily influenced by external trends and fashion.

Yet another source of bias comes from the fact that government officials may see the world differently by virtue of simply having taken the oath of office. Just as people may hold biased beliefs because they use their own benchmarks for gauging the appropriate viewpoint on issues about which they know very little (such as evaluating the impact of a national policy according to the impact it has in their own community), politicians may also update their beliefs according to their own experiences (known as the "where you stand is where you sit" hypothesis).[22] Hence, an economist who advocates free trade and is then appointed labor minister may change his or her opinion after spending time in the new position and dealing with people on a daily basis whose jobs have been negatively affected by trade, while very rarely encountering people who have gained jobs or whose living standards have improved as a result of the country's free trade policy. Politicians may also make decisions by following simple heuristics, such as voting in the same way as persons like themselves.[23]

Finally, the political system, by virtue of the institutions that regulate its functioning, may favor the selection of policymakers from particular interest groups, such as labor unions. Because political institutions are usually the consequence of history and patterns of power, they generally favor certain groups in the allocation of power (e.g., through malapportionment). For example, in some countries in Latin America, political institutions ensure the overrepresentation of particular provinces and states at the national level, which tends to generate redistribution in favor of those provinces and states.[24]

Interestingly, not only are differences in how people and leaders perceive the world important, but the pace at which each person or leader reacts to new information is as well, because it may affect the formulation and enactment of public policies. If leaders react late when people have ceased to care about a particular issue, reforms ad-

---

[21] Caselli and Morelli (2004) show that politics tends to offer higher possibilities for bad politicians to enter into politics, because "low-quality citizens" have a comparative advantage in pursuing public office.

[22] Hanes (2007) surveys the bureaucratic politics literature, which shows how government advisors change their views according to the jobs they hold.

[23] Masket (2006) shows that the physical location of legislators in the chamber matters in terms of how they vote, because they tend to be influenced by how people sitting close by have voted.

[24] Arretche and Rodden (2004) find that the bargaining power of small (overrepresented) states in Brazil is bigger than that of other states, but this advantage translates into benefits only if the legislators from these states are part of the government coalition. Spiller and Tommasi (2007) show similar evidence for Argentine provinces.

dressing that issue may be more difficult to implement. A tardy response by politicians may waste a golden opportunity for reform. In the meantime, people become disenchanted by politicians' tardy responses to what they see as their more-pressing needs.[25] Data from opinion polls about people's satisfaction with certain public policies and the opinions of leaders on the most relevant problems facing their countries confirm that people and leaders do not always perceive problems with the same intensity. Moreover, people may react more rapidly to changes in certain variables, but become more quickly accustomed to the new levels after the changes than politicians do.[26]

Reactions to the issue of crime are a dramatic case in point. Objective indicators, such as homicide rates, appall both people and leaders, as shown in Figure 9.1. However, people seem to react more intensely to more recent changes. This phenomenon seems to explain why the percentage of people who are dissatisfied with the level of violence is higher in Uruguay than in Colombia, even though the homicide rate in Colombia is 15 times higher than that in Uruguay. People also become used to high levels of violence, which explains the relatively low level of concern in Colombia compared to that in other countries. In both Uruguay and Colombia, people may be reacting to change.

Leaders seem to understand better than the citizens they govern the differences between levels and change, which helps explain why they are more concerned in Colombia than in Uruguay about violence. However, in some cases they may react more slowly to surges in violence. Figure 9.1 shows the simple correlation between the objective indicators, in this case homicide rates, and how people (as measured in the Gallup World Polls) and leaders (as measured by a survey of business and po-

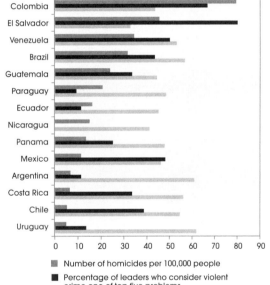

Figure 9.1 Homicide Rates and Security Perceptions of People and Leaders

- ■ Number of homicides per 100,000 people
- ■ Percentage of leaders who consider violent crime one of top five problems
- ▨ Percentage of people dissatisfied with security in their neighborhoods

Source: Authors' calculations based on Gallup (2007) and Consulta de San José (2008).
Note: Data on percentage of leaders considering violent crime a top-five problem not available for Nicaragua.

---

[25] Some hypotheses on why leaders may have a delayed response to a particular issue are (a) it takes time for information to accumulate; (b) people react more rapidly than statistics; (c) there is a status quo inertia and politicians are slow to respond; (d) rapid response may be seen as an argument showing that the government was not doing its job to begin with; and (e) leaders prefer to concentrate on more (politically) relevant issues and let others slip away over time.

[26] Data are from Gallup and a survey conducted by the IDB for La Consulta de San José (2008), a joint effort of the Copenhagen Consensus and IDB that aimed to identify the 10 best ways to invest hypothetical money to address key development problems.

litical leaders conducted by the Consulta de San José)[27] react. Countries are ranked from top to bottom in order of their homicide rates. As the figure shows, this order does not always correspond to either the public's degree of concern about the problem or the percentage of leaders who ranked it as one of the top five problems in their country. In El Salvador, leaders rank crime high on their agenda while the public does not. At the other extreme, in Uruguay, fewer than 10 percent of leaders rank violent crime as a top-five problem compared to over 60 percent of the public.

Using Information to Manipulate Perceptions

This chapter has argued that the beliefs and perceptions of people, politicians, and government officials may affect the demand and supply of public policies.[28] But these beliefs and perceptions are not necessarily exogenous. The literature on deliberative democracy has shown the benefits of deliberation under the basic premise that democracy revolves around the transformation rather than simply the aggregation of preferences.[29] In that context, preferences and positions are not givens and decisions are part of a complex process of negotiation and exchanges. Information can influence perceptions and, therefore, the demand for and supply of policies.

Ideally, deliberation can help fill in gaps in information and make for better choices and decisions. But it may also increase the ability of some people to manipulate others through the way they craft their messages, particularly when information is scarce. In a perfect world, inequality of information and specialization in the provision of information may be innocuous. Interest groups conduct research on the impact of their products, and as a result they generate information that others do not have. However, when there are conflicts between the interests of some and those of others, those who spend money to communicate may be trying to persuade others to hold beliefs that are not in their best interest.

How communication affects a particular person (e.g., a policymaker) depends on two things. First, it depends on whether he or she welcomes the new information. Second, it depends on his or her capacity to process the information received and to distinguish quality information from information that serves the purpose of the sender. To the degree that a person does not have this capacity, he or she may be more easily influenced by third parties. For example, in Latin America, most legislators have no previous legislative experience when they are elected, nor do they have institutional support in the legislature or at the party level.[30] These characteristics make them particularly susceptible to being influenced.

---

[27] Survey results are reported by Berkman and Cavallo (2006).

[28] As already mentioned, beliefs and perceptions are not the only determinants. Given the already prolific literature on the topic, this chapter has not considered the most obvious and studied determinants of deviations of public policy from people's preferences: the method of aggregation and government failures.

[29] There are no standard definitions of deliberation (Elster, 1998). For Przeworski (1998: 140), "'deliberation' is a form of discussion intended to change the preferences on the bases of which people decide how to act. Deliberation is 'political' when it leads to a decision binding on a community. . . . Finally, 'democratic political deliberation' occurs when discussion leads to a decision by voting."

[30] See Saiegh (forthcoming) for an analysis. Data provided by Manuel Alcántara (Universidad de Salamanca) show that in every Latin American country but Chile, more than 50 percent of legislators in 2003 had no previous leg-

Consequently, in a world where people and policymakers lack the capacity to generate their own information and test every single hypothesis they form or encounter, the flow of information, influence, and manipulation becomes very complex, with every actor trying to influence and convince the rest about the benefits of certain policies (Stokes, 1998).

How Elites Affect Public Opinion

Politicians usually, instead of pursuing people-chosen policies, try to frame information in a way that will enable them to win people's support for their policies. As Dick Morris, pollster for U.S. President Bill Clinton, acknowledged, "[legislators and the Clinton White House] don't use a poll to reshape a program, but to reshape your argumentation for the program so that the public supports it." Michael Deaver, a senior aide to U.S. President Ronald Reagan, made similar comments: "with [Reagan], polls were not used to change policy to follow the prevailing winds. Instead, they were tools to determine how to persuade people about an idea."[31]

Reshaping public opinion, which has become easier with the advancement of new technologies (such as radio and television), allows politicians to satisfy their electoral and policy objectives directly and indirectly by using public opinion to pressure other public officials. Some of the techniques used are tracking public opinion, managing press coverage, and "priming" the message. The "priming" approach concentrates on raising the priority and the weight that individuals assign to particular attitudes already stored in their memory.[32] The techniques for influencing opinion and actions do not have to be highly sophisticated to work. Research from other social science areas shows that simple actions, such as placing a sticky note on a written request, generate a much higher response rate, and that, for example, a server in a restaurant offering customers candy after a dinner significantly affects the tips he or she receives.[33]

Under certain conditions, part of the "manipulation" of public opinion may involve overselling ("promising too much") the impact and relevance of certain policies in order to gather support. This strategy has many risks. If the probability of success is low and promises are not satisfied, the unfulfilled expectations may decrease the sustainability of the policy change in question, prompting a reversion to the policy in place

---

islative experience. In some countries, such as Costa Rica, Mexico, Nicaragua, and Paraguay, the percentage was above 80 percent. Scartascini (2005) (based on data collected for the OECD/World Bank/IDB Database on Budget Practices and Procedures) shows that while most developed countries have legislative budget offices with more than 50 employees, only in a handful of Latin American countries do these offices have more than 25 (who usually are not even highly specialized).

[31] Quotes are taken from Jacobs and Shapiro (2000). While considerations like those underlying the quotes have not been fully fledged into theory, they are not new. According to Elster (1998), Schumpeter had already insisted that voters' preferences are shaped and manipulated by politicians. Alessandro (2006) provides evidence on how governments change the discourse.

[32] See Jacobs and Shapiro (2000: 50) for a list of references on the issue.

[33] A survey of research by Goldstein, Martin, and Cialdini (2008) reveals that placing a sticky note on a request for filling out a survey form generates more than twice the number of responses as having the request within the text of the survey. The same review finds that mints placed in the check tray presented to customers elicit much higher tips than mints placed in a basket for general consumption as diners exited the restaurant. Moreover, mints handed by a server directly to customers elicit even higher tips.

prior to the change.[34] Therefore, while manipulation may work, policymakers should be aware of the consequences that unfulfilled promises may engender.

Special Interests Affect Public Opinion and Politicians

Politicians are not the only ones who may be able to persuade the public to change its views or influence public opinion toward support for certain policies. Organized special interest groups may have similar tools at hand.[35] Strong issue campaigning, using techniques similar to those explained above, may tilt public opinion in an interest group's favor and affect how politicians vote on the issue.[36]

Interest groups may exploit other, less-organized groups by feeding them information that is favorable to their cause. This may be easier the bigger the informational gaps of the less-organized groups in regard to the issues at hand and the higher their susceptibility to being influenced. The case of education in Latin America is illustrative of this point. Many parents tend to disregard information on the quality of schools in their evaluations. For teachers' unions, which are strongly organized in many Latin American countries, this provides an opportunity to gain parents' support when pushing governments for new hires by persuading them that quantity is what matters. The example of education policy in Peru is revealing. While public expenditure on secondary education has increased by more than 50 percent in that country in the last few years, the increase has had minimal impact on education quality (in fact, test scores have actually dropped).[37] Despite these abysmal results, proposals to restructure the education system have been effectively blocked by teachers' unions.

Interest groups may also target politicians directly to achieve the enactment of the policies they want. Such groups have a number of ways to manipulate public officials to go along with their positions: (1) through campaign contributions and mobilization of grassroots groups that "buy" the support of politicians; (2) by convincing politicians about the benefits of their proposal or the drawbacks of the existing policy or other policy options on the table; and (3) by persuading politicians that public opinion is in favor of (or against) the policy in question.

The Media May Influence Policymakers and Citizens Alike

The media can have many positive effects in each different stage of the policymaking process by providing information to policymakers and voters alike.[38] The media can also

---

[34] This may be even more so when presidents have to move away quite considerably from promises they have made during their electoral campaigns, as was the case with, for example, Carlos Menem in Argentina and Alberto Fujimori in Peru. See Forteza and Tommasi (2006) and Stokes (2001).

[35] Large multinationals have access to advertising and the media that surpasses that of many governments. For example, research laboratories' advertising expenditure on the 50 most popular prescription drugs surpassed US$1.5 billion in the United States in 2000 (NIHCM, 2000). This amount is nevertheless smaller than the advertising budget of Coke, which may top US$2 billion (Ledbetter, 1998; Smith, 2006).

[36] Stokes (1998: 128) presents, as an example of this, the way special interests manipulated public opinion against the clean air act in the 1990s.

[37] Carranza, Chávez, and Valderrama (forthcoming) provide detailed data on the evolution of secondary education public expenditure and standardized test scores in Peru.

[38] See Hughes (forthcoming) for an analysis of the role of the media in policymaking in Latin America.

act as a watchdog and provide additional tools for enforcing policymakers' promises. People may also be able to put their own situations into perspective by comparing it to that depicted in media reports. Some embryonic research on this important but still understudied issue suggests that media exposure has an impact on people's perceptions of issues concerning national policies or the status of economic affairs in a country. For example, higher media exposure seems to make people more aware of national affairs and the differences between their situations and the situations of others.[39] Interestingly, exposure to media may also have an effect on social behaviors beyond those surveyed here. According to La Ferrara, Chong, and Duryea (2008), social attitudes, as presented in soap operas, may affect decisions on matters such as childbearing.

The media also play a role in public debate, and do not merely broadcast debates between political and private actors. On the one hand, the media help set the agenda of the public debate by deciding which issues they will and will not cover.[40] On the other, when they decide to cover a particular issue, their effect is rarely unbiased. First, they may be co-opted by political actors or private interest groups, each of which can buy advertising and "air and press time" in the media. Second, even in the context of "independent media," political reality may be distorted because economic pressures to draw audiences create incentives to emphasize political conflict as an entertaining way to present an otherwise dull political debate. Third, in similar fashion, the media tend to present those issues that may be more interesting but are not necessarily more important than the ones they choose not to present. For example, they may increase awareness of low-probability events (e.g., a plane crash) while leaving unreported other events of higher probability (e.g., traffic fatalities).[41] Fourth, by introducing certain topics into the public domain, they may generate a cascade effect on the relevance of issues related to that topic. It takes only a couple of noteworthy examples to create the impression that the public in general is for or against a particular measure. For example, a demonstration by a few people can be reported as widespread opposition in order to draw attention to it.

A Dialogue for Quality

If both people and policymakers see reality through a clouded prism, their reaction to new information is different, and the information on which they base their decisions may be biased, how can policymakers ensure that the policymaking process results in policies that improve people's choices, take people's preferences and beliefs into account, and effectively improve people's quality of life?

Increasing the amount of information available to people and policymakers is the first building block of the process. Clearly, incomplete and asymmetric information may have a negative effect and lead to biased opinions. Better access to information may

---

[39] See Higueras and Scartascini (2008) for an exercise involving Latin American countries. Marquis (2006) shows that the media have a role in determining behaviors in some people—citizens who qualify as "askers"—but not in others.

[40] Stimson (2004) looks at the issue of agenda setting. For Jacobs and Shapiro (2000), press coverage is largely driven by forces external to the press, such as the behavior of authoritative government officials.

[41] Lewis (2001, chap. 4) provides a note of caution regarding the actual impact of the media on public opinion. While he acknowledges that public opinion polls respond swiftly to the media's coverage of a particular issue, he also contends that people may not actually change their private views that dramatically.

help people make sounder decisions. Also, if citizens and policymakers can discern the source of information, they can more easily discriminate between objective advice and self-serving opinions.

Because the benefit of gathering information is usually low for both voters and policymakers, so the cost should be as well. Increasing the amount of available information involves simple measures, such as increasing the transparency of government actions (e.g., posting budget data on the Internet), and more complex ones, such as fostering a more competitive press, which may increase the availability of dissonant voices and level the playing field among different actors. An even more complex measure, because it may depend on deeper institutional reform, is to try to make political labels and party programs meaningful. This should reduce information costs for voters and generate conditions for competition among parties, providing a wide—but not excessive—array of options among which citizens can choose.[42]

More information may be to no avail if actors do not have the capacity to process it. On the public's side, building human capital matters; however, as has been painfully demonstrated, people must have incentives to demand education and politicians must have enticements to offer it, and to improve the quality of what is offered. Additionally, increasing the capabilities of policymakers will make them less subject to the whims of interest groups and partial information provided by the media. The evidence seems to support these claims. More capable legislatures and bureaucracies tend to be correlated with better public policies in Latin America.[43]

Capabilities should be increased on at least two fronts. First, inputs should be increased and the "type" of policymakers improved. That is, material and human resources—which have traditionally been the focus of donors' assistance—and policymakers' skills should be increased at the same time. Second, policymakers should be given incentives to invest in their capabilities; for example, increasing their expected tenure in office might create the conditions for policymakers to develop their skills, both by providing them with the actual time to develop these skills through experience and by increasing their incentives to do so (Stein and Tommasi, 2007).

Better-informed and more capable policymakers should help alleviate the problem of undue influence, but the door could still be left open for manipulation by interest groups with privileged access to policymakers. Therefore, political arenas should be more open, to provide access to everybody, not just interested parties or incumbents. But open arenas will work only if there are parties interested in participating in the discussions. Reducing participation costs (and solving collective action problems) may generate discussions among a broader set of actors. Because resource-rich interest groups have greater possibilities of influencing policy and public opinion, providing other groups with similar access to public opinion, the media, and policymakers may be appropriate.

More open arenas and better discussion should be complemented by an accountability system that helps thwart attempts to manipulate public discourse and poli-

---

[42] For example, voters in the Brazilian state of São Paulo were faced in the 2002 elections with 703 candidates for the post of federal deputy in the legislature, six candidates for the presidency, 1,424 candidates for state deputy and 25 candidates for two senatorial posts. It almost goes without saying that making an informed decision in such a situation is practically impossible.

[43] IDB (2005) and Stein et al. (2008) show the relevance of legislative and bureaucratic capabilities in the Latin American context.

cies. Enforcement may come from both inside and outside sources. Inside, actors who participate regularly in exchanges can punish those who deviate from previous agreements or norms developed over time. For example, two political parties that alternate in government at regular intervals may be able to pursue more stable policies by adopting, in their interaction over time, mutually beneficial strategies for punishing deviations of this kind. The most common outside source of enforcement is an independent judiciary (or similar control agency) that can create mechanisms to keep policymakers and interest groups at bay. The evidence indicates that both mechanisms (repeated interactions and judicial independence) improve the quality of the resulting policies (IDB, 2005; Stein et al., 2008; Scartascini, Stein, and Tommasi, 2008).

Decentralization of decision making may reinforce the effect of the mechanisms mentioned above. While providing voters with more information about the actions of the government, such decentralization can also help policymakers gather firsthand information about the preferences of voters. Moreover, it may provide more open arenas for deliberation and reduce participation costs because it is easier for citizens to organize around local issues and participate in local policy decisions. Since voters can punish local leaders relatively easily, decentralization can also increase accountability. All told, decentralization may be a useful way to bring policies closer to people's preferences.[44]

This volume has revealed a wealth of information provided by public opinion surveys that allow policymakers to see the world through their constituents' eyes. The public's point of view adds color, and often stark contrast, to the essentially black-and-white picture painted by traditional objective indicators. It can serve as a complement to the statistical skeleton and can help governments build more dynamic development programs and more effective political strategies.

However, important issues remain. One challenge is to find a way to track systematically the pulse of public opinion and ensure that it feeds continuously into the public debate. Some vehicles for tracking have been suggested in this volume. Chapter 8 proposes a system for monitoring the quality of urban life that could nourish an informed dialogue between politicians and the public and help establish priorities in individual cities. Chapter 4 introduces the idea that assigning a value to what matters to people could help prioritize public spending. In all cases, the effort should be ongoing so as to provide input over time that capitalizes on the dynamic nature of public opinion.

Perhaps even more pressing is the need to ensure that information flows are multidirectional so that people are equipped to express well-founded opinions. This chapter has exposed the biases behind both the public's and policymakers' opinions and raises a red flag against taking either at face value. Better information in open arenas can help ensure that the public's contribution is based on a solid foundation. Ignoring the public interest is clearly a danger, as is designing public policy to please a potentially misinformed populace. Countries in Latin America are in the process of reforming some of their most fundamental institutions, advancing the decentralization process and increasing transparency and accountability. The seeds of a deliberative democracy are being planted. Now is the time to help them grow into healthy, participative systems with strong roots, capable of delivering quality policies for a better quality of life.

---

[44] See Cristini, Moskovits, and Moya (2008) for detailed references.

References

Abt Associates Inc. 2008. The Quality of Education in Latin America and the Caribbean Region: The Case of Peru. Document prepared for the Inter-American Development Bank Research Network, Abt Associates, Cambridge, MA.

Acevedo, Germán, Patricio Eskenazi, and Carmen Pagés. 2006. Unemployment Insurance in Chile: A New Model of Income Support for Unemployed Workers. SP Discussion Paper No. 612. World Bank, Washington, DC.

Ades, Alberto F., and Edward L. Glaeser. 1995. Trade and Circuses: Explaining Urban Giants. *Quarterly Journal of Economics* 110(1) February: 195–227.

Ahsan, Ahmad, and Carmen Pagés. 2007. Are All Labor Regulations Equal? Assessing the Effects of Job Security, Labor Dispute and Contract Labor Laws in India. SP Discussion Paper No. 0713. World Bank, Washington, DC.

Alcázar, Lorena, and Raúl Andrade. 2008. Quality of Life in Urban Neighborhoods in Metropolitan Lima, Peru. Inter-American Development Bank, Washington, DC, and Group for the Analysis of Development (GRADE), Lima. Unpublished.

Alesina, Alberto, Reza Baqir, and William Easterly. 1999. Public Goods and Ethnic Divisions. *Quarterly Journal of Economics* 114(4) November: 1243–84.

Alesina, Alberto, Rafael Di Tella, and Robert MacCulloch. 2004. Inequality and Happiness: Are Europeans and Americans Different? *Journal of Public Economics* 88(9–10) August: 2009–42.

Alessandro, N. 2006. Foreign Policy: What Does the Government Say, and Why? An Analysis of Swiss Government Discourse in Federal Ballots' Leaflets. Paper presented at the European Consortium for Political Research (ECPR) Joint Sessions of Workshops, April 25–30, Nicosia, Cyprus.

Alfonso, Mariana, Suzanne Duryea, and María Victoria Rodríguez-Pombo. 2007. Reproductive Empowerment and Quality of Life. Inter-American Development Bank, Washington, DC. Unpublished.

Allardt, Erik, and Hannu Uusitalo. 1972. Dimensions of Welfare in a Comparative Study of the Scandinavian Societies. Scandinavian Political Studies, Bind 7. Available at http://www.tidsskrift.dk/visning.jsp?markup=&print=no&id=95959.

Alpízar, Francisco, Fredrik Carlsson, and Olof Johansson-Stenman. 2005. How Much Do We Care about Absolute versus Relative Income and Consumption? *Journal of Economic Behavior & Organization* 56(3) March: 405–21.

Altinok, Nadir, and Hatidje Murseli. 2007. International Database on Human Capital Quality. *Economics Letters* 96(2) August: 237–44.

Andalon, Mabel, and Carmen Pagés. 2008. Minimum Wages in Kenya. IZA Discussion Paper No. 3390. Institute for the Study of Labor (IZA), Bonn, Germany.

Argyle, Michael. 1999. Causes and Correlates of Happiness. In Daniel Kahneman, Ed Diener, and Norbert Schwartz, eds., *Well-Being: The Foundations of Hedonic Psychology.* New York: Russell Sage Foundation Publications.

Ariely, Dan. 2008. *Predictably Irrational.* New York: Harper-Collins.

Arregui, Patricia, ed. 2006. *Sobre estándares y evaluaciones en América Latina.* Grupo de Trabajo sobre Estándares y Evaluación. Santiago: GTEE/PREAL.

Arretche, Marta, and Jonathon Rodden. 2004. Política distributiva na Federação: estratégias eleitorais, barganhas legislativas e coalizões de governo. *Dados* 47(3): 549–76.

Arrow, Kenneth J., Amartya K. Sen, and Kotaro Suzumura. 2002. *Handbook of Social Choice and Welfare,* Volume 1. Amsterdam: North-Holland.

Astorga, Pablo, Ame R. Berges, and Valpy Fitzgerald. 2005. The Standard of Living in Latin America during the Twentieth Century. *Economic History Review* 58(4) November: 765–96.

Attanasio, Orazio, and Miguel Székely. 1999. An Asset-Based Approach to the Analysis of Poverty in Latin America. Working Paper No. R-376. Latin American Research Network, Inter-American Development Bank, Washington, DC.

Auerbach, Paula, Maria Eugenia Genoni, and Carmen Pagés. 2007. Social Security Coverage and the Labor Market in Developing Countries. IZA Discussion Paper No. 2979. Institute for the Study of Labor (IZA), Bonn, Germany.

Auguste, Sebastián, María Echart, and Francisco Franchetti. 2008. The Quality of Education in Argentina. Latin American Research Network, Inter-American Development Bank, Washington, DC. Unpublished.

Autor, David H. 2003. Outsourcing at Will: The Contribution of Unjust Dismissal Doctrine to the Growth of Employment Outsourcing. *Journal of Labor Economics* 21(1): 1–42.

Autor, David H., John J. Donohue III, and Stewart J. Schwab. 2004. The Employment Consequences of Wrongful-Discharge Laws: Large, Small, or None at All? *American Economic Review* 94(2): 440–46.

———. 2006. The Costs of Wrongful-Discharge Laws. *Review of Economics and Statistics* 88(2): 211–31.

Autor, David H., William R. Kerr, and Adrian D. Kugler. 2007. Does Employment Protection Reduce Productivity? Evidence from US States. *Economic Journal* 117(521): 189–217.

Ball, Richard, and Kateryna Chernova. 2008. Absolute Income, Relative Income, and Happiness. *Social Indicators Research* 88(3) September: 497–529.

Bartelsman, Eric J., John Haltiwanger, and Stefano Scarpetta. 2004. Microeconomic Evidence of Creative Destruction in Industrial and Developing Countries. Tinbergen Institute Discussion Papers 04-114/3. Tinbergen Institute, Amsterdam.

Bell, Linda A. 1997. The Impact of Minimum Wages in Mexico and Colombia. *Journal of Labor Economics* 15(3) July: 102–34.

Bentham, Jeremy. 1781. *An Introduction to the Principles of Morals and Legislation.* Available at http://socserv.mcmaster.ca/econ/ugcm/3ll3/bentham/morals.pdf.

Berkman, Heather, and Eduardo Cavallo. 2006. The Challenges in Latin America: Identifying What Latin Americans Believe to Be the Main Problems Facing Their Countries. Research Department, Inter-American Development Bank, Washington, DC. Unpublished.

Bernasconi, Andrés. 2002. El sistema de supervisión y mejoramiento de la calidad de la educación superior de El Salvador: estudio de caso. Education Unit, Sustainable Development Department, Inter-American Development Bank, Washington, DC.

Bertrand, Marianne, and Sendhil Mullainathan. 2001. Do People Mean What They Say? Implications for Subjective Survey Data. *American Economic Review* 91(2) May: 67–72.

Besley, Timothy J., and Robin Burgess. 2004. Labor Regulation Hinder Economic Performance? Evidence from India. *Quarterly Journal of Economics* 119(1) February: 91–134.

Betcherman, Gordon, N. Meltem Daysal, and Carmen Pagés. 2008. Do Employment Subsidies Work? Evidence from Regionally Targeted Subsidies in Turkey. IZA Discussion Papers 3508. Institute for the Study of Labor (IZA), Bonn, Germany.

Betcherman, Gordon, Karina Olivas, and Amit Dar. 2004. Impacts of Active Labor Market Programs: New Evidence from Evaluations with Particular Attention to Developing and Transition Countries. SP Discussion Paper No. 0402. World Bank, Washington, DC.

Betcherman, Gordon, and Carmen Pagés. 2007. *Estimating the Impact of Labor Taxes on Employment and the Balances of the Social Insurance Funds in Turkey.* Synthesis Report. World Bank, Washington, DC.

Bitrán, Ricardo, Rodrigo Muñoz, Liliana Escobar, and Claudio Farah. 2008. Governing a Hybrid Mandatory Health Insurance System: The Case of Chile. In William D. Savedoff and Pablo Gottret, eds., *Governing Mandatory Health Insurance: Learning from Experience.* Washington, DC: World Bank.

Blanchflower, David G., and Andrew J. Oswald. 2004. Well-Being over Time in Britain and the USA. *Journal of Public Policies* 88(7–8) July: 1359–87.

———. 2007. Hypertension and Happiness across Nations. IZA Discussion Paper No. 2633. Institute for the Study of Labor (IZA), Bonn, Germany.

Blomquist, Glenn C., Mark C. Berger, and John P. Hoehn. New Estimates of Quality of Life in Urban Areas. *American Economic Review* 78(1) March: 89–107.

Bogotá Chamber of Commerce. 2007. *Observatorio de movilidad de Bogotá y la region.* No. 1, December.

Borges Martins, Roberto. 2004. Desigualdades raciais e políticas de inclusão racial: um sumário da experiência brasileira recente. Social Policies Series No. 82(LC/L.2082-P). Social Development Division, United Nations Economic Commission for Latin America and the Caribbean (ECLAC), Santiago.

Bosch, Mariano, and William F. Maloney. 2007a. Comparative Analysis of Labor Market Dynamics Using Markov Processes: An Application to Informality. IZA Discussion Paper No. 3038. Institute for the Study of Labor (IZA), Bonn, Germany.

————. 2007b. Gross Worker Flows in the Presence of Informal Labor Markets: Evidence from Mexico: 1987–2002. IZA Discussion Paper No. 2864. Institute for the Study of Labor (IZA), Bonn, Germany.

Bourguignon, François J. 2003. From Income to Endowments: The Difficult Task of Expanding the Income Poverty Paradigm. DELTA Working Paper 2003-03. Département et Laboratoire d'Economie Théorique et Appliquée (DELTA), Paris.

Bourguignon, François, and Satya Chakravarty. 2003. The Measurement of Multidimensional Poverty. *Journal of Economic Inequality* 1(1) April: 25–49.

Bratsberg, Bernt, and Dek Terrell. 2002. School Quality and Returns to Education of U.S. Immigrants. *Economic Inquiry* 40(2) September: 177–98.

Brennan, Geoffrey, and Loren Lomasky. 1993. *Democracy & Decision: The Pure Theory of Electoral Preference.* New York: Cambridge University Press.

Brickman, Phillip, and Donald T. Campbell. 1971. Hedonic Relativism and Planning the Good Society. In Mortimer H. Appley, ed., *Adaptation-Level Theory: A Symposium.* New York: Academic Press.

Brown, Gordon D. A., Jonathan Gardner, Andrew J. Oswald, and Jing Qian. 2005. Does Wage Rank Affect Employees' Wellbeing? IZA Discussion Paper No. 1505. Institute for the Study of Labor (IZA), Bonn, Germany.

Buchanan, James M., and Roger D. Congleton. 1998. *Politics by Principle, Not Interest: Towards Nondiscriminatory Democracy.* New York: Cambridge University Press.

Buchanan, James M., and Gordon Tullock. 1962. *The Calculus of Consent: Logical Foundations of Constitutional Democracy.* Ann Arbor: University of Michigan Press.

Bulatao, Rodolfo A., and Patience W. Stephens. 1992. Global Estimates and Projections of Mortality by Cause, 1970–2015. Policy Research Working Paper No. 1007, World Bank, Washington, DC.

Byrnes, Steve. 2005. The Hedonic Treadmill. Unpublished. Available at http://leverett.harvard.edu/w/media/4/47/Byrnes-treadmill.pdf.

Calderón, Julio. 2001. Análisis comparativo de la población beneficiada y la no beneficiada por el Plan Nacional de Formalización. In Instituto Nacional de Estadística e Informática (INEI), *¿Ha mejorado el bienestar de la población?* Lima: INEI.

Canadian Treasury Board. 2005. *Canada's Performance: The Government of Canada's Contribution.* Ottawa, Ontario. Available at http://www.tbs-sct.gc.ca/report/govrev/05/cp-rc-eng.pdf.

Caplan, Bryan. 2007. *The Myth of the Rational Voter: Why Democracies Choose Bad Policies.* Princeton, NJ: Princeton University Press.

Cárdenas, Mauricio, Vincenzo Di Maro, and Carolina Mejía. 2008. Understanding the Role of Educational Perceptions and Victimization on Well-Being. Latin American Research Network, Inter-American Development Bank, Washington, DC. Unpublished.

Carlsson, Fredrik, Gautam Gupta, and Olof Johansson-Stenman. 2005. Keeping Up with the Vaishyas: Caste and Relative Standing. Working Papers in Economics 171. Department of Economics, Göteborg University, Göteborg, Sweden.

Carranza, Luis, Jorge Chávez, and José Valderrama. Forthcoming. Who Decides the Budget? Political Economy Analysis of the Budget Process in Peru. In Mark Hallerberg, Carlos Scartascini, and Ernesto Stein, *Who Decides the Budget? A Political Economy Analysis of the Budget Process in Latin America.* Washington DC: Inter-American Development Bank.

Caselli, Francesco, and Massimo Morelli. 2004. Bad Politicians. *Journal of Public Economics* 88(3–4) March: 759–82.

CEDLAS (Center for the Study of Distribution, Labor and Social Affairs) and World Bank. 2008. Socio-Economic Database for Latin America and the Caribbean (SEDLAC). The Statistics; Section 7, Employment (updated July 20). Available at http://www.depeco.econo.unlp.edu.ar/cedlas/sedlac/statistics.htm#employment.

Central Bank of Mexico. 2008a. Indice general de salarios sueldos y prestaciones medias. Available at http://www.banxico.gob.mx/polmoneinflacion/estadisticas/laboral/laboral.html.

———. 2008b. Índices de Precios al Consumidor y UDIS. Available at http://www.banxico.gob.mx/SieInternet/.

Central Bank of Nicaragua. 2008. Salario real: Nacional. Available at http://www.bcn.gob.ni/estadisticas/basedatos/datos/4.5.3.3.htm.

Chaiken, Shelly, and Yaacov Trope. 1999. *Dual-Process Theories in Social Psychology.* New York: Guilford Press.

Chong, Alberto E., and José Galdo. 2006. Training Quality and Earnings: The Effects of Competition on the Provision of Public-Sponsored Training Programs. RES Working Paper No. 555. Research Department, Inter-American Development Bank, Washington, DC.

Clark, Andrew. 2004. What Makes a Good Job? Evidence from OECD Countries. DELTA Working Papers No. 2004-28. DELTA (Département et Laboratoire d'Economie Théorique et Appliquée), Paris.

Clark, Andrew, David Masclet, and Marie-Claire Villeval. 2006. Effort and Comparison Income: Experimental and Survey Evidence. IZA Discussion Paper No. 2169. Institute for the Study of Labor (IZA), Bonn, Germany.

Clark, Andrew, and Andrew J. Oswald. 1994. Unhappiness and Unemployment. *Economic Journal* 104(424) May: 648–59.

Clark, Andrew, and Fabien Postel-Vinay. 2005. Job Security and Job Protection. IZA Discussion Paper No. 1489. Institute for the Study of Labor (IZA), Bonn, Germany.

Consulta de San José. 2008. Available at http://www.iadb.org/res/consultaSanJose/index.cfm.

Cowan, Kevin, Alejandro Micco, and Carmen Pagés. 2004. Labor Market Adjustment in Chile. *Economía* 5(1) Fall: 219–66.

Cox Edwards, Alejandra. 2007. Labor Market Reforms in Latin America: Consequences and Costs. Paper presented at the Copenhagen Consensus Center and Inter-American Development Bank Roundtable, Consulta de San José. California State University, Long Beach.

Coyne, Christopher, and Peter J. Boettke. 2006. Happiness and Economics Research: Insights from Austrian and Public Choice Economics. In Yew-Kwang Ng and Lok-Sang Ho, eds., *Happiness and Public Policy: Theory, Case Studies, and Implications.* New York: Palgrave Macmillan.

Cristini, Marcela, Cynthia Moskovits, and Ramiro Moya. 2008. La economía política de la provisión de bienes públicos: descentralización, participación y percepciones en América Latina y el Caribe. Inter-American Development Bank, Washington, DC. Unpublished.

Cristini, Marcela, and Ramiro Moya. 2008. Ciudades y calidad de vida en América Latina y el Caribe: Evolución histórica y comparación internacional. Inter-American Development Bank, Washington, DC. Unpublished.

Cruces, Guillermo, Andrés Ham, and Martín Tetaz. 2008. Quality of Life in Buenos Aires Neighborhoods: Hedonic Price Regressions and the Life Satisfaction Approach. Working paper for the Project on Life in Urban Neighborhoods in Latin America and the Caribbean. Inter-American Development Bank, Washington, DC, and Center for the Study of Distribution, Labor and Social Affairs (CEDLAS), La Plata, Argentina.

Cummins, Robert A. 1997. *Comprehensive Quality of Life Scale—Adult.* 5th ed. Melbourne: School of Psychology, Deakin University.

Curi, Andréa Zaitune, and Naércio Aquino Menezes-Filho. 2008. The Relationship between School Performance and Future Wages in Brazil. Latin American Research Network, Inter-American Development Bank, Washington, DC. Unpublished.

Curtis, Sian L., Ian Diamond, and John W. McDonald. 1993. Birth Intervals and Family Effects on Postneonatal Mortality in Brazil. *Demography* 30(1) February: 33–43.

Cutler, David M., and Edward L. Glaeser. 1997. Are Ghettos Good or Bad? *Quarterly Journal of Economics* 112(3) August: 827–72.

Cutler, David M., and Mark McClellan. 2001. Productivity Change in Health Care. *American Economic Review* 91(2) May: 281–86.

Dachs, J. Norberto W., Marcela Ferrer, Carmen Elisa Flórez, Aluisio J. D. Barros, Rory Narváez, and Martín Valdivia. 2002. Inequalities in Health in Latin America and the Caribbean: Descriptive and Exploratory Results for Self-Reported Health Problems and Health Care in Twelve Countries. *Pan American Journal of Public Health* 11(5–6) May: 335–55.

DANE (Departamento Administrativo Nacional de Estadística). 1998–2002. Encuesta Nacional de Hogares. Available at http://www.dane.gov.co/index.php?option=com_content&task=category&sectionid=19&id=74&Itemid=256.

de Botton, Alain. 2004. *Status Anxiety.* London: Hamish Hamilton.

de Figueiredo, Rui J. P. Jr., Pablo T. Spiller, and Santiago Urbiztondo. 1999. An Informational Perspective on Administrative Procedures. *Journal of Law, Economics, and Organization* 15(1) April: 283–305.

de Quadros, Ciro A. 2004. A Century of Vaccines and Immunization in the Americas. In Ciro A. de Quadros, ed., *Vaccines: Preventing Disease and Protecting Health.* Washington, DC: Pan American Health Organization.

de Soto, Hernando. 2000. *The Mystery of Capital: Why Capitalism Triumphs in the West and Fails Everywhere Else.* London: Black Swan.

Deaton, Angus. 2007. Income, Aging, Health and Wellbeing around the World: Evidence from the Gallup World Poll. NBER Working Paper No. 13317. National Bureau of Economic Research, Cambridge, MA.

Di Tella, Rafael, Robert J. McCulloch, and Andrew J. Oswald. 2003. The Macroeconomics of Happiness. *Review of Economics and Statistics* 85(4) November: 809–27.

Di Tella, Rafael, and Hugo Ñopo. 2008. Happiness and Beliefs in Criminal Environments. Inter-American Development Bank, Washington, DC. Unpublished.

Diener, Ed. 2005. Guidelines for National Indicators of Subjective Well-Being and Ill-Being. *Social Indicators Network News (SINET)* No. 84 November: 4–6.

Diener, Ed, and Carol Diener. 1995. The Wealth of Nations Revisited: Income and Quality of Life. *Social Indicators Research* 36(3) November: 275–86.

Diener, Ed, Carol L. Gohm, Eunkook M. Suh, and Shigehiro Oishi. 2000. Similarity of the Relations between Marital Status and Subjective Well-Being across Cultures. *Journal of Cross-Cultural Psychology* 31(4): 419–36.

Diener, Ed, Shigehiro Oishi, and Richard E. Lucas. 2003. Personality, Culture, and Subjective Well-Being. *Annual Review of Psychology* 54 February: 403–25.

Diener, Ed, and Martin E. P. Seligman. 2004. Beyond Money: Toward an Economy of Well-Being. *Psychological Science in the Public Interest* 5(1): 1–31.

Diener, Ed, Eunkook Suh, Richard Lucas, and Heidi Smith. 1999. Subjective Well-Being: Three Decades of Progress. *Psychological Bulletin* 125(2): 276–302.

Dolan, Paul. 2006. Happiness and Policy: A Review of the Literature. Report prepared for Department for Environment, Food and Rural Affairs (DEFRA), Whitehall, England.

Doyal, Len, and Ian Gough. 1991. *A Theory of Human Need.* New York: Guilford Press.

Drazen, Allan. 2000. *Political Economy in Macroeconomics.* Princeton, NJ: Princeton University Press.

Duclos, Jean-Yves, David E. Sahn, and Stephen D. Younger. 2006. Robust Multidimensional Poverty Comparisons. *Economic Journal* 116(514) October: 943–68.

Duesenberry, James S. 1949. *Income, Saving and the Theory of Consumer Behavior.* Cambridge, MA: Harvard University Press.

Duryea, Suzanne, Sebastián Galiani, Hugo Ñopo, and Claudia Piras. 2007. The Educational Gender Gap in Latin America and the Caribbean. RES Working Paper No. 600. Research Department, Inter-American Development Bank, Washington, DC.

Easterlin, Richard A. 1974. Does Economic Growth Enhance the Human Lot? Some Empirical Evidence. In Paul A. David and Melvin W. Reder, eds., *Nations and Households in Economic Growth: Essays in Honor of Moses Abramovitz.* Stanford: Stanford University Press.

ECLAC (United Nations Economic Commission for Latin America and the Caribbean). 2004. *Social Panorama of Latin America 2004.* Santiago: ECLAC.

———. 2007. *Social Panorama of Latin America 2007.* Santiago: ECLAC.

———. 2008. CEPALSTAT: Latin America and the Caribbean Statistics. Available at http://websie.eclac.cl/sisgen/ConsultaIntegrada.asp.

ECLAC (United Nations Economic Commission for Latin America and the Caribbean) and CELADE (Latin American Demographic Center). 1996. Déficit habitacional y datos censales sociodemográficos: una metodología. Series B, No. 114, ECLAC, Santiago.

The Economist. 2008. The Caribbean: Sun, Sea and Murder. *The Economist*, January 31, The Americas section. Available at http://www.economist.com/research/articlesBySubject/displaystory.cfm?subjectid=348942&story_id=10609414.

Eggleston, Elizabeth, Amy Ong Tsui, and Milton Kotelchuck. 2001. Unintended Pregnancy and Low Birthweight in Ecuador. *American Journal of Public Health* 91(5) May: 808–10.

Elacqua, Gregory, and Rodrigo Fábrega. 2006. El consumidor de la educación: El actor olvidado de la libre elección de escuelas en Chile. In Santiago Cueto, ed., *Educación y brechas de equidad en América Latina.* Fondo de Investigaciones Educativas. Santiago: Partnership for Educational Revitalization in the Americas (PREAL).

Ellison, Christopher G. 1991. Religious Involvement and Subjective Well-Being. *Journal of Health and Social Behavior* 32(1) March: 80–99.

Elster, Jon. 1997. The Market and the Forum: Three Varieties of Political Theory. In James Bohman and William Rehg, eds., *Deliberative Democracy: Essays on Reason and Politics.* Cambridge, MA: MIT Press.

———. 1998. *Deliberative Democracy*. Cambridge, England: Cambridge University Press.

———. 2007. *Explaining Social Behavior: More Nuts and Bolts for the Social Sciences*. New York: Cambridge University Press.

European Communities. 2000. *The Urban Audit—Towards the Benchmarking of Quality of Life in 58 European Cities*. Final report, 3 vols. Brussels: European Communities.

European Foundation for the Improvement of Living and Working Conditions. 2004. *Quality of life in Europe: First European Quality of Life Survey 2003*. Luxembourg: Office for Official Publications of the European Communities.

Eveleth, Phyllis B., and James M. Tanner. 1976. *Worldwide Variation in Human Growth*. New York: Cambridge University Press.

Fashoyin, Tayo. 2004. Tripartite Cooperation, Social Dialogue and National Development. *International Labour Review* 143(4): 341–72.

Fay, Marianne. 2001. Financing the Future: Infrastructure Needs in Latin America, 2000–05. Policy Research Working Paper No. 2545. World Bank, Washington, DC.

Fay, Marianne, and Anna Wellenstein. 2005. Keeping a Roof over One's Head: Improving Access to Safe and Decent Shelter. In Marianne Fay, ed., *The Urban Poor in Latin America*. Washington, DC: World Bank.

Fearon, James D. 1998. Deliberation as Discussion. In Jon Elster, ed., *Deliberative Democracy*. Cambridge, England: Cambridge University Press.

Felson, Richard B., and Mark D. Reed. 1986. Reference Groups and Self-Appraisals of Academic Ability and Performance. *Social Psychology Quarterly* 49(2): 103–9.

Ferre, Zuleika, Néstor Gandelman, and Giorgina Piani. 2008. Quality of Life in Montevideo. Inter-American Development Bank, Washington, DC. Unpublished.

Ferrer, Guillermo. 2006. Educational Assessment Systems in Latin America: Current Practice and Future Challenges. Partnership for Educational Revitalization in the Americas (PREAL), Washington, DC.

Ferrer-i-Carbonell, Ada. 2005. Income and Well-Being: An Empirical Analysis of the Comparison Income Effect. *Journal of Public Economics* 89(5–6) June: 997–1019.

Ferrer-i-Carbonell, Ada, and Paul Frijters. 2004. How Important Is Methodology for Estimates of the Determinants of Happiness? *Economic Journal* 114(497) July: 641–59.

FGV (Fundação Getúlio Vargas). 2008. Family Income, Intra-Household Redistribution and Health Perceptions. Paper prepared for the Latin American Research Network, Inter-American Development Bank. FGV, São Paulo.

Finseraas, Henning. 2006. Income Inequality and Demand for Redistribution: An Empirical Analysis of European Public Opinion. Paper presented at the annual meeting of the American Political Science Association, August 31–September 3, Philadelphia, Pennsylvania.

Flores, Carolina, and María Soledad Herrera. 2008. Understanding Quality of Life in Latin America and the Caribbean: Satisfaction, Quality of Education and Income Inequality. Latin American Research Network Paper. Inter-American Development Bank, Washington, DC.

Flores Lima, Roberto. 2006. El servicio de intermediación laboral como instrumento para promover la inclusión social y de género en el mercado laboral en México. Document prepared for the Fondo Enlace de Inclusión Social. Inter-American Development Bank, Washington, DC.

Flórez, Carmen E., and Victoria E. Soto. 2007. La fecundidad y el acceso a los servicios de salud reproductiva en el contexto de la movilidad social en América Latina y el Caribe. Documento CEDE 2007-16. Centro de Estudios sobre el Desarrollo Económico (CEDE), Bogotá.

Fogel, Robert W. 1994. Economic Growth, Population Theory and Physiology. *American Economic Review* 84(3) June: 369–95.

Fong, Christina M. 2006. Prospective Mobility, Fairness, and the Demand for Redistribution. Department of Social and Decision Sciences, Carnegie Mellon University, Pittsburgh, Pennsylvania. Unpublished.

Forteza, Alvaro, and Mario Tommasi, with Germán Herrera. 2006. Understanding Reform in Latin America. Global Research Project on Understanding Reform: Synthesis of Country Studies from Latin America. Global Development Network. Available at http://decon.edu.uy/~alvarof/URLA_Forteza_Tommasi_250406.pdf.

Frank, Robert H. 1985. The Demand for Unobservable and Other Nonpositional Goods. *American Economic Review* 75(1) March: 101–16.

———. 1999. *Luxury Fever: Why Money Fails to Satisfy in an Era of Excess*. New York: Free Press.

———. 2005. Does Money Buy Happiness? In Felicia A. Huppert, Nick Bailis, and Barry Keverne, eds., *The Science of Well-Being*. New York: Oxford University Press.

Frey, Bruno S. 2008. *Happiness: A Revolution in Economics*. Cambridge, MA: MIT Press.

Frey, Bruno S., Simon Luechinger, and Alois Stutzer. 2004. Valuing Public Goods: The Life Satisfaction Approach. CESifo Working Paper Series No. 1158. Center for Economic Studies, Munich, Germany.

Frey, Bruno S., and Alois Stutzer. 1999. Measuring Preferences by Subjective Well-Being. *Journal of Institutional and Theoretical Economics* 155(4): 755–78.

———. 2002. What Can Economists Learn from Happiness Research? *Journal of Economic Literature* 40(2) June: 402–35.

———. 2007. Should National Happiness Be Maximized? IEER Working Paper No. 306. Institute for Empirical Research in Economics, University of Zurich.

Frijters, Paul, John P. Haisken-DeNew, and Michael A. Shields. 2004a. Money Does Matter! Evidence from Increasing Real Income and Life Satisfaction in East Germany Following Reunification. *American Economic Review* 94(3) June: 730–40.

———. 2004b. Investigating the Patterns and Determinants of Life Satisfaction in Germany Following Reunification. *Journal of Human Resources* 39(3) Summer: 649–74.

Galasso, Emanuela, Martin Ravallion, and Agustin Salvia. 2004. Assisting the Transition from Workfare to Work: A Randomized Experiment. *Industrial and Labor Relations Review* 58(1) October: 128–42.

Galiani, Sebastian, and Ernesto Schargrodsky. 2007. Property Rights for the Poor: Effects of Land Titling. Business School Working Papers Series. Universidad Torcuato Di Tella, Buenos Aires.

Gallup. 2006. Gallup World Poll. Available at http://www.gallup.com/consulting/worldpoll/24046/about.aspx

———. 2007. Gallup World Poll. Available at http://www.gallup.com/consulting/worldpoll/24046/about.aspx.

Gandhi Kingdon, Geeta, and John Knight. 2004. Community, Comparisons and Subjective Well-Being in a Divided Society. Centre for the Study of African Economies Working Paper Series No. WPS/2004-21. Centre for the Study of African Economies (CSAE), Oxford, England.

Gasparini, Leonardo, Walter Sosa Escudero, Mariana Marchionni, and Sergio Olivieri. 2008. Income, Deprivation, and Perceptions in Latin America and the Caribbean: New Evidence from the Gallup World Poll. Latin American Research Network, Inter-American Development Bank, and Center for the Study of Distribution, Labor and Social Affairs (CEDLAS), La Plata, Argentina.

Gaviria, Alejandro. 2007. Social Mobility and Preferences for Redistribution in Latin America. *Economía* 8(1) Fall: 55–88.

Gaviria, Alejandro, and Carmen Pagés. 2002. Patterns of Crime Victimization in Latin American Cities. *Journal of Development Economics* 67(1) February: 181–203.

Gaviria, Alejandro, and Ernesto Stein. 2000. The Evolution of Urban Concentration around the World: A Panel Approach. RES Working Paper No. 414. Research Department, Inter-American Development Bank, Washington, DC.

Georgiadis, Andreas, and Alan Manning. 2008. Spend It like Beckham? Inequality and Redistribution in the UK, 1983–2004. VoxEU.org, January 5. Available at http://www.voxeu.org/index.php?q=node/850.

Giedion, Ursula, Beatriz Yadira Díaz, Eduardo Andres Alfonso, and William D. Savedoff. 2007. The Impact of Subsidized Health Insurance on Access, Utilization and Health Status in Colombia. Global Health Financing Initiative, Brookings Institution, Washington, DC.

Gigante, Denise P., Bernardo L. Horta, Rosângela C. Lima, Fernando C. Barros, and Cesar G. Victora. 2006. Early Life Factors Are Determinants of Female Height at Age 19 Years in a Population-Based Birth Cohort (Pelotas, Brazil). *Journal of Nutrition* 136 February: 473–78.

Gilbert, Alan. 2001. La vivienda en America Latina. Inter-American Institute for Social Development (INDES), Inter-American Development Bank, Washington, DC. Unpublished.

Gindling, Thomas H., and Katherine Terrell. 2007. The Effects of Multiple Minimum Wages Throughout the Labor Market: The Case of Costa Rica. *Labour Economics* 14(3) June: 485–511.

Goldstein, Noah J., Steve J. Martin, and Robert B. Cialdini. 2008. *Yes! 50 Scientifically Proven Ways to Be Persuasive*. New York: Free Press.

Graham, Carol. 2002. *Happiness and Hardship: Opportunity and Insecurity in New Market Economies*. Washington, DC: Brookings Institution Press.

———. 2008. Happiness and Health: Lessons—and Questions—for Public Policy. *Health Affairs* 27(1) January/February: 72–87.

Graham, Carol, Andrew Eggers, and Sandip Sukhtankar. 2004. Does Happiness Pay? An Initial Exploration Based on Panel Data from Russia. *Journal of Economic Behavior and Organization* 55(3) November: 319–42.

Graham, Carol, and Andrew Felton. 2005a. Does Inequality Matter to Individual Welfare? An Initial Exploration Based on Happiness Surveys from Latin America. CSED Working Paper No. 38. Brookings Institution, Washington, DC.

———. 2005b. Variance in Obesity Incidence across Countries and Cohorts: A Norms Based Approach Using Happiness Surveys. CSED Working Paper Series No. 42. Brookings Institution, Washington, DC.

Graham, Carol, and Stefano Pettinato. 2000. Happiness, Markets, and Democracy: Latin America in Comparative Perspective. CSED Working Paper No. 13. Brookings Institution, Washington, DC.

———. 2002a. Frustrated Achievers: Winners, Losers, and Subjective Well-Being in New Market Economies. *Journal of Development Studies* 38(4) April: 100–40.

———. 2002b. *Happiness and Hardship: Opportunity and Insecurity in New Market Economies*. Washington, DC: Brookings Institution Press.

Graham, Carol, and Sandip Sukhtankar. 2004. Is Economic Crisis Reducing Support for Markets and Democracy in Latin America? Some Evidence from the Economics of Happiness. CSED Working Paper No. 30. Brookings Institution, Washington, DC.

Griliches, Zvi, and Iain M. Cockburn. 1994. Generics and New Goods in Pharmaceutical Price Indexes. *American Economic Review* 84(5) December: 1213–32.

Groot, Wim. 2000. Adaptation and Scale of Reference Bias in Self-Assessment of Quality of Life. *Journal of Health Economics* 19(3) May: 403–20.

Grossman, Gene M., and Elhanan Helpman. 2001. *Special Interest Politics*. Cambridge, MA: MIT Press.

Guimarães Castro, María Helena. 2002. El caso de Brasil. Paper presented at the Inter-American Development Bank seminar "Higher Education and Science and Technology in Latin America and the Caribbean," March 8, Fortaleza, Brazil.

Gwatkin, Davidson R., Shea Rutstein, Kiersten Johnson, Eldaw Suliman, Adam Wagstaff, and Agbessi Amouzou. 2007. *Socio-economic Differences in Health, Nutrition, and Population within Developing Countries: An Overview.* Washington, DC: World Bank.

Gyourko, Joseph, Peter Linneman, and Susan Wachter. 1999. Analyzing the Relationships among Race, Wealth, and Home Ownership in America. *Journal of Housing Economics 8* (2) June: 63–89.

Hall, Gillette, and Harry A. Patrinos. 2005. *Indigenous Peoples, Poverty, and Human Development in Latin America: 1994–2004.* Washington, DC: World Bank.

Hall, Luis J., Roger Madrigal, and Juan Robalino. 2008. Quality of Life in Urban Neighborhoods in Costa Rica. Inter-American Development Bank, Washington, DC, and Centro Agronómico Tropical de Investigación y Enseñanza (CATIE), Turrialba, Costa Rica. Unpublished.

Hanes, Madalina C. 2007. Where You Stand, Where You Sit and How You Think: Bureaucratic Roles and Individual Personalities. Paper presented at the Southern Political Science Association Annual Meeting, New Orleans, Louisiana.

Hanushek, Eric A., and Ludger Woessmann. 2007. The Role of Education Quality in Economic Growth. Policy Research Working Paper 4122. World Bank, Washington, DC.

Hastings, Justine S., Thomas J. Kane, and Douglas O. Staiger. 2006. Parental Preferences and School Competition: Evidence from a Public School Choice Program. NBER Working Paper No. 11805. National Bureau of Economic Research, Cambridge, MA.

———. 2007. Preferences and Heterogeneous Treatment Effects in a Public School Choice Lottery. NBER Working Paper No. 12145. National Bureau of Economic Research, Cambridge, MA.

Heckman, James J., and Carmen Pagés. 2004. Introduction to Law and Employment. In James J. Heckman and Carmen Pagés, eds., *Law and Employment: Lessons from Latin America and the Caribbean.* Chicago: University of Chicago Press.

Hernani-Limarino, Werner L., Wilson Jiménez, Boris Arias, and Cecilia Larrea. 2008. The Quality of Life of Urban Neighborhoods in Bolivia: A Case of Study of the Great La Paz and Santa Cruz. Inter-American Development Bank, Washington, DC. Unpublished.

Higueras, Lucas, and Carlos Scartascini. 2008. The Role of the Media in Public Perceptions. Inter-American Development Bank, Washington, DC. Unpublished.

Hirsch, Fred. 1976. *Social Limits to Growth.* Cambridge, MA: Harvard University Press.

Hirschman, Albert O., with Michael Rothschild. 1973. The Changing Tolerance for Income Inequality in the Course of Economic Development. *Quarterly Journal of Economics* 87(4) November: 544–66.

HMIE (Her Majesty's Inspectorate of Education). 2006. *How Good Is Our School?* The Journey to Excellence: Part 3. Livingston, Scotland: HMIE. Available at http://www.hmie.gov.uk/documents/publication/hgiosjte3.pdf.

Hopkins, David. 2007. Quality Assurance and Large Scale Reform: Lessons for Chile. Synthesis Report from the International Seminar on Regulatory Models and Quality Assurance Systems. Santiago, December 2006. Inter-American Development Bank, Washington, DC, and OECD, Paris.

Hopkins, Ed, and Tatiana Kornienko. 2008. Status, Affluence, and Inequality: Rank-Based Comparisons in Games of Status. Unpublished. Available at http://homepages.ed.ac.uk/tkornie2/hopkins-kornienko-rank-2008.pdf.

Hughes, Sallie. Forthcoming. The Role of the Latin American News Media in the Policymaking Process. In Carlos Scartascini, Ernesto Stein, and Mariano Tommasi, eds., *Political Institutions, Actors, and Arenas in Latin American Policymaking.*

Hyman, Herbert H. 1960. Reflections on Reference Groups. *Public Opinion Quarterly* 24(3): 383–96.

Iaies, Gustavo, ed. 2003. *Evaluar las evaluaciones: una mirada política acerca de las evaluaciones de la calidad educativa.* Buenos Aires: IIPE–UNESCO.

Ibarrarán, Pablo, and David Rosas Shady. 2008. Evaluating the Impact of Job Training Programs in Latin America: Evidence from IDB Funded Operations. Inter-American Development Bank, Washington, DC. Unpublished.

IDB (Inter-American Development Bank). 2001. *Competitiveness: The Business of Growth.* Economic and Social Progress in Latin America: 2001 Report. Washington, DC: IDB.

———. 2004. *Unlocking Credit: The Quest for Deep and Stable Bank Lending.* Economic and Social Progress in Latin America: 2005 Report. Washington, DC: IDB.

———. 2005. *The Politics of Policies.* Economic and Social Progress in Latin America: 2006 Report. Washington, DC: IDB.

———. 2006a. *Education, Science and Technology in Latin America and the Caribbean: A Statistical Compendium of Indicators.* Washington, DC: IDB. Available at http://www.iadb.org/sds/SCI/publication/publication_761_4357_e.htm.

———. 2006b. Health Sector Evaluation, 1995–2005. Draft, Office of Evaluation and Oversight, Inter-American Development Bank, Washington, DC. Available at http://www.iadb.org/IDBDocs.cfm?docnum=1015137.

———. 2006c. *Living with Debt: How to Limit the Risks of Sovereign Finance.* Economic and Social Progress in Latin America: 2007 Report. Washington, DC: IDB.

———. 2007. *Outsiders? The Changing Patterns of Exclusion in Latin America and the Caribbean.* Economic and Social Progress in Latin America: 2008 Report. Washington, DC: IDB.

———. 2008. Sociometro. Available at http://www.iadb.org/res/sociometro.cfm.

Idler, Ellen L., and Ronald J. Angel. 1990. Self-Rated Health and Mortality in the NHANES-I Epidemiologic Follow-Up Study. *American Journal of Public Health* 80(4) April: 446–52.

Idler, Ellen L., and Yael Benyamini. 1997. Self-Rated Health and Mortality: A Review of Twenty-Seven Community Studies. *Journal of Health and Social Behavior* 38(1) March: 21–37.

Idson, Todd L. 1990. Establishment Size, Job Satisfaction and the Structure of Work. *Applied Economics*, 22(8) August: 1007–18.

ILO (International Labour Organization). 2008a. ILOLEX: Database of International Labour Standards. Ratifications. Available at http://www.ilo.org/ilolex/english/newratframeE.htm.

———. 2008b. Hours of Work. Available at http://laborsta.ilo.org/.

Immergut, Ellen M., Karen M. Anderson, and Isabelle Schulze. 2007. *The Handbook of West European Pension Politics*. Oxford: Oxford University Press.

Jacobs, Lawrence R., and Robert Y. Shapiro. 2000. *Politicians Don't Pander: Political Manipulation and the Loss of Democratic Responsiveness*. Chicago: University of Chicago Press.

Jalan, Jyotsna, and Martin Ravallion. 2003. Estimating the Benefit Incidence of an Antipoverty Program by Propensity-Score Matching. *Journal of Business and Economic Statistics* 21(1) January: 19–30.

Jha, Prabhat, Frank J. Chaloupka, James Moore, Vendhan Gajalakshmi, Prakash C. Gupta, Richard Peck, Samira Asma, and Witold Zatonski. 2006. Tobacco Addiction. In Dean T. Jamison et al., eds., *Disease Control Priorities in Developing Countries*. 2nd ed. New York: Oxford University Press and Washington, DC: World Bank.

Joyce, Theodore J., Robert Kaestner, and Sanders Korenman. 2000. The Effect of Pregnancy Intention on Child Development. *Demography* 37(1) February: 83–94.

Kahn, Lawrence M. 2007. The Impact of Employment Protection Mandates on Demographic Temporary Employment Patterns: International Microeconomic Evidence. *Quarterly Journal of Economics* 117(521): 333–56.

Kahneman, Daniel, and Alan B. Krueger. 2006. Developments in the Measure of Subjective Well-Being. *Journal of Economic Perspectives* 20(1) Winter: 3–24.

Kahneman, Daniel, Alan B. Krueger, David Schkade, Norbert Schwarz, and Arthur Stone. 2004. Toward National Well-Being Accounts. *American Economic Review* 94(2) May: 429–34.

Kahneman, Daniel, and Amos Tversky. 1981. The Framing of Decisions and the Psychology of Choice. *Science 211(4481)* January: 453–58.

———, eds. 2000. *Choices, Values, and Frames*. Cambridge, MA: Cambridge University Press.

Kenny, Anthony, and Charles Kenny. 2006. *Life, Liberty, and the Pursuit of Utility: Happiness in Philosophical and Economic Thought.* Thorverton, England: Imprint Academic.

Kertesi, Gábor, and János Köllo. 2003. Fighting "Low Equilibria" by Doubling the Minimum Wage? Hungary's Experiment. IZA Discussion Paper No. 970. Institute for the Study of Labor (IZA), Bonn, Germany.

Kohler, Hans-Peter, Jere R. Behrman, and Axel Skytthe. 2005. Partner + Children = Happiness? The Effects of Partnerships and Fertility on Well-Being. *Population and Development Review* 31(3) September: 407–45.

Komlos, John H., and Jörg Baten, eds. 1998. *The Biological Standard of Living in Comparative Perspectives: Proceedings of a Conference Held in Munich, 18–23 January 1997.* Stuttgart, Germany: Franz Steiner Verlag.

Kugler, Adriana D. 2004. The Effect of Job Security Regulations on Labor Market Flexibility: Evidence from the Colombian Labor Market Reform. In James J. Heckman and Carmen Pagés, eds., *Law and Employment: Lessons from Latin America and the Caribbean.* Chicago: University of Chicago Press.

La Ferrara, Eliana, Alberto Chong, and Suzanne Duryea. 2008. Soap Operas and Fertility: Evidence from Brazil. BREAD Working Paper No. 172. Bureau for Research and Economic Analysis of Development, Durham, North Carolina.

Lam, David A. 2006. The Demography of Youth in Developing Countries and Its Economic Implications. Policy Research Working Paper 4022. World Bank, Washington, DC.

Layard, Richard. 2003. The Secrets of Happiness. *New Statesman,* March 3. Available at http://www.newstatesman.com/200303030016.

Ledbetter, James. 1998. New Coke Order. Fairness and Accuracy in Reporting (FAIR), April 14. Available at http://www.fair.org/index.php?page=2731.

Lemos, Sara. 2004. The Effect of the Minimum Wage on the Formal and Informal Sectors in Brazil. IZA Discussion Paper No. 1089. Institute for the Study of Labor (IZA), Bonn, Germany.

Levine, Ruth, and the What Works Working Group. 2006. *Millions Saved: Proven Successes in Global Health.* Washington, DC: Center for Global Development.

Levy, Santiago. 2008. *Good Intentions, Bad Outcomes: Social Policy, Informality and Economic Growth in Mexico.* Washington, DC: Brookings Institution Press.

Lewis, Justin. 2001. *Constructing Public Opinion: How Political Elites Do What They Like and Why We Seem to Go Along with It.* New York: Columbia University Press.

London Sustainable Development Commission. 2005. *2005 Report on London's Quality of Life Indicators.* London: Greater London Authority. Available at http://www.london.gov.uk/mayor/sustainable-development/docs/lsdc_indicators_2005.pdf.

Lora, Eduardo. 2008. Percepciones de salud en América Latina. Background paper for *Beyond Facts: Understanding Quality of Life.* Development in the Americas 2009. Inter-American Development Bank, Washington, DC. Unpublished.

Lora, Eduardo, and Juan Camilo Chaparro. 2008. The Conflictive Relationship between Satisfaction and Income. RES Working Paper No. 642. Research Department, Inter-American Development Bank, Washington, DC.

Lora, Eduardo, and Mauricio Olivera. 2005. The Electoral Consequences of the Washington Consensus. *Economía* 5(2) Spring: 1–61.

Lora, Eduardo, and Ugo Panizza. 2001. Structural Reforms in Latin America under Scrutiny. RES Working Paper No. 470. Research Department, Inter-American Development Bank, Washington, DC.

Luttmer, Erzo F. P. 2005. Neighbors as Negatives: Relative Earnings and Well-Being. *Quarterly Journal of Economics* 120(3) August: 963–1002.

Madrigal, Lucia, and Carmen Pagés. 2008. Assessing Quality of Employment in Developing Countries. Background paper for *Beyond Facts: Understanding Quality of Life*. Development in the Americas 2009. Inter-American Development Bank, Washington, DC. Unpublished.

Maloney, William F. 2004. Informality Revisited. *World Development* 32(7): 1159–78.

Maloney, William F., and Jairo Núñez Méndez. 2004. Measuring the Impact of Minimum Wages: Evidence from Latin America. In James J. Heckman and Carmen Pagés, eds., *Law and Employment: Lessons from Latin America and the Caribbean*. Chicago: University of Chicago Press.

Manzi, Jorge, Katherine Strasser, Ernesto San Martín, and Dante Contreras. 2008. Quality of Education in Chile. Inter-American Development Bank Research Network, Washington, DC. Unpublished.

Marini, Alessandra, and Michele Gragnolati. 2003. Malnutrition and Poverty in Guatemala. Policy Research Working Paper 2967. World Bank, Washington, DC.

Marmot, Michael, and Richard G. Wilkinson, eds. 2006. *Social Determinants of Health*. 2nd ed. Oxford, England: Oxford University Press.

Marquis, Lionel. 2006. Patterns of Support for the Welfare State: Lessons Learned from 10 Years of Direct Democratic Votes in Switzerland. Paper presented at the Joint Session of Workshops, April 25–30, Nicosia, Cyprus. Available at http://www.essex.ac.uk/ECPR/events/jointsessions/paperarchive/nicosia/ws23/Marquis.pdf.

Marshall, Jeffrey H. 2007. Poverty, Policy, and Schooling in Rural Guatemala. Sapere Development Solutions, West Lafayette, Indiana. Unpublished. Available at http://www.sapere.org/GuatemalaData.htm.

Marshall, Jeffrey H., and Valentina Calderón. 2006. Social Exclusion in Education in Latin America and the Caribbean. Sustainable Development Department, Technical Papers Series. Inter-American Development Bank, Washington DC.

Martinelli, César, and Susan Parker. Forthcoming. Deception and Misreporting in a Social Program. *Journal of the European Economic Association*.

Masket, Seth E. 2006. Where You Sit Is Where You Stand: Using GIS to Measure the Influence of Seating Proximity on Legislative Voting. Paper presented at the annual meeting of the Midwest Political Science Association, April 20, Chicago.

Marx, Ive. 2005. Job Subsidies and Cuts in Employers' Social Security Contributions: The Verdict of Empirical Evaluation Studies. Paper presented at "Changing Social Policies for Low-Income Families and Less-Skilled Workers in the E.U. and the U.S.," April 7–8, University of Michigan, Ann Arbor.

Mazza, Jacqueline. 2000. Unemployment Insurance: Case Studies and Lessons for Latin America and the Caribbean. Working Paper No. 411. Research Department, Inter-American Development Bank, Washington, DC.

———. 2003. Servicios de intermediación laboral: Enseñanzas para América Latina y el Caribe. *Revista de la CEPAL* 80: 165–83.

McBride, Michael. 2005. An Experimental Study of Happiness and Aspiration Formation. Department of Economics, University of California, Irvine. Unpublished.

McKinsey and Company. 2007. How the World's Best-Performing School Systems Come Out on Top. Available at http://www.mckinsey.com/clientservice/socialsector/our practices/philanthropy.asp.

Medici, André C. 1999. Uma década de SUS (1988–1998): progressos e desafios. In Loren Galvão and Juan Díaz, eds., *Saúde sexual e reprodutiva no Brasil: dilemas e desafios*. São Paulo: Hucitec.

Medina, Carlos, Leonardo Morales, and Jairo Núñez. 2008. Quality of Life in Urban Neighborhoods in Colombia: The Cases of Bogotá and Medellín. Inter-American Development Bank, Washington, DC. Unpublished.

Menezes-Filho, Naércio Aquino, Raphael Bottura Corbi, and Andréa Zaitune Curi. 2008. Working Conditions and Quality of Life in Latin America. Background paper for *Beyond Facts: Understanding Quality of Life*. Development in the Americas 2009. Inter-American Development Bank, Washington, DC. Unpublished.

Menezes-Filho, Naércio Aquino, André Portela Souza, Creso Franco, Fábio Waltenberg, Aloísio Araújo, Gabriel Buchmann, Marcelo Néri, Paulo Picchetti, and Vladimir Ponczek. 2008. *The Quality of Education in Brazil*. Final report to the Inter-American Development Bank. Instituto Futuro Brasil and Escola de Economia de São Paulo–Fundação Getúlio Vargas, São Paulo.

Merchant, Kathleen, and Reynaldo Martorell. 1988. Frequent Reproductive Cycling: Does It Lead to Nutritional Depletion of Mothers? *Progress in Food and Nutrition Science* 12(4): 339–69.

Merton, Robert K. 1957. *Social Theory and Social Structure*. New York: Free Press of Glencoe.

Micco, Alejandro, and Carmen Pagés. 2006. The Economic Effects of Employment Protection: Evidence from International Industry-Level Data. IZA Discussion Paper No. 2433. Institute for the Study of Labor (IZA), Bonn, Germany.

Michalos, Alex C. 1985. Multiple Discrepancies Theory. *Social Indicators Research* 16(4): 347–413.

Mizala, Alejandra, and Miguel Urquiola. 2007. School Markets: The Impact of Information Approximating Schools' Effectiveness. NBER Working Paper No. W13676. National Bureau of Economic Research, Cambridge, MA.

Montenegro, Claudio E., and Carmen Pagés. 2004. Who Benefits from Labor Market Regulations? Chile 1960–1998. In James J. Heckman and Carmen Pagés, eds., *Law and Employment: Lessons from Latin America and the Caribbean.* Chicago: University of Chicago Press.

———. 2007. Job Security and the Age-Composition of Employment: Evidence from Chile. *Estudios de Economia* 34(2) December: 109–39.

Mossey, Jana M., and Evelyn Shapiro. 1982. Self-Rated Health: A Predictor of Mortality among the Elderly. *American Journal of Public Health* 72(8) August: 800–8.

Mueller, Dennis C. 2003. *Public Choice III.* Cambridge, MA: Cambridge University Press.

Nelson, Joan. 2008. Public Perceptions and Demand for Higher Quality Education. Inter-American Development Bank, Washington, DC. Unpublished.

Néri, Marcelo C., Samanta dos Reis Sacramento Monte, and Luisa Carvalhaes Coutinho de Melo. 2008. A Perceived Human Development Index. Centro de Políticas Sociales, Fundação Getúlio Vargas (FGV), and Inter-American Development Bank, Washington, DC. Available at http://www.iadb.org/res/laresnetwork/projects/pr 307finaldraft.pdf.

Ng, Yew-Kwang, and Lok Sang Ho. 2006. *Happiness and Public Policy: Theory, Case Studies and Implications.* New York: Palgrave Macmillan.

NIHCM (National Institute for Health Care Management). 2000. Prescription Drugs and Mass Media Advertising. Research Brief. NIHCM, Washington, DC. Available at http://www.nihcm.org/~nihcmor/pdf/DTCbrief2001.pdf.

Núñez, Javier. 2007. Living under a Veil of Ignorance. Department of Economics, University of Chile, Santiago. Unpublished.

OECD (Organisation for Economic Co-operation and Development). 2001. *Knowledge and Skills for Life: First Results from PISA 2000.* Paris: OECD.

———. 2004. *Learning for Tomorrow's World: First Results from PISA 2003.* Paris: OECD.

———. 2007. *PISA 2006: Science Competencies for Tomorrow's World.* Volumes 1 and 2. Paris: OECD.

———. 2008. OECD.StatExtracts. Available at http://stats.oecd.org/wbos/index.aspx.

Olson, Mancur. 1965. *The Logic of Collective Action.* Cambridge, MA: Harvard University Press.

Oswald, Andrew J. 1997. Happiness and Economic Performance. *Economic Journal* 107(445) November: 1815–31.

Pagés, Carmen, Gaëlle Pierre, and Stefano Scarpetta. 2007. Job Creation in Latin America and the Caribbean: Recent Trends and the Policy Challenges. World Bank, Washington, DC. Unpublished.

Pagés, Carmen, and Marco Stampini, 2007. No Education, No Good Jobs? Evidence on the Relationship between Education and Labor Market Segmentation. IZA Discussion Paper No. 3187. Institute for the Study of Labor (IZA), Bonn, Germany.

PAHO (Pan American Health Organization). 1998. *Health of the Indigenous Peoples Initiative: Progress Report.* Washington, DC: PAHO.

———. 2002. *Health in the Americas, 2002 Edition.* Washington, DC: PAHO.

———. 2007. *Health in the Americas, 2007 Edition.* Washington, DC: PAHO.

Palloni, Alberto, and Kenneth Hill. 1997. The Effect of Economic Changes on Mortality by Age and Cause: Latin America, 1950–90. In Georges Tapinos, Andrew Mason, and Jorge Bravo, eds., *Demographic Responses to Economic Adjustment in Latin America.* Oxford, England: Oxford University Press.

Palloni, Alberto, and R. Wyrick. 1981. Mortality Decline in Latin America: Changes in the Structure of Causes of Death, 1950–1975. *Social Biology* 28(3–4) Fall/Winter: 187–216.

Parker, Susan W. 2000. Elderly Health and Salaries in the Mexican Labor Market. In William D. Savedoff and T. Paul Schultz, eds., *Wealth from Health: Linking Social Investments to Earnings in Latin America.* Washington, DC: Inter-American Development Bank.

Parker, Susan W., Jere R. Behrman, and Luis Rubalcava. 2008. The Quality of Education in Latin America and the Caribbean Region: The Mexican Case. Inter-American Development Bank Research Network, Washington, DC. Unpublished.

Parker, Susan W., Luis N. Rubalcava, and Graciela M. Teruel. 2008a. Health in Mexico: Perceptions, Knowledge and Obesity. Paper prepared for the Latin American Research Network, Inter-American Development Bank, Washington, DC.

———. 2008b. The Quality of Life in Latin America: Working Conditions. Background paper for *Beyond Facts: Understanding Quality of Life*. Development in the Americas 2009. Inter-American Development Bank, Washington, DC. Unpublished.

Pebley, Anne R., and Paul W. Stupp. 1987. Reproductive Patterns and Child Mortality in Guatemala. *Demography* 24(1) February: 43–60.

Perry, Guillermo E., William F. Maloney, Omar S. Arias, Pablo Fajnzylber, Andrew D. Mason, and Jaime Saavedra-Chanduvi. 2007. *Informality: Exit and Exclusion.* Washington, DC: World Bank.

Persson, Torsten, and Guido Tabellini. 2002. *Political Economics: Explaining Economic Policy.* Cambridge, MA: MIT Press.

Piras, Claudia, and William D. Savedoff. 1999. Does Growth Lead to Growth? Income Effects on Adults' Height. Office of the Chief Economist, Inter-American Development Bank, Washington, DC. Unpublished.

Powell, Andrew, and Pablo Sanguinetti. 2008. Quality of Life in Urban Neighborhoods in Latin America. Research Department, Inter-American Development Bank, Washington, DC. Unpublished.

Pritchett, Lant. 2004. Towards a New Consensus for Addressing the Global Challenge of the Lack of Education. CGD Working Paper No. 43. Center for Global Development (CGD), Washington, DC.

Przeworski, Adam. 1998. Deliberation and Ideological Domination. In Jon Elster, ed., *Deliberative Democracy*. Cambridge, MA: Cambridge University Press.

Pulley, LeaVonne, Lorraine V. Klerman, Hao Tang, and Beth A. Baker. 2002. The Extent of Pregnancy Mistiming and Its Association with Maternal Characteristics and Behaviors and Pregnancy Outcomes. *Perspectives on Sexual and Reproductive Health* 34(4) July/August: 206–11.

Rama, Martin. 2001. Consequences of Doubling the Minimum Wage: The Case of Indonesia. *Industrial and Labor Relations Review* 54(4) July: 864–86.

Ramos, Carlos Alberto. 2002. Las políticas del mercado de trabajo y su evaluación en Brasil. Macroeconomía del desarrollo serie, No. 16. United Nations Economic Commission for Latin America and the Caribbean (ECLAC), Santiago.

Rehm, Jürgen, Dan Chisholm, Robin Room, and Alan D. Lopez. 2006. Alcohol. In Dean T. Jamison, et al., eds., *Disease Control Priorities in Developing Countries*. Washington, DC: World Bank.

Reid, Michael. 2008. *Forgotten Continent: The Battle for Latin America's Soul*. New Haven, CT: Yale University Press.

Reinert, Kenneth A., Ramkishen S. Rajan, Amy Joycelyn Glass, and Lewis S. Davis, eds. Forthcoming. *The Princeton Encyclopedia of the World Economy*. Princeton, NJ: Princeton University Press.

Rex, Tom R. 2006. Job Quality in 2004 and the Change between 2001 and 2004. W.P. Carey School of Business, Arizona State University, Tempe, Arizona.

Ribero, Rocio, and Jairo Núñez. 2000. Adult Morbidity, Height, and Earnings in Colombia. In William D. Savedoff and T. Paul Schultz, eds., *Wealth from Health: Linking Social Investments to Earnings in Latin America*. Washington, DC: Inter-American Development Bank.

Rivera, Juan A., Simón Barquera, Teresa González-Cossío, Gustavo Olaiz, and Jaime Sepúlveda. 2004. Nutrition Transition in Mexico and in Other Latin American Countries. *Nutrition Reviews* 62(Suppl. 1): 149–57.

Rodríguez-Pombo, María Victoria, and Carlos Scartascini. 2008. Do People and Policymakers Think Alike? Research Department, Inter-American Development Bank, Washington, DC. Unpublished.

Rojas, Mariano. 2008. Relative Income and Well-Being in Latin America. Facultad Latinoamericana de Ciencias Sociales (FLACSO), Sede Mexico and Universidad Popular Autónoma del Estado de Puebla, Mexico. Report for the Latin American Research Network, Inter-American Development Bank, Washington, DC.

Rosero-Bixby, Luis. 2004. Spatial Access to Health Care in Costa Rica and Its Equity: A GIS-Based Study. *Social Science and Medicine* 58(7) April: 1271–84.

Rueda Robayo, Miguel, and Carlos Scartascini. 2008a. Determinants of Support for Labor Regulations in Latin America. Research Department, Inter-American Development Bank, Washington, DC. Unpublished.

———. 2008b. Labor Regulations around the World: New Evidence. Research Department, Inter-American Development Bank, Washington, DC. Unpublished.

Rugiero Pérez, Ana María. 1998. Experiencia chilena en vivienda social 1980–1995. *Boletín del Instituto de la Vivienda* 13(35) November: 3–87.

Ruhm, Christopher J. 2000. Are Recessions Good for Your Health? *Quarterly Journal of Economics* 115(2) May: 617–50.

———. 2003. Good Times Make You Sick. *Journal of Health Economics* 22(4) July: 637–58.

Saiegh, Sebastian M. Forthcoming. Active Players or Rubber-Stamps? An Evaluation of the Policy-Making Role of Latin American Legislatures. In Carlos Scartascini, Ernesto Stein, and Mariano Tommasi, eds., *Political Institutions, Actors, and Arenas in Latin American Policymaking*.

Saint-Paul, Gilles. 2000. *The Political Economy of Labour Market Institutions*. Oxford, England: Oxford University Press.

Samaniego, Norma. 2002. Las políticas de Mercado de trabajo y su evaluación en América Latina. Macroeconomía del desarrollo serie, No. 19. United Nations Economic Commission for Latin America and the Caribbean (ECLAC), Santiago.

Sapelli, Claudio Nelson, and Bernardita Vial. 1998. Utilización de prestaciones de salud en Chile: ¿Es diferente entre grupos de ingreso? *Cuadernos de Economía* 35(106): 343–82.

Savedoff, William D. 2007. Challenges and Solutions in Health in Latin America: An Alternative View for the Consulta de San José. Conference paper sponsored by the Copenhagen Consensus Center (CCC) and the Inter-American Development Bank. CCC, Copenhagen, and IDB, Washington, DC.

———. 2008. A Moving Target: Universal Access to Healthcare Services in Latin America and the Caribbean. Paper presented at the workshop "Health and the Quality of Life in Latin America," January 14, Washington, DC.

Scartascini, Carlos. 2005. Budget Practices and Procedures Database: The Role of the IDB and Preliminary Results. Paper presented at meeting of Public Policy and Transparency Network on Development Effectiveness and Results-Based Budget Management, March 23–24, Washington, DC.

Scartascini, Carlos. 2008. The Role of Opinions and Beliefs in Public Policy. Research Department, Inter-American Development Bank, Washington, DC. Unpublished.

Scartascini, Carlos, Ernesto Stein, and Mariano Tommasi. 2008. How Do Political Institutions Work? Veto Players, Intertemporal Interactions, and Policy Adaptability. RES

Working Paper No. 645. Research Department, Inter-American Development Bank, Washington, DC.

Sen, Amartya. 1985. *Commodities and Capabilities*. Oxford, England: Oxford University Press.

———. 1987. *The Standard of Living*. Cambridge, England: Cambridge University Press.

———. 1999. *Development as Freedom*. New York: Random House.

Senik, Claudia. 2004. Relativizing Relative Income. DELTA Working Paper 2004-17. Département et Laboratoire d'Economie Théorique et Appliquée (DELTA), Paris.

Shaw, James W., Jeffrey A. Johnson, and Stephen Joel Coons. 2005. U.S. Valuation of the EQ-5D Health States: Development and Testing of the D1 Valuation Model. *Medical Care* 43(3) March: 203–20.

Shrotrya, Vijay Kumar. 2006. Happiness and Development: Public Policy Initiatives in the Kingdom of Bhutan. In Yew-Kwang Ng and Lok Sang Ho, eds., *Happiness and Public Policy*. New York: Palgrave Macmillan.

Silber, Jacques. 2007. Measuring Poverty: Taking a Multidimensional Perspective. FEDEA WP 2007-14. Foundation for Applied Economic Research (FEDEA), Madrid.

Smith, Rich. 2006. Coke Is an Idiot. *Motley Fool,* June 12. Available at http://www.fool.com/investing/value/2006/06/12/coke-is-an-idiot.aspx.

Smith, Sidney C. Jr. 2007. Risk Factors for Myocardial Infarction in Latin America: Sobrepeso y Obesidad. *Circulation* 115(9) March: 1061–63.

Soares, José Francisco, Cláudio de Moura Castro, and Cibele Comini César. 2000. Escolas secundarias de Belo Horizonte: As campeas e as que a oferecem mais ao aluno. Belo Horizonte, Brazil. Unpublished.

Soares, Rodrigo R. 2007. On the Determinants of Mortality Reductions in the Developing World. NBER Working Paper 12837. National Bureau of Economic Research, Cambridge, MA.

Spiller, Pablo T., and Sanny Liao. 2006. Buy, Lobby or Sue. NBER Working Paper No. 12209. National Bureau of Economic Research, Cambridge, MA.

Spiller, Pablo T., and Mariano Tommasi. 2007. *The Institutional Foundations of Public Policy in Argentina*. New York: Cambridge University Press.

SSS (Secretaría Nacional de Salud). 2008. Sistema Nacional de Información en Salud. Mexico. http://sinais.salud.gob.mx/infraestructura/.

Stein, Ernesto, and Mariano Tommasi. 2007. The Institutional Determinants of State Capabilities in Latin America. In François Bourguignon and Boris Pleskovic, eds., *Annual World Bank Conference on Development Economics Regional: Beyond Transition*. Washington, DC: World Bank.

Stein, Ernesto, Mariano Tommasi, Carlos Scartascini, and Pablo Spiller. 2008. *Policymaking in Latin America: How Politics Shapes Policies*. Cambridge, MA: Harvard University Press, and Washington DC: Inter-American Development Bank.

Stevenson, Betsey, and Justin Wolfers. 2008. Economic Growth and Subjective Well-Being: Reassessing the Easterlin Paradox. IZA Discussion Paper No. 3654. Institute for the Study of Labor (IZA), Bonn, Germany.

Stimson, James A. 2004. *Tides of Consent: How Public Opinion Shapes American Politics.* Cambridge, England: Cambridge University Press.

Stokes, Susan C. 1998. Pathologies of Deliberation. In Jon Elster, ed., *Deliberative Democracy.* New York: Cambridge University Press.

———. 2001. *Mandates and Democracy: Neoliberalism by Surprise in Latin America.* New York: Cambridge University Press.

Strauss, John, and Duncan Thomas. 1998. Health, Nutrition and Economic Development. *Journal of Economic Literature* 36(2) June: 766–817.

Stutzer, Alois. 2004. The Role of Income Aspirations in Individual Happiness. *Journal of Economic Behavior and Organization* 54(1) May: 89–109.

Szalachman, Raquel. 2000. Perfil de déficit y políticas de vivienda de interés social: situación de algunos países de la región en los noventa. Serie financiamiento para el desarrollo 103 (LC/L.1417-P). United Nations Economic Commission for Latin America and the Caribbean (ECLAC), Santiago.

Tatsiramos, Konstantinos. 2004. The Effect of Unemployment Insurance on Unemployment Duration and the Subsequent Employment Stability. IZA Discussion Paper No. 1163. Institute for the Study of Labor (IZA), Bonn, Germany.

Taymaz, Erol. 2006. Labor Demand in Turkey. World Bank, Washington, DC. Unpublished.

Tedesco, Juan Carlos, ed. 2005. *¿Cómo superar la desigualdad y la fragmentación del sistema educativo argentino?* Buenos Aires: IIPE-UNESCO.

Thaler, Richard H., and Cass R. Sunstein. 2008. *Nudge: Improving Decisions about Health, Wealth, and Happiness.* New Haven, CT: Yale University Press.

Theil, Henri. 1964. *Optimal Decision Rules for Government and Industry.* Amsterdam: North-Holland.

Thomas, Duncan, and Elizabeth Frankenberg. 2002. Health, Nutrition and Prosperity: A Microeconomic Perspective. *Bulletin of the World Health Organization* 80(2) June: 106–13.

Tiebout, Charles M. 1956. The Pure Theory of Public Expenditures. *Journal of Public Economy* 64(5): 416–24.

Tinbergen, Jan. 1956. *Economic Policy: Theory and Design.* Amsterdam: North-Holland.

Tversky, Amos, and Daniel Kahneman. 1974. Judgment under Uncertainty: Heuristics and Biases. *Science* 185(4157) September: 1124–31.

Uauy, Richard, Cecilia Albala, and Juliana Kain. 2001. Obesity Trends in Latin America: Transiting from Under- to Overweight. *Journal of Nutrition* 131(3) March: 893–99.

UN (United Nations). 2008a. Millennium Development Goals Indicators. Available at http://mdgs.un.org/unsd/mdg/Data.aspx.

———. 2008b. World Urbanization Prospects: The 2007 Revision Population Database. Department of Economic and Social Affairs, Population Division, United Nations. Available at http://esa.un.org/unup/.

UNDP (United Nations Development Programme). 2007. *Human Development Report 2007/2008: Fighting Climate Change: Human Solidarity in a Divided World.* New York: UNDP. Available at http://hdr.undp.org/en/media/HDR_20072008_EN_Complete.pdf.

UN-Habitat (United Nations Human Settlements Habitat Programme). 2003. Global Urban Indicators Database 1998. Available at http://ww2.unhabitat.org/programmes/guo/guo_indicators.asp.

Urquiola, Miguel, and Valentina Calderón. 2005. Apples and Oranges: Educational Enrollment and Attainment across Countries in Latin America and the Caribbean. Education Network, Regional Policy Dialogue. Inter-American Development Bank, Washington, DC.

Valdivia, Martín. 2002. Public Health Infrastructure and Equity in the Utilization of Outpatient Health Care Services in Peru. *Health Policy and Planning* 17(Suppl. 1) December: 12–19.

van Praag, Bernard M. S. 1985. Linking Economics with Psychology: An Economist's View. *Journal of Economic Psychology* 6(3) September: 289–311.

van Praag, Bernard M. S., and Ada Ferrer-i-Carbonell. 2007. *Happiness Quantified: A Satisfaction Calculus Approach.* New York: Oxford University Press.

van Praag, Bernard M. S., Paul Frijters, and Ada Ferrer-i-Carbonell. 2003. The Anatomy of Subjective Well-Being. *Journal of Economic Behavior & Organization* 51(1) May: 29–49.

Vandell, Kerry D. 1995. Market Factors Affecting Spatial Heterogeneity among Urban Neighborhoods. *Housing Policy Debate* 6(1): 103–39.

Veblen, Thorstein. 1899. *The Theory of the Leisure Class*. New York: Modern Library.

Veenhoven, Ruut. 2000. The Four Qualities of Life: Ordering Concepts and Measures of the Good Life. *Journal of Happiness Studies* 1: 1–39.

———. 2007. Measures of Gross National Happiness. Paper presented at OECD Conference on Measurability and Policy Relevance of Happiness, April 2–3, Rome.

Vegas, Emiliana, and Jenny Petrow. 2007. *Raising Student Learning in Latin America: The Challenge for the 21st Century.* Washington, DC: World Bank.

Waaler, Hans T. 1984. Height, Weight and Mortality: The Norwegian Experience. *Acta Medica Scandinavica* 215 (Suppl. 679): 1–56.

Wagstaff, Adam. 2002. Inequalities in Health in Developing Countries: Swimming Against the Tide? Policy Research Working Paper 2795. World Bank, Washington, DC.

Wald, Nicholas J., and Malcolm R. Law. 2003. A Strategy to Reduce Cardiovascular Disease by More than 80 Percent. *British Medical Journal* 326 (7404) January: 1419.

Waltenberg, Fábio D. 2008. Benchmarking of Brazil's Education Performance Using PISA 2003. Research Department, Inter-American Development Bank, Washington, DC. Unpublished.

Wantchekon, Leonard. 2003. Ethnicity, Gender, and the Demand for Redistribution: Experimental Evidence from Benin. New York University, New York. Unpublished.

Ware, John E. Jr., 1998. Overview of the SF-36 Health Survey and the International Quality of Life Assessment (IQOLA) Project. *Journal of Clinical Epidemiology* 51(11) November: 903–12.

Wassmer, Robert W. 2002. An Economic View of Some Causes of Urban Spatial Segregation and Its Costs and Benefits. California State University, Sacramento. Unpublished.

Watson, Tara. 2005. Metropolitan Growth and Neighborhood Segregation by Income. Williams College, Williamstown, MA. Unpublished.

Willms, J. Douglas. 2006. Learning Divides: Ten Policy Questions about the Performance and Equity of Schools and School Systems. Working Paper No. 5. UNESCO Institute for Statistics, Montreal, Canada.

World Bank. 2007. World Development Indicators Online. Available at http://web.world bank.org/WBSITE/EXTERNAL/DATASTATISTICS/0,,contentMDK:20398986~menuP K:64133163~pagePK:64133150~piPK:64133175~theSitePK:239419,00.html.

———. 2008. *Doing Business in 2008*. Washington, DC: World Bank.

WHO (World Health Organization). 2002. *The World Health Report 2002: Reducing Risks, Promoting Healthy Life.* Geneva: WHO.

———. 2004. *The World Health Report 2004: Changing History.* Geneva: WHO.

———. 2008. WHO-UNICEF Estimates of DPT3 Coverage (updated August 26). Available at http://www.who.int/immunization_monitoring/en/globalsummary/timeseries/ tswucoveragedtp3.htm.

WHO Multicentre Growth Reference Study Group. 2006. Assessment of Differences in Linear Growth among Populations in the WHO Multicenter Growth Reference Study. *Acta Pædiatrica* 95(s450) April: 56–65.

Index

H

Q

R